The Insider's Guide to America Online

The Insider's Guide to America Online

♦ ♦

by Meg Booker

with the Insider Team

Kimberly Brown

Curt Degenhart

D.C. Denison

Jen Muehlbauer

Developed by Songline Studios for America Online

Distributed by O'Reilly & Associates, Inc.

The Insider's Guide to America Online

by Meg Booker, Kimberly Brown, Curt Degenhart, D.C. Denison, and Jen Muehlbauer

Printed in the United States of America.

Published by O'Reilly & Associates, Inc., 101 Morris Street, Sebastopol, CA 95472

Editor: Kimberly Brown

Book design and illustrations: Studio 180

Cover design: DKG Design

Production: Miriam Adkins

Indexing: Seth Maislin

This book is printed on acid-free paper with more than 50% recycled content, 10% post-consumer waste. O'Reilly & Associates is committed to using paper with the highest recycled content available consistent with high quality.

ISBN: 1-56592-372-3 ISBN: 1-56592-373-1 (CD insert)

This book was very much a collaborative effort. The entire Insider Team would like to thank:

Gretta Olton for her fun design and vision.

Mim Adkins for her dedication, effort, and sense of style.

Kirsten Alexander, Todd Bairstow, Hilary Goldhammer, Andy Howatt, and Maura Welch for their creative contributions.

Greg Rahal, Sheryl Avruch, Jane Ellin, and Nancy Kotary for crossing all the t's and dotting all the i's. Seth Maislin for his indexing expertise.

Sue Willing from O'Reilly and Jim Nicholas and Lisa Rhoa from IPC for their flexibility and patience.

Steve Block, Tim O'Reilly, and Dale Dougherty for staying focused on the Big Picture.

Bonnie "King Penguin" Hyland, Eleanor Eyre, and the gang from Turtle Express for helping keep the gears moving.

Brad Schepp and Judy Carpinski for their experience and guidance.

All the staffers at AOL who took the time to read individual chapters, share their insights, or get us what we needed:

Frank Irving, Marta Grutka, Laura Sheahen, Doug Miller, Mark Rogers, Marc Appleman, Ellen Taylor, Alison Nixon, Rob Shenk, Amy Burk, Natalie Farsi, Geoff Smith, Alex Whalen, Kara Wade, Steve Gaitten, Paul Murphy, Cheryl Davis, Adam Rugel, Susan Pirie, and MaryLynne Ashley.

And a special thanks to Miriam E. Grossman, who got this ball rolling.

Contents

Using AOL Effectively

How to Use this Book 3

The Nature of the Online World 3
Make the Insider's Guide Your Launching Pad 4
Take an Integrative Approach to AOL's Resources 4
Text Conventions in this Book Help You Navigate the Service 5

Getting Beyond the Basics 6

Where to Start if You're New to AOL
(or Need a Refresher on the Basics) 6
Decrease the Amount of Junk Email 6
Enliven Your Email with Rich Text 7
Send a Secret Email 7
Share Your Favorite Places with Hyperlinks 8
Beware Trojan Horses 9
End Your Message Board Posts with a Signature 10
Just the FAQs: Join Internet Discussions 10
Emoticons Help Say What You Mean 11
Tailor the AOL Newsreader to Your Preferences 12
Create a Private Room for a Family Reunion 13
Gather Together in Your Screen Name 13
Devise Your Own Form of "Push" Technology 13
Record Chats with the Log Manager 14
Use Sounds in Chat Rooms 15
Volunteer to be a Chat Room Ranger 16
Ignore Bothersome Chatters 17

Report Password "Phishers" 18
Hide from Other People's Buddy Lists 18
Instant Message People Over the Internet 19
Get Unstuck: Bypass the Hourglass 19
Search More Effectively 20
Find Information in the Top Window 20
Capture Text Online Instead of Taking Notes by Hand 21
Get the Helper Programs You Need 21
Find Help Online Before Picking Up the Phone 22

Customize Your AOL Experience 23

Start Up AOL with Your Favorite Place 23
Customize the Go To Menu 23
Change the Sounds of Incoming Mail, Buddies, and Downloaded Files 24
Set Your Mail, Web, and Chat Preferences 25
Install Must-Have Browser Plug-Ins 25
Use Voice Email Software to Speak, Rather than Type, Your Mail 26

Using AOL at Work 26

Install AOL at Work 26
Separate Business from Your Personal Life 27
Share Files with Colleagues Using Your FTP Space 28
Log Onto AOL When Away from Home 29
Timeshift: Make AOL Work While You Sleep 30
Telecommute from Your Home Office 30
Build Your Company's Web Site 31
Page Someone through AOL 31

AOL NetFind: Not Your Average Search Engine 32

Quickly Locate What You Need on the Internet 32
See Which Web Sites are Worth the Effort 32
Read the Essential Guide to Newsgroups 33
Make Your Life Easier with NetFind's Time Savers 33
Find a Person's Address and Send them a Card Through the Web 34
Locate a Business 34
Kids Can Find Things on Their Own 35

The Insider's AOL 4.0 Sneak Preview

Pictures Are Added 38

Create an Online Photo Album 38
Insert Pictures in Email 39

Email is Enhanced 39

Spell Check Your Mail and Catch Grammatical Errors 39
Create Your Own Personalized Stationery 40
Compose Individualized Greeting Cards 41
Store Friends' and Relatives' Pictures in Your Address Book 41
Attach Multiple Files to Email Messages 42

Chat is More Fun 42

Use Rich Text in Chat 42

AOL Becomes Even Easier and More Efficient to Use 43

Leave Electronic Bread Crumbs to See Where You've Been. 43
Move the Toolbar and Add Your Own Icons 43
Print Out the Quick Reference Guide 44
Get Immediate Answers to the Top 25 Questions
Asked About AOL 44
Switch Screen Names Without Disconnecting 45
Get the Screen Name You Want 45
Choose Where You Want to Put Your Favorite Place 46

Experience More Multimedia 46

Enjoy Multimedia Content That Is "Streamed" In 46
Find Popular Plug-Ins and Active X Controls Built In 47
Design More Advanced Web Pages 47

AOL Carries a Security Blanket 48

Conduct Secure Transactions with the
Highest Level of Encryption Available 48
Establish an Internet Site Ratings System 49
Lock Your Personal File Cabinet with a Password 49

3 Keeping Current: News and Weather Reports on AOL

Get National and World News When You Want It 52

Get News as It Happens 52
Get Focused with ABC News 52
Keep Up with the Times 53
Search for the News You Want 53
Photojournalists Capture News in Pictures 53
Interact with Newsweek Magazine 54
Understand Market and Investment News 55

Get an Accurate Outlook on Weather 55

Local Forecasts Whenever You Want Them 55
Plan for International Travel 56

Get Really Local News 56

Plan a Trip to Orlando 56
News About the Windy City from the Chicago Tribune 56
Find the News in Your Own Digital City 57
Find a Job in the Southwest 58
Consumer Reports Looks Out for You 58

Get Informed and Get Involved in Politics 59

Get Political News You Can Trust 59
Visit the White House Forum 59
Contact Your Congressional Representative 60
Get Live Gavel-to-Gavel Coverage from C-Span 60

Learn More About Political Parties 61

Hang Your Hat with the Democrats 61
Join the Republicans 61
Explore the Libertarian Platform 61

Engage in Political Debate 62

Air Your Opinions 62
Politics Gets a New Look 62
Speak Your Mind About Politics, Religion, and Current Events 63

Lighten Up with Online Satirists 63

Cut Washington Down to Size 63
Editorial Cartoons Draw on Congressional Figures 64

4 Build Your Business and Guide Your Career

Startup and Succeed in Your Small Business 66

Get Your Own Business Going (and Keep it Running!) 66
Brainstorm and Build Your Startup 67
Work from Home. 67
Put Your Business on the Web. 68
Government Assistance: The Small Business Administration. 69
Talk Business Live with Pros. 69
Get Forms and Templates in the Business Owner's Toolkit 70
Learn Guerrilla Marketing Techniques from the Pros. 70
Incorporate Your Business Online 71
Join the Multi-Level Marketing and Direct Selling Forum 71

Current Business News: What's Going On in Your Field? 72

Business Week: Get Live Advice 72
Make Your Home Office More Efficient 72
Inc. Online: Grow Your Company 73

Manage Your Career 73

About Work: Tools to Help You Get the Job You Want 73
Consult Career Experts. 74
Find a Job, Get Promoted, or Move On 75
Working Parents Need Extra Help 76

Women Mean Business 76
Get a Job Through AOL's Classifieds 76
City by City: Relocation and Job Prospects 77

5 Managing Your Money: Personal Finance on AOL

Information for Investors 80
How to Invest Online 80
Investing for Beginners 81
Find Out About Funds 82
Research Companies Before You Buy Their Stock 83
For Serious Stockholders 84
The Latest Market Facts and Figures 85
Get News You Need 86

Analysts and Advisors 86
Invest Wisely with the Motley Fools 86
Get Sage Mutual Fund Advice 87
Investment Insights with a Focus on Canada 88
Make the Most of Online Investments 89
Take an Economics Lesson 89
Five Lunches to Financial Knowledge 90
Control Your Investments 94
Get Informed and Get Ahead 94
Network with Other Online Investors 95
News from Wall Street, Tokyo, and Cyberspace 96

Financial Resources Everyone Can Use 97
Get Your Money Questions Answered 97
Recommended Reading for Money Management 97
Understanding Insurance 98
Balance Your Checkbook and Pay Your Bills Online 99
Choose the Best Mortgage, Loan, or Credit Card 99
Do Your Own Taxes 100
Plan for the Future 101

Computing, Software, and the Internet

How to Work and Play Hard: Support Forums and Help Areas 104

Find All the Support Forums Under One Roof. 104
Find PC Help for Ordinary People 104
Tools to Help You Fight PC Viruses 104
Get Your PC Questions Answered. 105
Give Your Browser a Tune Up 106
Use Windows More Effectively 106
Learn C++, Visual Basic, and Assembly 107
Top Answers to Common Computer Questions 107
Program and Use Databases 108

Get More from the Internet. 108

Learn to Use the Internet Like a Pro 108
Become an Internet Power User. 108
Talk, Listen, and Learn in Internet Discussion Groups 109

Find and Use the Software You Want, In a Flash 110

Find the Right Software for You 110
Get Software Recommended by the PC Staff 110
Locate Your Downloaded Files 111

Produce a Video, Scan Images, and Retouch Your Grandma's Pictures 112

Learn and Understand Multimedia 112
Scan Your Own Images 113
Create Graphic Arts and Images 113
Get Photoshop Plug-Ins, Filters, and Tools. 114
Find, Use, and Create Music and Sound 114
Learn to Create Virtual Reality 114

Get Published, Spread the News, or Put Out Your Own Scandal Sheet 115

Publish It on Paper or on the Web 115
Publish on the Internet with AOL's Personal Publisher 115
Create Web Page Art and Graphics 116
Take Classes in the Online Classroom 116
What Do You Want to Publish on the Web? 117

Keep Up-to-Date with Leading Computing News and Magazines 118

Get Timely Computing News 118
Get Associated Press Computer News Every Day 118
Be a Better Computer Consumer 118
Ziff-Davis Hardware Tips and Software 119
Interviews with Industry Leaders and Innovators 120

Be a Better Computer Shopper 120

Buy Computer Software, Hardware, and Peripherals 120
Get Products and Support Directly from a Company 121
Comparison Shop for Computers, Etc. 121
Read CD-ROM Reviews Before You Buy 122

7 Live and Learn: Reference on AOL

Look It Up 124

When You Don't Know Where to Look 124
Choose Your Encyclopedia 125
Facts and Figures, Everyday and Obscure 126
Test Drive a Flashy Online Library 126
When "Common Knowledge" Isn't Common 127

Reading and Writing 127

Master the Written Word 127
Tell Wall Street Bulls from Bears 128

Dictionaries from A-Z 128
Have More Fun with Words 129

Computer Reference 129

Check the Computer-to-English Dictionary 129
How to Download (and What to Download!)` 130

Science Studies 131

Jobs for Science Scholars 131
Eureka! Up-to-the-Minute Scientific Discoveries 131

Dive into History 132

Attack the Study of Military History 132
Celebrate Black History Month Anytime 132
Remember the Holocaust 133

Where in the World 133

Your City's Report Card 133
Find Anyone Anywhere 134
My Country 'Tis Online 135

Take a Class Online 135

Attend the University of California at Home 135
Broaden Your Horizons Without Thinning Your Wallet 136

Homework Help and College Preparation 136

Win Big at the Science Fair 136
Make College Applications Less Painful 137
Prepping for the Big Standardized Test 137
How to Survive College 138
Financing Those Expensive Four Years 138
Get Help with Homework 139

Lessons for Teachers and Parents 140

Use Computers to Help Kids Learn 140
Running a Successful Home School 140
Make the Classroom Come Alive 141

Professional Resources for Educators 142
Fun Lessons for Kids 143

Learn Something New Every Day 143

Fact of the Day 143
Word of the Day 143
Quote of the Day 144
Historical Happening of the Day. 144
Snappy Answers to Silly Questions 144

8

Here's to Your Health

Springboards to Great Health 148

Start Here! 148
Don't Just Survive, Thrive! 149
Learn New Strategies for a Better Body 149
How to Focus on Your Health 150

How to Connect with Online Communities 150

Empower Yourself! 150
Find Deaf AOLers 151
How to Help Yourself 151
Join an Extended Family of Cancer Survivors 152
How to Kick the Habit for Good 152

Add to Your Body of Knowledge 153

The Next-Best Thing to Med School 153
Towards a Healthier, Happier You 154
Arm Yourself with AIDS Information 156
How to Research Cancer at Home 156
For Doctors Only! 156

House Calls from Physicians and Healers 157

AOL User, Heal Thyself 157
Ask Doctor D! 157

Learn from Healthcare Pros . . . 158
How to Get Free Professional Advice . . . 158

Healthy Body . . . 159

Diabetes Demystified! . . . 159
How to Stop the Pain . . . 159
Quit Smoking! . . . 160
Work Towards a Healthier Heart . . . 161
Spread the Word about Breast Cancer . . . 161

Healthy Mind . . . 162

Get to Know Your Brain . . . 162
Recognize Depression, Then Cope with It . . . 162

9

It's All In the Family on AOL

Family First: Resources for Nuclear, Blended, and Nontraditional Families . . . 166

Connect with Other Parents . . . 166
Start an Email Loop . . . 167
Explore Parent Resources . . . 168
Find Support and Advice . . . 168
Find the Perfect Name for Baby . . . 169

Browse Family-Related Magazines . . . 170

Dive Into Family Life . . . 170
Fine Tune Your Family's Computing . . . 170

Family Activities . . . 171

Find Family Fun . . . 171
A Place to Chill . . . 171
Find the Best Movies, Books, and Software for Your Family . . . 172
Launch Your Kids on Their Own Online Adventure . . . 173

Kids Only: An AOL Just for Children

Define the Parameters of Your Child's Online Experience 176

Set Parental Controls 176
Give Your Children Their Own Screen Names 176
Establish a Separate Child Account 176
Teen Accounts Range Further 177
Use Custom Controls 177

Let the Games Begin! 178

Trek the Trivia Trails 178
Construct a Computerized Game Room 178
Kids Quest After Knowledge 179

Make Homework Help a Favorite Place 179

Ask a Teacher 179
Look It Up! 180
Explore Your World 181
Discuss Homework Problems with an Online Tutor 181

Art Galleries for Kids Abound 182

Post Your Pictures on the Big Fridge 182
A Classic Children's Magazine Invites Readers to Create Their Own Pages 182
Kids' Creative Community at Blackberry Creek 183
How to Amaze Kids with AOL 184
Fill in Coloring Books Online 188
Write-On! 188
Fill in the Blank 188
Kids' Humor is Taken Seriously 189
Get Your Name in a Super Story 189

Enter the Clubhouse 189

Check Out the Music Scene 190
Pen Pals Connect Here 190

Add to Your Collection 190
Create Your Own Club. 191

Sporting Around 191

Meet the All-Stars 191
Learn Sports Tips and Tricks 192
Tackle Sports Jargon. 192
Chat About Your Favorite Sports 192
Play . . . Games!. 193

What's New in the News? 193

Kids Report the News 193
Subscribe to the Kids Only Newsletter 194

Kids Inspiring Kids 194

11 It's All Fun and Games

Some Games Are Free; Some Carry Added Fees. 195

What's in the Gaming Chapter? 196

Strategy and Action: Smart and Fast-Paced. 197

Experience Dogfighting Action 197
Join Warriors in MultiPlayer BattleTech 197
Hang Out in a Virtual Pool Hall. 198
Improve Your Chess Game 198
Simulate Modern Naval Warfare. 199

**Roleplaying and Persona Games:
Be Someone (or Something) Else 199**

Where Is the Adventurer's Hub? 199
Be a Vampire 199
Enter a World of Never-Ending Quests for Glory and Loot 200

Rolemaster: Magestorm 200
Free-Form Gaming Has Fewer Rules 201
Find Your Gaming Niche in the Gaming Forums 201

Video Games: Get Reviews, Buyers' Guides, and Strategies . . . 202

Review Before You Buy; Get Gaming Tips 202
Purchase and Download Games 202
Download Free Add-Ons and Demos 203
Join AOL's Most Popular Gaming Community 203

Trivia: Test Your Knowledge 204

Trivial Pursuit Interactive: Head-to-Head Competition 204
Which Trivia Game Suits Your Interests? 204
Trivia with an Attitude 205
Parent Soup: The Game 205

Puzzles, Cards, and Board Games: Challenge Yourself 206

Solve the New York Times Crossword 206
Unscramble Words, Head-to-Head 206
Poker with Sights and Sounds of a Real Casino 206
Interactive Word Puzzles with a Twist 207
Assess Your Mind; Test Your Brain 208
Word-Matching, Quiz-Show Style 208
Mix Bingo and Slots to Get Slingo 209
Enjoy Classic Card Games 209

Sports: Games and Contests 209

Play Simulated Sports Matches in Fantasy
and Simulation Leagues 209
How Well Do You Know Your Sports? 210
Tee Off with Golf 210
Meet Other Basketball Fans 210
Predict the Quarterback's Next Move 211
Manage (or Invent) Your Own Teams 211

The Sports Channel: Fans, Fantasy, and Fitness

News, Scores, and Commentary 214

Get Up-to-the-Minute Sports Information 214
Travel the Wide World of Sports on ABC 214
Read CBS SportsLine Commentary 215
Log into The Sporting News 216
Get Complete Previews 216
Tap into Great Local Coverage 217

Talk Sports, Whenever You Feel Like It 217

Express Yourself in the Grandstand 217
Talk to the Pros in Athlete Direct 218
Sports Chat, Live 219
All-Night Sports Chat 219

Where Buck Goes 220

Find Complete Coverage of the Big Events 220
Follow the Recruiting Wars 220
Link Up to the World of Golf 221
Get Up-to-Speed with Stock Car Racing 222
Courtside Insights from a B-Ball Expert 223
Preview Hockey Combat 223
Check Your Baseball Stats 223
Read No-Frills Tennis Coverage 224
Find Your Favorite NFL Team 224
Kickin' It with AOL Soccer 225
Download Your Sports 226
Shop for Sports Collectibles 226

Games and Contests 227

Indulge Your Sports Fantasies 227
Show Off Your Sports Knowledge 227

Get Fit 228
Find Out the Basics 228
How to Bulk Up. 229
Get Information and Support 229

Explore the Great Outdoors. 230
Find Places to Go. 230
Make the Most of Your Time Outdoors 230
Get in the Hunt and Go Fish 231
Prepare for Ski Trips. 232

Get Extreme 232
Find Athletic Adventures 232
Wage War with Paint 233
Get on Your Bike and Ride! 233

13 Maximize Your Entertainment Options

Meet the Stars 236
Chat with the Queen of Nice 236
Advice from Oprah 236
Stay Up Late with David Letterman 237

What's on TV? 238
Tune into ABC. 238
How to Find Sci-Fi Hotspots 238
Take a Trip Down Memory Lane 239
Sample Both Flavors of Music TV. 239
Catch Up with the Soaps 240

At the Movies 240
Thumbs Up or Thumbs Down?. 240
Make the Most of Your VCR 241
How to Plan Your Evening. 241

Entertainment Mags and Gossip Rags 242
How to Break into the Biz 243

Music to our Ears 243

Who Shares Your Taste in Music? 243
Jam with Other Musicians 244
Don't Buy the Whole CD from a One-Hit Wonder 245
Fun in the Aisles of Online Record Stores 245
How to Make a Boring Day Fun 246
Find a Concert, Then Chat About It 248
Rolling Stone Offers Something Old, Something New 248
Music Fans Unite 249

Explore the Art World 250

Getting from Main Street USA to Broadway 250
Take a Crash Course in Culture 251
Visit Museums from Home 251
All Things Considered, You Prefer NPR 252

The Laugh Track 252

Interactive Comedy at the "Online Mardi Gras" 252
Knock Knock, Joke's There 253

Comics Draw a Big Crowd 253

Become the Superhero in a Marvel Adventure 253
Meet the Whole Warner Bros. Family 254
Get a Grand Tour of the DC Universe 255
If It's Animated, It's Here 255

What's Happening Now? 256

Live Events, Right This Minute! 256
Plan Ahead for Great Live Events 256

Where to Find Online Originals 257

Try This Trivia Game, If You Dare 257
What to Do When You Can't Sleep 257

Find Something Different to Do 258
The Inside Track on Hollywood and Washington. 258
Celebrate Your Lack of Willpower 259
Keeping Your Kids Entertained 259

14

A View of the World: AOL's International Flair

Get a Taste of Foreign Culture. 262

Explore Irish Heritage 262
Learn Japanese Customs and Etiquette 262
Read News from Israel 263
Say G'day to Australia 263
Visit Every Nation Under the Sun 264
Tell Us How Your Family Came to America 265
Dine with the Global Gourmet 265
Captivating Travelogues Tell You Where to Go 266
Encounter the Parisian Lifestyle 266

Talking with People Around the World: Make International Friends. 267

Connect with Members Overseas 267
Chat in a Foreign Language 267
AOL Is Getting the World Wired 268
Get a Passport to Love 269

Global Fun and Games 269

Brush Up on Your Latin—and French, German, Spanish 269
Around the World in 80 Mouse Clicks 270
Flaunt Your Knowledge of International Trivia 274
Name That Flag 274
Play with Our Neighbors to the North 274
Meet the International Channel Insiders 275
Sneak a Peek at Japanese Animation 276
Discover Royalty Around the World 276

Sample the Virtual Baguette 276
Become an Aficionado of German Cinema 277

15 The Great Escape: Travel Resources on AOL

The World Is Your Oyster: How to Know Where to Go 280

Find the Key Guide to Florida. 280
Prepare for European Travel 281
Plan Your Itinerary. 281
Camp Across America 282
Find the Cruise That's Right for You. 283
Viva Las Vegas 283
The Practical Traveler. 284

Taking the Kids, Pets, and Other Stowaways 286

Families Share Their Travel Experiences and Advice 286

Bargain Hunting and Reservation Booking 287

Learn the Art of Budget Travel 287
Keep Business Travel Costs Down. 287
Be Your Own Travel Agent 288
Book an Entire Vacation Online 289
Make the Most of Frequent Flyer Miles 289

Traveling Savvy, Safe, and Stylish 290

Become an Independent Traveler. 290
Ask Arnie About Specific Travel Needs 290
Map Out Your Journey 291
Travel Safe with Advisories from the State Department 292
Find Needed Travel Supplies Online 292

Vacations Off the Beaten Path. 293

Gays and Lesbians Venture Over the Rainbow 293
Design an Exotic Getaway 293
Get Cozy with Lanier's Bed and Breakfast Guides 294

Add These Dependable Planning Tools to Your Favorite Places. 294
Subscribe to the Official Travel Channel Newsletter. 294
Get a Complete Vacation Plan 295
Vacation in the Magic Kingdom 295

16 At Your Leisure: Explore Your Interests on AOL

Satisfy Your Appetite for Eating, Drinking, Cooking, and Entertaining 297
Expand Your Cooking Repertoire 297
Transform Everyday Dishes into Gourmet Meals 298
Educate and Entertain the Kids with Cooking 298
Learn More About Vegetarianism 299
Pore Through Beer and Wine Reviews. 299
Host a Wine Tasting Party 300

Turn Your House into a Home. 301
Get Help with Selling or Buying a Home. 301
Calculate How Much House You Can Afford 301
Pick the Perfect School for Your Children 302
Take Excellent Care of Your Pet 303
Build Your Dream Home 304
Derive Interior Design Inspiration 304
Consider Doing Your Own Home Improvement 305
Learn Backyard Basics 305
Grow an Organic Garden. 306

Listen to Your Literary Voice. 306
Get Sneak Previews of Upcoming Novels. 306
Unearth Your Family Roots 307
Buy Books Online 308
Improve Your Writing with Critiques and Contests 308
Turn Your Writing Habit into a Career 309

Indulge Your Zeal for Wheels. 309

Visit the Auto Center 309
Research Before Buying a Car 310
Find the Inside Scoop on the Auto Industry 311
Buy Your Next Car Online 311

Take Flight with Aviation Areas 312

Hone Your Knowledge of Specialty Aircraft 312
Read All About Aviation 312

Become a Savvy Techno-Shopper 313

Choose TV and Video Equipment with Confidence 313
Get a Personal Perspective on New and Used Stereo Systems 313

Focus on Photography and Art 314

Ask Todd About Marketing Your Art 314
Learn to Take Stunning Travel Photos 314
Exchange Photography Advice and Equipment 315

Enrich and Improve Your Craftsmanship 316

Get a Handle on Woodworking Tools 316
Patch Up Your Quilting Skills 316
Join an Online Crafting Community 317
Download Craft and Sewing Patterns 317
Prepare to Tie the Knot 318

Meet the Martial Arts Masters 319

Learn the Dojo 319
Let Martial Arts Experts Train You 319
Get a Closer Look at the Ultimate Fighting Championships 320

Explore Mystical Powers and Other Psychic Phenomena 320

Uncloak the Mysteries of the Mind and Universe 320
Learn to Use Metaphysical Powers 320
Get a Free Psychic Reading 321

Communities: Finding Friendship, Advice, and Support

What Do You Believe? ... 324

Explore the World's Religions and Beliefs ... 324
Connect with the Christian Community ... 324
Discuss Faith with the Catholic Community ... 325
Your Jewish Heritage ... 325
Where's Your Faith on AOL? ... 326
Atheism-Agnosticism Forum ... 327

Racial Harmony ... 328

Hispanic Schools, Cities, and Success Stories ... 328
Black Voices ... 329
Your Heritage Is Represented ... 329
NetNoir: The Soul of Cyberspace ... 330

Queer Connections ... 331

Find Queer Fellowship at onQ ... 331
PlanetOut: Fun and Informative ... 331

Women's Network ... 332

Network with All Kinds of Women ... 332
Magazines for Women Who Do Too Much ... 333
Coping with Your Divorce ... 334

Generations ... 334

Where the Teens Are ... 334
Teens Exist on the Outer Edge ... 335
What Teens Do Online ... 336
Remember When with Baby Boomers ... 338
Seniors Congregate Around Their Computers ... 338
Prepare for Retirement with AARP ... 339

AOL Salutes the Military 340
Services for Servicepeople 340
Find an Old Army Buddy 340
Remembering Veterans 340

Community Service 341
Help Build Better Communities 341
Youth Get Involved 342
Do Something. . . Volunteer 342

Find a Match That Fits 343
Fall in Love@AOL 343
See Who You're Chatting With 343
Meet Your Neighbors 344
Find Love Overseas 344
Dating Resources for the Gay Community 344
Meet Christian Singles 345
Connect at the Jewish Matchmaker 345
Keep Your Online Relationship Alive 346

That's a Wrap 347

AOL Members' Choice Areas and Web Sites 351

AOL Shopper's Guide 355

Index 367

Who is Meg???

Blank screen. black coffee. It's 8 a.m. in Dulles, Virginia, and I'm just kicking off my shoes, crossing my legs and hunkering down over my keyboard. I do this every morning for AOL and for you. I give you the inside scoop on making the most of AOL in the *AOL Insider* (**KEYWORD: Insider**). It's a great job. It better be. I invented it. You see, I kept popping up above my cubicle (a practice known as prairie-dogging) brimming over with AOL tips and inside info about navigating the service. My cubiclemates finally made me sit, stay, and write it all down. Tada! The Insider was born.

◆ ◆

When I began working for AOL I set up an account for my mom. At first she was slow to try it. "What am I going to do with America Online?" she asked warily. I was astonished. What do you do with AOL? For me AOL had already become completely enmeshed with my life—like my telephone or my newspaper. After all, it's always there, ready to be my personal mail slave, research tool, and news provider. I resolved it right then and there on the phone with Mom. I had to be an evangelist for AOL —forces were driving me to it. Shortly after that, I started the prairie dogging thing.

Like every red-blooded American, I'd like to think I'm a one-of-a-kind. But the reality is, I'm probably a lot like you. Only my dog thinks otherwise. To him I am the center of the universe . . . as it should be with dogs and their people.

Like most of you I work hard—often longer hours than would be recommended by the family doctor. And I have a hard time fitting everything in to a given day, week, or month.

"I'll be showing you how to do things with AOL that matter in your real life—things that save you time, get you connected, and help you get answers."

Like: mailing birthday presents on time, getting my car tuned up, choosing the most cost-effective long distance carrier, and having a variety of 20-minute meal options in the freezer. And then there's catching the good movies, must-see TV, and reading all the Oprah book selections. There's hanging out with my friends, getting fitted for a bridesmaid dress, and just ONCE a month doing nothing for a while. In short, the pace can seem breakneck.

And like many of us, I up and moved away from my extended family. Thereby removing myself from all those people who help you move, plan a wedding shower, loan you tools, babysit, give too much advice, drop in unannounced, or are there when you need a shoulder to cry on. My family is from Spokane. I live in Virginia. My sister is in San Francisco. And my brother's in France. Funny thing is we're actually a really close family.

So that's a peek at what it's like to be Meg. For me, AOL is part of the glue I use to hold my life together. It keeps me in contact with my family every day. It saves me time and energy with shopping, planning, and decision-making because I can research my options online. It provides me with great advice, because it's filled with genuine people who aren't afraid to reach out and help.

I know a lot about AOL. First, because it's my job . . . but second because I use it all the time. And, if you haven't figured this out by now, I hate keeping things to myself. So whenever you see me online, I'll be showing you how to do things with AOL that matter in your real life—things that save you time, get you connected, and help you get answers.

Oh, and I make it a personal rule to have as much fun as possible no matter what I'm doing. So this will be anything but boring. ;)

Using AOL Effectively

So enough about me. More about AOL. *Your* AOL. I'll show you how to put America Online to work in your everyday life, but it's up to you to implement the tools and personalize the online experience. So log on. Try out the tutorials. Explore the keywords. Write in the margins of this book and make it your own. Consider me your AOL personal trainer, committed to making you a real Insider, and let's get started.

How to Use this Book

The Nature of the Online World

The online world moves fast. Really fast. It's especially difficult to keep up with constantly changing content and new technology developments when you're trying to set the details on paper. You know just from browsing the Web and getting those "404 File Not Found" error messages that the nature of online material is ephemeral.

With this in mind I brainstormed about the best way to approach writing this book so it wouldn't depreciate like a new car being driven out of the showroom. So to make the most of *The Insider's Guide to AOL*, here are some tips.

Make the Insider's Guide Your Launching Pad

Many people are unaware of the vast resources available through AOL. But you don't have to live on AOL 60 hours a week like I do to develop expertise in using the software and services on it. Here in this book I'm teasing out the best areas to date and the hidden nuggets and tools to be found within them.

I'm also going for the big picture—how AOL constructively fits into your life. Because you will always be able to find instructions for the simplest tasks online, I will direct you to an area itself, usually with a keyword, rather than reprint the steps verbatim. You can always print out instructions before attempting to install a new browser plug-in or gaming software.

I will, however, explain and lead you through the more complicated stuff. After reading this chapter you may want to jump to Chapter 6, which discusses Computing, Software, and the Internet. It points you toward the key resources for optimizing your hardware and customizing your software.

Take an Integrative Approach to AOL's Resources

Most people tell their friends and colleagues, "I'm on AOL." My vision is for you to tell people, "I *use* AOL." To go beyond email and just surfing the Web to do your banking, take college courses, set up neighborhood watches, and get solid medical advice all online. To that end, I've included several task-oriented scenarios that show how you can integrate the resources across the service to get things done.

For example, when planning a trip you'd obviously go to the Travel Channel. But you can also go to a database in Health for tips on preventing motion sickness, find little-known tricks for making the most of DisneyWorld in the Learning and Research Channel, and learn foreign language idioms in the International Channel.

This entire book is designed to help you adopt this functional approach to AOL, making it practical—making it work for you.

Text Conventions in this Book Help You Navigate the Service

It's frustrating to post a query on a message board one day and not be able locate that same message board later to see if anyone's posted an answer. To combat that problem I use style formats throughout this book to emulate the structure of the online areas. This should give you a visual clue as to levels of depth within an area.

The title of the main screen of an area will be italicized; the keyword to reach that area will be bolded. For instance, if I'm talking about my own area, *AOL Insider Tips*, and I urge you to visit it often by adding **KEYWORD: AOL Insider** to your customized Go To menu, you can see the one-to-one relationship between an area and its keyword.

Elements within an online area that lead to a subsection are capitalized. Sometimes I'll give you a path to reach a tool that involves clicking on a particular button. Those button names will be capitalized. Example: *AOL Insider Tips*, at **KEYWORD: Insider**, is where I keep my fingers on the Pulse of AOL with access news and other systems information. Click on the Very Cool button to take a tour of Insider lessons on the best ways to access AOL.

You should also be aware that this book was written for members who are currently working on AOL 3.0 for the PC, though all the keywords can be accessed on a Mac. There's no difference in the content and ways in which Mac users can use AOL. If you're on a Mac you'll just need to substitute your keyboard commands for the ones printed herein.

The best way to understand AOL's structure is to go online and explore. Visualize each keyword leading to a main screen, and its buttons and folders leading into deeper levels of that same area.

Getting Beyond the Basics

Where to Start if You're New to AOL (or Need a Refresher on the Basics)

Beginners, huddle up. The first secret to using AOL is this: it's easy. Clear navigation, tons of online help, and tutorial areas will get you up and running in no time. I'm not going to belabor the basics here in the book because there is so much instruction available online and I want to concentrate on teaching you the advanced techniques. The *Member Orientation* area at KEYWORD: **Discover AOL** has step-by-step instructions on how to use the software and navigate the service. Various tours explain standard AOL tasks such as:

- Attaching files to email
- Organizing your Filing Cabinet
- Using Instant Messages (IMs)
- Joining scheduled conferences and chats
- Storing Favorite Places
- Downloading from software libraries
- Using the Internet

What follows in this section are some advanced tips to bump your skill level up a notch and maximize AOL software capabilities. Most are actually quite simple, just little known or not commonly used. If you're unfamiliar with any of these terms or tasks, KEYWORD: **Discover AOL** will describe them in full.

Decrease the Amount of Junk Email

Many businesses use email as a direct marketing vehicle, often resulting in "spam," or junk mail in your email box. AOL has instituted some practices to help rid your inbox of unsolicited mail. At KEYWORD: **PreferredMail**, you can see the list of addresses AOL has blocked from sending mail to members. *PreferredMail* is conveniently preset to assure that you won't get inundated with junk mail from known spammers. But they can be hard to keep up with. You can also take a proactive approach by reporting spam. Forward the mail to screen name TOSspam just once, and TOSspam will study the junk mail it receives to determine which junk sites to block.

Enliven Your Email with Rich Text

Most email programs only allow you to write messages in a standard character set comprised of upper- and lowercase letters and limited control characters. This character set is known as ASCII (pronounced as-kee) or plain text, and it looks pretty boring. Meanwhile, in AOL email you can use stylistic flourishes to bold, italicize, and underline your text; align it to the left, right, center, or justify it; change the font size; and add color to the text and background. These formatting tools appear when composing email in a bar between the header and body of the message. You'll also find them in the AOL notepad, which you can access with the keyboard shortcut Ctrl-N. A useful way to format your text in email is to emphasize important points or change the color of your comments when replying to someone else's messages so they can differentiate your text from theirs. Coworkers have even helped edit parts of my book using this method! Remember that non-AOL members receive mail over the Internet in ASCII text, so they won't be able to see your creative formatting.

Send a Secret Email

To send a Blind Carbon Copy (BCC) of a message means you're sending someone a copy of an email someone *else* is getting, without the original recipient's knowledge. It's kind of like talking to someone on the phone with someone else secretly listening on another extension. To use the BCC function in email, simply put the screen name in the CC: field in parentheses. If there are multiple recipients getting a Blind Carbon Copy, put each separate name in parentheses. That way, when the message is sent, the person listed in the To: field won't see who's been copied on it.

Email will be greatly enhanced in AOL 4.0, and one of the features being added is a BCC button. But you can still achieve the same effect in AOL 3.0 with parentheses.

Share Your Favorite Places with Hyperlinks

If you subscribe to an official channel newsletter you're certainly familiar with "clicking on the blue underlined words" to access the areas the newsletter describes. HTML, the language of the World Wide Web, is what makes hyperlinks work; but you don't have to know the language to use these links in your email. You just need your Favorite Places folder.

For instance, if you have a buddy you think would love to get the Personal Finance newsletter *Checks and Balances*, you could send him to **KEYWORD: Newsletter** and tell him to click on the "AOL Official Channel Newsletters" folder, *then* on "Personal Finance: Checks and Balances." Or you could make it a one-step process. That area has a heart in the upper right-hand corner of its title bar, which means you can make it a Favorite Place. Once you've added it to your Favorite Places folder, compose your email:

"Hey, Steve. I know you're a busy guy so I thought this newsletter might help you balance your monthly budget more quickly and easily." Now, highlight the word "newsletter" in your text and open your Favorite Places folder. Simply drag and drop the heart anywhere onto the body of the email. When you release the mouse, the word "newsletter" will automatically become blue and underlined. If you want to double-check that the link works, double-click on it, then select the "Launch" button from the dialog box that pops up. Then send your mail on to Steve or Mom or your account manager or whomever, knowing that your link works. Or you can send it to yourself first to triple-check it.

Beware Trojan Horses

Never download a file from a stranger. If you get email from an unfamiliar screen name with an attachment, it could be a "trojan horse."

According to *Que's Computer and Internet Dictionary* (KEYWORD: **Que's Dictionary**), a trojan horse is "a program that appears to perform a valid function but contains, hidden in its code, instructions that cause damage (sometimes severe) to the systems on which it runs."

Sometimes someone will send out a program that, once downloaded onto your computer, will record your AOL password and report it back to the sender. The text of the email may read something like, "Hey remember me? We chatted a few weeks back. Well, here's that picture of me I promised to send." But then attached to the email is a file with the .exe executable extension, not the typical .gif or .jpg picture file extension. This is one clue that someone's trying to send you a trojan horse.

Do not download the file. Instead, forward it to screen name TOS Files. You have to forward the exact mail you received, rather than cut and paste the message into a new one for TOS Files to examine the attachment. And AOL staffers will never send you an attachment unless you specifically request that information be sent to you that way. Usually, they will upload files to a library where you can retrieve them yourself.

AOL has also incorporated a new download sentry: an automatic warning about the potential danger of email attachments from unfamiliar senders which will serve as a helpful reminder. And remember that simply opening an email that has an attached file will do you no harm. You won't get a virus simply by *reading* an email. The virus or trojan horse is transmitted when the file is downloaded. So as long as you don't download that file, you'll be fine. To learn more about how to protect your hard drive from corruption visit KEYWORD: **Virus**.

End Your Message Board Posts with a Signature

The new design of threaded message boards on AOL allows you to automatically append all of your posts with a signature, or "sig." This is helpful if you post often and want other members to have business contact information. Or maybe you'd like to express your personality with a quote. As you post regularly, members will become familiar with your signature and recognize you on the boards.

Go to **KEYWORD: Usenet** and click on "Set Preferences." Among the options there you'll see a space to type your signature. Save it by clicking the OK button. Now when you reply on newly designed message boards (the ones with a background graphic of push pins), you can personalize your post simply by checking off the Use Signature option.

Just the FAQs: Join Internet Discussions

If you've been posting on AOL message boards actively for a while you'll probably enjoy Usenet newsgroups on the Internet. At **KEYWORD: Newsgroups** you can join Internet discussions on almost any topic imaginable.

The keys to starting out on Usenet, though, are the FAQs. (FAQ is shorthand for Frequently Asked Questions.) Before you begin posting to a newsgroup it's wise to read the FAQ so old-timers don't have to keep supplying the same answers over and over again. And "lurking," reading posts for at least two weeks before posting, is also a good rule to follow. These precautions may save you from asking embarassing questions or offending someone in the Usenet community—which could land you in an online argument known as a "flame war."

What do members discuss in newsgroups? Everything! You can Search All Newsgroups to find one on a topic you're interested in, or browse them under Add Newsgroups to see what's available.

Emoticons Help Say What You Mean

Sometimes it can be difficult to communicate effectively online because the listener can't hear the intonation in your voice or read your body language. If you say something jokingly, the reader wouldn't be able to tell and might take offense. A good way to avoid that is by using emoticons, or "smileys," which are happy faces turned on their side and mean, for example, "I'm just kidding!!"

Some examples of emoticons are:

:) = smile
;) = wink
:D = broad grin or laugh
{{ }} = a big hug; wrap around someone's screen name, i.e. {{screen name}}
:* = kiss
:(= frown
:'(= crying
:X = my lips are sealed
:P = sticking out tongue
:-~| = has a cold
O:) = angel
}:> = devil
B-) = Batman
=:o] = Bill Clinton

Another convention of online conversations are shortening common phrases to their initials:

LOL = Laughing Out Loud
ROTFL = Rolling On The Floor Laughing
BRB = Be Right Back!
BTW = By The Way
IMHO = In My Humble Opinion
GMTA = Great Minds Think Alike
WTG = Way To Go!
OIC = Oh, I See.

Tailor the AOL Newsreader to Your Preferences

Keeping up with all the postings on an active newsgroup requires the effort of checking **KEYWORD: Usenet** often and sorting through a deluge of information. But there are several features of the newsreader you can adjust to minimize your effort.

First, use Set Preferences for all your newsgroups. You may not need all the header information in each message if posters consistently sign their missives with a signature. Otherwise, you'll probably want to see the originating email address in order to reply directly to the author and not the entire group. (Headers list the subject line, sender's full name and email address, time and date stamp, and message ID. Meanwhile, signatures typically include more useful information such as the poster's company and title, phone number, and fax number, in addition to name and email address.) But if you find headers superfluous you can either move them to the end of attendant messages or ignore them altogther. The Preferences here also allow you to sort postings by date or alphabetically by subject line and list them by either their proper Internet name or by a general description.

The default expiration on posts is 14 days. That means you have to be sure to read your groups every two weeks to get every message. But you do have the capability to extend a message's shelf life so that you can check in monthly, if you like. Just click on the newsgroup you're subscribed to and open it. The Preferences button at the bottom of the newsreader will lead you to a dialog box. Where it says, "Show messages no more than 14 days old," just type in the number 30. If you have a daily habit of checking your newsgroups you can lower the number to one or two days to get only the freshest posts.

A convention of newsgroup communication is to quote a bit of someone's post when responding to it, so readers know what you're referencing. To do this quickly, highlight the text you wish to quote before hitting the Reply button. This is also a good trick for replying to email. Remember, it's a good rule to post only a small portion of the original post's text—not the entire post.

Create a Private Room for a Family Reunion

When a family is spread out geographically you can pull them together online and save some money on phone bills. Email your relatives with the date and time you plan to meet (including time zone), and the name of the private room you're going to create. Before the meeting time, click on the chat icon in the tool bar to go to the main lobby, then click on "List Chats." Select Private Rooms, and type in the name you sent everyone. That's all you need to do to create the room. And that's all your loved ones need to do to get to it. Now you can catch up with far-flung family members without interruption.

Gather Together in Your Screen Name

Your Buddy List pops up immediately after logging on so you can see right away if your friends are online. And typically a tracking instinct leads you to hunt them down with the Locate button (keyboard shortcut Ctrl-L) or fire off an IM (Ctrl-I). But that requires contacting each person separately. With the Buddy Chat button you can bring them all to you *en masse* with one concise message.

If you have set up groups of screen names you can invite the entire gang to a private chat room just by highlighting the title of the group in your list and clicking on Buddy Chat in the lower right corner. Planning on a chat conference? This is a great way to get everyone in the same chat room without having to round them up individually.

If you close your Buddy List window you can always bring it up again quickly with **KEYWORD: BuddyView**.

Devise Your Own Form of "Push" Technology

When "push" comes to shove, you want to deliver information to a specified audience quickly and efficiently. You may have heard the buzz about push technology being developed by many online companies, including

AOL. The purpose is to save people from searching for the information they want by sending it straight to them. Mailing lists are a simplistic yet effective form of push. They are different than "spam" (unsolicited advertisements) because members subscribe to mailing lists, thereby requesting the email.

Another modified form, and an innovative use of AOL tools not many people have thought of, is using Buddy Chat to broadcast timely messages. You see, a private chat room isn't the only place you can gather online buddies. You can also invite them to a keyword or Favorite Place. Switch the button at the bottom of the Buddy Chat dialog box from Private Chat Room to Keyword/Favorite Place and then enter your information in the box.

If you're doing research on the stock market and want to share a hot tip with a bunch of people instantly, just drag and drop the Favorite Place heart from the area you're in straight into the Buddy Chat dialog box. This way you can alert many members to crucial dispatches instantly.

Record Chats with the Log Manager

Scheduled chats with people knowledgeable about a certain topic are illuminating and invaluable. To make the most of them, keep a log.

Before you head into a chat where you hope to get specific information or questions answered, turn on the log manager. From the File menu, select Log Manager. You can choose to open a log for either a chat or a session. A session log records the text of every screen you open until you close the log. A chat log records all the dialogue in a chat you visit until you close the log.

Select Open Log and name the file, i.e. "taxes.log" if you're participating in a Personal Finance chat on filing your income taxes. Now when you chat the entire dialogue will be kept in a text file, even if you change chat rooms. To close the log, return to the Log Manager dialogue box through the File menu.

Open the log as you would any other text document and you have a transcript of the chat to print and read offline. This is a simple way of keeping the minutes of an online meeting—without a secretary.

Use Sounds in Chat Rooms

Not all of what I know about AOL comes from working here. Admittedly, I get a lot of cool ideas about how to use the software from one of the best help areas on the service: the Tips and Tricks chat room. Volunteers called Rangers lead these chats to help members learn how to use system functionality. An especially helpful Ranger explained how to use sound effects in chat, so I thought I'd share his instructions here.

"In order to hear a sound that is being played in a chat room, you must have the same .wav file with the same name installed on your computer hard drive. You can already hear many sounds played in the chat room because America Online comes preinstalled with basic sounds, such as 'tada,' 'gotmail,' 'ding,' 'filesdone,' 'welcome,' and 'goodbye.' If you wish to hear any other sound being played in the chat rooms, you will have to add that sound directly to your AOL Directory.

"To install sounds, the first thing you have to do is get a .wav file that is appropriate for a chat room. Short sound samples are best since long-playing sound .wavs interrupt the discussion flow of a chat room, both for you and for anyone else who may have the same sound installed on their hard drive. Chat Sound samples should be restricted to a few short noises or six or seven words of speech. [The .wav files in the Sound Room of **KEYWORD: Creative Computing** are all short enough for regular chat room use.]

"The other thing you can do is ask people to mail you interesting looking sounds that you see played in the chat rooms. Trading sound files with friends is one good way to make sure that you both have the same sounds with the same names.

"When you go to download a chat sound, make sure it is compatible with your system. AOL Windows users must use .wav files. If the .wav file that you plan to download is "zipped" (look for a .zip at the end of the file name), make sure that your AOL automatic unzipper is enabled. (See "Download Preferences" in the Download Manager under your File menu.) Or you can download an unzipping program from **KEYWORD: Filesearch**. Download your .wav file to your AOL Directory (don't put it in a subdirectory) and unzip it to this directory. Your sound sample is now installed and ready to use.

"To play a .wav in a chat room remember these easy steps. . .

- Type {S <—always use a Capital
- Then on the same line, type the .wav name
- Example: {S tada
- Then hit Enter

"Do not ever play a .wav you may have saved to a floppy disk or diskette in your A or B drive, nor should you play .wav files saved on a CD drive because this will cause system problems online and other people will not be able to hear your sound even if they have that sound installed in their AOL directory."

This last point is important. Attempting to play sounds off a disk or CD drive is a violation of the Terms of Service. So don't do it. You're sure to get TOSsed out of the chat. Remember that in order for someone to hear a specific file, they must have the *exact* file name.

Volunteer to be a Chat Room Ranger

We're always looking for experienced, eager members who are looking to contribute more to the AOL community. At **KEYWORD: Leaders** you'll see many opportunities to volunteer in the Help Wanted Listings, including the Ranger position responsible for hosting chats. You should consider applying through the forms at *The Virtual Leader Academy* if you meet the following requirements:

- Have been an AOL member for at least six months

- Must be at least 18 years of age—proof is required
- Have no Terms of Service or Billing violations
- Type at least 25 words per minute
- Are familiar with AOL's features
- Are a team player

Some of the responsibilities and expectations include:

- Being available for the required training
- Attending required meetings
- Maintaining of confidentiality about team matters
- Having the willingness to adhere to all AOL policies
- Completing minimal paperwork on a timely basis
- Keeping current on team policy and procedures

There are also some system requirements to make sure you've got the equipment to do the job reliably. If you'd like a chance for an online interview, send a completed application to RngerAPP. There are many positions open so applications are accepted at any time.

Ignore Bothersome Chatters

Managing mutiple IMs while simultaneously participating in a chat room can be overwhelming—especially if someone you don't want to converse with keeps sending annoying messages. Fortunately, there's a way to get rid of them.

In the listbox to the right of the chat room, highlight the screen name that's bugging you. A dialogue box pops up with a number of options:

- "message": send that person an IM
- "get info": view their member profile
- "ignore": block IMs from this person

Simply click the "ignore" option and close the window to stop receiving those unwanted Instant Messages.

Or you can block all incoming IMs by turning them off. Type "$im_off" in the To: field of an outgoing IM, type at least one character in the body of the message, and send it. To turn IMs back on, simply send an IM to "$im_on."

Report Password "Phishers"

AOL will never send an IM asking for your password. You know this. What you may not know is the procedure to report people who do.

When a password "phisher" claiming to be an AOL staffer makes up some fictitious reason why they need your password, *don't* close the IM window. Leaving the window open, go to **KEYWORD: TOS**. (If you're in a chat, click the "Notify AOL" button.) Select "Report a Violation," then "Password." (If you went to Notify AOL click on the "Report Password Solicitations" button.) Then cut and paste the phisher's screen name and the full text of the message in the IM, and send off the report.

When you get really good at it, you can tease the miscreant first: "Don't you need my credit card number, too? And my social security number? Mother's maiden name? Shoe size? Would you like some fries with that?" ;)

Hide From Other People's Buddy Lists

The beauty of Buddy Lists is immediately knowing when someone has logged on so you can IM them or join the chat room they're in. This is great for seeing friends and family you want to catch up with. But there are times when you'd like to log on without anyone, or certain people, knowing. To maintain your privacy, all you need to do is set your Buddy List preferences.

AOL gives you several options for your Buddy List participation. First, you have to go to **KEYWORD: Buddy** and set your Preferences there. By default, the "Allow all members to add me to their lists" option is selected. If you don't want *anyone* to have you on their Buddy List, you can select the next option: "Block all members from adding me to their lists." You may also specify members who are allowed to add you to their lists. This would be useful if you don't want anyone in a chat room to add you to a Buddy List, but would like your relatives and friends to have you appear as one of their buddies. Or vice versa. Click the "Allow only the members below" option and type the screen names of the people you choose in the box just under the option. You may also select to block specific AOL members from adding you to their lists. Do this by clicking the button for "Block only the members below" and type their screen names into the space provided.

Instant Message People Over the Internet

AOL's Instant Messaging technology has been expanded so you can reach anyone on the Internet instantly, not just other AOLers. The beauty of it is, you don't have to do anything extra to use the Instant Messenger. Once your friends register you can send them IMs and put them on your Buddy List, regardless of what online service or ISP they may use to get online. At **KEYWORD: Instant Messenger** there's a form to notify your non-AOL buddies about this technology so you can start using it with them.

AOL members can choose which incoming messages to accept from outside the service. And along with the regular blocking feature, you can issue warnings to the sender of annoying or unwanted messages. When the limit of warnings is reached, the user gets bumped from the network for a fixed period of time.

Get Unstuck: Bypass the Hourglass

The speed of your connection, level of online traffic, and amount of artwork all determine how quickly you get into an area. If it's taking too long to access and your patience wanes, you don't have to be stuck staring at that hourglass.

Click on the AOL symbol in the upper left corner, above the menu bar. Highlight the Restore option, then move the cursor over to the Members pull-down menu to the right. Select any area from there, such as Member Services. The area will open, freeing up your cursor from timer mode so you can go on to other work. At a later time you may want to return to the area that you couldn't access before, when traffic is lighter or the area has become available.

Search More Effectively

Narrow your searches in Find with the special "operator" word "not". For instance, a search for "music NOT classical" will result in a list of musical areas excluding classical. However, if a search for the name of a particular, obscure composer doesn't bring up anything, the next logical term to search would be "classical music."

You don't need to be a perfect speller, either, to find what you're looking for. Combining characters with special search functions, like the question mark, tilde, and asterisk, along with your phrase can help modify your search. Look under the Hot Search Tips in Find Help for specific instructions.

Be sure to check the proper directory for the information you're looking for:

AOL areas	=	KEYWORD: **Find**
Members	=	KEYWORD: **Directory**
Web sites	=	KEYWORD: **NetFind**
Software	=	KEYWORD: **File Search**
Business	=	KEYWORD: **Switchboard**

Find Information in the Top Window

Tucked away in the Edit menu is a highly useful tool that will save you from digging through your file cabinet. Find in Top Window will provide a quick search for a phrase or screen name in whichever window is currently active. If your personal filing cabinet is the active window, you can search for a piece of mail from a particular person instead of scrolling through all your saved mail. If the News area is active, do a search for "White House" using Find in Top Window to get the latest update from Washington.

Capture Text Online Instead of Taking Notes by Hand

The Research and Learning Channel houses indispensable volumes of educational information, writing guides, career databases, dictionaries, encyclopedias, and more. These online resources make research extremely fast and simple. Find famous quotations, word origins, scientific facts, and historical timelines here.

Shorten the note-taking process. Open a session with the Log Manager and quickly gather text into one file by opening all the areas relevant to your topic. Then you can edit the single document and print out a compilation of all the information you looked at in various places online.

Get the Helper Programs You Need

When downloading files from a library you may see terms like "unzipping program" or "vbrun.dll" listed in the requirements to run the downloaded program. To get these "helper files," go to KEYWORD: **File Search**.

You can search for either the type of file you're looking for, "file compression," or for the exact file name, "winsock.dll." Once you've downloaded the required files, you can return to the accounting software file or meeting scheduler program you were originally after and get it installed and working properly.

At KEYWORD: **File Search** you can also get a "zipping program," such as PKZip. This will allow you to compress and send multiple files to someone in a single email attachment.

Find Help Online Before Picking Up the Phone

There are often times when you need advice and you just want to get on the horn and call someone who might know how to help you with your modem or explain what an error message really means. But before you jump to the phone to call technical support, use all the online help resources first. It's a step that will likely save you a great deal of time and frustration.

Many questions and problems have been encountered by members before you, and some of them have left their solutions on the *Members Helping Members* message board. **KEYWORD: MHM** is a great place to get help from people who might have first-hand experience with your problem—from the member perspective. If you find live help more reassuring, head to the chat rooms. List Chats, and select Tips and Tricks. This is the premier place to get immediate assistance from knowledgeable members and experienced volunteers.

KEYWORD: Help is the best general resource. Here is Step-By-Step Assistance on a range of topics such as using Netscape through AOL, setting up and configuring AOL for use with a Local Area Network (LAN), and uploading files to a software library. Quick Answers are provided for questions on accessing AOL, accounts and billing, and troubleshooting common problems. It's wise to print out the instructions before following them, so you have them handy if you get stuck.

The essential thing to know about *Member Services* is that it is the only way to reach Member Help Interactive. The people who service members here online are the same people who answer the phones for technical support. But reaching them online means that you don't have to wait on hold. It may take a little while for them to get to you, but while you're waiting you can continue working.

There isn't a direct keyword to reach Member Help Interactive. This is because so many common questions are already answered in *Member Services*. The Step-by-Step Assistance section will run a series of questions by you. If none of the questions presented are yours, you don't come to a dead end. Instead, the area now knows that you've done everything you can to get the answer yourself and puts in a request to an AOL staffer for technical support. All you have to do is wait for them to respond to the IM. Even though they're usually helping up to five people at a time, the process doesn't take long, and you can get the direction you need. The best part about getting help through an IM is that you can save or print the directions, and leave the IM window open while you try out the suggested instructions. If you are still having problems, just return to the IM window and that same staffer will continue to help you.

Customize Your AOL Experience

Start Up AOL with Your Favorite Place

In addition to adding a Favorite Place heart to your folder and sharing it with friends in email, you can drag and drop a Favorite Place to your desktop. When you want to log on to AOL, just click on your Favorite Place and after signing on you'll automatically go to that area.

Customize the Go To Menu

You can assign personalized keyboard shortcuts to get to your most frequently visited areas even quicker than by using the Favorite Places folder. Pull down the Go To menu and select Edit Go To Menu. A grid will appear where you can enter the titles and keywords of ten favorite places. For instance, in the first line enter Political as the title and the keyword. After saving the customized menu you can use the keyboard shortcut Ctrl-1 to pull up the latest headlines in political news.

You can also type URLs in the keyword line while editing the menu. Set up the fifth line as *http://www.aol.com/netfind* to use Ctrl-5 to instantly access AOL NetFind. Or get the Favorite Place heart to an area that doesn't have its own keyword, like your local five-day forecast. You can't drag and drop the heart into the Edit Go To grid, but you can still get the location. Open your Favorite Places folder, highlight an area, and click "Modify." Then cut and past the URL into your personalized Go To menu. Now instead of having to open that Favorite Places folder you can just hit Ctrl-6 or 7 or 8 or whatever number you've assigned to check the weather forecast for your city.

Change the Sounds of Incoming Mail, Buddies, and Downloaded Files

"You've got mail." It's the mantra of the nineties. It's also a sound that I was becoming desensitized to because of the constant stream of incoming email. So I changed it. In fact, I changed the sounds of an incoming IM, incoming buddies, confirmation of a downloaded file, welcome, and goodbye so that I now have an entire sound scheme comprised of Bogart sound bytes from *Casablanca*.

Go to **KEYWORD: Filesearch** and click on the "Shareware" button. Mark off the Music and Sound option to find .wav files, and type in any kind of sound you're looking for, be it the voice of John Wayne or animal sounds or silly cartoon noises. Often many related sound bytes are collected in zip files so you don't have to gather them individually. My search for "Bogart" brought up eight different collections.

Download the file to any directory you wish and unzip it, if it's a collection. (AOL will automatically unzip most files when you sign off.)

Now go to the Control Panel of your PC and double-click the Sounds icon. There you'll see a list of "events" on your computer that can be announced with a sound. All the AOL events are stored there as well. Simply highlight the event, such as Welcome, type in the path to the sound file you want to assign to it, and click OK. Now the next time you log on you won't hear that vintage voice, but "Here's looking at you, kid," or whatever sound byte you assigned to the Welcome event instead. You can change the sounds whenever you like and make them more personal. I never hear that "Goodbye" anymore. I find it much more pleasant to log off to "Louie, I think this is the beginning of a beautiful friendship."

Set Your Mail, Web, and Chat Preferences

You've probably already set your AOL preferences at KEYWORD: **My AOL**, but I think it's a good area to emphasize. Here is where you determine how you want graphics presented to you and where you store your password to your computer. Set up your Personal Filing Cabinet to save copies of all incoming and outgoing email, even if you delete if from your mailbox. Adjust the size of the text on the screen. Decide if you want the Channel menu to greet you every time you sign on. Multimedia, chat, Web, marketing, and download preferences can all be established at *My AOL*. Work your way through the list to give yourself the most comfortable online experience possible and tailor the software to work in the same way you do.

Install Must-Have Browser Plug-Ins

The cool tools you can install to enhance your Web browsing experience can be downloaded from KEYWORD: **MM Showcase**. Click on the Plug-Ins/Controls section to get Shockwave™ by Macromedia®, the RealAudio Player™ by Progressive Networks®, VDOLive™ by VDOnet Corporation®, and Microsoft's ActiveX controls that bring Web content alive. Some Web sites which take advantage of these streaming technologies have features that can only be viewed when you have these plug-ins and controls installed, including games, radio shows, and movies. The *Multimedia Showcase* stores all the latest versions in one convenient place.

Installing plug-ins is not an involved process. Most companies offering these free downloads have followed a consistent, systematic process. Print out the instructions for reference. Ensure you have the system requirements to run the application. (They'll be enumerated in the instructions.) Make note of the directory where you download the file. You'll have to exit AOL to begin the installation of a plug-in, and it's wise to close any other applications you may have running. When you double-click on the file, a step-by-step guided tour will prompt you for information and lead you through the installation. You'll most likely have to restart your machine. Then when you next sign on to AOL and fire up your browser, you can reap the benefits by experiencing the Web's most cutting-edge technologies. Anytime you want to upgrade your plug-ins or find new ones, just return to the *Multimedia Showcase*.

Use Voice Email Software to Speak, Rather than Type, Your Mail

If your PC has a sound card and a microphone, you can use BONZI Software's Voice E-Mail™ AOL add-on. It enables you to actually talk through email, as well as include pictures, all from within AOL. You can send an unlimited number of Voice E-Mail™ messages, as there is no monthly fee nor per-message charges. At the time of this writing the program was being offered for a one-time user fee of $49.95, which you can pay online with a credit card. Not only does it sound like a cool tool to use, it might save many a member's posture since they won't have to cradle the phone on their shoulder and type simultaneously.

Using AOL at Work

Install AOL at Work

You can install the same AOL account on as many computers as you wish. This means you can have access to the same account at work as you have at home. Just remember that when you're logged on at work, no one at home whose screen name is attached to your main account will be able to log on.

If your company has a TCP/IP connection, there's a clear advantage to logging on at work; instead of connecting through a modem you can access AOL through a higher speed network connection. You can check with your system administrator to see what kind of connection your company has. If it's TCP/IP, here's how to install AOL:

1. Establish your Internet connection as you normally would (contact your system administrator if you have questions about this).
2. Install AOL on a computer connected to that network. During the registration process, put in your own screen name and password when AOL prompts you for a registration number and password.
3. Don't bother setting up a modem or local access number—they're both unnecessary with TCP/IP. Just click "Cancel."
4. Click "Setup" on the Sign On screen, then select "Create Location."
5. Name the location TCP/IP, then skip down to the Network box.
6. Select TCP/IP, then click "Save" and exit the Setup.

Installing AOL at work can help with timeshifting. Check your mail on a lunch break or log on at quitting time for a current commuter traffic report.

Separate Business From Your Personal Life

An excellent use of multiple screen names is keeping online business activities separate from personal ones. That way you can filter business email from notes from friends and maintain several different stock portfolios. Establish a professional persona in the member profile for one screen name, then let loose and show your more personal side with the other four.

Share Files with Colleagues Using Your FTP Space

You know AOL will host your Web site and provide tools to help you write HTML files. But were you aware that you can also store other files like Word documents, spreadsheets, and pictures to make them available to friends and coworkers? Instead of sending out email after email with an attached file, just upload them to **KEYWORD: My Place**. Then when someone needs a file you have, they can simply go get it themselves.

Here's how it works: If you put something in *My Place*, it's saved to your FTP (File Transfer Protocol) space. So it's in your personal little chunk of our servers. Now, all other people have to do to read it is to visit your FTP space.

For instance, if you have a spreadsheet with charts of third quarter revenues you need to share with colleagues around the country, just tell them the name of the file, such as "3qtr.xls."

Then they can go to your FTP space to download the report. They can do this either by bringing up a keyword box and typing in "http://members.aol.com/yourscreen-name/3qtr.xls" to get the file. Or they can download it by:

- Going to **KEYWORD: FTP**
- Clicking on "Go To FTP"
- Choosing "Other Site"
- Then typing in "members.aol.com/yourscreen-name" to see all the files in your directory

Non-AOL members can also access this space. Anyone able to run anonymous FTP or a Web browser can access your site. Browsing of AOL user names is not allowed, so someone wishing to access your space needs to know your screen name.

For example, a non-AOL member would have to FTP to the *members.aol.com* site, then immediately input the "cd/screenname" command.

AOL also provides you with a Private directory to store confidential files. Only people who have the exact file name can get to them. Unless you tell someone the exact name of the file in your private directory, they won't be able to find it. This protects any business documents or private correspondence you want to share with a small group of people.

Log Onto AOL When Away From Home

Before going on a business trip within the U.S. get the AOL access numbers for the cities nearest your destination. Search the list of numbers at KEYWORD: **Access** by area code. Write down the access numbers in the area you'll be visiting, and make a note of the speed and network (AOLnet, for example) for each number. You may also print the entire list by clicking on the printer icon at the top of your screen. Then change your Setup to dial those numbers by adding a new "Locality." You'll automatically have that location ready to go once you've reached your destination.

To create a new location file to store alternate local access numbers:

1. Click "Setup" on the Sign On screen.
2. Click "Create Location."
3. Delete the default name (New Locality) and type a name for the new location file. You can use the city you're visiting or call it "Mom and Dad's house" or whatever you want.
4. Type the local access numbers that you got from the *Accessing America Online* area in the Phone Number fields.
5. Verify that the correct network is selected for each local access number you are using, i.e. AOLnet.
6. Verify that the appropriate speed is selected for the new number and your modem. (Select the highest rate at which your modem can transmit data, up to 33.3 bps for AOLnet numbers.)
7. Click "Save."

If your travel takes you out of the country you can connect with the numbers found at KEYWORD: **Intl Access**.

Timeshift: Make AOL Work While You Sleep

Two tools that can make AOL work for you while you're away from your desk are Flash Sessions and the Download Manager. At **KEYWORD: Flash Sessions** you can click on the "Walk Me Through" button for a lesson on how to set up a session. With Flash Sessions you can tell your computer to retrieve unread email and newsgroup messages and send outgoing ones. Just schedule the session for a convenient time and leave AOL open. At the designated time AOL will sign on, grab your mail, send your messages, and log off. You can schedule a Flash Session to get everything at night while you're sleeping and then wake up to read all your files offline in the morning without worrying about trying to connect to AOL.

Flash Sessions will also retrieve any software or files from your Download Manager. Whenever you're working online and find a sound file, utility, application, or browser plug-in you want, just click on "Download Later." Then when your Flash Session is activated at night, all the time your computer spends downloading those files will be time you can spend doing something else.

I should mention that in AOL 4.0 Flash Sessions will be called Automatic AOL. Just so you know.

Telecommute from Your Home Office

One of the reasons for conducting your business on AOL is that you can work in the comfort of your own home. The online world has made telecommuting a very popular practice. For details on helpful areas and ways to do business on AOL, consult Chapter 4, *Build Your Business and Guide Your Career*. You'll find ways to carve out a quiet space at home to build an office, how to network while working alone, and how to manage your career or vocation while getting ample family time. The WorkPlace Channel has essential resources especially for entrepreneurs and job coaches for people looking to shift careers.

And because AOL has access numbers all over the world, your office is quite portable. You don't necessarily have to incur long distance charges as you would by hosting your business on a local Internet Service Provider (ISP).

Build Your Company's Web Site

In the WorkPlace Channel you'll also find **KEYWORD: PrimeHost**. Using this service will get your company Web site up in ten minutes to establish your professional presence on the Web and stay competitive. Templates allow you to build the site quickly and easily and additional resources here help you promote it. *PrimeHost* aims to be a "turnkey solution to doing business on the Internet." For example, Storefront is a product offered by PrimeHost that will enable you to sell inventory through your Web site. At the time of this writing the cost for the service was $99 per month. There is also an additional fee of $100 payable to InterNIC, the organization that regulates all domain name registries.

To learn more about creating your company's Web site read Chapter 4: Build Your Business and Guide Your Career.

Page Someone through AOL

KEYWORD: Page has just got to be the coolest tool I've ever found on AOL. You can actually page someone through this area. Just type in their pager number, select the paging company (either AT&T or MobileComm), type your message, and send it off. Filling out the message field is required to send a page. After you click the "Send" button, "sound waves" from the satellite dish picture represent a wait cursor, so you know that the page is still being sent.

You can store pager numbers in the address book in this area, and add the person's email address as well.

AOL NetFind: Not Your Average Search Engine

Quickly Locate What You Need on the Internet

Powered by the Excite search engine, AOL NetFind pares down the time it takes you to find Web sites, newsgroups, businesses, and individuals. It's the most comprehensive way to locate who and what you need on the Internet.

NetFind's columnist, Casey, is your personal guide to NetFind and offers many practical searching tips, including Seven Simple Steps for Finding What You Want. For example, #2: Be Specific, suggests you use more descriptive, exact words to conduct a search. Casey's in-depth explanations and example searches lend a friendly face to this search engine and make it more personable than one that dumps a list of useless links in your lap.

See Which Web Sites are Worth the Effort

NetFind proffers reviews of Web sites in various categories and rates them on a scale of 1 to 4, from If You're Desperate to Must See. Excite's editors place reviews into categories such as Arts, Entertainment, Movies, Magazines, and Sports.

For example, AOL NetFind rates *Business Week* as a 4-star site. Well, actually, a 4-magnifying glass site: "One of the bibles of the working establishment, *Business Week* brings the world up to speed on activities in board rooms around the world, daily news from Wall Street, the latest high-tech breakthroughs, and advice on where (or where not) to invest your money. Defying common practice, *BW* publishes its entire U.S. and international editions every Thursday night in addition to its online-only features."

Read the Essential Guide to Newsgroups

The Newsgroup resources on NetFind are a great complement to the newsreader at **KEYWORD: Usenet**. On NetFind you'll see reviews of 500 Newsgroups that explain what audience the groups are directed toward and rate the level of activity and quality of the postings. The Newsgroup Finder will locate the Internet addresses of groups you're searching for. You don't have to know the hierarchical name of a group; just do a search for the topic you're interested in.

Although not mandatory for participating in Newsgroups, a highly recommended and appreciated step is reading the FAQ, or list of Frequently Asked Questions, that goes with a particular Newsgroup before diving into the conversation. The Ohio State FAQ Archive is a good place to start, and there's a link right here. Also, be sure to read the etiquette handbook stored here to save yourself from embarrassment or angry replies. Learn what's considered "off-topic" for a certain group and limit your messages to the subject the group was designed to address. Don't compose posts in all capital letters—it's considered shouting online. And don't quote someone's page-long post only to say, "Me, too." It wastes bandwidth, annoys people, and is considered very bad form.

Make Your Life Easier with NetFind's Time Savers

One of the best features of AOL NetFind is its Time Savers section. In this you can accomplish tasks with a package of dependable, powerful Web resources. These are the "tried-and-true" sites popular with AOL members and Internet users alike. Time Savers can help you:

- Find a new apartment or a realtor
- Plan a trip
- Go out on the town
- Stay on top of the news
- Avoid mall crowds by shopping online
- Get customized maps

- Find a job
- Buy a car
- Manage your money
- Reconnect with a long-lost friend
- Participate in government

Time Savers provides links not only to pivotal Web sites, but also to substantial Newsgroups where postings are relevant and of real worth.

Find a Person's Address and Send them a Card Through the Web

Type in a name plus a city and state in the Switchboard area and click "Find" to track down the phone numbers and addresses of old friends, old flames, and close relations. You can also add or modify your own listing so others can find you. It's free to register to become a Switchboard member, and you can enter as much or as little personal information as you want. For instance, you could include your email address and phone number, but not disclose your physical address. When you get your password, you can login and modify your listing if your information changes.

If you find someone on Switchboard and they have an email address registered, you can send them a note right then and there. Or you can send a greeting card for around $4 or a letter for $3 through "snail mail." Compose your message online and it will be printed out, addressed, and mailed to your friend, relative, or colleague. I'm a big fan of the Anne Geddes postcards—you know, the babies in the flower pots. There's also some really silly "FunMail" you can send through the site, such as a summons to perform in a talent show and a golf-etiquette violation.

Locate a Business

Switchboard's Find a Business on NetFind is a flexible directory. It allows you to search for a business either by name or by the category you would find it under in the Yellow Pages. An added benefit of searching for a company online is that you can get an interactive map to direct you to the exact location. To find a business, just type in the name or select the category from the pull-down menu. Input the city and state and you'll get contact information for the business you're looking for.

Scroll down the site to find the link to American City Business Journals; it's a must-see. Updated daily, this Web site connects you to local trade journals in real estate, banking and insurance, high tech, and other industries. You can also access critical demographics information here.

Kids Can Find Things on Their Own

NetFind Kids Only is a special area of the site set aside for children. The best feature is the Top Sites, where kids can find games, news, sports, and more. The Exploratorium Web site has been a long-standing favorite, and for good reason. Kids can participate in an exhibit that illustrates how animals along the Amazon River blend into their surroundings. Or they can do their own cow's eye dissection, much like the one displayed in the actual museum in San Francisco. NetFind for Kids is also an excellent resource for Web-based games to educate and entertain your children.

Whew. Who knew there was so much to say just about the functionality of AOL, much less the content? Well, now you do. Practice using these techniques to streamline your use of online time and become more effective. Also keep them in mind while you're reading the rest of the chapters on how to use AOL areas in accomplishing every day tasks. Remember to use the

Download Manager when exploring software catalogued in the games and computing chapters (Chapters 11 and 6). Turn on your Log Manager to record important chats with financial analysts and guidance counselors listed in the personal finance and business chapters.

Another key to making AOL function in your life effectively is the tactic I mentioned earlier in this chapter: take an integrative approach to AOL's resources. In working through this book you will develop a familiarity with all of AOL's content, not just your Favorite Places. And you'll learn to jump from one channel to another to find all the relevant information you need in places you might have overlooked previously. I've given tons of channel jumping examples in the margins of this book to show you what I mean to help you uncover some hidden gems. Try them!

AOL is truly a comprehensive and convenient tool to get stuff done, if you know how to use the service fully. And that's what this book is for. So continue reading and testing out your new-found knowledge online. And don't forget to visit *my* area at **KEYWORD: AOL Insider** for more tips. You should also subscribe to the Advanced Tips newsletter at **KEYWORD: Tip of the Day** to have additional tricks delivered straight to you via email.

The Insider's AOL 4.0 Sneak Preview

I'm really excited about the dynamic enhancements being made to AOL with the upcoming 4.0 version. From what I've seen so far, they're going to make exploring AOL and the Internet faster, more responsive, and more interactive than ever before. A great deal of sophisticated multimedia technology has been added to offer a more cutting-edge online experience. Member feedback has also been incorporated to improve the software, resulting in a more simplified, intuitive installation and registration process. Personal File Cabinet passwording and multi-redial capability have also been added. AOL 4.0 will automatically redial each of your access numbers five times.

Of course I could only get my hands on a working beta at the time of this writing, so some of the features I discuss here may change. Keep checking my area at **KEYWORD: AOL Insider** to find out when you can upgrade to 4.0 and get added tips on how to use the new software.

The recommended system requirements for using AOL 4.0 upon its availability are as follows:

Windows 3.1

- 12 megabyte system configuration
- 486-based or better PC
- 30 megabytes available hard disk space
- 640x480, 256 colors or better screen
- 14.4 or faster modem

Windows 95

- 16 megabyte system configuration
- Pentium-based PC
- 30 megabytes available hard disk space
- 640x480, 256 colors or better screen
- 14.4 or faster modem

Macintosh

- 12 megabyte system configuration
- System 7.1 minimum
- 68040 or PowerPC Macintosh
- 30 megabytes available hard disk space
- 640x480, 256 colors or better screen
- 14.4 or faster modem

Pictures Are Added

Create an Online Photo Album

A major change to AOL with the 4.0 version is the addition of a Picture Gallery. You can display a collection of pictures or modify a single picture all within AOL.

To create a photo album, just store all the pictures you want grouped together in the same folder on your hard drive. Then, in AOL 4.0, go to the File pulldown menu and select "Open Picture Gallery." A dialog box will ask you for the folder where your pictures are stored and what type of files you're looking for: either "Pictures of All Types" or snapshots stored on a Kodak Picture Disk. Select the proper picture source, then click "Open Gallery." A grid will open, showing thumbnail versions of six of your pictures. If you have more than six in a folder, the Picture Gallery will tell you the total at the bottom and an arrow will appear, allowing you to move forward and backward through the Gallery. It's just like flipping through pages in a photo album.

You can open a picture by clicking on the thumbnail version in the Gallery. A picture toolbar allows you to fine-tune and tweak the picture before you send it off to friends. You don't have to open the picture in a separate paint program. You can rotate the picture counterclockwise 90, 180, or 270 degrees, flip the picture over left-to-right or top-to-bottom, crop it, remove the color information, and make other adjustments. When you've got the picture in the shape you want it, just Save it within the picture editor. If you liked it better in its original form, a button at the bottom will allow you to undo all your changes and restore the picture to the way it was. To share it with friends, click the "Insert in Email" button. This will generate an email with the picture automatically inserted in the body of the message.

Insert Pictures in Email

You can also simply drag a picture directly from the Picture Gallery and drop it into an email. The embedded picture will automatically appear when the recipient opens the message. There's no longer a need for them to download an attached file to view pictures you send them.

Pictures can be inserted from digital cameras and scanners as well. Parents will be able to control whether children can use this feature at KEYWORD: **Parental Controls**.

Email is Enhanced

Spell Check Your Mail and Catch Grammatical Errors

Email in AOL 4.0 has a new look. Three tabbed folders create easier access to your New Mail, Old Mail, and Sent Mail. And when you start to compose a new message you'll see that the email toolbar has been expanded. Added to this new toolbar is a feature members have been clamoring after for a while: a spell checker.

The spell checker also looks for errors in your grammar and can be used whether you compose your email online or offline.

You can also customize your grammar and punctuation preferences. Go to My AOL on the toolbar and select Preferences from the pulldown menu. Click the "Spelling" button and choose "Advanced." This allows you to tell the spell checker to follow or ignore particular rules of grammar. Back under Preferences you'll also see buttons that enable you to set a default font for your email text and add foreign languages to your dictionary.

To spell check your mail, type your message and then click the button on the toolbar with the "ABC" and checkmark on it. It works the same way the spell checker in your word processor does.

You can set up your preferences to perform an automatic spell check before sending mail. Click on the Mail Center in the toolbar and select Mail Preferences. Here you can choose to perform a spell check before sending mail, save your mail to your personal file cabinet, and show addresses within mail as hyperlinks.

The Edit pulldown menu in AOL 4.0 also includes direct links to *Merriam Webster's Collegiate Dictionary* (**KEYWORD: Collegiate**) and *Thesaurus* (**KEYWORD: THESAURUS**) which you can use when composing mail online.

Create Your Own Personalized Stationery

Additional elements of the toolbar enhance the presentation of your email. In addition to the spelling and grammar check for accuracy, you can use the new fonts to stylize your text and drop pictures into the background of your messages.

A wonderful application of these new features would be to create your own online stationery. Center your logo at the top of the page for company memos. Change the font throughout a letter to emphasize different lines and give them more expression and context. Trying to relate the story of a bad date? Try using different colors to distinguish the comments in a he said/she said manner, so your reader doesn't get confused about who said what.

Another option with the new email in AOL 4.0 is the ability to add a picture as a background picture. Place your cursor in the body of the email and go to the Edit pulldown menu. Highlight "Insert" and select "Background Picture" from the side menu (or right mouseclick once and select "Background Picture"). The picture will fill the body of the email, and repeat itself for as long as you continue to type. As with background pictures for Web pages, the best pictures to use for a background in email are small pictures that tile well. The graphic file formats supported for this feature are .art, .jpg, .gif, and .bmp. And use the text colors in the toolbar to make sure your message contrasts well enough with the background to be legible.

If you try to embed a picture and wrap your text around it like a magazine-style layout, it won't work. When you send the email, headers are added that crop the top of your picture and shift the typed message down the page. You may be able to play around with your pictures and the spacing of your text, but it's best to use a tiled picture. You can find many of them to download for free from Web page resources, such as **KEYWORD: On the Net**.

Compose Individualized Greeting Cards

Another stylish way to send a message is with a greeting card you design yourself. With several different templates to work from, you will be able to quickly personalize a birthday, anniversary, or "thinking of you" card that includes pictures and sounds. AOL 4.0 makes it easy to incorporate multimedia into your everyday correspondence.

Store Friends' and Relatives' Pictures in Your Address Book

A simple way to remember your friends' special days is also included right in the new email features. The new address book will be expanded so you can store not just names and email addresses, but also your friends', relatives', and colleagues' personal data such as birthdays, anniversaries—even pictures of them. A notes field lets you keep track of any relevant information you need to record. For instance, this is an excellent place to store contact information that you would find in someone's signature file, or "sig," at the end of a message board posting. With the notes field, your email address book on AOL can do double duty as a personal phone book.

You can drag and drop names from the address book directly to mail you're composing or from mail you've read to your address book. A Blind Carbon Copy button is also added, though you can already use this feature manually in previous versions. See the section entitled "Send a Secret Email" in the first chapter of this book.

Attach Multiple Files to Email Messages

With AOL 4.0 you can attach multiple files to an email message without having to zip them first. Once you select the files you want to attach, the files are automatically compressed to speed their transmission across the network.

Chat is More Fun

Use Rich Text in Chat

When you type in chat rooms your text can be bolded, italicized, or underlined in AOL 4.0. You can change the font or the color of the words, even midway through a sentence. This can help you express what you *really* mean, in addition to using emoticons. Keep in mind that some lighter colors may be more difficult to read against the white background on some monitors. Use colors that create a strong contrast for legibility.

AOL Becomes Even Easier and More Efficient to Use

Leave Electronic Bread Crumbs to See Where You've Been

A new streamlined toolbar makes access to AOL areas and the Web seamless. You don't have to open the Web browser separately (as you do with the Globe icon in AOL 3.0). Instead, the place for typing in the location of where you want to go combines both AOL areas and Web sites. With 4.0 you simply type either the keyword or the URL into the box within the toolbar and click on "Go." This box also serves as a dropdown list that stores the last 25 areas or Web sites you visited, kind of like Hansel and Gretel leaving bread crumbs behind to find their way home. So if you forgot to mark an area as a Favorite Place, you can return very easily.

AOL 4.0 includes Microsoft's Internet Explorer as the integrated Web security browser on all computer platforms (16-bit PC, 32-bit PC, and Macintosh). With the integrated Internet Explorer, you have a Web browser that includes 128-bit SSL encryption in the U.S. (overseas it's 40-bit SSL encryption), the benefit of which I'll explain later in this chapter.

Move the Toolbar and Add Your Own Icons

The toolbar has been re-designed so you can move it from the top to the bottom of your screen. This is great if you temporarily want more room on your screen. A simple toolbar preference enables you to place the toolbar in either place.

The *really* cool thing about the new toolbar is that you can customize it to add more icons. Open an area that you want to place on your toolbar, such as **KEYWORD: Pet Care** or the genealogy forum at **KEYWORD: Roots**. Now drag and drop the Favorite Place heart up onto your toolbar. A selection box will pop up so you can Choose Button Art to represent that area on your toolbar. You can select the sun behind the clouds to represent your local weather, or a car to indicate local traffic reports. Note that in order to add Favorite Places to your toolbar your monitor resolution should be set to 800x600 pixels. To remove a customized icon, hold down the Ctrl key on your keyboard, and drag the icon off the toolbar onto any other place on your screen.

Print Out the Quick Reference Guide

When you install AOL 4.0, you can print out a Quick Reference Guide that familiarizes you with AOL and helps you make the most of your online experience. Useful for both beginners and seasoned members, the Guide covers a broad range of topics including the basic concepts of how to get around, how to communicate with others, new features available, and much more.

That guide is just to get you up and running. You'll also soon find new Quick Reference Guides that list all the areas on AOL. While this Insider's Guide tackles AOL content in a task-oriented way, Quick Reference Guides in an upgrade area will list everything in each channel from A–Z. This will be particularly handy even for experienced users, since the face of AOL will change along with the debut of the AOL 4.0 software. Areas will be rearranged and put into new channels, or categories, to make it easier to find them.

Remember, you can always do a search for a topic of interest with **KEYWORD: Find**.

Get Immediate Answers to the Top 25 Questions Asked About AOL

Upon installing AOL you'll find a list of the top 25 questions and their answers. This will allow you to get help immediately for the most commonly asked questions.

These answers will also be available online in a searchable database in the Member Services area at **KEYWORD: Help**.

Switch Screen Names Without Disconnecting

AOL 4.0 also simplifies connectivity. With 4.0 you'll be able to move between screen names in your account without disconnecting your modem. Instead of signing off, click on "My AOL" from the toolbar. Then select "Switch Screen Name." A listbox will pop up with all the screen names attached to your account, and indicate which ones have new mail to be read and the type of account (General, Child, Teen, etc.). Highlight the screen name you want to use and click the "Switch" button. Before signing on with the new screen name, a box will show you how many minutes you've already been online and which pricing plan you have. Click "OK," then enter the password for the new screen name and click "Switch." This means everyone in the family can check their mail during one session without having to reconnect.

You can also schedule a single Automatic AOL session (formerly known as a Flash Session) to retrieve and send mail and newsgroup postings and download files for all five screen names. Go to My AOL on the Toolbar and select Automatic AOL from the pulldown menu.

Get the Screen Name You Want

AOL's membership growth doesn't just affect access; it also means more and more screen names are being used. Just as we've expanded access to accommodate new users, AOL is expanding the number of characters you can use in your screen name. Soon your screen names can be up to 16 characters long. This will give you more naming options and the chance to create more meaningful names. Every account will still allow you five screen names. Using them all is a good way to filter your email.

Choose Where You Want to Put Your Favorite Place

With AOL 4.0 you will have more flexibility when you find an area worth remembering. When you click on the Favorite Places heart in the title bar of an AOL area or Web site, you can now choose what you want to do with the link to that place. You can add it to your Favorite Places folder, send it in an email message, or put it in an IM. (You can do all of these things now in AOL 3.0, but 4.0 just makes it easier.) In 4.0 if you're already composing an email message, a link to your Favorite Place is inserted at the current point in the message. Otherwise, an email message is automatically generated with a subject and a link to the place; all you need to do is address the message and send it off.

Experience More Multimedia

Enjoy Multimedia Content That Is "Streamed" In

"Streaming" content allows you to see and hear multimedia as soon as you enter an area—without waiting for large multimedia files to download, or worse, having to retrieve them yourself. Sounds and pictures begin to play even as the files are being transmitted to your computer. It's like listening to "Pomp and Circumstance" at a commencement ceremony; the song doesn't play *after* all the graduates have arrived, it ushers them in.

Good examples of streaming technology can be found at KEYWORD: **Slideshows**. And at KEYWORD: **News** you can see how ABC News streams in their broadcasts. You'll be seeing it used more regularly in AOL areas, and the player you need is automatically downloaded, so you don't need to install it manually.

Another new format you may come across is AOL's Artdoc. With this new technology, AOL presents text, pictures, sounds, and slideshows with an elegant look and feel. Check it out at KEYWORD: **Artdoc**.

Find Popular Plug-Ins and Active X Controls Built In

Microsoft's Internet Explorer is the browser that's integrated into AOL 4.0. Along with it comes support for Active X technology, both bundled into the browser and built into AOL areas. This means online content comes to life with multimedia effects, interactive objects, and sophisticated applications. Additional features you can enjoy with the latest browser are animated GIFs (pictures), marquees that display moving banners of text, simplified frame navigation, 128-bit Secure Sockets Layer (SSL) encryption security (explained later in this chapter), background sound, and the latest HTML 3.2 tags, including, table cell colors, font faces, multi-column tags for side-by-side columns, and spacers.

And when installing AOL 4.0 from a CD-ROM, you can automatically install the following plug-ins:

- Shockwave Essentials™ by Macromedia® provides both Shockwave Director® (a player for rich multimedia, games, and streaming audio), and Shockwave Flash™ (a player for small and fast Web animations).
- VDOLive™ by VDOnet Corporation® enables anyone on the Web to receive live and on-demand video broadcasts and news reports, regardless of the speed of their modem.
- QuickTime and QuickTime VR from Apple Computer allow you to watch downloaded movies.

If you're a "gotta have it now" kind of person and you want to play with these technologies immediately, go to **KEYWORD: MM Showcase** and consult the section "Install Must-Have Browser Plug-Ins" in Chapter 1, *Using AOL Effectively*, in this book.

Design More Advanced Web Pages

Not only can you enjoy the added effects of advanced Web publishing on other people's sites, you can also design your own Web pages knowing that the AOL audience will be able to view them in their optimal form.

With AOL 4.0 comes Personal Publisher 3.0. This new version of the Web page design tool will help you create and edit custom pages that include sophisticated features such as tables, picture maps, and formatted text. And the ability to graphically manage multiple pages makes it easier to keep tabs on your work.

AOL Carries a Security Blanket

Conduct Secure Transactions with the Highest Level of Encryption Available

AOL is the first online service and Internet access provider to automatically provide members with a Web security browser, Microsoft's Internet Explorer, which features 128-bit SSL encryption for the highest level of security on the Internet. Only available for use in the U.S. and Canada, the advanced security of 128-bit SSL encryption scrambles information into code that is virtually uncrackable in the industry today. This means you can continue to bank and shop online safely.

When you communicate with a secure server using SSL, messages are automatically encrypted before they are sent across the Internet. A secret key on the server decrypts the messages when they arrive.

You can set your Web preferences to have AOL give you warnings:

- Before sending information over an open connection
- If you're changing between secure and unsecure mode
- About invalid site certificates
- Before accepting "cookies"

"Cookies" are electronic files used by Web sites to record your preferences. For instance, if you shop for jazz and classical CDs in an online music store, that merchant can avoid showing you the collections of country and rap music.

Just go to My AOL on the toolbar, select Preferences, and choose the "Web" button. The above warnings can be turned on or off under the "Advanced" tab.

Establish an Internet Site Ratings System

Also under the Web preferences at My AOL is a tab for "Content." Here you can enable the content advisor, which offers ratings on Web sites to help you control what kind of Internet content users of your computer are allowed to view. Enabling and disabling this ratings system requires a password, so kids won't be able to turn off the ratings when they log on. You can set your specific level of tolerance for categories such as language, nudity, sex, and violence separately. Of course, the best way to monitor what you're children view online is to browse the Web along with them. No program can match an involved parent.

Lock Your Personal File Cabinet with a Password

Another oft-requested feature has been incorporated into the new version of AOL. You can now make sure the contents of your Personal File Cabinet are hidden from anyone using your computer by assigning a password to it. You won't have to worry about your kids or any guests using your computer opening any of your mail or newsgroup postings.

9 9 9 9 9

There are truly some powerful tools being added to AOL, especially some of the new multimedia features. I hope what I've written in this chapter gives you some ideas not just about what to expect from AOL 4.0, but ways to use the new technology effectively.

Regardless of the version you're using, you'll be able to apply the techniques that appear in following chapters. Why? Because despite the ongoing advancements inherent in the online medium and the ever-growing online community, AOL remains easy to use. As you read on in the *Insider's Guide*, you'll see what I mean: no matter where you start, AOL's technology and content are designed to work together, to help you accomplish your everyday tasks more efficiently.

Keeping Current: News and Weather Reports on AOL

It used to be that casually flipping through the morning edition while leisurely sipping your coffee was enough to be informed about the world around you. Then life sped up. With streams of data and bits of information flying in from every direction every second of the day, how do you manage it all and relate it to your own daily life?

Here's where AOL really changes your way of working and getting news. Hourly news dispatches at **KEYWORD: News** are stored in one convenient spot so you can get the news as it happens with just a mouseclick. In this chapter, you can learn how to have the news fed directly to your desktop. Customized news dispatches deliver only the articles you want to your email box.

And on AOL, forums provide message boards where local news refers to your exact neighborhood. Digital Cities provide forums where you can help establish a neighborhood watch and places where small mom-and-pop stores can advertise to their target market cheaply.

You can get either the five-day forecast for your area or the expected weather for next week's business trip to Hong Kong. What makes accessing news and weather on AOL ideal is that you never have to wait for that "film at 11."

Get Today's News on a Constant Feed

At **KEYWORD: News Ticker**, the top headlines from Today's News come streaming along the top corner of your screen, on top of the window you already have open. While you're doing other work, you can keep an eye out for an interesting story. When you see a headline that interests you, click on it to read the story in full, or just wait five seconds for a new headline to appear, all while reading your mail, checking your portfolio, or browsing the Web.

Get National and World News When You Want It

Get News as It Happens

The hourly newswire reports at **KEYWORD: News** keep you abreast of world events nearly as they happen. Once you're at *News*, you can jump directly to the sections of the news that are important to you, such as U.S. and World news, Politics, Weather, Sports, Business, or Entertainment.

You can also access *News* right from the toolbar, which creates an easy way to check what's happening throughout the day. This is especially useful if you're following the events of a trial or a natural disaster where friends and family may be located.

Only on AOL

ABC News puts AOL slide show technology to great use, broadcasting reports on your desktop. You'll find them in a link from **KEYWORD: News**.

Get Focused with ABC News

What makes the *ABC News* area stand apart from other news services on AOL is its use of slide show technology. Digitized versions of broadcast reports recount current events with voice-overs, interviews, and images that automatically appear on your screen. The slide show starts up as soon as you click on the link to the area from *News* or select the Slide Shows section from the *ABC News* Web site. Each slide show gives you news when you want to see and hear it. Conveniently, there is a pause button for times when you need to turn up the volume on your speakers. Something else you can't do with TV news: rewind or fast-forward the slide show manually.

The News To Use section of the Web site illustrates how big news stories affect your everyday life, like which dogs are biting more people these days and why email is helping kids and teachers with schoolwork. It puts top news stories in context, providing a practical and informative resource.

Chatter Box

Every week ABC News correspondents log on from Hong Kong, the Middle East, or wherever they are stationed and take questions regarding affairs in their particular locale. **KEYWORD: ABC News Live** connects you to these live discussions.

Keep Up with the Times

The New York Times has long been considered the newspaper of record for the nation. At **KEYWORD: Times** the offerings are extensive: all the major sections from the print version are here, including the *Sunday Magazine*. Page One covers top stories, then moves on to cover National News, Sports, Business, and the New York Metro area.

A popular feature for New York residents, tourists, and anyone who loves the arts is the Arts & Entertainment Guide. You can find extensive book and movie reviews, theater listings, and a Dining Guide.

I recommend *The Times*' own searchable database to find what you want right away, to help tailor the paper's far-reaching coverage to your specific needs.

Do You Remember...?

KEYWORD: NYT Looks Back has collected stories that serve as a time capsule, commemorating historical milestones or epochs. Jackie Robinson: Breaking the Color Barrier. Heroine Worship: The Age of the Female. Hong Kong's Return to China.

This compendium of windows on the past is provided to AOL members exclusively, and is not found on the *New York Times* Web site.

Search for the News You Want

When you want to follow a particular story every day, such as stock market fluctuations or the details of the President's latest proposals, **KEYWORD: News Search** can

Photojournalists Capture News in Pictures

Located in the *News* area and updated every Friday, Pictures of the Week provides a colorful and often dramatic complement to the area's top stories. Snapped by Reuters and Associated Press photographers, quality photos at **KEYWORD: Editor's Choice** are displayed in gallery format so you can spend as much or as little time studying a picture and its caption as you'd like, or even click a link to more related photos.

Another useful tool: sports fans will enjoy the sports gallery, organized by sport, which contains a bit more commentary.

Meet... Newsmakers and Shakers

Appearing in featured profiles at **KEYWORD: NYT People** are chefs, actors, business people, and others who have made a name for themselves in their respective industries.

help you get the latest reports instantly. This news search engine allows you to enter the words you want to read about, such as "Dow Jones" or "Clinton budget," and get all the recent news headlines about those subjects. *News Search* is updated 24 hours a day, using newswires such as the Associated Press, Reuters, Business Wire, PR Newswire, and Sportsticker.

The most recent articles are first. Simply choose the headline that seems most relevant, click, and read the story. News articles are kept online for a minimum of three days.

The Help & Info button can help you learn some better searching techniques, if you're having trouble coming up with articles.

Attention AOL Shoppers!

KEYWORD: **Magazine Outlet** has truly great bargains on subscriptions to news, business, computing, and numerous other magazines with big savings off the newsstand price.

Interact with Newsweek Magazine

Traditional print and broadcast journalism strive for objectivity, relaying information without a strident opinion or an invitation for feedback. The sole opportunity for personal voice in a mainstream newspaper is to write a letter to the editor and hope it gets printed. But that's not the case online.

KEYWORD: **Newsweek** includes most of the articles from its print magazine with a very important addition. *Newsweek Interactive* is a prime example of a publication that successfully blends both print and online media. The best feature is My Turn online, where a controversial question is posited in an original article and a symposium is begun on a dedicated message board. You can debate the current week's issue with other members and if your comments are insightful and coherent, they may be incorporated into a follow-up article that summarizes members' viewpoints. In this way, *Newsweek*'s quality, in-depth reporting is fully and successfully blended with member-contributed ideas.

Insider's Tip

See your opinions on top news issues incorporated into an article at KEYWORD: **Newsweek**, a publication that makes the most of the online medium.

And this online version of *Newsweek* reflects the look and feel of the print publication. The area works like a magazine, as you "flip" through the stories laid out in standard columns. You can quickly produce a printed copy if you find that reading lots of information online is difficult.

Understand Market and Investment News

Extensive, specific, timely information drives the *Market News Center* (KEYWORD: **MNC**). Throughout the day, this area provides the NYSE averages and the most active stocks on the NYSE and AMEX. You can also get the stocks with the biggest gains and the biggest losses and find indices for S & P, NASDAQ, and Dow. Search through the Currencies section to find out what the hourly foreign exchange rates are, or verify the new issue pricing for U.S. corporate bonds.

The best aspect of the area is the collection of graphs. Look at DJIA, NASDAQ, Long Bond, and the Japanese Yen charted throughout the day.

9 Understand Wall Street Jargon

For those of us who don't know the difference between small-cap and mid-cap funds, the Stock Market Terms dictionary at KEYWORD: **WSW** might help. After looking up words in this reference you'll be able to decipher a typical broker's vocabulary.

Get an Accurate Outlook on Weather

Local Forecasts Whenever You Want Them

KEYWORD: **Weather News** brings you current conditions, forecasts, satellite images, and the latest weather news in any area nationwide. *Weather News* is useful if you're traveling in the U.S. and need to know what conditions you'll encounter, or if you're planning a picnic right in your own backyard.

Weather News lets you find the weather in any region simply by typing a state, town, area code, or zip code. You'll get the latest weather conditions, plus a local forecast and handy links to related content like maps and satellite and radar images. No matter what time of day or night, your personal weather forecast is available. And a peculiar yet powerful resource is the garden area where you'll find the last freeze dates for each growing zone.

You can also find local weather forecasts in the many Digital Cities on AOL.

Insider's Tip

KEYWORD: **Newsstand** collects all the magazine areas on AOL in one spot. *Business Week Online*, *Consumer Reports*, and even hobby publications are gathered here.

Good Stuff!

The Weather Classroom at **KEYWORD: Weather** has fascinating facts about hurricanes, tornadoes, and insightful weather safety tips. Weather History covers the top ten snowstorms that rampaged across the East Coast, including the infamous "Blizzard of '78."

Plan for International Travel

KEYWORD: Intl Weather reports the conditions across the globe so you can prepare for a foreign climate. A good use of Web technology, the ubiquitous Web cams capture pictures of the weather in Dublin and London, which are updated every 30 seconds. Maps here cover entire continents as well as specific cities, so you can get an idea of what your journey will be like as well as what conditions will be when you arrive at your final destination.

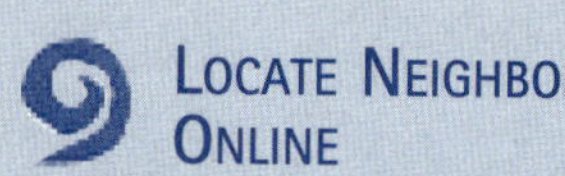

LOCATE NEIGHBORS ONLINE

Digital City provides a forum for major cities across the country and internationally. Type in your city as a keyword and you have access to local news that covers your suburb, the five-day forecast, movie listings, and hometown sports news.

The best part of these Digital Cities are the residents you'll meet on the message boards and in chats. It's a great chance to meet in real life the friends you make online, since they could live just around the block.

Get Really Local News

Plan a Trip to Orlando

The *Orlando Sentinel Online* at **KEYWORD: OSO** can help you appreciate local Florida news.

The best thing about the *Orlando Sentinel Online* is that members contemplating a move or a vacation to Florida can take their pick from among the dozens of features about recreation, dining, and real estate. This area also has a link to **KEYWORD: Black Voices** which highlights afro-centric news in Florida, as well as Chicago and Hampton Roads, Virginia.

News About the Windy City From the Chicago Tribune

KEYWORD: Chicago Tribune brings you each day's local news from the *Chicago Tribune*, plus searchable archives of world, national, and business news. A great sports section (go Bulls!) entices fans with the downloadable graphics and photos of the players in action. The *Tribune*'s op-ed writers have their own section which includes syndicated columnist Bob Greene and Jeff MacNelly, political cartoonist.

Visitors and business travelers will find the Best of Chicago especially useful for articles on dining, sights, shopping, and the music scene.

Find the News in Your Own Digital City

Want to know what's happening in your neck of the woods? **KEYWORD: Digital City** brings local coverage to many metro areas such as Cleveland, Minneapolis-St. Paul, and Philadelphia. New cities are constantly being added, so check your nearest metropolitan mecca simply by typing in the city name as the keyword, such as **KEYWORD: Boston**, or **KEYWORD: LA**. Each city has online versions of its own local news sources, from both the worlds of print and broadcast journalism. For instance, Seattle has the *Seattle Times*, the *Tacoma News Tribune*, and the *Seattle Daily Journal of Commerce*, and Boston has the *Herald*, *Patriot Ledger*, New England Cable News, and WB56.

Your *Digital City* is also the optimal source for weather information because it is highly localized and current. Multimedia five-day forecasts prepare you for what's coming weatherwise.

Another key to news resources in Digital Cities are the message boards, usually arranged according to neighborhood. You can find out not only what's going on downtown, but what's happening on your block by checking in with other wired neighbors. An effective use of this forum would be setting up an online neighborhood crime watch. Many people also post to cities they grew up in and have since moved from to see if their favorite hangouts still exist.

You can see how these message boards are particularly helpful when you sample other "local" city sites that are cropping up all over the Web. Many of them, like *Sidewalk.com*, merely provide listings of events and business addresses categorized by type or service. Clearly, the real resource of Digital Cities are the residents themselves.

Insider's Tip

KEYWORD: Classifieds is an easy way to buy or sell a car, a computer, real estate, or even hunt for a job. The Find a Buyer section offers instructions on how to place a premier ad.

Good Stuff!

An interesting feature of the Web that has now become ubiquitous is the "Web cam." You can get live, updated pictures of local areas to put right on your desktop. Try going to **KEYWORD: NetFind** and searching for "Web cam" plus the name of your city to find a familiar view. Or watch the sun set over the Golden Gate Bridge with a plethora of Web cameras focused on San Francisco.

Using the *Tribune*'s excellent search, it is also possible to track down hard-to-find information from archives that reach back to 1985—a boon for researchers, scholars, and the just plain curious.

9 Create a Personalized, Automated News Search

You don't have to scour several news sources yourself to follow subjects you're interested in. Just create a *Personalized News Profile*. At KEYWORD: **News Profile** you can set up an automated search to cull stories you'd be interested in. You get news from the Associated Press, PR Newswire, Business Wire, and others. These dispatches are sent directly to your email box to give you the very latest updates on the news you want to track.

Find a Job in the Southwest

KEYWORD: **Arizona Central** is a combination of the *Arizona Republic* and the *Arizona Business Gazette*, providing some powerful online resources to augment offline ones in this hot locale.

Teens are a segment of the population often overlooked by print newspapers, but they have their own section here. In addition to advice columns on managing stress and finding community services, a chat forum, and entertainment, college-bound students will find a resource for all the schools located in the state.

The business section is a great tool for residents. A business calendar and job listings are here, as well as a unique approach to restaurant reviews, taken from the

Consumer Reports Looks Out for You

You can trust KEYWORD: **Consumer Reports** to give you unbiased product comparisons and help you become a smarter consumer. With their reviews you learn what's safe and what's suspicious. For instance, you can find evaluations of child car seats, comparisons of answering machines' reliability, or analyses of the picture quality of different brands of 35mm film. All the test reports are both specific and extensive.

Consumer Reports also includes financial tips on topics such as 401(k) mistakes to avoid, how to finance remodeling costs, where to get lower auto insurance rates, and how to secure the lowest possible airfare.

perspective of a business person with the time constraints of a business lunch in mind.

Get Informed and Get Involved in Politics

Get Political News You Can Trust

KEYWORD: **Politics** is the hub for all AOL areas related to discussion of the American government. Here you can read the latest political news from the country's top publications, an op-ed page with columns from leading analysts, and detailed coverage of events and people in the political sphere.

Politics also offers daily coverage of the President, party news, scandals, and human rights.

Good Stuff!

It's "Not just politics as usual" at KEYWORD: **GEORGE**, a magazine that puts a refreshing spin on political news.

Visit the White House Forum

Featured as a Member's Choice area, KEYWORD: **White House** is where you can send email to the President with your thoughts on his nominations or bills currently being debated on Capitol Hill. To receive a response from the White House, be sure to fill out the entire form, including your name and U.S. postal address.

You can read briefings, speeches, and congressional reports on any current issue in a number of categories, such as Budget, Appointments, or Housing. These official memorandums and documents are excellent ways to get government news directly from the source.

White House press releases can help you see exactly what President Clinton has said about the economy, the military, or the environment before it appears in newspapers.

Check out the transcript of the President's weekly radio address and read press releases to learn the latest from thc Oval Office.

Channel Jumping

Activists and grassroots organizations congregate in the Interests Channel. To learn more about which areas will help you find volunteer opportunities to put your political and social beliefs into action, read Chapter 17: *Communities: Finding Friendship, Advice, and Support.*

Contact Your Congressional Representative

Only on AOL

At KEYWORD: **Buzzsaw**, you can share the day's scathing humor—or groans—with your pals simply by checking the Send to a Friend box in the corner of the screen.

Keep tabs on your representation in government by reading the news and updates in *Congressional Quarterly's American Voter*, KEYWORD: **CQ**. When men and women are pounding the campaign trail during an election, you're sure to hear where they stand on the issues. With *Congressional Quarterly*, you can know exactly what decisions your representatives are making once they've been elected.

In On the Job you can learn about what action your state's representatives have taken. Type in the name and *Congressional Quarterly* will tell you the legislator's background information, bills sponsored, and votes recently taken. If you don't know who your representatives are, you can look them up in the Library section and get their proper physical and email addresses.

VoteWatch is just one of many tracking tools here. You'll also find Senate news, political analysis, and speeches reprinted verbatim. What's important about this area is that you gain a critical knowledge that can help cut through vapid campaign slogans and sound bytes.

Get Live Gavel-to-Gavel Coverage From C-Span

Good Stuff!

Not everything at KEYWORD: **White House** is serious: you and your kids can get a guided tour of 1600 Pennsylvania Ave. from Socks the Cat. Just follow the link to the White House Web site.

A public service created by the American cable television industry, *C-Span* gives viewers access to the proceedings of the U.S. House of Representatives and Senate. At KEYWORD: **C-Span** you'll find the schedule of floor activity in Congress for the week, so you can find out when certain bills are being discussed. This isn't the glossiest or most compelling congressional news area online, but if you're trying to follow specific legislation, it's a reliable tool.

Parts of *C-Span Interactive* are geared toward teachers, and prove to be the most useful of the area. A library of lesson plans and teaching aids are stored in the software library, and a mailing list is available to deliver you program alerts and further teaching tips. You can also take a virtual tour behind the scenes.

Learn More About Political Parties

Hang Your Hat with the Democrats

You can use the *Democratic Party Online*, **KEYWORD: DNC**, as a springboard for contacting Democratic parties through AOL and on the World Wide Web.

The real strength of this area is the large number of sites of interest to Democrats, and how easily it allows you to access both Presidential and Congressional news bulletins, Democratic chat areas, and party organizations such as the Young Dems and the College Dems.

If you want to become a member of the Democratic Party, you can discover how to do so and use the membership button on the main page to sign up.

Join the Republicans

KEYWORD: RNC brings you to the *Republican National Committee* area for news, information, and commentary by political reporters.

Useful at the RNC are the forums that allow you to do some talking, or perhaps debating, on all the hot-button issues of the current political scene. Chances are you can find folks to grind axes with or make a friend in the process.

In addition, there's even a way to join the GOP online: just fill out the convenient form, and you're in.

Explore the Libertarian Platform

Representing the third largest political party in the United States, the *Libertarian Party Forum* is the hub for those wanting to curb taxation and limitations on personal freedom. **KEYWORD: Libertarian** puts members into contact with organizations and publications focused on the political and social movement that is centered on individual rights.

Good Stuff!

Drop a line to the Vice President, the Secretary of State, the First Lady, or even the President himself. **KEYWORD: White House** gives you easy access to top government officials.

BEYOND DONKEYS AND ELEPHANTS

Political agendas and inclinations are more diverse than you might think. **KEYWORD: Politics** has links to Web sites for numerous parties for you to research. While the Democrats, Republicans, and Libertarians have their own keywords on AOL, you'll be able to find even more political parties with the Web links in the *Politics* area, such as these:

- Independence Party
- Reform Party
- Democratic Socialists of America
- Labor Party
- Socialist Party
- Progressive Labor Party
- Creators Rights Party
- U.S. Taxpayers Party

Especially enlightening are the official Libertarian Press Releases and the State and Local Announcements sections. The links to numerous Libertarian Web sites can help you understand the philosophies of the party, provide context for where it has been, and predict where it is going.

Engage in Political Debate

Air Your Opinions

Once you've availed yourself of all the news and political resources on AOL you can discuss your informed views both live in chats and on message boards. KEYWORD: **Great Debate** features Hot Topics for discussion, such as fairness of the media, conspiracies, school prayer, and timely issues like the federal budget.

Chatter Box

Fierce political discourse rages on in *The Great Debate*'s chat room. Take the Floor to make your opinions known and grapple with other members over the tough issues of the day.

Politics Gets a New Look

The image of three-year-old John F. Kennedy, Jr. saluting his fallen father has been emblazoned on the country's consciousness since that tragic Presidential assassination. Now the grown-up John-John runs a magazine that aims to inject America's youth with enthusiasm for political involvement. The glossy look and feel of Kennedy's print publication is carried through in *George Online*, its often irreverent cover shots depicting celebrity mock-ups of historical figures. It appears that KEYWORD: **George** aspires to add an entertainment value to political discourse, especially with a fast-paced, real-time trivia game. If your youngsters appear apathetic at the dinner table when pressing congressional issues enter into the discussion, you might try sending them to *George* to spark interest.

Meet. . . JFK, Jr.

As the editor of *George* magazine, America's favorite son brings interviews with prominent statesmen and women online. You can find his own articles at KEYWORD: **George**.

Particularly engaging is the Pundit's Corner, where you can read the opinions of CNN's Robert Novak, Tony Snow of *Fox News Sunday*, *USA Today* columnist Susan Estrich, and Mark Shields of the *Lehrer Newshour*. Each week you can join two of the Pundits as they debate the issue live every Monday at 9 p.m. EST. You can even become a special guest on People's Pundit yourself—if you have something particularly interesting and intelligent to say in one of the chat rows or in the message boards.

UNDERSTAND FOREIGN NEWS, IN-DEPTH

The Dispatches section at **KEYWORD: ABC News** takes you to the source—whether it's Jerusalem, China, Hong Kong, Tehran, or London. ABC correspondents post articles while out on assignment. What's most impressive is that they frequently include video and sound clips to complement their pieces and bring you closer to their own experience of the news.

You'll be able to understand the context of the story even more fully by following links to regional maps, plus on-topic synopses of countries' histories, government, and population.

Speak Your Mind About Politics, Religion, and Current Events

When you want to share your views with other Democrats, Republicans, Libertarians, and all manner of political independents, go to **KEYWORD: Freethought**. No topic is off-limits.

Use the *Freethought Forum's* Discussion message boards to argue with other freethinkers about controversial issues. Does God exist? Is Rush Limbaugh full of good ideas or hot air? Atheism, affirmative action, abortion, gay and lesbian rights, and smokers' rights: these subjects generate a lot of discussion. You needn't hold back your opinions, though keeping your language within AOL's Terms of Services is a good idea.

Lighten Up with Online Satirists

Cut Washington Down to Size

If the Democrats, Republicans, and other newsmakers have got you down, check into **KEYWORD: Buzzsaw**, the political area that cuts Washington down to size.

Columnist Bill Shein provides equal-opportunity political humor—that means everyone gets nailed. What's especially funny: the lists on such topics as humorous movie sequels, phone behavior, and celebrity scandals. In this world of death, taxes, and campaign promises, humor is the best defense.

Good Stuff!

At KEYWORD: **Dilbert**, you'll find that sarcastic yet naive office worker, forever doomed to his oppressed life in cubicle-city in one of America's most popular comic strips.

Editorial Cartoons Draw on Congressional Figures

KEYWORD: **Intoon** is where editorial cartoonist Mike Keefe spoofs America's top leaders and current issues with his own brand of humor.

Think you're just as funny? Try your hand at political satire, even if you can't draw a stick figure, by entering the weekly Hot Air contest. The real fun of *Intoon with the News* is creating your own scintillating captions. Mike provides the picture and you enter your text in the word balloon for a chance to win a black and white print of a Mike Keefe cartoon and some public recognition of your sharp wit.

Quick delivery, customized layout, and search engines for simplified research: you can see the advantages of getting your news through AOL.

AOL also has many magazines online. A great place to find them all is KEYWORD: **Newsstand**. These areas are useful when you want the news placed in a specified context to see how it affects your business concerns, financial investments, travel plans, or purchasing decisions.

News specific to particular interests, such as entertainment reports or health updates, is typically stored in a link right off the main screen of the corresponding channel. And to find out what's happening in the channels themselves, subscribe to their free newsletters. At KEYWORD: **Newsletters** a folder at the top of the listbox houses all the Official Channel Newsletters. Delivered directly to your email box, these missives highlight notable and timely features throughout the channel, including links so you can reach them easily.

Build Your Business and Guide Your Career

I admit it: I love my job. Saying "love" and "job" in the same sentence is almost blasphemous in these days of corporate downsizing, frozen wages, and job insecurity. Perhaps I'm unusual in that I can't wait to come to work, although, like many of you, I probably put in too many hours. One of the best things about my job is finding ways to help you boost your ability to use AOL in every aspect of your life. Of course, that includes using AOL to find a job, get a promotion, or change careers. You can even use AOL to start your own business.

AOL's new WorkPlace Channel aims to help you solve sticky career problems and get what you truly want out of your line of work. It's your "office-in-a-box," as one WorkPlace Channel Insider tells me.

The goal of WorkPlace is to inspire and educate business owners, aspiring entrepreneurs, and people who seek to advance their own careers. If you're a first-time job seeker, WorkPlace can show you how to land a job you want. Or if you don't have a clue about what you'd truly like to do, the resources on AOL can help you figure that out, too. The tools on AOL can help you create new business and professional opportunities no matter what your chosen line of work is. Career switchers can also find plenty of help on AOL.

Get Free Business and Career Newsletters in Your Email Box

When you're starting a business or looking for the career that's right for you, you need all the help you can get—especially if it's free. Several newsletters can help you out. The *Business Strategies Forum*'s weekly newsletter is full of advice on home-based business, taxes, marketing, and goings-on in the forum itself. Career changers and seekers can get *About Work*'s information on industry chats, software, and guides to recommended job listings sites. Go to **KEYWORD: Newsletters**, then just click "Finance" in the list of topics that appears.

Insider's Tip

Since WorkPlace is a totally new channel, there will probably be even more useful tools to use and explore after this book goes to press. Be sure to check KEYWORDS: **Your Business** and **Your Career** for the newest offerings.

One of the best things about most of the areas in WorkPlace are the communities of like-minded people. You are encouraged to join in the community that best suits you. Meet other chefs, lawyers, writers, or dental hygienists! Share knowledge with fellow entrepreneurs. Get templates and model proposals for starting up your own company.

WorkPlace is divided into two main networks: KEYWORD: **Your Business** is a one-stop shop for complete business information, including startups. KEYWORD: **Your Career** brings you tools to help you track down a job, get a promotion, or move on to another, better job.

Startup and Succeed in Your Small Business

Get Your Own Business Going (and Keep it Running!)

The entrepreneur and business owner's main hub is KEYWORD: **Your Business**. They've got everything to help you start a small business. If you're already running a company but just need some answers to urgent questions, *Your Business* is the place. Network and meet other business people in your industry. *Your Business* is like an online CEO's office—full of tools, information, and the knowledge to help you make your dream of a successful small business come true.

Your Business is organized around several subcategories to make it easier to navigate.

KEYWORD: **Professions** takes you to the *Professional Forums* where you can congregate with people in your field in over 100 categories, from accountants and architects to insurance agents and jewelers.

Meet Others in Your Field

Here's just a handful of the more than 100 forums you'll find at KEYWORD: **Professions:**

- Biotechnology
- Carpets & Rugs
- Construction
- Consultants
- Delivery Services
- Energy & Oil
- Hotels & Motels
- Photography
- Publishing
- Restaurants
- Sales & Marketing

Get up-to-the-minute news in your line of work, jump directly to relevant Internet resources, or discuss issues in your field with fellow professionals. What's especially good here is that each forum develops its own community of highly dedicated members who help each other tap into professional networks or deal with the kinks of doing business.

To meet others in your geographical area, use KEYWORD: **Regional**. The links to Internet resources are copious; if you're looking for specific business information in a particular state, this is a place to start.

For banking products, Web hosting, and business magazines, you might try KEYWORD: **Business Store**.

Brainstorm and Build Your Startup

Get help coming up with business ideas that won't flop in a section entitled Business Idea Center at KEYWORD: **Strategies**. How about success coach, newsletter publisher, or medical biller? And that's just a slice of the

Work From Home

If you've ever wanted to own your own business and work from home, KEYWORD: **Strategies** has a section on Home Business & Startups that is geared to help. Are you working from home illegally? Business Strategies' own Janet Attard says you'd better be sure to check the zoning laws to find out whether home businesses are allowed in your community. Or get tips on how to avoid the pitfalls of working non-stop and sneaking in just a bit more work after dinner, since your office is literally down the hall.

KEYWORD: **AboutWork** also has work from home tools. In their Work From Home section, click on the Work From Home Kit for advice on starting your home business, like this reason why businesses often fail: giving up too soon. Of course you need that special drive and self-direction, but after you pick up many of those skills right here, move on to the list of hot new home businesses you can try (how about computer tutor, copywriter, or greeting card designer?).

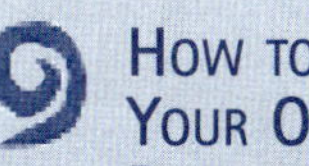

How to Start Up Your Own Business

Wouldn't you know it? KEYWORD: **Startup** is the hub for startup help. Find links to the top 20 home businesses, an interactive worksheet to let you know what your startup is going to cost you, and business software to download. All of the other startup areas mentioned in this chapter can also be found by going to KEYWORD: **Startup** and following the links.

tips you'll find in the *Business Strategies Forum*: you can also earn ways to promote your business, such as offering to be a speaker in your area of expertise, or discuss which gift baskets really sell with other "basketeers."

Learn how to design a successful new product, develop a newsletter to enhance marketing, and build a good business plan with the tools at **KEYWORD: AboutWork**, in the sub-section Start Up Help. One of the *About Work* experts, entrepreneur Marcia Layton, writes a weekly column full of essential advice for anyone thinking about starting a business or seeking to improve one.

Learn Web Publishing

Increasingly, putting your business on the Web is an important marketing tool, and a way to sell new products to demographically lucrative customers. Forrester Research has predicted that by the year 2000 consumers will spend $546 billion online. But what happens when you can't afford professional services? Learn the basics yourself in the Computing Channel at **KEYWORD: On the Net**. Take a class on WEBing Your Business. Sit in on a course on Web Basics which covers HTML tags, counters, and uploading to FTP. Advanced topics include using CGI on AOL, and Getting Started with Java—some of the hottest trends right now in Internet publishing and applications.

Put Your Business on the Web

You need a Web site to stay competitive and target more customers if your business is to enter the 21st century. **KEYWORD: PrimeHost** takes you to AOL's own professional-level Web hosting service. For $99 a month, you can have a basic—though professional-looking—site up in about ten minutes.

You'll have to design and maintain the site yourself, but *PrimeHost* has tutorials and templates that make creating a basic site easy. On the other hand, if you don't want to be bothered by designing and maintaining your site, *PrimeHost* may not be for you. *PrimeHost* is best for small businesses that want a Web publication but don't want to pay—literally—tens of thousands of dollars for it.

If you're not scared to learn about FTP (file transfer protocol), HTML forms, and maybe even a little CGI programming, you can give your pages the exact look you want. Use AOL's free page layout tool, AOL Press, to design and update your pages as well as send them to AOL for hosting.

When you want to sell products online and accept credit card payments, you can upgrade your account to the *PrimeHost Commercial Service*, at **KEYWORD: PHcomm**. This service is currently $199 a month, plus a startup fee.

Government Assistance: The Small Business Administration

Good, solid, helpful advice—and it comes from the Federal Government, believe it or not. The Small Business Administration has been known for decades as a source of guidance for small businesses. Tons of easily accessed information is available on their Web site, which you can access via **KEYWORD: SBA**. If you go to the Web site, you'll find tons of updated information: business plan outlines, marketing questions, home-based business help, and answers to the most common questions about starting a business.

Get quick contact phone numbers and addresses to the many SBA resources like the Small Business Answer Desk at (800) 8-ASK-SBA. Or locate your nearest SBA Business Information Center (BIC).

The SBA is well known for its 7A loan guarantee program. Read all the fine print and surprise your

Upgrade

Add your favorite small business area to the new tool bar. Just drag and drop the Favorite Places heart from the area up onto the tool bar and choose an appropriate icon to represent the location.

Talk Business Live with Pros

Get a front-row seat when business professionals hold live conferences at **KEYWORD: Business Talk**. Talk business as often as possible in what's clearly one of the best interactive resources for anyone starting or managing his or her own company.

Get advice directly from pros and other entrepreneurs at **KEYWORD: Lunch**. You can meet every day at 1:00 p.m. ET to talk about common topics like marketing and writing business proposals.

Weeknights at 8:00 p.m. ET, **KEYWORD: Dinner** takes you front-and-center with special guests from the world of business. Ask questions about such topics as managing your self-employment, scams on the Net, or hiring the right people.

Insider's Tip

Keep a record of your Business Talk chats using AOL's Log Manager feature. On the **File** menu, click "Log manager." You can then save what's said in a file on your hard drive to read or print out later.

banker at your next appointment. You can also read about other loan programs, minority programs, home-based businesses, and special services for women entrepreneurs.

Another valuable service is How to Start a New Business. There are links to business plan outlines, marketing information, and booklets on scores of different business categories.

Get Forms and Templates in the Business Owner's Toolkit

Good Stuff!

Got your own small business and need quick yet quality news? The SOHO daily news at **KEYWORD: CCH** keeps you on top of topics important to you, including tax changes, investment fraud, and technology.

Both entry-level and experienced entrepreneurs can use the resources in the *CCH Business Owner's Toolkit*, **KEYWORD: CCH**. Model business documents, financial spreadsheet templates, and checklists help guide employee management, worker safety and compensation, and marketing strategies. What's easily accessible here could take months to track down elsewhere.

The best thing about the *Toolkit* is the Small Business Library: covered in detail are issues such as Financing Your Business, Controlling Taxes, Building Personal Wealth, and Getting Out of your company.

Learn Guerrilla Marketing Techniques From the Pros

Attention AOL Shoppers!

Get instant marketing weapons, business tips, and interactive examples from the *Guerrilla Marketing Software Library* at **KEYWORD: Guerrilla**.

Find some pretty successful yet slightly unorthodox methods of making your business stellar at **KEYWORD: Guerrilla**. Small business owners, salespeople, and marketers of all kinds come to the official online companion to the best-selling Guerrilla book series in which the editors suggest often radical and never-before-imagined tactics you can use to get your business bubbling.

Special Daily Guerrilla Communiqués bring little ideas to keep you on track every day, like "If you're serious about doing business through your own Web storefront, do it from your own domain name address."

Don't miss the Weekly Tales from the Front Lines: Guerrilla editors select the smartest reader business strategies each week. One on "following up" tells how the more contact you have with a customer, the more satisfied they'll be and the more loyalty they'll have for your product.

Get help from sought-after Guerrilla marketer and president Jay Levinson and internationally recognized technology writer Charles Rubin, just two of the columnists who share their strategies for successful selling in *The Weekly Guerrilla.*

Incorporate Your Business Online

The Company Corporation is the largest direct incorporation service in the U.S. and number one for incorporating businesses in Delaware, the state of choice for most New York and American Stock Exchange companies.

Over 145,000 businesses have used the services to gain the benefits of incorporation which *The Company Corporation* can provide in all 50 states. By incorporating you are able to separate your personal from your business assets, gain special tax shelters, allow for continuation of your business, receive dividends 80 percent tax-free, and raise capital more easily.

Their quick, low-cost online services are located at **KEYWORD: Incorporate**. You pay no legal fees when you form your corporation. You pay no processing fees if *The Company Corporation* is your registered agent. You pay less than you normally would for ongoing service, including statutory representation.

YOUR BUSINESS NEWS

You're only one click away from the top business news at **KEYWORD: Business News.** Click to jump to the Dow Jones Business Center, full of breaking reports on tax law, mergers, and indexes. Small business news is at *CCH*'s The Daily News. Other quick links include Worth Magazine, The Nightly Business Report, and the New York Times Online.

Join the Multi-Level Marketing and Direct Selling Forum

Network with others in your industry and share tips and hints about multi-level marketing and direct selling at **KEYWORD: MLM**. Special featured articles can help you learn techniques to grow your business as well as learn how to avoid scams. Some articles provide welcome inspiration on such MLM and direct marketing necessities as how to make contacts with customers, using Internet advertising, and perseverance.

The many company-specific message boards are helpful if you want to ask questions about growing specific businesses. But beware: advertising is allowed only in designated areas of the forum and even an ad in your signature file at the end of your post will get your message pulled from the boards.

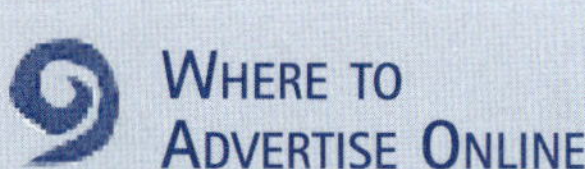

WHERE TO ADVERTISE ONLINE

AOL Classifieds is the perfect forum for getting your service or product advertised online. You can place an ad at KEYWORD: **Classifieds** in categories similar to those in a traditional newspaper: real estate, employment, computing, and business, for example.

You may also want to consider putting an ad up on the largest online billboard currently available—the World Wide Web. KEYWORD: **PrimeHost** leads you to a service that will help you build and maintain a commercial Web site with the professional look and feel you want.

Current Business News: What's Going On in Your Field?

Business Week: Get Live Advice

All the editorial content—news, market reports, inside observations, and opinions—from the world's largest business magazine is found at KEYWORD: **Business Week**. The live conferences with the editors and contributors are energetic, giving you the chance to interact with journalists and commentators who really know the business world—you can't do that in the print version. Click on the Talk and Conferences button for frequent business school chat, conferences on how to hire the right people, or knowledgeable discussion of hot growth companies.

The all-encompassing archives of stories go back to 1991 so you can find the article on, for instance, the growth potential of the Internet, Beijing, and any other topic you seek.

Make Your Home Office More Efficient

Slash your accounting fees. Discover the top ten Web businesses. KEYWORD: **Home Office Computing** is a serious business technology publication for entrepreneurs who rely on their personal computers. Whether the topic is getting new clients, hiring an employee, or getting the most out of your computer, you will find a mix of technology and business coverage. Each months' feature articles on legal matters, marketing strategies, financial concerns, and office design are directed to operators of small businesses.

The index and search features of past issues of the magazine are really useful, helping you zoom in on articles with tips on saving money on taxes and keeping clients happy. The number of archived articles is very large, so be as specific as possible when you perform your search to keep from choking on a glut of articles.

Channel Jumping

KEYWORD: Met Home has several articles on how to design a home office that fits your decor and supports your work ethic. Find design ideas as well as furniture resources here.

Inc. Online: Grow Your Company

Inc. Online is an electronic consultant to those of you who are starting and running your own company. *Inc. Online* goes beyond *Inc. Magazine* to bring you resources that are only available online. After all, with new technologies come new ways of doing business.

At **KEYWORD: Inc** you go directly to *Inc.*'s special Web site where you have full access to *Inc. Magazine* and its editors, including monthly columns on running a business from successful entrepreneur Norm Brodsky. The interactive worksheets allow you to instantly calculate whether your personal finances are in order, or calculate the true cost of your PC. Only in the online magazine will you get special features like Online Entrepreneur and "Zinc," a section featuring companies run by 20-something entrepreneurs.

Meet... entrepreneur Norm Brodsky

He's a veteran entrepreneur whose six businesses include an Inc. 100 company and a three-time Inc. 500 company. Get what he calls "street-smart" advice for your business in his monthly Inc. columns.

Manage Your Career

About Work: Tools to Help You Get the Job You Want

Why is looking for a job such hard work that it's sometimes harder than the job itself? **KEYWORD: AboutWork** eases

Chatter Box

Every Wednesday night at 9 p.m. ET in the Career chat room, a sub-area under **KEYWORD: AboutWork**, you can join Ron Linder to discuss his eight-step system for successfully finding a new job.

the burden with its tools to help you find a job you'll be happy with.

Jobs, Jobs, Jobs has advice on writing dreaded cover letters and top-notch job searching tips. Especially helpful are the tools to help you get to know yourself better. Just by taking a few online tests, you can gain some insight into your preferences and your career inclinations that you might not previously have realized.

You can get tips like how to prepare for informational interviews: tip number four is "save your best contacts until you are ready to approach them, after you

Meet... career coach Barbara Reinhold

Consultant, author, and the director of the Career Development Office at Smith College, Barbara answers your questions about tough work situations in message boards and in her regular column at *About Work*.

Consult Career Experts

Some of the best resources in WorkPlace are the real career professionals who answer your questions in live career chats and in message boards. Barbara Reinhold is *About Work*'s guest career coach and she's got quite a following in her message boards. You can get her sage advice on difficult bosses, dead-end jobs, and researching companies. She is the author of the book *Toxic Work: How to Overcome Stress, Overload and Burnout and Revitalize Your Career.*

Another good career professional is "Shift Coach" Hope Dlugozima. Hope is the author of *Six Months Off*, a how-to guide for would-be sabbatical takers. She answers your questions on revamping your nine-to-five world, giving your career a makeover, and perhaps ending up with a better life in the process. Join her at the *About Work* chat room every Tuesday at 8 p.m. ET to get your questions answered, or post on her well-utilized and insightful message boards.

To get to *About Work*'s career experts, go to **KEYWORD: AboutWork**, then click "Ask the Experts" to see a list of professionals waiting to help you.

have laid some ground-work by establishing your goal and objectives and researching your targets."

About Work even provides a list of questions to ask. For instance, if you are a career switcher investigating a new field, you might ask your informational interviewer, "How would you suggest I overcome a lack of experience in this particular area?"

Learn the three Rs of job interviewing: Research, Rehearse, and Relax, from pros who have been in the career business for decades. Download some surprisingly helpful flashcards to walk through common interview situations such as how to answer questions about your personality, ways to discuss your work experience, and how to negotiate a salary.

Keyboard Yoga

Relax and reduce anxiety and anticipation. Anyone looking for a new job could use a little help fighting stress. For well-done, step-by-step guides to resting your back, exercising your eyes, and breathing, go to KEYWORD: **Virtues**, then click "Keyboard Yoga."

Find a Job, Get Promoted, or Move On

As this book goes to press, a new area is being designed at KEYWORD: **Your Career**. Much of what I've mentioned in this chapter will be collected and organized so that you can drop in for some high-powered information gathering, networking, and tools to help you with your career. You will be able to get directly to the employment classifieds, link to quality resources on the Web, and get newly designed Business News.

A section called Business Research looks particularly useful to both business owners and employees. You'll be able to search for and purchase articles and reports from trade publications, get analyst reports, do demographic research, and obtain company profiles.

There will most likely be a fee to access some of the research services. However, many of the fee-based tools will be of the type previously available only to corporate libraries. Now you'll be able to be more knowledgeable than your competition. You can research prospective employers, partners, and business contacts. Business owners will be able to research potential partners, competitors, and suppliers, and examine business opportunities and industry reports.

Working Parents Need Extra Help

Learn how to balance a job and a family and meet other working parents. Work at home—with all the extra organization, scheduling, and difficulty of staying motivated—and still find ample time to spend with the kids. *Parent Soup* has a special section for Working Parents. Go to **KEYWORD: Parent Soup**, then click "Index," then click "Working Parents."

You can also get live, ready advice from national experts in chats several times a week. Maybe you'd also like to share some tips of your own or tricks for staying on track and dealing with pressure. For the live chats, go to **KEYWORD: Parent Soup Chat**, then look for the chat of your choice in their lineup.

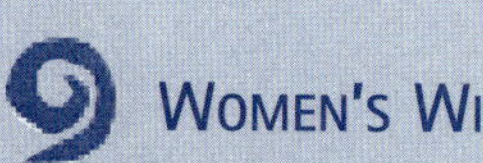

WOMEN'S WIRE

The popular Web site at *http://www.women.com* has a section devoted to work issues. Find your niche with a career quiz or get advice from the "biz shrink." You can learn here how your company rates in terms of family-friendly benefits packages, child care availability, and salaries for women. Career and small business forums foster networking with other wired women, and you can glean some advice with profiles from women who are succeeding in their industries.

Women Mean Business

Women discover how to make it up and out through the glass ceiling, join women's business networks, and learn strategies to get promoted in their own forum at **KEYWORD: Strategies**. The sub-section Women Owned Businesses contains information and tools to help with loans, rights, and organizations focused on women in the workplace.

Another area, *The Women's Network*, also has great work resources, like a listing of the 100 best companies for women; among them are AT&T, Eastman Kodak, and Procter & Gamble.

If you're examining a particular field, use the ever-growing collection of about 40 well-done articles—reported on by women, for women—that includes TV writer, graphic designer, therapist, headhunter, and computer programmer. Follow **KEYWORD: Women**, then go to the section called "Work."

Get a Job Through AOL's Classifieds

AOL's new classifieds at **KEYWORD: Classifieds** have a section for employment that merits the attention of both members looking for jobs and employers looking for employees. The hundreds of listings give you options: search by region, or you can use the search function to scour the entire database for a job in your field. Employment ads are $20.00 per month as of this writing. If you're promoting yourself with an ad, stay posted for the amount of time you specify.

You can also find businesses in your area in literally hundreds of specific categories: it's just like looking through a frequently updated phone directory. For example, get lists of all the auto-repair shops or attorneys' offices in your area. What makes this feature great is that you can get a door-to-door map or printable driving directions to each business just by entering your street address. To use the business directory, click on "Locate a Business." Maybe the businesses you find won't be hiring immediately, but you can get leads for jobs down the line.

Good Stuff!

Get a job on the Net. **KEYWORD: NetFind** has great resources for job seekers. Click "Time Savers," then "Find a Job" for a list of Web sites like Career Mosaic and America's Job Bank.

City by City: Relocation and Job Prospects

What if there were a place somewhere in North America with better job potential than your current location's, and you didn't know it? Do you want information on the new city you and your family are being relocated to? Want to know what your salary will buy in your new hometown? Use **KEYWORD: Places Rated** to get job statistics and prospects—and thousands of other facts—about cities throughout the U.S. You can discover which jobs are among those that account for half of all new jobs created. Cashiers, retail salespeople, janitors, and waiters and waitresses. Which occupations are on the outs? Farmers, typists, bookkeepers, and bank tellers.

In addition to your job prospects, you can get information about the livability of 343 officially defined metropolitan areas where 75 percent of Americans live. Rated are: costs of living, job outlook, housing, transportation, education, health care, crime, the arts, recreation, and climate.

Channel Jumping

Get insider information about a city direct from the city itself before you relocate. **KEYWORD: Digital City** brings scores of cities to you so that you can learn more about them.

So how's your startup coming along? Ready to open up shop? Or have you decided to switch careers? Take some time to investigate AOL's WorkPlace with as much enthusiasm as you would explore your career options. Both in the WorkPlace Channel and in the job world, there's obviously a lot out there to choose from; now it's up to you to decide what catches your eye.

Just remember to circle back to the hubs, **KEYWORD: Your Business** and **KEYWORD: Your Career**, for little refreshers every once in a while. We could all use as much help as we can get when it comes to staying happy in our jobs, moving up the ladder, or getting our own business dreams out of our imaginations and into reality.

Managing Your Money: Personal Finance on AOL

Anyone who has money—and you do, even if you think you don't have enough—needs to read this chapter. You might already know about some of AOL's wildly popular, up-to-the-minute investing areas, like *Quotes and Portfolios* and the *Dow Jones Business Center*. By reading this chapter, you'll learn how to use them better, and maybe find some new favorites. If you're not an investor, don't be intimidated—the Personal Finance Channel has plenty of advice for day-to-day money management, saving for college, and getting out of debt.

The first section of this chapter, "Information for Investors," is full of facts and statistics. Why wait for tomorrow's newspaper to get today's stock quotes? You'll find out how to get the latest data from the *Market News Center*, how to use the *Company Research* area to inform your stock-buying decisions, and how to set up an online portfolio for 24-hour trading. Learn all about mutual funds from *Sage*, one of the best mutual fund resources online anywhere. Travel to the *New York Stock Exchange* in minutes and get financial news in a flash.

Advisors and Analysts helps you find expert advice and guidance that may improve your investing experience and boost your business. Some of these people are well-known, like the *Motley Fool*'s David and Tom

And the Winner Is . . .

Why is the *Motley Fool* so popular? Because it is both informative and amusing—no easy trick. Visit **KEYWORD: Fool** to see why so many members consider it the best place on AOL.

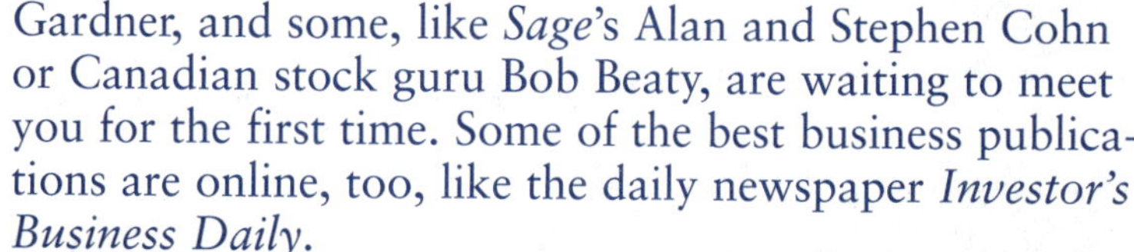

Gardner, and some, like *Sage*'s Alan and Stephen Cohn or Canadian stock guru Bob Beaty, are waiting to meet you for the first time. Some of the best business publications are online, too, like the daily newspaper *Investor's Business Daily*.

The last part of this chapter, "Financial Resources Everyone Can Use," can help improve your quality of life by stretching your paycheck as far as it will go. You won't find anything complicated here—just ordinary goals like buying a car, paying the bills, and choosing the right insurance. Once you get a handle on the day-to-day necessities, you can learn how (and how much) to save for the future. And if you decide to venture into the investment world with your newfound dollars, you'll have the rest of this chapter to help get you started.

To find the information that matters to you, try navigating the Personal Finance Channel with **KEYWORD: PF Search**. Choose the topics you want to search for, and even limit the amount of time you want AOL to spend on your quest. After all, time is money.

Look Up Jargon

Even if you always forget whether a bull market is good or bad, you can understand financial lingo as long as you're logged on to AOL. *Wall Street Words*, **KEYWORD: WSW**, is a dictionary of business and financial terms that clearly explains the most complicated terminology.

Information for Investors

How to Invest Online

Why trade on AOL instead of through a real-life broker? Because the *Brokerage Center* has longer hours (24 hours a day, to be exact) and often has lower prices. Commissions vary, but some brokers offer big discounts for online traders. If this sounds appealing, **KEYWORD: Broker** tells you more about investing online. New to the investment world or to the Internet? How to Invest Online explains jargon and helps you choose a broker. There are many firms on AOL to choose from, including Charles Schwab, Waterhouse Securities, PC Financial Network, and Ceres Securities. It's perfectly safe, and it's not even complicated.

Insider's Tip

At **KEYWORD: ExpressNet**, American Express cardholders can get current account information, access Membership Rewards points balances, purchase Travelers' Cheques, pay bills, and make reservations online.

To view your investments' progress, jump to **KEYWORD: Quotes**. With a few clicks, you can view the latest price for a particular stock, the day's high and low prices, volume traded, and other information. AOL can automatically track your stocks and funds for you. You can

Insider's Tip

Use *AOL NetFind* to explore the wealth of financial resources on the World Wide Web. *NetFind* also saves you time by listing some of the best sites. You can get there at *http://webcrawler.com/AOL/finance/stocks/*.

Investing for Beginners

Investing can be intimidating, but not if someone has properly explained it to you.

At the Fool's School, KEYWORD: **Fool**, the wise-guy investors of *Motley Fool* teach you what you need to know about investing, like how to value stocks.

The Sage School at KEYWORD: **Sage** has a lot of beginning-level information to make mutual funds less mysterious.

The Investor Education section of KEYWORD: **IBD** is a 28-part investment tutorial. It starts at the beginning by defining "stock" and progresses gradually from there.

KEYWORD: **MoneyWhiz** has quick Savings and Investing resources like 10 Big Investor Mistakes, 5 Investing Rules, and 3 Things to Know About Bonds.

In KEYWORD: **Money U**'s Investments section, Ric Edelman answers member questions about real estate investment trusts (REITs), treasuries, and transferring mutual funds to your kids.

KEYWORD: **AAII** features a more intermediate-level Investing Basics section with a focus on book recommendations and risk. It also contains an extensive library of FAQs, articles, and Web links.

Investor 101 sounds simple, but since it's from the pros at KEYWORD: **Worth**, look at it after you've been through the other beginner resources. Find out how to read a financial statement and rate your 401(k).

After you understand the basics, you can start taking advantage of AOL's many resources for investors.

The Buzz on Wall Street

Part of what draws investors to the stock market is its exciting unpredictability. The View Noteworthy Stocks button at KEYWORD: **Earnings** leads you to a daily update of Wall Street surprises. Find out about companies that didn't live up to expectations as well as those that beat the street, and get positive and negative revisions for both followed and underfollowed companies.

also use this feature to research stocks and funds before you buy.

To view your portfolio, all you have to remember is **KEYWORD: Portfolio**. See how much money you've made or lost in one investment, view your total portfolio, or check whether a stock or mutual fund is at your buying or selling price. You can create multiple portfolios to keep track of different sets of investments for different purposes, like one portfolio for a college fund and one for retirement.

Good Stuff!

Long- and short-term investors and anyone planning for retirement can get ideas from the sample portfolios at **KEYWORD: Fundworks**. Find out why some experts advise against bond funds.

Just remember: the *Brokerage Center* is where you get started or choose a brokerage firm. The *Quotes* area is where you get the facts about your investments and potential investments. The *Portfolios* area lets you look at your investments, get updates, and make changes to your portfolio.

Find Out About Funds

If you've been saving for retirement, you probably have some mutual funds. But how much do you know about them? For a summary of AOL's mutual fund resources, including links to more than a dozen fund companies, go to **KEYWORD: Mutual Funds**. But don't neglect the individual areas that make up the *Mutual Funds Center*.

Chatter Box

How much is there to say about mutual funds? Plenty. Find out just how much with the chats at **KEYWORD: Funds Live**.

KEYWORD: Sage is a frequently updated mutual funds area. Their Sage School has an interactive tutorial, Mutual Funds 101, that starts by explaining what a mutual fund is and progresses to explanations of dollar cost averaging and asset allocation. The people at *Sage* archive FAQs and past articles, organizing them by type of fund (large cap, international, etc.). They also evaluate brokerage firms, spotlight up-and-coming funds, offer a free newsletter, and answer members' questions about IRAs, 401(k)s, and other funds.

A guide to fund categories, instructions on viewing a prospectus, and excerpts from the book *Investing from Scratch* can all be found at **KEYWORD: Fundworks**. For help choosing funds, investigate some model portfolios: click on "Features" and look for FundWorks Models.

Scheduled talks in the 401(k) Café chat room add to the interactivity of this useful area.

The mutual fund mavens at *Morningstar*, **KEYWORD: Mstar**, rate the top 25 funds in over 30 categories such as aggressive growth, European stock, and small company funds. Additional data comes from Individual Fund Reports for over 8,000 funds, grouped by ranking and investment objective. If you get confused, you can consult *Morningstar*'s glossary of mutual fund terms.

KEYWORD: Online Investor's weekly Guide to Mutual Funds column keeps you up-to-date with online mutual fund resources. When you're ready to set up an online portfolio, **KEYWORD: Fund Portfolios** can help. Don't miss the links to sample portfolios for four common goals: college, a new home, retirement, and "income right now."

Insider's Tip

KEYWORD: Fund Brief, like the name says, is a quick way to get mutual fund tips. Find the top five performers, rate your fund manager, and decide whether an A, B, or C class share is better.

Research Companies Before You Buy Their Stock

The online exchanges aren't the only places to get stock information. Find out about firms at **KEYWORD: Company Research**. It organizes many company research areas, some of which I've described next.

KEYWORD: Stock Reports leads you to a database of over 6,000 companies with stocks listed on the NYSE, AMEX, and NASDAQ. Type in a company's name or ticker symbol, and you'll be able to examine over 50 fundamental data points. The *Stock Reports* area also features AAII Special Screens, each of which attempts to identify different companies to fit different investment styles.

KEYWORD: Edgar shows investors how to understand the information reported in two primary SEC reports, the 10K and 10Q. A 10K is the key SEC report submitted annually which provides a comprehensive overview of the company. A 10Q is the quarterly financial report submitted every three months, which shows the investor a continuing view of a company's financial position during the year.

Disclosure Financial Statements, **KEYWORD: Financials**, provides a searchable database of balance sheets,

Research a Company's Track Record

The *Historical Quotes* area, **KEYWORD: Charts**, shows you where a company has been so you can assess where it might be going. Just type in a company's name or symbol to get its individual history, reaching back as far as 1910. Don't buy stock without doing your history homework here.

incomes, and cash flow statements for almost all public U.S. companies and many in the international market. You can also attempt to predict the future of a company at KEYWORD: **First Call**. The *First Call* area brings you estimated earnings, buy/hold/sell recommendations, growth rates, and price/earnings data on more than 5,000 North American companies daily, weekly, or monthly. Click "Earnings & Estimates" or use KEYWORD: **Earnings** to go right to that database.

Since history repeats itself, don't forget the past. Track a company's prior performance back to 1910 with KEYWORD: **Charts**. At the *Historical Quotes* area, members can get a company's stock history reports by the year, month, or day. The Preferences let you download data

Good Stuff!

The mutual fund experts at KEYWORD: **Sage** will answer your message board questions within 48 hours. They can do that because they have an enthusiastic staff of 75, at last count.

For Serious Stockholders

Eat or be eaten at KEYWORD: **Shark Tank**. Here, members get tips from stock professionals and learn how to trade aggressively. "Trading can be a dangerous game," says host Rev Shark, "but no one feasts better than a savvy Shark." You can show off your stock-picking prowess with the Stock of the Month contest, or trade strategies with other sharks in busy message boards and three different chat rooms.

For more stockholding competition, try the Penny Picks contest at KEYWORD: **Beaty**. Or go to KEYWORD: **IBD**, click on "Community," and take the Stock Challenge. See who picks winners and who loses their shirt.

KEYWORD: **DP** has information about technical analysis, including a Technical Analysis Short Course—a series of short lessons with text and pictures—to help newcomers learn the basics. Find daily charts, the chart of the week, and charting software support. Technical analysis may seem esoteric at first, but the experts at *Decision Point* insist that it's not hard to learn.

Meet. . . Rev Shark

Your favorite Shark goes head-to-head with three other investment gurus every week. Watch the sparks fly at KEYWORD: **Conference Call.**

in Quicken or MetaStock format and enhance graphs with volume bar charts, a 50-day moving average, and an overlay of the stock's strength relative to the S&P 500 index.

Has a company you're researching made headlines lately? At **KEYWORD: Company News**, you can read all the news articles that have mentioned that company in the last 30 days.

Additional tools for company research are contained in other areas. For instance, **KEYWORD: Online Investor** has an archive of companies that they've examined closely within the past month.

Insider's Tip

Two more ways to get the latest at **KEYWORD: MNC**: the Before the Bell section focuses on news that emerges before the market's opening bell. After the Bell lists news put out in the evening, after the market closes.

The Latest Market Facts and Figures

There are several easy ways to get the latest stock quotes (with only a 20-minute-or-so delay). The first option jumps out at you from the main screen of the Personal Finance Channel. **KEYWORD: Finance** features real-time market indices right on the front screen, so you don't have to go looking around for the latest from the Dow Jones, S&P 500, and NASDAQ.

Another cool way to track market indices is **KEYWORD: Chartomatic**. Select a stock market index, such as the NASDAQ Industrial Index or Dow Jones Composite Average, or click on the S&P 500 icon to chart one of the stocks that make up the S&P 500 index. If you're going to be online for a while, leave *Chart-O-Matic* open and it will automatically update itself every few minutes. Write some email or catch up on a message board, then check back to see how the market has changed in the meantime.

Good Stuff!

Get basic information about over 11,000 companies from **KEYWORD: Company Profile**.

Get a comprehensive look at the market with the *Market News Center*. **KEYWORD: MNC** brings you recent quotes, graphs, and news items in the following categories: Stocks & Mutuals, Bonds & Money, Currencies, Futures, U.S. Economy, and International.

To check out individual stocks, your best bet may be **KEYWORD: Quotes**. Enter the symbol of the stock you want to check, and its most recent status pops up.

Get News You Need

The financial newspapers and magazines on AOL are great (they come later in the chapter), but some days you just don't have time to read *all* about it. On those days, it's easy to skip the feature articles and dive right into the headlines.

Channel Jumping

Additional international economic news can be found at the *Economic Intelligence Unit*, **KEYWORD: EIU**.

KEYWORD: MNC takes you to the *Market News Center* main screen, where you'll find graphs and breaking stories. Stocks and mutual funds are covered, of course, with information on markets at a glance, today's most active stocks, and recent big gains and losses.

KEYWORD: MNC Bonds shows you bond indices, money market rates, and U.S. Treasuries statistics. Keep tabs on the mark or the yen with **KEYWORD: MNC Currencies**. Track pork bellies, crude oil, soybeans, and other commodities at **KEYWORD: MNC Futures**. Graphs show you the latest activity in futures like Eurodollars, gold, and corn.

News about the U.S. economy, including jobs, sales, and economic indicators, is at **KEYWORD: MNC Economy**. For a global focus, go to **KEYWORD: MNC International**. It connects you to international stock indices and stock reports from countries all over the world.

Analysts and Advisors

Invest Wisely with the Motley Fools

Attention AOL Shoppers!

Buy investing tools, subscribe to financial news publications, and find Foolish book recommendations at **KEYWORD: FoolMart**. Pick up a jester tie while you're there.

The *Motley Fool* has always been one of AOL's most popular areas, and with good reason. It's informative enough to be worth your time and amusing enough to keep you interested. It's also big enough that I can't mention all its best features, but here are a few of the highlights of **KEYWORD: Fool**.

Dueling Fools is a bulls vs. bears debate between two Fool staff members, and you can vote for the winner. The Daily Double describes a company whose stock has more than doubled over the last year, reviews the business, and talks about why it has done so well. The Daily

Double's evil twin, the Daily Trouble, talks about a company whose stock has dropped by over 50% in the past year. Lunchtime and Evening News updates fill you in during your lunch break login or after-dinner online time.

Have a minute? Read a Fribble, a short opinion piece written by either a Fool staffer or an AOL member. Fribbles are usually about investing or the online universe, but "if you know the Meaning of Life or can make quantum mechanics fun in fifty lines or less, then send it in," say the Fools.

Insider's Tip

Get the latest issue of *Business Week* several days early at **KEYWORD: BW**. The full text of the magazine goes online before it reaches any newsstand.

Fribbles are just one indication that member participation is important here. The Fools keep their fans amused with an interactive trivia game and stock market simulation contests. The Chat section not only lists the chat schedule, but keeps track of the ten busiest message boards and archives the transcripts of past chats. The Fool Chat room is as informative and entertaining as you'd expect—if you can get into it. The room is also so popular that the message "We're sorry. The Conference Room is full" will become a familiar sight. The message boards are just as busy, but always accessible (and usually eloquent). The Post of the Day spotlights a clever message board remark that you might otherwise miss.

There are several ways to make sure you get the most out of the *Motley Fool*. New users might appreciate the suggestions of Nine Nightly Stops in Fooldom. To see all of their offerings, click the Index button at the bottom of the screen. Most Fool screens have a Search button at the bottom that helps you dig through all the resources to find the ones that interest you. The Search button also calls up their FAQs—Foolishly Answered Questions—about investing and the area itself.

Good Stuff!

Review closing market prices and the best Foolish content of the day with the Fool-A-Day email newsletter. It's free to subscribe at **KEYWORD: Fool**.

Get Sage Mutual Fund Advice

Sage, in some ways, is like the *Motley Fool* of the mutual fund world. **KEYWORD: Sage** is well-written, comprehensive, community-oriented, and will probably teach you a thing or two no matter how much you already know.

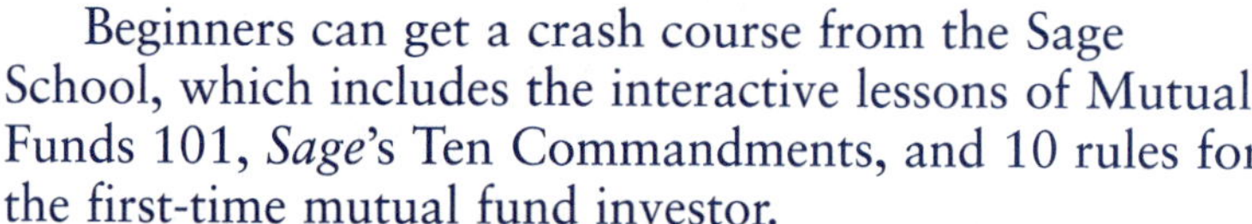

Beginners can get a crash course from the Sage School, which includes the interactive lessons of Mutual Funds 101, *Sage*'s Ten Commandments, and 10 rules for the first-time mutual fund investor.

Insider's Tip

The investment wiseguys at KEYWORD: **Fool** also have some advice about basic personal finance (getting a job, buying a car, doing your taxes) in the Fool School section.

When you get beyond the basics, use the table of contents to make sure you don't miss anything. Find FAQs for many mutual funds and send retirement and investment questions to a Sage expert to receive a reply within 48 hours.

The Portfolio Models section lets you follow the progress of sample portfolios like the Gray-Haired Baby Boomer Portfolio and Funds of the Stars. The Mutual Fund Superhighway section keeps an eye on top funds and shows you some of the best fund-related Web links out there.

"We have so much to say and so little space to say it," write the Sages, "that we have been forced to leave a lot of our *Sage* Wisdom off-line." But don't despair—subscribing to *Sage*'s free bi-weekly newsletter will fill in all the gaps and highlight useful information that you might have missed while browsing *Sage*'s vast resources.

Investment Insights with a Focus on Canada

Good Stuff!

You can find additional Canadian financial data in the country profiles at KEYWORD: **EIU**.

Members of AOL Canada probably already know about *Beaty & Company*, but it's time that everyone else knew, too. The columnists are the main draw at KEYWORD: **Beaty**. Fred Langan explains developments in economics and politics and how they relate to your finances. Kevin Cork tackles personal financial planning. Kerry Harman shares her 15 years of experience as an investment advisor, and Alexander McLean explores international investing. Bob Beaty is the most unpredictable—his main topic is stocks, but he's also written about beer, "clients from hell," the Internet, funeral homes, and trucks.

For more Canadian financial resources, such as mutual fund facts and a link to the Vancouver Stock Exchange, click the Finance button on the bottom of Beaty & Company's main screen. You'll be transported to AOL Canada's Business & Finance Channel.

Make the Most of Online Investments

The two market enthusiasts who run *Online Investor* don't recommend stocks, but they give you the ideas you need to pick them yourself. Be patient. Diversify your portfolio. Do your homework. Know what you own, and know yourself. For more detail, see the Ingredients for Investment Success at KEYWORD: **Online Investor**.

Like the name implies, *Online Investor* focuses on stockholders who trade online. The Guide to Company Research column is a weekly look at investment resources, especially the ones on AOL. Past columns found in the archives explain trading jargon, help you choose an online broker, show you how to find stock recommendations, and teach you how to read stock graphs. Their other weekly column examines mutual fund investment.

Online Investor also features analyst ratings and a guide to translating them into English, earnings information, and a Company Spotlight that tells members about companies which might be "the next big thing."

Meet...
The Online Investors

The experts at KEYWORD: **Online Investor** encourage you to ask them all your investing questions. Even if you think the question is stupid, they won't.

Take an Economics Lesson

Fans of the insightful weekly journal *The Economist* will enjoy the work of their affiliates at the *Economic Intelligence Unit*. KEYWORD: **EIU** analyzes international economics, politics, and business from the inside. The Hong Kong message boards are monitored by experts on the Asian economy, and prominent speakers like Guillermo Perry, World Bank Chief Economist for Latin America, have visited the chat room to discuss global issues. Find news by country, region (like Asia-Pacific and Western Europe), or jump right to the latest alerts from all countries. Don't just find out what's going on; find out why.

For more international business and financial news, jump over to the International Channel. At KEYWORD: **International**, under News & Business you'll find currency conversions, exchange rates, global market quotes, and banks of the world.

Attention AOL Shoppers!

KEYWORD: **Magazine Outlet** has great deals on financial magazines like *Forbes*, *Fortune*, *Inc.*, *Money*, *Worth*, and many others.

Five Lunches to Financial Knowledge

"MAKE YOUR MONEY WORK FOR YOU!"

I've always loved that phrase. It only seems fair: I work hard for my money, I have the right to tell it: Get To Work! The unfortunate reality, however, is that I've got lazy money. I think it just sort of hangs around at the bank all day, sleeping and watching television. And I only have myself to blame: I haven't had the motivation and the discipline to really get in there and learn how to manage my financial assets.

But I'm happy to say that my dough's lazy, crazy days are over. . .

Recently, I spent one week of lunch hours exploring personal finance resources online. I've always known that the Personal Finance Channel (KEYWORD: **Finance**) is one of the most popular and practical destinations on AOL, but I had never really checked it out. But now I had a plan: if a spoonful of sugar makes the medicine go down, think how much financial savvy I could digest with a whole carton of fried rice!

LUNCH 1:

Blueberry yogurt, a sandwich, iced tea, and the Personal Finance main channel screen.

There's a ton of info here at KEYWORD: **Finance**, but these guys know how to structure information. The Welcome Kit that popped up on my first visit suggested that I start by subscribing to their two newsletters: *Checks & Balances* and *The Investor*. Done.

From there I moved onto Financial Planning (KEYWORD: **PF Planning**), where I matriculated into Ric Edelman's Money University (KEYWORD: **Money U**). I like their motto: "The fun way to learn personal finance." *MU* is designed to look like an online campus. I checked into some very helpful classes on credit cards, insurance, elder care, mortgages, even wills and trusts.

MoneyWhiz (**KEYWORD: MoneyWhiz**) is also packed with step-by-step answers to personal finance questions. As I finished off my yogurt, I learned how to get the best deal on credit cards.

Parent Soup's *Resource Library* (**KEYWORD: Resource Library**) also has a Money area with helpful tips on spending and budgeting.

After all this worthy, responsible planning, I felt as if I deserved some financial fantasy time. So I stopped in at *Your Business* (**KEYWORD: Your Business**). This area calls itself "The Entrepreneur and Business Owner's Resource," and it really delivers, with a bunch of buttons leading off to topics like The Dream, Getting Started, and Tools and Reference.

LUNCH 2:

Vegetarian fried rice, frozen yogurt, iced tea, and Online Personal Finance Calculators.

Now these are cool! I spent my entire lunch hour at the Calculators Web site, an easy click from the Personal Finance Planning screen. My favorites: the Credit Card Calculators (where I answered the question, "Should I consolidate my debt?"), the Budgeting Calculators (where I calculated "What's it worth to reduce my spending?"), and my personal favorite, the Savings Calculator that tackled the question: What will it take to become a millionaire? (For me? You don't want to know. But let's just hope I live well into the 22nd century.)

LUNCH 3:

A large baked potato, a lemonade, and the AOL Banking Center.

The *AOL Banking Center* (**KEYWORD: Bank**) allows you to choose from more than 30 financial institutions, and the best part is that your choice doesn't have to be on the way home from work. I was impressed by what these institutions offered: the ability to download balances, pay bills, balance your check book, etc. (continued)

CCH Business Owner's Toolkit (KEYWORD: **CCH**) also features an entire office supply closet of important info, like how to deal with office equipment and how to market your product. From there I checked out *Guerrilla Marketing Online* (KEYWORD: **Guerrilla**) for some good tips on getting an idea into the marketplace.

(Lunch 3, continued)

BankRate Monitor (KEYWORD: **BMR**) and *MoneyWhiz* (KEYWORD: **MoneyWhiz**) helped me sort them out by offering unbiased views of the whole online banking scene.

AOL has also teamed up with CheckFree, Intuit, Online Resources, and Visa Interactive to give financial institutions the ability to offer their customers a choice of a variety of interface options that best suit their needs. Since I've used Quicken, I checked out Intuit's new product, *BankNow* (KEYWORD: **BankNow**). You know, I'm not going to miss mailing checks at all!

LUNCH 4:

Pad Thai, coffee, and Motley Fool.

By Thursday, I felt like I was on firm financial footing. I was ready to speculate. And that led me to (where else?) *Motley Fool* (KEYWORD: **Fool**). My first stop was the Lunchtime News, not because I needed up-to-the-midmeal financial news, but because, hey, I was eating lunch!

Then I backtracked a little to a couple of really cool intros: 13 Steps to Investing Foolishly, and Fool's School. These *Motley* guys may be foolish, but when it comes to money, they're downright sensible!

They also have a bead on the best financial info on AOL and the Internet. I checked out *Online Investor* (KEYWORD: **Online Investor**) for help with understanding daily market news. (I liked their capitalized warning: "DO NOT BUY ANY STOCK UNTIL YOU HAVE INVESTIGATED IT TO YOUR COMFORT LEVEL.") Then I went over to Sage (KEYWORD: **Sage**) to learn how to invest in mutual funds.

Before I went back to work, I checked out a few solid financial news sources—for when my investment plans really take off: *Company News* (KEYWORD: **Company News**) searches a 30-day archive of Reuters, PR Newswire, and Business Wire by company ticker symbol; *Company Research* (KEYWORD: **Company Research**) features stock reports, financial statements, earnings and estimates, and historical stock quotes.

Some of the advice I got from these Start-Your-Own-Business areas was downright inspirational. In fact, I began to think that, yeah, maybe someday I will work for myself. Maybe I'll start a chain of Chinese steamed dumplings shops. Why not? Or how about a publishing company that specializes in books that will help you get to sleep—really, really boring novels. Could be a market there, wouldn't you say? Or do you think I should keep my day job?

LUNCH 5:

Garden salad, mineral water, and the Future.

I know, this last meal seems unusually restrained, but I had to put myself in a sober, responsible mood, because the lunchtime topic was taxes and retirement planning.

I started with a keyword that is probably not on anyone's list of Saturday night entertainin' sites: **Taxes.** But, once I forced myself to enter the *Tax Planning* area, I was impressed with the information: tax news, forms and schedules, IRAs and Keoughs, tax software, Web sites, and tax-related articles from *Worth*, *BusinessWeek,* and other first-rate publications.

Feeling virtuous, I clicked over to the retirement resources in KEYWORD: **PF Planning**. Plenty of solid info here from the American Association of Retired Persons (AARP) and the American Association of Individual Investors (AAII). I checked to see if they had anything from the AAPYW (the American Association of Procrastinating Young Women), but no luck. I did find a cool 401(k) Café at *FundWorks* (KEYWORD: **FundWorks**), which gave me all the info I needed for this great tool.

Control Your Investments

Read a comparison of technical analysis software, learn the basics of cash flow analysis, and protect yourself from financial information service rip-offs. That's only some of the information in one of the subsections of **KEYWORD: AAII**. The *American Association of Individual Investors* is a nonprofit organization for individuals managing their own investments, and *AAII Online* provides plenty of tools that can help.

Insider's Tip

KEYWORD: Business News is a shortcut to industry news, company research, consumer briefs, and business news from the *New York Times*.

You'll learn how to avoid brokerage firm fraud, why you should avoid penny stocks, how to buy treasuries without a broker, and how to file a complaint against a broker. Compare differences between sector funds, learn how to value stocks, and start understanding industry analysis. Download a table of positive free cash flow firms, or visit the Software Library for a varied selection of downloadable investment software.

One of the most useful features of AAII is the frank discussion of online investing resources. Message board topics include the pros and cons of various financial Web sites, investment software, and online brokerage firms. The experiences of other members will help you use technology to your full financial advantage.

Get Informed and Get Ahead

Good Stuff!

KEYWORD: IBD includes a daily databus, a graphic representation of important business trends like intranet use.

Investor's Business Daily's concise articles seem designed for life in the fast lane: economy briefs are clearly labeled by country, and To the Point condenses important business news items into one- or two-sentence blurbs. But if you have the time, don't miss the longer, more in-depth articles at **KEYWORD: IBD**.

The meatiest part of *Investor's Business Daily* is Markets & Investing. The Investor's Corner column looks for the larger meaning of market headlines, and Company in the News analyzes an individual company's progress. Other news columns focus on mutual funds, futures, the NYSE, AMEX, and NASDAQ markets.

Network with Other Online Investors

Financial chat rooms and message boards are organized at **KEYWORD: PF Live**. Check the chat schedule for discussions on specific topics like active and passive fund management, portfolio tracking, and making money in profes-sional speaking. There are other chat rooms you can drop by any-time—some times are busy, like during lunch and after work, and some times are slower. You'll usually find something going on in these rooms:

- Investment Chat is for general investing discussion and is often crowded.
- Market News Chat is for discussing today's most important market events.
- The Shark Tank chat room is the place to talk to other aggressive traders.
- Fool Chat is a popular, often moderated room for serious investors with not-so-serious personalities.
- Fund Talk and Stock Talk have bustling scheduled chats but tend to be empty at other times.
- Conference Call is an interesting chat event: "Four Investors. Four Philosophies. Who's Right? You Decide." Watch the debate every Thursday night at **KEYWORD: Conference Call**.

These chats are certainly engaging, but don't get so involved you miss all that the message boards have to offer. The Stock Talk boards (**KEYWORD: PF Live**) and the Fool Community boards (**KEYWORD: Fool**) are both excellent, well-populated resources for discussing investments and getting information from other investors. The Fools even supervise their boards to make sure "problem posts" don't interfere with your conversation.

Channel Jumping

You won't get the kind of return you do from investing, but smart shopping still pays. Get the most for your money with help from the consumer advocates at **KEYWORD: Consumer Reports**.

Meet...
Ric Edelman
One of the nation's most highly-respected financial advisors can be your financial advisor, too. Best-selling author Ric Edelman dispenses advice at KEYWORD: **Edelman**.

Any businessperson, market maven or not, will benefit from the business news here. News For You offers practical advice on topics like business communication and home finance. Stay abreast of technological changes that will affect the workplace with the Computers & Technology section. The IBD University has Investor Education Modules and a Stock Challenge where you can enter to win free months of AOL. To find the most relevant articles for your career, search the *IBD* archive.

News from Wall Street, Tokyo, and Cyberspace

The *Dow Jones Business Center* isn't just about Wall Street. In addition to the NYSE and AMEX, KEYWORD: **Dow Jones** gives ample coverage on international stocks, the national economy, and world business news. This easy-to-navigate area even has keywords for each of its subsections so you can skip right to your main interests. Or make it even easier and subscribe to their free email newsletter to receive market updates twice a day.

Click the Markets button or use KEYWORD: **DJ Markets** to see Dow 30, NASDAQ, S&P 500, long bond, soybean, and dollar statistics that are only minutes old. Click the Analysis/Statistics icon for news and commentary about up-and-coming stocks and the changing business world.

The Economy & Nations section, KEYWORD: **DJ Economy**, spotlights the U.S. economy, while KEYWORD: **DJ Intl** tells you what's new in the global economy, including Web links that will get you closer to the country of your choice. In these fast-moving times, you'll benefit from KEYWORD: **DJ Tech**'s news about telecommunications, computers, and the Internet. Industry and company news is available so you can keep an eye on your competition.

Visit KEYWORD: **Best of Dow Jones** for selected articles about personal finance, career development, and small businesses. Surprisingly, there are also articles about travel, entertainment, and health. Business news isn't just important—it's everywhere.

CUT WEDDING COSTS

Sure, it should be one of the happiest days of your lives, but does it have to be so darn expensive? KEYWORD: **PF Planning**'s Family Finance section features a guide to cutting wedding costs. Can the bride fit into her mother's wedding dress? Maybe. Will your guests mind if you serve chicken instead of beef? Probably not. Will a DJ cost less than a live band? Almost definitely. You get the idea. You'll also find money-saving tips for the honeymoon.

Financial Resources Everyone Can Use

Get Your Money Questions Answered

At **KEYWORD: Edelman**, financial expert Ric Edelman has plenty of advice for ordinary people trying to keep their heads above water. Encourage adult children living at home to contribute rent money. Choose financial stability over a costly fairy-tale wedding. Don't do your holiday shopping with credit cards (you'll spend up to 32% more). And whatever you do, don't buy a condo.

Edelman may use a "tough love" approach sometimes, but it's also very user-friendly. Many of his columns are based on member questions. The articles are easy to understand, and questions posted in the message boards often get personalized attention from Edelman or his staff of experts. Problems like overwhelming debt and difficulty saving for retirement are common. You'll also find advice about paying for college, managing credit cards, paying the mortgage, and planning for your future.

To have money tips delivered to your email box every week, subscribe to the free Edelman Advisor newsletter. The newsletter is also a good way to keep up with Edelman's chat room appearances.

Free Advice from the Wall Street Journal

For an amazing money management resource, follow this trail: **KEYWORD: PF Planning** > Learning the Basics > Wall Street Journal Lifetime Guide to Money.

You'll find generation-specific financial planning advice, information on putting together a financial safety net, tips on boosting your savings, and a guide to choosing a financial planner, if you need one.

Insider's Tip

Do bank fees drive you nuts? **KEYWORD: MoneyWhiz** has suggestions for dodging them. Keep a large balance in your account, limit your check-writing and ATM use, and order your checks from an outside distributor.

Recommended Reading for Money Management

Don't let the name fool you. You don't have to be a whiz at all to take advantage of *MoneyWhiz*. In fact, it's for anyone who wants to have more money left over at the end of the month. This area gives you the advice you need to teach yourself how to pay all the bills, and maybe even save some of your hard-earned salary for the future.

KEYWORD: MoneyWhiz covers topics like debt management, checking accounts, ATMs, car financing, mortgages, taxes, saving, and investing. The content is mostly

Channel Jumping

For advice on affording your kid's tuition, try **KEYWORD: Road To College** and **KEYWORD: RSP**. I've also written about the tricky task of paying for college in Chapter 7, *Live and Learn*.

Insider's Tip

KEYWORD: Insurance links to the Web sites of several top insurance carriers, including Prudential, Colonial Penn, Lincoln Benefit Life, and the Teachers Insurance and Annuity Association.

Good Stuff!

KEYWORD: Vanguard has an article called "Keeping Life Insurance out of Your Estate" that might help you get more out of your policy.

in the form of easily readable feature articles, but you can also find personal interaction in the message boards.

Here are just two down-to-earth lessons from *MoneyWhiz*: Did you know that debit cards really *are* better for consumers than credit cards or checks? They can be used anywhere in the country, you don't have to show ID, and you control your debt by never having an outstanding balance that accumulates interest. How do you handle the family budget when one of you is a spender and the other is a saver? Try three checking accounts: a joint account for mutual expenses like rent, and one account each for you and your mate's separate spending money.

Understanding Insurance

KEYWORD: Insurance can make everyone's life easier with all the insurance resources it has gathered into one area. If you have insurance or need insurance, this is one-stop shopping for all the relevant information. You'll learn the difference between different types of home insurance policies, get tips for saving money on automobile insurance, and participate in chats with insurance professionals.

You're guaranteed to learn something important at the *Insurance Center*. For instance, what's the most vital insurance you can have? Some experts say disability insurance, even though less than 15% of US workers have it. Your insurance needs also depend on which of these four categories you fall into: single, married without children, married with children, and married with adult children. Moms and dads might want Parent Soup's perspective on selecting family health insurance, investing in life insurance, setting up a trust, and writing a will. They can find it in this area. Singles might appreciate this tip from *MoneyWhiz*: if you're single, you usually don't need life insurance.

Balance Your Checkbook and Pay Your Bills Online

More convenient than an ATM card, more powerful than a locomotive, can leap long teller lines in a single bound . . . it's **KEYWORD: Bank**. The *Banking Center* makes online banking easy for everyone. Choose one of 30 participating banks, and get ready to pay your credit card bills, check your balance, or make mortgage payments on AOL, 24 hours a day.

There are many measures being taken to ensure the safety of your money. First of all, you'll have an online banking password (different from your AOL password) and a PIN number that only you know. As long as you keep these to yourself, you're safe. Don't worry about hackers, either. Web transactions scramble your banking information using the highest-level security available. Non-Web AOL transactions never go over the Internet and are protected by AOL's private security system. The banks that use *BankNOW* technology (**KEYWORD: BankNOW**) combine 1024-bit RSA encoding with triple-DES encryption—it's akin to sending your postal mail in a safe.

Channel Jumping

Thinking of moving? Real estate listings, mortgage information, and ways to research your new neighborhood are all at **KEYWORD: Real Estate**.

Choose the Best Mortgage, Loan, or Credit Card

Don't settle for a bank with high interest rates—unless you're looking for a CD or money market account, that is. **KEYWORD: BankRate** has gathered data from banks all over the U.S. to help you find the best banking deals. Just because you don't have time to do all the research doesn't mean you should get stuck paying too much interest on your loans.

Bank Rate Monitor features state and national rates (highs, lows, and averages) so you can see how your neighborhood bank compares. Mortgage information includes rate, annual percentage rate, and points for one-year, 15-year, or 30-year mortgages. Credit cards are divided into the categories of gold cards, conventional cards, the best deals nationwide for people who carry a balance, and good cards for those who pay their bills in

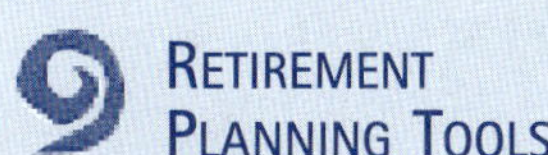

Retirement Planning Tools

KEYWORD: Fidelity offers a free Retirement Toolkit. Interactive worksheet and software help you evaluate your needs, figure out how much money you should save for retirement, create an investment strategy, and decide whether to include an annuity in your financial plan.

Tax Tip of the Day

KEYWORD: **Tax Channel** offers Tax Tips that will help you survive the cruel month of April. Learn:

- Which tax forms you should save
- What to do if you need an extension
- How to deduct moving expenses
- What to do if you are audited
- How to get deductions by donating unwanted items to charity

full every month. You'll find the bank name, phone number, interest rate of the card, amount of the annual fee, and number of interest-free days allotted. Bank Rate Monitor also evaluates auto loan rates, CDs and MMAs, personal loans, and home equity lines of credit (HELOCs). All these acronyms can be confusing, but clicking on any of them brings up a glossary of terms.

Do Your Own Taxes

Filing your tax return might seem like a Herculean task, but you can do it without hiring an accountant. All you need is a little help from KEYWORD: **Tax**. The *Tax Planning* area connects you to software reviews that help you choose the best program for you and even gives you your choice of downloadable tax software that gets the job done. To save time, you can download federal and state tax forms, schedules, and instructions.

If you're having trouble deciphering tax codes, experts are available to answer your questions in message boards and chats. For example, a member wrote, "My father-in-law passed away earlier this year, and he expressed a desire to have some of the insurance money go to his daughter. What is the best way for her mother to transfer a portion of the money to her daughter?"

The same day, another member answered, "One way is for your mother-in-law to make an out and out gift. If total gifts from mother to daughter exceed $10K for the year, a gift tax return has to be filed." Yet another member added, "If Mom-in-law wishes to give more than the $10K a year . . . she can give your wife $10K inclusively and she can also give YOU the same amount. If she gives more than that, she MUST file a gift tax return, since it is doubtful tax is due . . . ."

If April 15 comes and your tax return remains unfiled, there's still hope. You can learn how to get an extension until August 15, but make sure you file in time for your new summer deadline. It's possible to get a second extension until October, but it's more difficult.

Plan for the Future

The *Advice and Planning* area, **KEYWORD: PF Planning**, organizes resources for family finance, retirement planning, credit, debt, and other basics that everyone needs to know about. It's hard to think about saving money when you're scrambling to come up with this month's rent or mortgage payment, but this area will help.

For example, as you probably know, it's never too early or late to plan for retirement. Start investing in your company's 401(k) as soon as you can (it's a tax break, too!) and visit the Retirement Planning section to find out more. Parents can use the Family Finances section to learn how to pay for everything from braces to college to weddings. You'll also find information that will help you save, invest, pay debts, and land a better job.

Good Stuff!

Obviously, raising kids isn't cheap. Parent Soup's resident money expert, PSNeale, answers members' questions about making ends meet at **KEYWORD: PS Money**.

The best part may be that you can meet your financial goals without crunching any numbers—just use the Financial Planning Calculators. Mortgage calculators address questions like how much you can borrow, how much your payments will be, how much you can save in taxes, and whether you should refinance. Auto loan calculators settle debates like new versus used, buying versus leasing, and financing versus paying cash. Should you consolidate debts? What will it take to pay off your credit card balance? How much money should you be stashing away to save for a car, a home, college, or retirement? Plug in your numbers and let AOL do the math.

The fast-paced financial world is exciting, but it can be hard to keep up. For the latest headlines, use **KEYWORD: PF News**, which also connects you to informative areas like the *Market News Center*. You can read about other tricks for finding news in Chapter 3, *Keeping Current: News and Weather Reports on AOL*.

Sometimes I'm too busy to do anything but check my email. On those days, I'm thankful for AOL newsletters like *Checks & Balances* (for general money-management) and *The Investor* (specifically for investing and business). These and other free newsletters deliver the latest news about your interests to your email box, and highlight particularly noteworthy online areas. After reading a newsletter, I can often convince myself that I have a *few* minutes to look at the areas I've just read about. Newsletters ensure that you don't miss any online information about your interests, from entertainment to health, and they make sure you hear that "You've got mail" message much more often. Visit KEYWORD: **Newsletters** and subscribe to a few. If you decide a newsletter you've been reading isn't what you're looking for, unsubscribing is easy.

Insider's Tip

KEYWORD: **NBR** has information on mutual funds, women and investing, and taxes.

The Personal Finance Channel isn't the only place to make the most of your money, either. The Shopping Channel (KEYWORD: **Shopping**) has lots of great deals, and the discerning reviews published in the Entertainment Channel help you make the most of your leisure dollars. And now that members don't get charged by the hour for AOL access, it's economical to explore it all.

Computing, Software, and the Internet

The jumping-off point for all my computing needs and desires is **KEYWORD: Computing**. It's all here: from technical support and classes to Internet publishing. You'll also find tools to help you select a new computer, new software, or peripherals.

Dive deep into whatever computer or software pool you desire. In the area called *Download Software* I search through thousands of files for shareware programs or the latest upgrades. To help you get the most out of the software you can download on AOL, I've provided information on the software libraries later in this chapter. I also want to be up on the current trends in computing, so I go to **KEYWORD: CS Hot**. There I find the staff's daily picks of the best software tools, events and classes, and computing news.

And then there's shopping. I can get consumer information and research products on AOL, order online, and then have what I buy home-delivered. Check the section later in this chapter on choosing and buying computers and peripherals. **KEYWORD: Computing Superstore** is available 24 hours a day.

I certainly don't know how to program my computer, but with AOL I can troubleshoot problems with my modem or my speakers. AOL's support forums, described in the next section, have all the tools I need to keep my machine running smoothly.

Access AOL at Blazing Fast Speeds

Maybe you thought your 28.8kbps modem was fast. But now in select cities you can access AOL at twice the speed of mere mortals with the new x2 modems from U.S. Robotics. To start, big cities like New York and Chicago are up and zipping on AOL. As the field trials progress, AOL plans on adding hundreds of locations. Check **KEYWORD: x2** to learn more, and to find out whether your area has a new, free x2 access number.

LIVE COMPUTING HELP AND HOW-TOS

Get tips from other members and staff in live forums at **KEYWORD: CompLive.** Even if you're not having trouble with Windows, or your printer works perfectly, you can join in to relax with like-minded folks. Here's a sampling of the live Personal Computing chats:

- Multimedia
- Applications
- Graphics
- 3-D
- Printers
- Computing Help
- Web Design
- Windows 95/NT/3.1
- Youth Tech

Insider's Tip

Get Meg's Top Tips every day at **KEYWORD: AOL Insider**. Learn to create your own Go To menu, ignore chat room participants, or use parental controls.

How to Work and Play Hard: Support Forums and Help Areas

Find All the Support Forums Under One Roof

KEYWORD: Forums is AOL's launchpad for PC, software, and Internet help.

Developers, graphic artists, multimedia lovers, musicians, Windows users, telecommuters, and networkers all have their own forums. Get essential information from pros and AOL members who know the ins and outs of Windows and Mac operating systems and applications. Electronic music and sound production, personal digital assistants, and graphic arts are other areas where you can pick up information and how-tos.

Find PC Help for Ordinary People

KEYWORD: Home PC calls itself "the computer magazine for the rest of us." *Home PC* makes no secret of the fact that it is aimed at a lay audience—its articles are mostly jargon-free and easy to understand. The best features at *Home PC* are Consumer Labs and Ask Dr. PC.

Consumer Labs puts a new twist on the standard product reviews: a special consumer panel, not techies, use, review, and rate products. In the monthly column you can find reviews of products like portable drives and trip-making software.

Ask Dr. PC is the place to come for quick, non-techie advice for PC problems. Come here for answers that won't confuse you.

Tools to Help You Fight PC Viruses

How do you spell relief when viruses invade your computer, your life, and your sanity? The answer is at **KEYWORD: Virus**.

The *PC Virus Information Center* brings you answers to the questions you have about PC viruses. Best of all, you'll find information on how to avoid "catching" them. The Virus Reference provides step-by-step instructions you can use to avoid infection, ways to be ready in case your machine gets infected, and what you can do if infection has already occurred.

Other virus resources come from the companies themselves, such as McAfee at KEYWORD: **McAfee.** A search at KEYWORD: **Software** will also help you find Dr. Soloman's Software and Symantec, some of the big players in virus protection. Try the demos before you buy.

If you do things right, your computer will be better protected and virus-free.

Insider's Tip

Find what you're looking for. Click FIND on the Tool Bar, or go to KEYWORD: **Find**. Type in a search word and you'll get a whole list of areas to choose from.

Get Your PC Questions Answered

AOL apprehension? Fear of trying? Try the friendly guides at KEYWORD: **PC Help**. The *PC Help Desk* is where you can take a refresher course at Download 101, learn to convert files, and become expert at locating information. You'll also find live help chat—indispensable for those rare times when you've gone through the FAQs and tutorials and you still don't quite have the answer.

A great feature at the *Help Desk*: post your PC question on the Message Board and you'll have an official response via email within 72 hours.

KEYWORD: **Discover AOL** takes you on a walk-through of a number of AOL's services like email, message boards, downloading files, chat rooms, and using the Internet. Think of it as a quick member orientation, or—if you're a seasoned Insider—a reorientation. Even Meg needs a little refresher course every now and again.

Send your newbie friends to KEYWORD: **LearnAOL**, where people with little online or AOL time under their belt can get quickly, and easily, up to speed.

Optimize Your PC

Find out if your system is a speed-demon or a sloth at KEYWORD: **WinMag.** Download WinTune, a free program for Windows 95 or NT, in *WinMag*'s software section. It can help you decide how to make your system run faster and more efficiently. Discover whether your hard drive needs optimization, or whether you could use a quicker CPU. By comparing your configuration to the many others in the program, you'll see just where it stacks up, or doesn't.

Chatter Box

The Windows Forum Conference Areas at **KEYWORD: Win** bring you live assistance for Windows 3.1, 95, and NT. Check the schedule for times when the professional staff are online.

COMPUTER SUPPORT

AOL has many support and users' forums for getting help or learning to use new software. At **KEYWORD: Forums,** here's what you have to choose from:

- Applications Forum
- Desktop & Web Publishing
- Developers
- Games
- Graphic Arts
- Hardware
- Help
- Multimedia Zone
- Music and Sound
- OS/2
- Personal Digital Assistants
- Software Center
- Telecom & Networking
- User Group Forum
- Windows 95 Forum
- Windows NT Forum
- Mac Support Forums

Give Your Browser a Tune Up

Browser Tune is one of the most useful tools you'll find at **KEYWORD: WinMag**, short for *Window's Magazine*. Find out where your browser shines or fails and where it could use

Use Windows More Effectively

Windows is covered in so many ways, each of which you can find by clicking on "Windows" at **KEYWORD: Forums**. Windows users and aficionados of any flavor—Windows 95, Windows NT, or Windows 3.1—get software, patches, tips, tricks, and news from people who really know their stuff. Each Windows version has its own Reference Guide full of questions and answers for booting, dial-up networking, desktop problems, printing woes, memory issues, and more. You'll also find a connection to the Microsoft Windows Home Page.

Post a message to the Windows Forum community and get your questions answered. **KEYWORD: Win95** covers Microsoft's latest OS, while **KEYWORD: WinNT** covers the higher end of the spectrum. **KEYWORD: WCE** covers the handheld products. And you can be sure that when the next versions appear, there will be areas for those, too.

In Software, you won't want to miss the staff's Recommended Utilities: everything here has been selected because of its special value or popularity.

In Computing Companies, you can find technical support as well as program patches, press releases, and support message boards.

Interact live with other Windows users in the forum's conference rooms during the three regularly scheduled chats: Mondays are for Windows NT, Tuesdays for Windows 95, and Thursdays cover Windows 3.x.

some improvement. It doesn't matter whether you're using AOL's default browser (MS Internet Explorer), Netscape, or another browser. Maybe you need to make a few optimizations in its options, or you might improve your Internet experience with a few plug-ins. Find Browser Tune in the section titled WinMag on the Web.

In addition, Windows users can find reviews of new products, how-to columns, analysis, and opinions from the experts that can help guide you to a smarter purchase.

Good Stuff!

Web University, at KEYWORD: **On the Net**, gives free online classes in Java and Javascript for those who want to be on the cutting edge of Internet publishing.

Learn C++, Visual Basic, and Assembly

Information that can help make developers more productive stocks the shelves at KEYWORD: **PC Development**. A handy tool is the Developer's Reference, where in one stop you can find numerous up-to-date links to programming resources on the Web. Need to talk to experts about your programming, or just want to hang out with others who share your programming interests? Drop by a nightly chat: Mondays cover Visual Basic; Tuesdays, Windows Programming; Wednesdays, DOS Development; Thursdays, C/C++; Fridays, Teen/Beginning Programming; and Saturdays are reserved for Special Topics.

Development companies show off the latest on their services, products, and training. Shareware, demos, and samples help you with every aspect of your coding.

Top Answers to Common Computer Questions

Kim Komando leads this very down-to-earth forum for computer users who don't know all the jargon, but who need help they can understand. The best things about KEYWORD: **Komando** are the easy-to-understand tips on upgrading, saving money, and basic computer survival.

Practical items such as discussions on whether airport x-ray machines damage magnetic media or whether to leave your computer on overnight come up daily here.

Meet. . . Computer Advisor Kim Komando

A TV host, a talk radio host, a syndicated columnist, an author, and the founder of the *Komputer Klinic* on AOL, KEYWORD: **Komando**, Kim really knows how to help you master your computer.

SURF SHACK: INTERNET INFORMATION IN A NUTSHELL

The Shack is your Internet center for information and support. There are links to just about all the Web-related resources on AOL. Get your own Web page up with page-building resources for all skill levels at KEYWORD: **Personal Publisher** or KEYWORD: **Prime Host**. You'll also find online courses in Web site creation and Java at KEYWORD: **On the Net** and KEYWORD: **Online Classroom.** Internet books and software await you at KEYWORD: **Computing Superstore.**

If a little inspiration is what you're looking for, publishers like you will also find a comprehensive list of members' favorite Web sites at KEYWORD: **Member Waves.**

♦ ♦ ♦ ♦ ♦ ♦ ♦ ♦ ♦ ♦ ♦ ♦

Insider's Tip

KEYWORD: **Modem** has the answers to questions about connecting to AOL. If you're having trouble, you may need a new modem profile to assist your modem in speaking AOL's language.

Among the many solutions in the Top Answers Collection are instructions on how to connect a VCR to your computer and advice about what to do when your color printer won't print color.

Program and Use Databases

With all the talk about macros, and queries, and forms, I've always thought that database gurus were a breed apart. The designers and programmers who make it easy for the rest of us to gather and use data go to KEYWORD: **Database**, where they keep up-to-date on developments in the field. Developers and administrators find plenty of database tools and techniques, and the software libraries offer downloadable support files, updates, source code, templates, and utilities. Connections to software companies will provide you with the latest information on applications such as Access, FoxPro, Delphi, Paradox, and others.

Get More from the Internet

Learn to Use the Internet Like a Pro

KEYWORD: **Net Highlights** brings you to one of AOL's doorways to the Internet. You'll find information and tips on surfing the Web, as well as what's up in the other parts of the Internet, like Newsgroups, FTP, and Gopher. If you're looking for some of the best links around, just click the "Best of" button for key Web sites and recommended Newsgroups, which are text-based discussions on nearly 30,000 topics of interest.

Become an Internet Power User

KEYWORD: **NetGuide** brings you up-to-date Internet news. Especially helpful is the Product Spotlight, due mainly to

Tim Hight's ongoing column that highlights new, unusual Internet and computing products. Phones that can receive email and VCRs that you can control from your computer are just two of Tim's recent finds.

Net Know-How is aimed at making you more proficient in using Internet and online services. Snap Guides give practical, topical advice on how to use the Net to improve your daily life. Your feedback is also important at *NetGuide*: Behind the Scenes encourages you to contribute to a *NetGuide* article by answering a poll or giving your opinion on the hot topic of the week.

DON'T DOWNLOAD FROM STRANGERS

If you've received email from someone you don't know, it is good advice not to download any attachments until you can confirm that it is virus-free. Although hackers are a small minority in the online community, they may try any means of corrupting your system, or gaining your online passwords. So if a stranger tempts you with free games, faster modem connections, or email versions of AOL software upgrades, don't be taken in. On the bright side, you can never get a virus just from reading email—only corrupt attachments are the culprits. And remember: AOL will never send software via email, and AOL staff will never ask for your password.

Talk, Listen, and Learn in Internet Discussion Groups

Discuss almost anything you want in literally tens of thousands of Internet discussion groups accessible worldwide. Nearly 30,000 Newsgroups (a.k.a. Usenet) and over 25,000 Mailing Lists cover the world: science, politics, hobbies, interests, computing, music, and cultures.

Mailing Lists and Newsgroups are among the oldest resources on the Internet, and they continue to be among the most popular. Some people find that the more time they spend online, the less time they spend on the Web—that is, you might find yourself surfing less, but participating more and more in Internet discussion groups.

KEYWORD: Mailinglists is your entrance to several good resources on getting the most from these email discussions. Especially helpful is AOL's own searchable directory of several thousand worthy discussion groups broken down by interest.

KEYWORD: Usenet is your gateway to Newsgroups. Millions of participants worldwide discuss a variety of interests. The groups are listed in hierarchies. For example, computing topics begin with "comp.", science-related groups begin with "sci.", and recreational and leisure groups begin with "rec.".

With AOL's newsreader, you can download a group's posts automatically using flashsessions and read them offline, whenever or wherever you choose. You

Good Stuff!

The searchable Mailing List directory at **KEYWORD: Mailinglist** has in-depth descriptions of each group so that you can make a more informed decision before you decide to subscribe to a list. Click "Browse the Directory" to take a look.

Insider's Tip

Use the **Download Manager** to download files automatically. With "Download Later," you can get the files you want even when you're doing something else, like writing email, getting stock quotes, or sleeping.

can also respond offline, and send in your posts the next time you log in.

Find and Use the Software You Want, In a Flash

Find the Right Software for You

Download just about anything at KEYWORD: **Software**. You can find freeware, shareware, and software to purchase with the AOL guarantee. Most of it is available for instant download, which is good if you want your software without going out to the store or waiting for the mail.

Use the search function to find programs and tools in a variety of categories: telecommunications, fun and games, graphics, multimedia, Internet, sound and music, networking, and business.

KEYWORD: **File Search** let's you search for shareware or products to purchase and download immediately. Once you've found the items you need, you can download either immediately or later on in your session using the Download Manager in the File menu.

For the most successful searching, it's a good idea not to search using the filename. For instance, *PKZip* or *vbrun300* might change slightly or new version numbers might be added. Your best option is to search using more general words that relate to or describe the file, such as "runtime module" for *vbrun300* or "uncompress" rather than *PKZip*.

Attention AOL Shoppers!

atOnce Software brings you over 2,000 business applications, games, and tools for your immediate purchase and download at KEYWORD: **atOnce**.

Get Software Recommended by the PC Staff

Perhaps the best thing about *Hot Files* is that you don't have to search for what you want; in fact, you might find something among the staff's picks that you didn't even know you wanted, like PKZip for compressing your files or MIDI files for Web pages. At **KEYWORD: Hot Files** you can get fun games, children's storybooks and sounds. Popular business and home applications and images are available daily and archived.

Good Stuff!

Get an expert opinion on kids' software by clicking on "Kids' Software" at **KEYWORD: Home PC**. Hundreds of reviews await parents interested in the best educational, fun stuff for kids.

Locate Your Downloaded Files

Where does your software go when you've downloaded a file from AOL? Sometimes we all have trouble remembering where a downloaded file went. Thankfully, most files end up in the same place: a special default directory in your AOL software for downloads called the AOLxx\DOWNLOAD directory. Whenever you download a file, it appears in your C:\AOLxx\DOWNLOAD directory unless you ask AOL to put the file into another folder of your choice. You should see this path in your Download Manager (on the File menu). Look for the line that says "Files will be downloaded to: C:\AOLxx\DOWNLOAD" where xx is the version number of your AOL software. If you use AOL V4.0, your download directory is C:\AOL40\DOWNLOAD.

You can change this directory by clicking the Select Directory icon, and then choosing the folder you want from the window that comes up.

If you're still having trouble locating a file you've downloaded, go to the Download Manager from the File menu on the AOL menu bar. Click "Show Files Downloaded." Select the file you're having trouble finding. Click the Show Status icon: you'll get a small box telling you where the file is on your computer.

Another way to locate downloaded files is with FIND in Windows. Click "Start" then "Find" then "Files or Folders," and type in the name of the file you're looking for.

Files Come Compressed for Faster Downloading

Most files you can download are compressed or "ZIPed" so they'll download faster. A ZIPed file can be easily recognized since its actual filename will end with a .ZIP (or .zip) extension. A single .ZIP file may contain only one file or dozens of separate files. Before the file's contents can be used, the file must be unzipped.

Your AOL software can automatically unzip most files you'll find in the software libraries: when you sign off, AOL unzips the files into folders that have the same name as the .ZIP file. For example, *software.zip* will be extracted into a folder called "software."

Produce a Video, Scan Images, and Retouch Your Grandma's Pictures

Learn and Understand Multimedia

You can be at the helm of a tidal wave of multimedia software and information in the *Multimedia Zone*, **KEYWORD: MM**. All the latest tools are here so that you can use and even develop your own tricky video clips, dancing animated bears, and funky noises on your computer.

One handy tool: the Multimedia Showcase, where you can download browser plug-ins and Active X controls that can enhance the way you use the Web. You can get Macromedia's Shockwave, which allows your browser to play special multimedia presentations that are found all over the Web. RealAudio gives your browser the ability to play CD-quality sound over your 28.8 connection, and pretty decent sound on a 14.4. VDO Live is an add-on that brings your browser streaming video. Once you've installed the necessary extensions, you can follow the links to quality sites that use the technology, like InternetTV, ABC News, and the Online Newshour from PBS.

In Multimedia Resources' Tips and Tricks, find tons of answers to frequently asked questions (FAQs) on numerous topics, such as multimedia for beginners, copyrighting your own creations, AVI, and MPEG. Test software before you buy in the software library. If you're yearning for more help, find links to support for game and application development, graphic arts, and music and sound.

If, like many others in these days of CD-ROMs and MMX, you are looking to buy a new multimedia machine, you can get information on the speediest processors, as well as which systems will give you the most bang for your buck in the discussion boards, the Industry Connection, and the PC Vendors Database.

Publishers and Designers Share Their Knowledge

As part of the *Desktop and Web Publishing Forum*, weekly chats cover making, downloading, and using fonts; business on the Web; HTML and stupid Web tricks; and programs like Pagemaker, Quark, Corel, and Photoshop. Check the schedule at **KEYWORD: PCDWP**, then choose Conference Room.

Scan Your Own Images

Since you can add images to your emails and Instant Messages (IMs), you might want to learn how to optimize them for use online. First you have to get them into your computer. You can get the images placed on disk when they're processed. Or, you can have more control over how they look if you learn to digitally scan them yourself at **KEYWORD: Scanning**. Images with large file sizes take a long time to download (and upload!), so you'll want to learn to compress them before you send them.

The *Imaging Resource Center* is the hub of information about scanning images. It's a reference manual of facts and tips, with graphical how-tos dealing with art imaging.

Find help and descriptions of hardware and software, lists of contact information for publications, and links to scanner manufacturers like Canon, Hewlett Packard, and Epson. The software libraries contain downloadable examples of scanned images, as well as utilities to make your images shine, like CorelDRAW add-ons.

No Scanner of Your Own? Get EZScan to Do It for You

Now that you can send electronic versions of your favorite photos in IMs or email, you will need to have them converted into a format your computer can read. For this you need either a scanner or a special disk from your photofinisher. If you don't have a scanner, **KEYWORD: EZScan** can scan them for you. Just send in your photos or slides, and they'll send them back to you via email.

Create Graphic Arts and Images

The *PC Graphic Arts Forum* is a hub of graphic activity for creating fine art. At **KEYWORD: PC Graphics**, doors open onto a gallery, a library, and a learning center featuring one of the largest software collections for graphic enthusiasts in the online world: over 28,000 images.

The Conference Center is especially helpful: artists and staff meet every night for friendly, fun, and informative discussions on computer art, Web art, 3-D, and CAD.

Software Libraries house graphic-related files, images, animation, applications, and utilities. Message boards cover topics ranging from general art discussion to commercial software. From the *PC Graphic Arts Forum* you can also get to Special Interest Groups (called SIGs) that range from VRML to CAD, from scanning and digital imaging to resources for print artists.

Channel Jumping

Find info on digital cameras at **KEYWORD: Popular Photography**. Click "Digital Imaging" to get ratings of the top digital cameras and some help on how to use them.

Don't Just Search, Find

Get to what you're looking for on the Internet with **KEYWORD: NetFind.** AOL and Excite have teamed up to bring you a powerful directory, which includes reviews and ratings of the best sites. You'll also find Newsgroup reviews on hundreds of topics. *NetFind for Kids* can also lead parents to parent-approved sites, on both AOL and the Internet.

Get Photoshop Plug-ins, Filters, and Tools

You can get new tools to help you touch up your graphical images and speed transmission times when you send them in email or in IMs. Graphics professionals and high-end amateurs love Kai's Power Tools, KPT Convolver, and powerful and creative plug-in filters and extensions for imaging software such as Adobe Photoshop and Fractal Design Painter. You'll find all these tools at **KEYWORD: MetaTools**. *MetaTools* also publishes KPT Bryce, an innovative 3-D landscape generator, and Kai's Power Goo. If you really want to learn more, you can mingle with the programmers and designers themselves to get advice and tips on any of *MetaTools* apps and plug-ins at their frequent chats.

Find, Use, and Create Music and Sound

The *PC Music & Sound Forum* at **KEYWORD: PC Music** has hundreds of ready-to-play music and sound effect files that you can use with almost any sound board. It's the middle ground between computer outlet and music store, providing information and tools to help get you up and

Insider's Tip

Leave it to *Youth Tech* staffer YTCC Byte to say this to Web designers: "Compress your graphics when possible. People don't want to stay looking at a screen saying 'loading' for hours!"

Learn to Create Virtual Reality

Find out about Virtual Reality Modeling Language in the technically robust area at **KEYWORD: VRML**.

All the technical tools an author needs can be found in the *VRML Resource Center*—browsers, plug-ins, and converters. You can get tips and tricks for creating a scene and converting it to VRML using one of the many existing converters available. Several modelers are also available that will translate directly to VRML. The authoring tools will have you in the VRML driver's seat in no time. There's so much here, your head just might be spinning—in 3-D.

running with MIDI. The libraries are packed with great software, MIDI patches, songs, and full-featured sequencers.

The *Composers' Coffeehouse* at KEYWORD: **Composer** is the hangout for anyone interested in making music, whether you're into composition, songwriting, lyrics, film and video scoring, producing, or any aspect of the business. Message boards are the best way to find other members with the same equipment or PC audio and multimedia interests.

Make Your Documents Look Great with New Fonts

If you've ever downloaded and installed a font only to find it isn't at all what you're looking for, the Font Petting Zoo, at KEYWORD: **PCDWP**, can help you out. The information at the Petting Zoo helps you install fonts with fewer problems, and you can preview exactly what a font will look like before you decide to download it.

Get Published, Spread the News, or Put Out Your Own Scandal Sheet

Publish It on Paper or on the Web

All the resources for desktop and Web publishers are under one roof at KEYWORD: **PCDWP**: the *PC Desktop and Web Publishing Forum*. You can also get to the area with KEYWORD: **Web Publishing** or KEYWORD: **Desktop Publishing**. Learn how to create your own Web site, write Java, and get tips on True Type fonts, Optical Character Recognition, and scanning. Particularly useful are the free online courses in HTML, Java, and CGI in the Online Classroom. See the section later in this chapter on Web classes for more information. And when you're in need of some tools, the DWP Library contains software for clip art, fonts, publishing help, online texts, and more.

Insider's Tip

Where are you located on the Web? Spread the word! If you upload to your server space on AOL, your URL will be: *http://members.aol.com/your_Screen_name*.

Publish on the Internet with AOL's Personal Publisher

To start, KEYWORD: **Personal Publisher** will let you create several different types of Web presences. You can add colorful backgrounds, clickable images, and items that can be easily rearranged and edited. Use the simple templates to create a personal home page, a business page, or a greeting card. By moving step by step and filling in the form, you can add text, photos, graphics, and sound to your page, all without knowing a thing about coding or HTML. Just follow the smart tutorial and whistle while you work. In no time you'll have a basic publication to show off.

Create Web Page Art and Graphics

The *Web Page Art Creation Center*, at **KEYWORD: WebArt**, is a branch of the *PC Graphic Arts Forum*. Create clip art, background textures, icons, buttons, and bullets for your Web sites. At the Clip Art center, designers and digital artists like you find tools and tips for your creations, as well as a library to display your works. Learn how to make transparent GIFs and animations.

Chatter Box

The Web is rapidly becoming a visual environment. Don't get left behind with staid text home pages. *WebArt*'s weekly chat helps you to learn all about creating great graphics for Web pages at **KEYWORD: WebArt**.

You can view and compare art created or modified using a computer. **KEYWORD: Artists Spotlight** is a gallery of some serious online artists. See who's highlighted this week in the spotlight, critique the works, and download pieces you like. Perhaps the information and artwork will be just the ticket to invite the muse over to your PC and inspire art of your own.

Take Classes in the Online Classroom

You know that with AOL, you're both online and on the Web. Now perhaps you're thinking about getting your own home page. Enroll at **KEYWORD: Online Classroom** and learn how. Make yourself more marketable with new job skills by learning how to build a Web page. You can also master spreadsheets by learning Microsoft Excel. Or get the fundamentals of other software to boost your productivity. At **KEYWORD: On the Net**, you can take a 30- to 90-minute course and learn, for example, all about AOL's *Personal Publisher*, "The Easiest Way to Get On the Web." There's a course on Web Basics which covers HTML tags, counters, and uploading files with FTP. You can also sign up for a class called WEBing Your Business. Advanced topics include Using CGI on AOL, and Getting Started with Java—some of the hottest trends right now in Internet publishing and applications.

Each online course is conducted live by one of the Computing Channel's staff members. You'll find all of the class materials you need right online. As of this writing, there is no additional fee above regular AOL charges for these educational opportunities.

Add Animation to Your Web Site

Get the tools to add movement to your Web site with animated GIFs. You don't need to know Shockwave or Java to make things stand out on your page; all you need are the tools at the *Animated GIF Resource Center*, **KEYWORD: AGIF.**

What Do You Want to Publish on the Web?

Depending on your familiarity with Web publishing, you can use your AOL server space for nearly any sort of Web page you choose. You've got 2 megs of space for each of up to five screen names—making that 10 megs per account. You might start with a few vanity pages about you and your family, then move to up to creating pages for your poetry. Finally, you could graduate to designing a small business site.

Feel free to use the tools that are right for you, like PageMill, FrontPage, or even AOL's free Web page designer, AOL Press (found at **KEYWORD: AOL Press**). Separate HTML editors and design applications like these can help you design professional-looking pages. Or you can use AOL's *Personal Publisher*, which is described elsewhere in this chapter.

When you're ready to publish, simply upload each of your files via **KEYWORD: My Place** or AOL's FTP tool at **KEYWORD: FTP**. Easy-to-follow online help guides you through each step of the upload process.

Now get going and publish, whatever your skill level with HTML.

Insider's Tip

AOL's own free, full-featured Web design tool, *AOL Press*, helps you create pages with many of the bells and whistles that the pros have, including image maps, tables, and forms. Download at **KEYWORD: AOL Press**.

Insider's Tip

KEYWORD: CleanUp helps you get your computer in top shape. Safely clean your keyboard, mouse, and CD-ROMs. Install and remove software easily. And learn how Zip drives can ease an overcrowded hard drive.

Keep Up-to-Date with Leading Computing News and Magazines

Get Timely Computing News

The best thing at **KEYWORD: Magazine Rack** is the detailed information in the magazines. Read the latest issues of your favorite computer magazine—*PC World*, *PC Computing*, *Windows Magazine*, *MacWorld*, *HomePC*, *The Cobb Group Online*, *Kim Komando's Komputer Klinic*, *ChipNet*, and *GamePro* are here. If you know what sort of information you're looking for, the search tools will help you come up with a list of articles on your topic, such as buying a quality printer or installing a Zip drive.

Get Associated Press Computer News Every Day

Every day at **KEYWORD: Newswire**, the top computing and Internet news stories from the Associated Press are posted. If you miss a day, you can sift through several stories from days past, too. Savvy computer users come here to read up on the constant changes in technology and culture.

Daily News from selected Web sites brings you articles from numerous well-respected sources such as *Interactive Week*, *iworld*, and Excite. Take a peek at what goes on at Microsoft, Netscape, Apple, and IBM. You'll also find gaming news and the ever-present weird news for a good laugh.

Attention AOL Shoppers!

KEYWORD: Magazine Outlet houses more magazines than the average newsstand. Get good deals on computing, gaming, and Internet magazines from scores of publishers.

Be a Better Computer Consumer

The most revered feature at **KEYWORD: PC World** is the monthly Top 20. Each month, you'll find *PC World*'s list of the Top 20 computing components in several categories. Find the Top 20 monitors, Top 20 printers, Top 20 desktop systems, and Top 20 laptops. It's all to help you be a better consumer. If you want more information, you can send questions directly to *PC World*'s editors in live chats or via the message board. Download and test-drive new software, or exchange software with other members with the site's Shareware feature.

And don't miss **KEYWORD: BuyersGuide**. Read top reviews of the top products before you buy in the Computing Superstore.

Insider's Tip

Would you like to win something, enter a contest, or go for a give-away? Just go to **KEYWORD: Home PC** and click on "Promos and Freebies" for links to tons of good, free stuff.

Ziff-Davis Hardware Tips and Software

Ziff-Davis has its finger on the pulse of computing. **KEYWORD: ZDNet** is an all-in-one computing arena where you'll find Ziff-Davis' top-rated magazines, help, and software—most of it shareware.

In a section called Mingle, you can interact with industry big-shots and Ziff-Davis editors—all of whom are willing to hear what you have to say, as well as provide some insightful advice about the major trends and issues in computing today.

Tweak can help you solve computer glitches and battle viruses. Download top-rated software and exclusive apps, utilities, and plug-ins in ZDNet's download area. A healthy living toolkit, anti-virus programs, and role-playing games are just a few items waiting in the giant software library. Shareware for education, business, finance, and hobbies are part of the editors' picks where you know you're getting the best of the best.

To stay on top of it all, read the latest news from Ziff-Davis publications like *Computer Life*, *FamilyPC*, *Computer Shopper*, *PC Computing*, *MacUser*, *MacWeek*, *Computer Gaming*, and many others.

Good Stuff!

The Weekly Byte™, AOL's official computing & software newsletter, has free tips and insider news from PC experts. Subscribe at **KEYWORD: C&S news**.

Meet. . .
Craig Crossman
At Computer America, Craig puts out a weekly radio show and writes a nationally syndicated column on computing. Every Wednesday at 9 p.m. you can win software during Craig's laugh-out-loud trivia contest. Find Craig online at **KEYWORD: Computer America**.

Interviews with Industry Leaders and Innovators

Craig Crossman is a nationally published columnist who embodies the true meaning of multimedia: he works in print, on the radio, and online. His weekly column and radio show, *Computer America*, are found at **KEYWORD: Computer America**. You can hear Craig talk live with industry insiders each Sunday. Guests have included computer company CEOs and software developers. Ask questions and get answers about DVD, removable hard drives, WebTV, laser printers, voice recognition, and telephony. And if you miss it live, the transcripts are always available in the archives.

Be a Better Computer Shopper

Sell Your Old Computer

In the computing sections at **KEYWORD: Classifieds**, you'll find more than 25,000 new and used items from laptop computers to RAM to Microsoft software. Search the ads to get a deal, or place your own ad. What you no longer use could be gold to someone else. You can place an ad for free in the bulletin boards, but they're not searchable and may get pushed out by other eager sellers. But when you buy a premiere ad, you decide how long you want it available.

Buy Computer Software, Hardware, and Peripherals

KEYWORD: Computing Superstore is where you can purchase computer hardware, software, and peripherals by many name brand makers. What's especially handy in the *Computing Superstore* is the ability to purchase and immediately download software so you'll be using it moments after you buy it. There's also mail order software and peripherals like printers, scanners, joysticks, and digital cameras.

Browse the *Computing Superstore* by category or search for what you want using search words. Categories include hardware, software, computing books, Internet tools, and digital imaging.

The Hot Deals of the Week also make the store worth a trip: depending on the week, visit for price breaks on cameras, memory, or anti-virus software. Before you buy, you can check up on best sellers and new products, news and reviews of the latest technologies, and related goods.

The Customer Service area can answer questions and help with online purchases. Everything purchased includes the AOL Guarantee of Total Satisfaction and

Security. Using your credit card, you can make purchases 24 hours a day, 7 days a week.

Get Products and Support Directly from a Company

Over 300 companies such as Adobe, Iomega, and US Robotics make up the *Company Connection*, a place to come if you need help, support, product information, or demo software. At KEYWORD: **Company Connection**, you've got direct access to the companies themselves. To find a company, use Company Search.

Perhaps the best parts of the *Company Connection* are the software libraries full of demos, patches, and software upgrades—you can often get a fix for your problem directly from the manufacturer, without having to wait on the phone or wait for an update to be sent via snail mail.

Internet Time Savers

KEYWORD: **Time Savers** can help you find a lost friend, get quality national and world news, fix your car, or get a personalized map. *Time Savers* is a must-stop for anyone looking for a job, planning a trip, or investing money.

Comparison Shop for Computers, Etc.

The rating and pricing service of computers and peripherals at KEYWORD: **Maven** is easy to use and can help you save money. The listings of desktop systems, notebooks, modems, monitors, and printers is exhaustive. What's more, quality is *Maven*'s focus, because *Maven* lists the National Software Testing Laboratory's (NSTL) microcomputer and accessory test results, all in an effort to keep AOLers well-informed before they buy.

With the PriceWizard you can search current models by price, power, or warranty, so you can find a machine with features you really want. You can organize the listings by price, by computer maker, or by NSTL quality rating. I want the best system at the lowest price, so I list them by price and then compare the ratings of the systems; I then look for systems that have the best mix of price and quality.

Computing Just for Teens

If you're not a teen, you might end up jealous over the community that teen founder Jeremy Wechsler heads up at **KEYWORD: Youth Tech.**

Youths chat, do some programming, play games, find Techie Pals, and enter contests. Surf the Web with *Youth Tech*, too, with Web reviews, gaming sites, and how-to sites for technologically inclined teens.

Read CD-ROM Reviews Before You Buy

There are thousands of CD-ROM titles on the market, and *Anders CD-ROM Guide*—at **KEYWORD: Anders**—can help you find the CD-ROM that's right for you. Choose from among over 700 reviews on titles like 101 Dalmations Animated Storybook, Final Doom, and Microsoft Golf 3.0.

The professional Anders staff and knowledgeable AOL members rate hundreds of ROMs in categories like reference and learning, kids-oriented software, games, and how-to guides. Each review is insightful and down-to-earth and tells you if what you're looking for is worthy of your money or is "just an expensive coaster."

As a bonus, you can also sample software from the Demo Area, where you can actually try before you buy. And at Rate-A-ROM, you can give your opinions on all the CD-ROMs you've tried out, and by rating discs, you become eligible to win software, too.

Insider's Tip

You probably hate spam—unsolicited email that gets sent to hundreds of thousands of Internet members. Help prevent blanket spammers: forward spam you receive to **SCREEN NAME: TOSSpam**, and AOL can set its software to block them out.

After you've done everything else, there might be a few things left to do that can make your computing more enjoyable and fun for you and your kids. **KEYWORD: Computer Camp** exists throughout the summer so that the young among us can learn new skills, like creating digital portraits, designing Web pages, or Java programming. Over 10,000 campers were involved when I last checked.

The new *Online Classroom* that I mentioned earlier in this chapter is just getting the final touches as I write this. But you should know that by the time this book is published, there will be a special area at **KEYWORD: Online Classroom** that's dedicated to online classes, tutorials, and reference information. And don't forget: **KEYWORD: HelpDesk** brings you tips and resources to answer your computing questions. You can get live computer help in the HelpDesk chat room or browse the computer tips.

Live and Learn: Reference on AOL

America Online has so many resources for finding reliable information that it can be overwhelming. So this chapter is all about finding the hidden gems that put the facts at your fingertips immediately. It's also about lifelong learning, whether for credit, home schooling, or just a natural curiosity.

The learning resources on AOL go well beyond the traditional classroom. The authors of "Parenting Your Aging Parents" teach a helpful online course of the same name (one of many non-credit classes here) and the University of California's Extension program offers over 150 for-credit classes via AOL, including a whole curriculum on Hazardous Materials Management!

In terms of reference resources, I don't just mean looking up the capital of North Dakota (Bismarck), but things you'd never guess were on AOL—and they aren't always found in the Research and Learning Channel.

For example, at **KEYWORD: Battered**, the Massachusetts Coalition of Battered Women Service Groups has numbers to call and information to read about domestic violence and how to obtain a protective order. Its "home base" is Digital City Boston. Even more on the topic of domestic violence can be found in the enormous *Better Health & Medical Network* database, at **KEYWORD: Better Health**, although it's in the Health Channel. Think creatively and it's likely you'll find what you're looking for.

Sit Back, Relax, and See the Sights

We know you're busy, but if you have four to eight minutes to spare, sit back for a guided tour of the Research Channel. Tours cover reference for business, fun, home, and students. **KEYWORD: RefTour** gets you started.

Need Legal Help?

Nolo Press Self Help Law Center, at **KEYWORD: Law Net**, was formed 25 years ago by two ex-Legal Aid lawyers. Fed up with the public's lack of affordable legal information and advice, *Nolo* began writing understandable, easy-to-use, self-help law books. Now, *Nolo* publishes books, form kits, software, and audio and videotapes that take the mystery out of law and make it available to everyone.

Channel Jumping

Did you know about the baseball encyclopedia on AOL? It's pretty well-hidden. Jump to **KEYWORD: STATS BB**, click on the "STATS" button, then click "Encyclopedia."

The *AOL Directory of Services* at **KEYWORD: Find** is my secret to finding the best of AOL quickly. It contains constantly updated descriptions of over 1,500 AOL areas.

So, settle in and we'll look at some of AOL's reference and learning areas: resources to help kids with homework (**KEYWORD: Homework**), searchable databases of financial aid for new high school grads as well as professionals looking for a sabbatical (at **KEYWORD: RSP**), and aids for understanding everything from computers to geography. Students, parents, teachers, and anyone else who loves knowledge: bring out your who, what, where, when, and how questions and let's get them answered.

Look It Up

When You Don't Know Where to Look. . .

It might seem obvious, but **KEYWORD: Reference** is the best place to start. The index organizes reference spots on AOL and the Internet, and includes an exhaustive listing of topics. It has descriptions of Web sites (so you don't waste time waiting for a page to load that you really didn't want to see in the first place), links that go right to the search engines of AOL areas like *Newsweek Interactive*, and both an alphabetical and topical list of areas.

Use the Reference Channel to connect to the experts who can answer your questions. For example, Kim Komando's Komputer Klinic was asked, "How do I get AOL to use Netscape as its browser?" Kim answers, "AOL cannot *default* to Netscape as its browser, but if you own AOL 3.0, just start up Netscape after you logged into AOL, and it'll work correctly. . . . If you have AOL 2.5 for PC, you need to download the separate *Winsock.dll*, but it's easier to upgrade to 3.0."

The *Macmillan Information SuperLibrary*, **KEYWORD: SuperLibrary**, is another good place to start. It links to quotations, extensive travel resources, the World Wide

Web Yellow Pages, and other areas described later in this chapter.

Choose Your Encyclopedia

AOL houses *three* general reference encyclopedias. Each has its own distinguishing purposes, so cut down your research time (and frustration) by knowing which to use first.

The *Columbia Concise Encyclopedia*, **KEYWORD: CCE**, is just that: concise. Enter a word or phrase, click "Search," and get a short article about your subject. The information isn't late-breaking, but it's solid. This easy-to-use encyclopedia is probably the best bet for younger students. It's also what I'd use to find basic information about a topic in my everyday, non-academic life.

Compton's Living Encyclopedia, **KEYWORD: Compton's Encyclopedia**, is more extensive, but remains user-friendly. You have more ways to find what you need—a table of contents or a search engine—but Compton's provides a detailed How to Search section to make sure no one gets lost. The "living encyclopedia" part is fun for kids and adults: click on "Multimedia Table of Contents" to find illustrated articles, or download songs, games, lesson plans, and maps from the Software Library. The Behind the Headlines section keeps you up-to-date with articles pertaining to current events. As for keeping the encyclopedia itself current, you can download monthly updates from Compton's Web site, which you can access from this area.

Good Stuff!

The searchable database at **KEYWORD: Medline** is one of AOL's best-kept secrets. You have access to over 3,500 medical journals around the world, and many medical articles published since 1990.

The *Grolier Multimedia Encyclopedia*, **KEYWORD: Grolier**, has the most bells and whistles of any AOL encyclopedia. This can make it harder to use, so remember the Help link at the bottom of the page. To search, browse the alphabetical table of contents, or search for keywords in article titles, picture captions, and/or the articles themselves. Articles are hyperlinked to related articles, pictures, and maps—one simple query could turn into an all-day learning tangent if you have the time. There's even a clubhouse for kids on the Grolier home page.

Facts and Figures, Everyday and Obscure

The astounding variety of both practical and scholarly information in the *New York Public Library Desk Reference*, KEYWORD: **Desk Reference**, makes it useful for everyone.

You can download graphics of symbols used in astronomy or the Braille alphabet. Post a query for a librarian. See a list of major foreign holidays. Learn first aid procedures. Download a perpetual calendar for any year between 1775 and 2076. Figure out how to remove different types of stains. Calculate your net worth, or make a budget. Learn the most landed-on spaces in Monopoly. Get tips on how to store and serve wines. Save face by mastering business etiquette.

These are just a few examples. Explore the *Desk Reference* for yourself to find the information you didn't know you needed.

Channel Jumping

In the mood for food? KEYWORD: **Cooking Club** and KEYWORD: **eGG** have so many recipes online, you may never buy another cookbook.

Test Drive a Flashy Online Library

A little-known research tool on AOL is the Electric Library at KEYWORD: **Research Zone**. The main focus is their easily searchable database of 150+ newspapers and hundreds of magazines, journals, and photographs (all updated daily). Plus, they offer tips on writing papers that deserve A's, and host an "idea directory" that helps even the most unwilling student get started on a paper topic and research in a number of subjects.

Built as a helpful tool for kids (with reading level noted for each piece), the Electric Library is equally handy for work-related research, especially collecting articles about potential partners and competitors. It's a lot easier to use than Lexis-Nexis (a big legal, news, and business information serivce) and a fraction of the price. So what if they meant it for homework? After a free 30-day trial, the Electric Library is subscription-based (about $10 a month or $60 a year, as of this printing), but many people think it's worth it. Take your free 30 days to find out if you agree.

Attention AOL Shoppers!

Buy legal books and software, investing guides, and the latest dictionaries at the *AOL Reference Store*, KEYWORD: **Reference Store**.

When "Common Knowledge" Isn't Common

Everyone knows some literary references, Bible stories, folksy sayings, and mythological characters, but nobody knows them all. Yet no one wants to admit ignorance (especially when everyone else seemed to get the joke about Achilles sulking in his tent), and that's why the *Dictionary of Cultural Literacy* exists. Look up those random facts at **KEYWORD: DCL** so you'll never have to ask anyone. While you're at it, find a few more allusions to throw into your next conversation with those name-dropping friends.

The *Dictionary of Cultural Literacy* will clear up obscure references, but is also a good general resource for subjects like science, politics, geography, medicine, technology, and history. "Cultural literacy" covers a lot of ground.

Insider's Tip

KEYWORD: net.help solves problems that arise in the ever-baffling world of email, FTP, gopher, newsgroups, mailing lists, and the Web.

Good Stuff!

At **KEYWORD: Komando**, Kim Komando archives the answers to the computing questions she hears the most. If she can't teach your computer to behave, no one can.

Reading and Writing

Master the Written Word

Everybody's a writer. Even if you're not a professional wordsmith, you probably have to produce academic papers, business reports, speeches, or email regularly. **KEYWORD: Reading & Writing** will help reluctant letter-writers and aspiring novelists alike write more clearly and correctly.

Two areas for quotations spice up your writing with wise words from others, and the *Merriam-Webster Thesaurus* ensures that you don't repeat yourself. But the specialty of *Reading & Writing* is its list of Web links, like the *MLA Style Guide* Web page and the On-Line English Grammar site.

After seeing everything available online, if you'd still rather have a dictionary or style guide that you can hold in your hand, you can buy them from the AOL Reference Store. And if you decide that you love writing

Insider's Tip

If you're unsure of spelling while looking up a word, just use an asterisk (*) in place of those unknown letters.

Good Stuff!

KEYWORD: Desk Reference has guides to Grammar & Punctuation and Words. Avoid common misspellings, find the right postal abbreviation, and learn tricks for crossword puzzles and Scrabble.

after all, jump to **KEYWORD: Writer's Club** to meet others who share your passion.

Tell Wall Street Bulls from Bears

Rule 10b-10, tenancy in common, hot money: the lexicon of Wall Street is intimidating. If you run across some confusing lingo in the Personal Finance Channel or in the Business section of the newspaper, head to **KEYWORD: WSW.** *Wall Street Words* helps individual investors understand

Can I Quote You on That?

As evidenced by *.sig* files everywhere, Netizens love quotations. Find them at **KEYWORD: WritersResources** (click on *Bartlett's Familiar Quotations*) and **KEYWORD: Quotation.** Not enough for you? Go to **KEYWORD: Newsgroups** and subscribe to *alt.quotations.*

Dictionaries from A-Z

The *Merriam-Webster Dictionary*, **KEYWORD: Collegiate**, works like a paper-bound dictionary, except faster. Type in the word, and the definition appears almost instantly. However, if you think you need only one dictionary, you might be surprised. To define specialized terms, check AOL dictionaries like these:

- **KEYWORD: Medical Dictionary** takes care of over 35,000 medical terms
- Financial mumbo-jumbo starts making sense at **KEYWORD: WSW**
- **KEYWORD: Que's Dictionary** and **KEYWORD: Computer Terms** tackle techno-babble
- Kids ages 8 through 12 can easily use **KEYWORD: Kids Dictionary**
- Break down the language barrier—any language—at **KEYWORD: Foreign Dictionary**
- To find a legal dictionary and encyclopedia, go to **KEYWORD: Legal** and click on Web Resources

Would you believe a cheese dictionary and a birdwatcher's dictionary exist? Find them all at **KEYWORD: Dictionaries.**

what they're getting into, and also helps Wall Street professionals keep up with the terms of the trade.

To track down your financial mystery word, you can search the dictionary two ways: look for your word in the dictionary entries only, or the entries plus their definitions. With the latter method, you can find other contexts in which your word is used. And if you don't know how to spell a word, you can use an asterisk (*) in place of the missing letters and *Wall Street Words* will try to fill in the blanks and define the word anyway.

Channel Jumping

The Food and Drink Network, **KEYWORD: FDN**, has a dictionary of wine terminology. In the future, they plan to include dictionaries for food, beer, and spirits.

Have More Fun with Words

The dictionary people at *Merriam-Webster* know that all work and no play makes Jack a dull AOL member. For the most fun you can have with words (within Terms of Service, of course), jump to their main screen at **KEYWORD: Merriam Webster**.

Language lovers will want to read transcripts of *Word for the Wise*, a two-minute National Public Radio show about the eccentricities of the English language. Why do we call liquor "grog?" What is the difference between "lay" and "lie," anyway? Yiddish words, words for phobias, traffic terms . . . it's an entertaining, random assortment of trivia.

The Merriam-Webster message boards discuss oxymorons (jumbo shrimp), and the answer to the puzzle about three words ending in -GRY. It seems like every aspect of English is examined, including slang—so you can catch up with the vocabulary of the younger set.

Attention AOL Shoppers!

Finish the crossword and win at Scrabble with help from the word game references at the *Merriam-Webster Bookstore*, **KEYWORD: Merriam-Webster**.

Computer Reference

Check the Computer-to-English Dictionary

Que's Computer and Internet Dictionary, **KEYWORD: Que's Dictionary**, is often used to decipher Internet acronyms: LOL, IMHO, BRB, IRL. It's great for showing computer

10 Useful Web Pages

There are a lot of useless Web sites out there, but here are a few that are worth your time:

- *www.learn2.com*
- *www.iTools.com/research-it/research-it.html*
- *www.ipl.com*
- *www.mapquest.com*
- *www.aol.com/search/*
- *www.si.edu/resource/start.htm*
- *www.refdesk.com/outline.html*
- *learning.turner.com*
- *www.stpt.com/refer.html*
- *www.careerpath.com*

newcomers the ropes, teaching netiquette, and explaining terms in plain English. If you don't know the meaning of the words "newbie" or "FAQ," you should get acquainted with Que's resources to save yourself some online embarrassment.

But even if you're an experienced user who tells newbies to RTFM, you still might need Que's Dictionary—fluent English-speakers have copies of *Webster's*, don't they? Que's Dictionary defines terms relating to UNIX, hardware, the Web, programming, and computer culture. It even throws in an insult or two. Just like a standard English dictionary that defines both "cat" and "phenomenology," the terms here span all levels of fluency and expertise.

How to Download (and What to Download!)

Does all this talk of "downloading" have you baffled? That's okay. **KEYWORD: Download101** was designed to walk you through the process. Not only does *Download 101* provide step-by-step instructions, it educates you about the dangers of viruses (but now that you know how to download, you can download a virus checker) and addresses AOL-specific issues like using FlashSessions and the Download Manager that comes with everyone's Personal Filing Cabinet. The lesson ends with seven exercises so new downloaders are able to practice what they've just learned.

No matter how long you've known how to download, it's often hard to find the right shareware (software with a free trial period) and freeware (free software, no strings attached). Go to **KEYWORD: Filesearch** and click on "Shareware" to look around. Members can search AOL's file libraries for software from the past week, month, or any time; choose from eleven categories of software; and narrow the search even further by looking for specific words or phrases.

This is the perfect place to quickly find sounds to use in chats, pictures to use as desktop wallpaper, programs to zip and compress files, and tons of games to play.

Science Studies

Jobs for Science Scholars

It can be hard to meet students and professionals in your field, especially those at other institutions. It's equally hard to find funding and summer projects. The *National Academy of Sciences* Web site has practical resources to make life as a student of science more manageable.

The *National Academy of Sciences*' Career Planning Center helps students find jobs, internships, funding, and even mentors. If you've had trouble finding someone in your department to give you the bottom line about your field, this is a way to network across the country. You'll also have access to an online guide for graduate school and career planning, and job opportunities at the National Academy of Sciences in Washington, DC.

Explore the rest of the Web site and **KEYWORD: NAS** for news about scientists using their knowledge to make the world a better place. The news articles and opinion pieces provide valuable background about science with a conscience.

SPACE: THE FINAL FRONTIER

The *National Space Society*, at **KEYWORD: Space**, is the place to talk with others about what life will be like in outer space. To make our future in space a reality, get active here.

The *Astronomy Club*, at **KEYWORD: Astronomy**, attracts everyone from students to scientists. Check in with The Lawnchair Astronomer, find Internet resources, and visit the Planetarium Chat Room.

Eureka! Up-to-the-Minute Scientific Discoveries

Sometimes a monthly magazine just won't do. On those days when scientists break new ground—like the day they cloned the sheep or first examined the Mars rock—rely on **KEYWORD: NYT Science** to fill you in.

The *New York Times Science News* lists the past week's big stories so you don't fall behind. Less pressing concerns like "Why do you get a headache when you drink a cold drink too fast?" can be addressed by Science Q&A.

Like the rest of the *Times*, the science section provides in-depth, reliable journalism to the online world for free.

Insider's Tip

Younger scientists should look to **KEYWORD: Science Fairs** for inspiration (and that extra competitive edge!).

Research on a Tangent

The *Annals of Improbable Research* area offers not only many laughs, but an annual prize—the IgNobel award for completely useless scientific research. The prizes are handed out by bona fide Nobel Laureates, too! You'll have to visit to fully appreciate the improbability at KEYWORD: **Improb.**

Dive into History

Attack the Study of Military History

Believe it or not, one of the best ways to research military history is brought to you by a TV station. The History Channel's *Military History Forum* (KEYWORD: **Military History**) is a catalog of information about battles from Biblical times to today. The coverage of more recent conflicts, like the World Wars, is complemented by photographs, recruitment posters, and other multimedia. Civil War re-enactors and Society for Creative Anachronisms members are encouraged to bring their historical hobbies to the Living History Forum.

Civil War buffs, re-enactors or not, will enjoy the forum devoted to the War Between the States. Some of the sites at KEYWORD: **Civil War** include trivia contests, a guide to visiting battlefields, genealogy tips for finding Civil War veterans in your family tree, and a surprisingly busy chat room (prepare to take some teasing whether you're from the North or the South).

The *Revolutionary War Forum* is smaller, but just as dedicated. The message boards at KEYWORD: **Rev War** are active, the archives are informative, and the Internet links will keep Revolutionary War enthusiasts, particularly re-enactors, very busy.

Good Stuff!

KEYWORD: **History** organizes all of AOL's history content and digs up a variety of history-related Web sites, like a medieval studies reference and photos from Time-Life.

Celebrate Black History Month Anytime

KEYWORD: **BHM** helps African-Americans teach themselves and their children about their heritage. Read about the rich culture of the Harlem Renaissance, remember the struggles and triumphs of civil rights leaders, and behold the beauty of the African American Art Gallery.

Resources at the *Black History Month* area come from all over AOL and the Web. NetNoir's *Black History Month* area celebrates black women, athletes, film stars, and political activists. Black History Reference is crammed with facts, from a timeline of important events to scholarships and grants. Find recipes for healthy soul food, insight into Afrocentric wedding traditions, book recommendations, and Digital City Atlanta's tribute to Martin Luther King, Jr.

Remember the Holocaust

Watching "Schindler's List" is a good start, but to learn more about the Holocaust, visit the *Holocaust* area at KEYWORD: **Jewish**. The area answers tough questions about this troubling period in history: questions like "When did the 'Final Solution' begin?" and "What did people in Germany know about the persecution?"

Read authentic Nazi documents, transcripts from the Nuremberg trials, and challenges to the arguments of Revisionists (those who claim the Holocaust did not happen). A glossary defines the terminology of the Holocaust and World War II, lists German military rankings (for instance, Oberstgruppenfuehrer = General), and explains the roles that world leaders like Winston Churchill played during this time.

Thought-Provoking World War II Resources

Study the end of World War II at KEYWORD: **Hiroshima**. At the *Hiroshima Remembered* area, you can learn about the cities of Hiroshima and Nagasaki, the decision to drop the atomic bomb, World War II in general, and the *Enola Gay*.

Where in the World

Your City's Report Card

If you're thinking of relocating, or you're curious how your current hometown compares to the rest of North America, the *Places Rated Almanac* can tell you. Cities and their suburbs get examined and ranked in nine different categories at KEYWORD: **Places Rated**. What's important to you? Cost of living, education, recreation, crime, weather, the arts, transportation, health care, or jobs? Find out how 351 geographic areas fare in all these categories, or search for the city of your choice.

For less official, more personalized feedback, people about to move often consult the Places Rated message boards. Locals give advice about which cities and sub-

Good Stuff!

KEYWORD: **Unofficial Vegas** thoroughly explains the art of casino gambling. Read it before you visit Vegas or Atlantic City.

Meet... the Massachusetts psychic
How many Massachusetts residents know that they have an official state psychic? Meet him at **KEYWORD: Cosmic Muffin**.

urbs offer affordable rent, have good schools, or are just all-around nice places to hang your hat. A member thinking of moving to Wichita, Kansas got the following varied opinions: "Wichita is a good town for raising a family," "There are many opportunities here," "If you are young and ready to get out and do things don't move here," and a response from a Places Rated Almanac representative claiming that "Wichita is the 'most normal' metro area in North America."

Another resource area would be your destination's Digital City. Message boards here cover specific neighborhoods or you can chat with the locals to get a sense of the city's personality.

Where to Retire?

Want to become a Florida "snowbird"? Decide where to spend your golden years with the *Retirement Places Rated Almanac*, **KEYWORD: RPR.**

Features include Tracking Crime Risk, Where to Find a Physician, and For Those Who Hate Humidity. So, hit the road in a motor home or make that move to some sunny beachfront property—after collecting the facts.

Find Anyone Anywhere

KEYWORD: Switchboard will help you find a high school buddy, a college roommate, or anyone else. Punch in the person's name (and city, if you know it) and you'll probably find his or her address and phone number. If the person you seek has provided the information, you can search within a group or organization, including fraternities, colleges, veterans' organizations, and professional groups. This helps if you know the John Smith you seek is a frat brother, a Mensa member, or a lawyer. If you don't like the idea of people everywhere being able to look you up, you can register at *Switchboard* and hide the information you'd rather keep private. For instance, you can set up a screening process, called "Knock-Knock," so that people trying to contact you have to send email to *Switchboard* instead. *Switchboard* forwards the mail to you, and you can answer it or ignore it.

Switchboard is useful for finding businesses across America, too. Search for a business by name, category, or distance from a certain location. There is also an 800 number directory so you don't waste time and money calling another state.

My Country 'Tis Online

Everything you learned about your state in third grade is reborn at **KEYWORD: USA**, like the state bird, state flower, state tree, state motto, and, of course, the capitals of all fifty states. Other resources for each of the states: quotations about the state, a link to its Web page, and maps and info from *Grolier's Encyclopedia*.

Unite the states, and you get important dates in U.S. history, the text of the Constitution, time zones, and national holidays. The unbelievable part of the *Fifty States* area is GILS (Government Information Locator Services)—a link to publicly available federal information from the CIA, the State Department, and other government agencies. That should pep up any history paper (or just satisfy patriotic nosiness).

Insider's Tip

You don't need an atlas or a globe to see maps of every country, state, and Canadian province. All you need is **KEYWORD: Maps**.

Take a Class Online

Attend the University of California at Home

If you can't be a full-time student, you can still take college-level classes—*for credit*—from the University of California at **KEYWORD: UCAOL**.

Here's how it works: you enroll in a class online, on the phone, or by fax or postal mail. When you enroll, you also buy your textbook, which you'll receive in about ten days. About a week after you enroll, you'll receive access to your electronic "classroom," including the online syllabus, Web links, course notes from your professor, message boards where students and teachers talk about the class, and a chat area where you can schedule office hours with your professor or study sessions with classmates. The only part of the course that happens offline is, in most cases, the final exam.

You have up to one year to complete each course, so the program is great for full-time employees, stay-at-home parents, and other busy people. Unfortunately, you can't get a degree this way, but the coursework can be

SAMPLE THE REST OF AOL'S COURSE CATALOG

KEYWORD: Corcoran offers a computer graphics certificate program.

- At **KEYWORD: NetNoir**, there are classes in African-American poetry
- "C" what you can learn at **KEYWORD: ProgrammersU**
- *Money University* (**KEYWORD: Money U**) claims to be "the fun way to learn personal finance"

applied towards degrees at other colleges—so check with the school of your choice to make sure they'll accept these credits.

Broaden Your Horizons Without Thinning Your Wallet

Good Stuff!

Culturefinder University is an online series of courses in four genres—classical music, musical theater, ballet and opera. Go to KEYWORD: **Courses** to find it.

Most of the classes at KEYWORD: **Campus** boast a tuition of about $25, making this one of the most cost-effective ways to master a subject. You won't get college credit, but if that doesn't bother you, look into the catalog of fascinating courses at *Online Campus*.

Some of *Online Campus*' practical classes teach about parenting, gardening, traveling on a budget, writing a resume, and cooking. You can learn a language, discover the secrets of your computer, improve your chances of getting published, or become a business whiz. Standard academic courses like math, science, and history are here, too.

Be on the lookout for classes being taught for the first time—they're free!

Homework Help and College Preparation

Win Big at the Science Fair

Insider's Tip

The educational database at KEYWORD: **ERIC** isn't just for teachers. Many pamphlets for parents are here in electronic form, including Gifted Children, Teens 14–20, Children with Special Needs, and Assessment Testing.

Want to encourage students to go beyond moldy bread for their science fair experiments? Try KEYWORD: **Science Fair**. Elementary and secondary school project suggestions, from observing insects to designing digital computers, are indexed here. *Science Fair* gives general pointers on putting together and displaying your masterpiece, and many project ideas include specific instructions for set-up.

If the project scores well locally, consider taking it to a state or regional fair, many of which are listed at this area with links to their Web pages.

Make College Applications Less Painful

If more high school students and their parents knew about *The Road to College*, there would be less anxiety in the world. **KEYWORD: Road to College** does everything possible to lower your stress level.

The section Choosing a College has calendars for both juniors and seniors to help schedule college planning tasks, like writing a resume and researching financial aid eligibility. The section also helps you get a taste of individual colleges, with school rankings, statistics, and links to their Web sites. But don't just go by the numbers—contact alumni at the *Alumni Hall* area, **KEYWORD: Alumni**, to get the inside track.

Once you've figured out where you want to go, visit the Applying to College section for help on getting in. You'll find links to great advice about when to apply, how to present yourself, what colleges are looking for, and the number of schools to apply to. You'll even get some clues about how to deal with those grueling essay questions—you can't put them off forever.

Good Stuff!

Parents who believe in Montessori schools are a small but dedicated bunch. Find feature articles, message boards, and a software library at **KEYWORD: Montessori**.

Prepping for the Big Standardized Test

Taking the SAT, TOEFL, MCAT, or GMAT is no fun, but it's possible to make it easier.

The *Princeton Review*, **KEYWORD: Princeton**, offers lots of insider information about the exams, the colleges themselves, and the most important thing: how to get in. You can take a practice SAT online. Using the information you provide, the Princeton Review's Counselor-o-Matic calculates an admissions rating to estimate your chances of admission at most colleges.

The Stanley Kaplan Virtual Campus, at **KEYWORD: Kaplan**, has similar helpful information for grad school applicants, international students, and high school students alike. Download Digital Test Booklets from the library or try Kaplan's Amazing College Simulator™, which helps identify what kind of student you'll be. The career center may help you land a job after graduation.

Getting Into College

In addition to Stanley Kaplan and Princeton Review, *Testprep.com* has an SAT-prep course online—and it's free.

The Applying to College area (**KEYWORD: Road to College**) has Tips on Getting Admitted that are really worth a read. Don't write an essay until you look over "Presenting Yourself in the Application."

♦ ♦ ♦ ♦ ♦ ♦ ♦ ♦ ♦ ♦ ♦

Even the College Board itself is here on AOL at **KEYWORD: CB**. This area's offerings include books about the new calculator policy for the SAT and PSAT. Many of the videos and books are geared more towards teachers than individual students, but isn't it a good idea to take your advice from the company that makes the test?

Here's a tip: don't underestimate the value of practice software and books. After a few rounds of practice tests, even the SAT doesn't seem so evil anymore.

How to Survive College

Congratulations! Now that you've been admitted, how can you get the most out of college? Forget researching your future school's course catalog and official materials—start with some insight into what college is *really* like. I laughed out loud at the College Glossary at **KEYWORD: Back to School** ("Coffee: Your new best friend"). Parents might want to skip this area, unless they're ready to admit that their college years were crazy, too. Tip: this keyword only works during back-to-school months, so make sure you catch it before the end of September.

Get additional realistic information at **KEYWORD: College Online**. The First Year section explains the important things: what to bring, dorm culture, getting along with your roommate, managing stress, and how to pass your finals with your sense of humor intact. In the message boards, other students direct you to the good hangouts in college towns, discuss the pros and cons of Greek life, and vent their angst about all aspects of those fun-but-turbulent times. To connect with like-minded students, look to the networks of women, African-Americans, Jews, Christians, Muslims, and international students.

Insider's Tip

New college grad? At **KEYWORD: Study**, click on the "Perfect World" icon for the 10-Step Program to landing a great job.

Financing Those Expensive Four Years

Plenty of parents have seen the T-shirts that say something like "My kid and all my money go to college."

Paying for college, however, doesn't have to bankrupt you. Now that the acceptance letter has been sent, go back to **KEYWORD: Road to College** for their Financial Planning information. The Financial Aid Calculator helps you estimate what the damage will be, and a Financial Aid checklist tells you what to do and when—junior year is the best time to start, but it's never too late.

KEYWORD: RSP might lead you to a great fellowship or scholarship. The database covers all different grade levels, artists in various media, and people with physical or social challenges. Search by a specific phrase or browse the categories just to get an idea of what's out there. The

Channel Jumping

Other resources for high school students, including ways to take a break from studying and have some fun, are at **KEYWORD: Teens**.

Get Help with Homework

Book reports, research, and even specific questions about math are made easier with AOL's age-appropriate homework resources. **KEYWORD: Homework** splits into *Homework Help for Kids*, *Homework Help for Teens*, and *Homework Help for Adults*. Volunteer tutors are available from 4 P.M. until midnight to help answer questions on many topics. Or, post a question and get an answer from a teacher within 24 hours. Kid-friendly research tools and Web sites to explore are also gathered in these areas.

Study Skills Service, **KEYWORD: Study**, offers the Study Smart plan for helping middle- and high-school students learn faster, study more effectively, remember longer, and get better grades on tests. The lessons are quick and clear and full of helpful information. Curriculum guides cover topics like "Mastering Writing Papers" and a Parents' Library covers topics like "Helping an Underachiever."

Compton's Living Encyclopedia, **KEYWORD: Compton's Encyclopedia**, gets you "Behind the Headlines" to learn about current events. The Research Assistant has explanations about the paper-writing process, from choosing a topic to citing sources.

Insider's Tip

Lots of overachieving tenth graders are prepping for the Ivy League and getting advice at "How to Get in to College." Find it at **KEYWORD: Road to College**'s Applying to College section.

Insider's Tip

KEYWORD: RSP will add you to their snail mail list and tailor the mailings to your financial aid needs and interests.

Financial Aid Library lists publications and directories that include information on grants, fellowships, scholarships, awards and prizes, loans, and internships. *RSP Focus* isn't just for undergrads, either—money is also available for research, training, creative activities, personal development, and emergency situations. The Money Trail, a message board, helps people in all financial and scholarly situations find each other.

African-American students shouldn't miss the scholarship and grant information at **KEYWORD: BH Reference**, and Hispanic students can benefit from the scholarships listed at **KEYWORD: Hispanic Online**.

Lessons for Teachers and Parents

TEACHING MADE EASIER

ERIC, Education Resources Information Center, is possibly the most comprehensive educational resource around. The whole ERIC database, complete with more than 850,000 abstracts of documents and journal articles on education research and practice, is open for business at **KEYWORD: ERIC** so people can do their own research. ERIC also lists over 700 lesson plans and provides archives of education-related mailing lists.

Use Computers to Help Kids Learn

In addition to being a distraction from homework, the Internet can be an educational tool. *The Electronic Schoolhouse*, **KEYWORD: ESH**, connects teachers and students around the world and involves them in interactive projects, surveys, pen pal programs, and other exchanges. The message boards allow teachers to trade thoughts and project ideas with other teachers from all over, including plans to connect classes with similar interests.

Educational undertakings range from month-long Quick Projects to more involved adventures that require advance registration. This area is changing as fast as teachers can get ideas, so go see for yourself what's out there in the world of online education.

Running a Successful Home School

Teaching your kids at home can be tricky, but **KEYWORD: Homeschool** will help you do your homework. Beginning homeschoolers in particular have plenty of resources to get them started, including Frequently Asked Questions and copies of every state's homeschooling laws.

Homeschool Academy holds online classes for parents in subjects like "Preparing Your Child for Reading & Screening for Reading Problems." The Academy's archives let you review past lessons, from pre-school to high school, in every academic discipline. Lessons for the kids are in the Homeschooling Forum's Lesson Libraries.

Your individual homeschooling situation, not to mention the political currents of the U.S., is always changing, so keep current with this forum. Are your homeschooling freedoms being legally challenged? How can you incorporate Internet technology into your curriculum? Are you burning out? Do you need to cut your budget? Get the answers from other homeschoolers and extensive documents.

Attention AOL Shoppers!

KEYWORD: Compu School has reviews of computer hardware and educational software especially for those families with students headed back to school.

Make the Classroom Come Alive

The subscription-based Scholastic area, **KEYWORD: Scholastic**, is full of teacher resources. For instance, you can find out if your class is "geo-smart" by playing Map Man's Geography Game. Regular chats with experts offer good ideas to use in K–12 classrooms.

Scholastic offers a special series called My Story. In this series, students participate in hands-on activities while learning about the 20th century's great events from the men and women who lived them. One installment, "We Remember Anne Frank," was developed for the 50th anniversary of the publication of *The Diary of Anne Frank*. After reading their stories, students submitted questions for Anne Frank's close friend and Holocaust survivor Hanneli Pick-Goslar, and for Miep Gies, the woman who hid the Frank family. Both women answered these letters, bringing a vibrant part of history alive for students. This type of project is a great way for educators to harness the power and connectivity of the online world.

Chatter Box

Informal chats with teachers in many subjects take place most weeknights at the *Electronic Schoolhouse*'s Schoolroom, **KEYWORD: ESH**.

Insider's Tip

The *Smithsonian* has an education Web site at *http://educate.si.edu*. Get lesson plans and resources for teaching art, languages, social studies, and science.

Insider's Tip

The Hit the Books section of **KEYWORD: College Online** has resources for college professors including software demos and Web links.

Professional Resources for Educators

When school lets out, teachers can log onto AOL to find out the latest developments in their profession.

The *National Education Association* area, at **KEYWORD: NEA Public**, is open to Union members and non-members alike, providing information about the organization, progressive learning methods, and a forum for teachers throughout the nation to show and tell their classroom experiences. A special area for members is accessible with a password.

Search for articles in the Education Database or find out what's going to be on Teacher TV, the half-hour weekly series co-produced by the NEA and the Learning Channel. You can order video copies of titles such as "Technology in the Classroom" and "Appreciating Diversity." Talk with other teachers about school safety, certification, and extra-curricular activities. There are more tools in the Professional Library to explore new concepts and sharpen your teaching skills.

The American Federation of Teachers can be found at *AFT Plus*, **KEYWORD: AFT**. AFT is a union of public and private school teachers as well as higher education faculty and professionals. Information for teachers, reviews of educational software, and a searchable database of current events are all available here. There are "schoolrooms" that are chat centers and forums for discussing a variety of educational issues. Again, some sectors of this site are accessible only to AFT union members.

And when learning and teaching wear you down, kick back with colleagues in the chat room at **KEYWORD: Teachers Lounge**. Exams, lesson plans, curriculum ideas, and good cheer are exchanged here.

Fun Lessons for Kids

When you send your kids to *ABC Classroom*, the creative sparks might start to fly. The Express Yourself Café encourages young people to submit their poems and short stories for publication online. Budding journalists get their news stories and columns published in KidViews. You'll see that **KEYWORD: ABC Class** is more than Afterschool Specials and Schoolhouse Rock.

The Teacher Resources section can also be used for learning outside the classroom. Home Math activities explain things like how to make a trip to the grocery store an opportunity for kids to learn sorting and classifying skills. Look up science experiments to do at home, take a virtual field trip to Disney World or a middle school in New York, or start a pen-pal exchange with Romanian teenagers.

Insider's Tip

KEYWORD: TEN links to Ask the Activities Expert, who has advice on picking a camp, birthday party themes, and more.

Channel Jumping

The Outer Edge teen area, **KEYWORD: TOE**, also has a place where young people can display their creative work, including writing and art. Budding authors will also enjoy **KEYWORD: Teen Writers**.

Learn Something New Every Day

Fact of the Day

Fact: everyone knows a factoholic. A brother or aunt, a co-worker, a parent—someone in your life regularly regurgitates statistics and factoids. Introduce that person to **KEYWORD: Knowledge Daily**—or just one-up them the next time you get together.

Knowledge Daily also links to other "of the day" areas I've described below. You may not wind up raking in tons of cash as a *Jeopardy!* contestant, but you'll probably improve at Scrabble and Trivial Pursuit.

Attention AOL Shoppers!

Buy Cecil Adams' books at **KEYWORD: Straight Dope** and find out the real lyrics to "Louie, Louie." There's even a cleaned-up book for the kiddies.

Word of the Day

It's easy to improve your vocabulary if you learn a new word every day—especially if they're interesting words, like the ones at **KEYWORD: Word of the Day**. Just think how smart you'll sound saying "kakistocracy" (which means "government by the worst men") instead of "those bums in Washington."

Quote of the Day

The New York Public Library's *20th Century Quotations* spotlights different words of wisdom every day at KEYWORD: **Quotation**. Click on "Find a Quote" to search the archives for a certain word, or to dig up eloquent utterances by a specific person. If you just want to browse for contemporary quotables, try the alphabetical subject listing and the message board folders like Looking for a Quote. Each individual 20th Century Quotation can be added to your Favorite Places folder so you never forget the good ones.

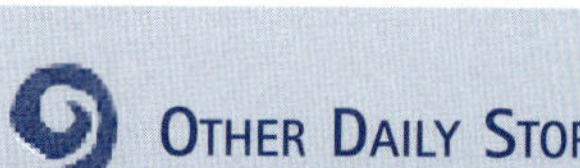

Other Daily Stops

How else can you learn something new every day?

- The hourly summaries at KEYWORD: **News** can teach you something new 24 times a day.
- The *Investor's Business Daily*, KEYWORD: **IBD**, educates investors and businesspeople every day.
- And of course, the *AOL Insider* column, KEYWORD: **Insider**, gives you daily tips on getting the most out of your AOL experience.

Historical Happening of the Day

At KEYWORD: **Fact A Day**, click on *Today in History* for the History Channel's perspective on today's date. Clicking on the big red and yellow H shows significant events that happened today. Clicking on the hourglass gives you the chance to search any day for that day's memorable events, celebrity birthdays, and hit songs. Find some trivia to include in a birthday card!

Snappy Answers to Silly Questions

Fact-A-Day gets its facts from his area, but it's worth an individual look. Cecil Adams' weekly wiseguy question-and-answer columns are so revered by fans around America that he has spawned his own newsgroup: *alt.fan.cecil-adams*. Now he has an AOL area, KEYWORD: **Straight Dope**.

You won't know how you survived before Cecil Adams, "the world's smartest human," answered all your profound questions like "What is the meaning of PEZ?"

and "What's the deal with Area 51?" Your brain will visibly swell from all your newfound knowledge about falling cats, sex in space, and pouring salt on garden slugs. Warning: it's hard to read this area without temporarily turning into a wisecracking sarcasm machine yourself.

Cecil's Junk Drawer contains Questions We Refuse To Answer (there aren't many), a compilation of reasons why smokers tap their cigarettes, and a continuing debate of the falling cat question. You can search the archives (a.k.a. "Cecil's Brain") to find information about Strange Beliefs, Random Mysteries, and other interesting subjects of questionable usefulness. Even the chats are bizarre. Members download from a library of *.wav* files which they can play during scheduled chats to liven things up. As if Straight Dope needed any more liveliness . . .

Channel Jumping

To subscribe to *alt.fan.cecil-adams* or any other Usenet newsgroup, visit **KEYWORD: Newsgroups**.

Of course, many other areas of AOL have their own specialized research sections. The *Company Research* area, **KEYWORD: Company Research**, has detailed stock market reporting and in-depth analysis of various companies and their investment potentials.

For those more interested in toddlers, the *Preschool/Early Childhood SIG* (Special Interest Group), at **KEYWORD: Preschool**, has excellent software and networking resources for the concerned parent or daycare provider. *Parent Soup*, at **KEYWORD: Parent Soup**, even has an A to Z Baby Name Finder. If the name you're seeking isn't defined here, send it in and the Baby Name expert will find it for you. Other great parenting resources, from dating to discipline, can also be found in the Soup.

What else can you find through AOL? Classified ads, at **KEYWORD: CLASSIFIEDS**, offer everything from used computer equipment to antiques to a used Harley Davidson classic motorcycle. The "Find" button on the top right of the AOL menu bar brings you to all sorts of other

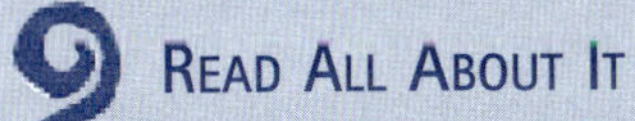

READ ALL ABOUT IT

He's smart, he's organized, and he really knows his way around AOL—so what if he's a 40-year-old man living in his mother's basement? He's Dr. Dewey, and he writes the free, biweekly reference newsletter *Know It All*. Go to **KEYWORD: Newsletters** to subscribe.

searchable areas on AOL, such as live events, personals, and member screen names and home pages.

I find that just about anything I want or need to find is located somewhere on America Online. After all, lots of people have done the searching before me, and added the missing resources over time. Thank goodness!

Here's to Your Health

Desk jockeys like me know that our lifestyles are unhealthy. I spend all day sitting down, I often eat fast food for lunch, and I'm keyboarding my way to Carpal Tunnel Syndrome—sometimes I feel about as fit as Dilbert. But I also know that we cubicle-bound workers can use AOL to improve our health.

Here's an example: I decided to see how much I could help my hay fever while staying safely indoors at my computer. After a few minutes I found "Focus on Seasonal Allergies" in the Archives of KEYWORD: **Healthfocus**. I learned that since my sniffles are most debilitating in the spring and early summer, I'm probably allergic to trees. Then I followed the link to my area's pollen count and learned that tree pollen is high this week . . . and rising next week. Uh oh. I'd better stay away from that big flowery tree in my backyard.

Next, I opted for some more advice at KEYWORD: **Columbia.net**. After flipping through their articles, I discovered "Understanding Allergies" and a few tactics for avoiding the springtime wheezing. Now I know not to wear my contacts during particularly high-pollen times.

KEYWORD: **Health Magazine** made it a breeze to find what I wanted—click on the "Search" button at the bottom, and choose "Search Health Online." I typed in "allergies," and voilà! Instant information. My trivia

Like a Bridge over Troubled Water...

The *Personal Empowerment Network*, KEYWORD: **PEN**, is a network of forums for self-help and helping others. An offshoot of the *Better Health & Medical Network*, PEN shares some of the same goals and content but focuses on the more support- and community-oriented forums. Don't miss it if you need a {{{hug}}} along with your information.

Health From Head to Toe

Here are some of the specialized topics at **KEYWORD: Better Health.** ::deep breath::

- Abdominal and digestive disorders
- Blood and lymph problems
- Brain or spinal cord problems
- Ear, nose, and throat concerns
- Eye and vision disorders
- Hormone and endocrine concerns
- Infectious diseases
- Kidney and urinary tract disorders
- Muscles, bones, and joints
- Reproduction and infertility
- Skin, hair, and nail disorders
- Teeth, gum, and mouth health

tidbit from this session: 50 million Americans have allergies.

I figured if I missed anything, **KEYWORD: Better Health** would lead me to it. It hooked me up to the Seasonal Allergies message board, some Web sites, and a bunch of allergy books from the *Better Health Bookstore* (**KEYWORD: Better Health Books**). As an experiment, I tried **KEYWORD: Allergies**, and it worked! I found Web links and some Health areas that were spotlighting allergies.

If you're not one of those sneezing 50 million, AOL still has the dirt on whatever your health concern may be—you just have to know where to find it. And after reading this chapter, you will. First hint: many conditions have their own index areas at **KEYWORD: Illnesses**. Now go out and get healthier!

Springboards to Great Health

Start Here!

On your mark, get set, go! **KEYWORD: Health** is like the *TV Guide* of many AOL health areas, letting you know what's on, where, and when. It's neatly organized into Illnesses & Treatments, Healthy Living, Support Groups & Experts, Health News, and Health Resources so you can find what you want in a flash.

Another good starting point is the *Better Health and Medical Network*, **KEYWORD: Better Health**. Forums concentrate on infertility, divorce, parenting, mental health, dieting, learning disorders, children's health, and a multitude of physical ailments. *Better Health* also links to Internet sites and stands on its own as an island of information. It's fun to wander aimlessly in this world of resources, but there's also an easy way to search for specifics—just double-click "Search Better Health Databases" to find anything.

Don't Just Survive, Thrive!

KEYWORD: Thrive's recipe finder turned up 10 uses for left-over zucchini, including four conveniently labeled "Fast!" Maybe you'd prefer Mexican, and tips on mixing the perfect margarita. Too busy to cook? Nonsense, says E-Z Eats for Busy People. Learning how to eat yummy-yet-nutritious food with Thrive@eats is just part of what makes *Thrive* interactive, insightful, entertaining, and most importantly, useful.

If food isn't your idea of fun, that's okay. Aisles of entertainment exist at the Thrive Store, packed with unusual items and novelties. Thrive@sex provides plenty of distraction, too. Voice your opinion in polls (is it okay to date someone 20 years younger?), enter contests, and hone your wit with games like the Top Seven Things Not to Say to Your Lover's Parents.

It's refreshing that *Thrive* tempers its self-improvement ideas with realism. For instance, Thrive@shape tells readers how to lose weight if they want to, but also devotes a section to feeling good about yourself regardless of your waistline. Other quality-of-life boosters include reasons Fido and Fluffy keep you well, and methods for blowing off steam before you blow your top.

Insider's Tip

To become a member of *Thrive*, fill out a confidential form that lets the *Thrive* team know your interests. There's even a "Don't email me—ever. I mean it" option if you want it.

Learn New Strategies for a Better Body

True or false: the date stamped on a food's packaging is a good indicator of when to throw it out. The Test Yourself section of **KEYWORD: Health Magazine** is chock-full of revealing quizzes about nutrition (the answer is false, by the way) and the state of your health. Take this opportunity to find out how sleep-deprived, fidgety, fit, or angry you are—the answers might be surprising. You may also be surprised at how easy, healthy, and money-saving it is to be an "Almost Vegetarian," even if you hate the sight of tofu.

Current and back issues of *Health Magazine* supply information about food, diet, and exercise. Relationship

Channel Jumping

No couch potatoes allowed! From outdoorsy adventures like back-packing and canoeing to extreme sports like ice-climbing and sky diving, **KEYWORD: Active Sports** will push athletes to their limits.

The Sporting Life

If you're ready for a little healthy competition, **KEYWORD: Fitness** will get you on the right track (and field). Find forums for tennis, squash, running, cycling, bodybuilding, backpacking, skiing, and walking for fitness. You may even find a workout buddy to help you sweat it out.

Meet... the Empowerment Team

Forum facilitators of the Empowerment Team at **KEYWORD: PEN** have personal profiles that let you get to know them, including—why not?—what kitchen appliances they'd like to be.

issues—vasectomies, sex therapy, and the decision whether or not to have children—are also tackled insightfully. The Remedies section offers tactics for slaying migraines, beating fatigue, and curing your common cold. If the articles don't answer all your questions, thoughtful advice columnists can probably help.

How to Focus on Your Health

In the past, **KEYWORD: Healthfocus** has spotlighted issues like heart disease, aging, and tension-producing holidays. The archives of past issues continue to be one of the best features of this electronic magazine. Explore the up-to-date articles on everything from auto safety to safe sex to safe drinking water.

Get involved by participating in opinion polls and interviews, exploring new ideas, joining debates, or writing a letter to the editor. The interactivity of *HealthFocus* plus the scores of downloadable files and heart-friendly recipes from the American Heart Association allow you to take control of your well-being.

How to Connect with Online Communities

Empower Yourself!

"It's an accessible world after all," say disabled travelers on the subject of Disney World, but a certain hotel in Cancun gets the thumbs down for their poor wheelchair ramps. For more travel tips and many other forms of camaraderie, jet over to **KEYWORD: Disability**.

Gather in the *disABILITIES Forum* to meet people living with blindness, Cerebral Palsy, Multiple Sclerosis, developmental disorders, Attention Deficit Disorder, and other challenges. Regularly scheduled chat room

Empowerment Conferences cover all these issues, and the Equal Access Café is always open for casual talks.

To get more involved, dig into disABILITY Organizations & Resources. Each organization provides an address, telephone number, and description of what they do.

Insider's Tip

Look in the Software Libraries of **KEYWORD: Disabilities**, under "ADA & Social Security," and you'll find back issues of the *Disability Notes* newsletter. It's a great way to keep tabs on government policies towards disabled Americans!

Find Deaf AOLers

If you're looking for Deaf and hard-of-hearing buddies, jump to **KEYWORD: Deaf**. Regularly scheduled chats for teens, late-deafened people, and general networking help the online Deaf community stay in touch.

Anyone, including hearing people—especially hearing people—will learn a lot in the comprehensive *Deaf and Hard of Hearing* message boards. The area has put together a separate message folder for what seems like every aspect of Deaf culture: mainstreaming, ASL, interpreting, cochlear implants, Deaf humor, travel, employment issues, and about 40 other topics.

How to Help Yourself

KEYWORD: Self Help has a lot to offer when it comes to finding support for health-related problems. Forums, web sites, and message boards have been established to help with difficult situations and conditions, including:

- Dieting, compulsive eating, and anorexia
- Panic, anxiety, and stress
- Smoking, alcoholism, and drug addiction
- Emotional abuse, sexual assault, and child abuse
- AIDS/HIV, cancer, and diabetes
- Cerebral palsy and multiple sclerosis

If you haven't sought help before now, the online world can be a safe place to start anonymously.

The area also lists Web links that might otherwise get lost in the WWW shuffle, such as the slew of well-organized information at the Deaf Resource Library and the active community at the Deaf Queer Resource Center. The Deaf World Web site boasts information in several languages, a live chat room, and Deaf Cyberkids for children and teenagers.

Join an Extended Family of Cancer Survivors

KEYWORD: Glenna hosts the popular Cancer chat room, for cancer sufferers and survivors, compassionate friends, grieving families, and anyone else living with cancer's effects.

The Cancer Community Forum was named after a real person: Glenna Tallman, who left many online friends when she died of cancer in 1994. When the people in *Glenna's Garden* say "community," it's clear that they mean it. "Each smile and outreaching hand makes a difference," says a member in the message boards, "that's why we're all here."

KEYWORD: Glenna helps you through every step when you or a loved one has cancer. Share the initial shock of being diagnosed ("I have said 'I have breast cancer' at least one hundred times to friends and family and I'm only 24 hours into the diagnosis," said one member), then learn how to deal with the changes ahead. The message boards are designed to help people connect, so there must be one that fits your needs: Family and Friends' Support, Kids with Cancer Connection, Gays' Network, folders for each type of cancer, and story-sharing boards like "The first thing I did was . . ."

How to Kick the Habit for Good

When you're recovering from an addiction, even "one day at a time" can seem like a lot. Your friends and family may not fully understand that, but people at **KEYWORD: A&R** do. So if you're panicking at 2 a.m. but don't want to wake people up with frantic phone calls, try the Friends of All chat room, which seems to always have a neighborly group in it.

Alcohol, drugs, gambling, eating disorders, and nicotine have their own sections at *Addiction and Recovery*. Other issues such as shoplifting, online addiction, and self-mutilation receive attention in the message boards—it's amazing to see so many groups of people who used to think they were the only ones with that problem. Teens in recovery have their own area as well.

Members in need can locate names and listings of organizations designed to help with recovery. Many people here firmly believe in 12-step programs, but many others have different approaches to beating their habits—you're bound to find a method of recovery you're comfortable with.

Good Stuff!

For life-in-the-fast-lane sorts, **KEYWORD: Thrive** offers Tips for Taming the Stress Monster. Find out what kinds of food can calm you, and gaze at the soothing pictures in the Gallery of Serenity.

Add to Your Body of Knowledge

The Next-Best Thing to Med School

Even if you're not a doctor, you can play one on AOL—or at least learn more about medical advances by examining **KEYWORD: Medline**. Physicians, students, researchers, and other medical professionals have long turned to the powerful *Medline* database for data on every medically-related topic imaginable, and that's because it's *huge*. When about 30,000 new articles get added every month, you know you've got a powerful resource on your hands.

Doctors love *Medline*, but you'll find it user-friendly even if your only medical training is watching *ER*. It's easy to accommodate everyone, because *Medline* has three ways to search the millions of records and abstracts available: Standard, Advanced, and Infostar. The Standard method uses keywords. The Advanced search allows you to narrow your search by looking for article titles, subject headings, concepts, author, institution, or year. The Infostar search engine is the most flexible, but also the most complex: you can incorporate MeSH headings, CAS registry numbers, and other specifics into your search.

Insider's Tip

Don't understand a medical term? Hop over to the *Reference Channel*'s **KEYWORD: Medical Dictionary** and let the good people at Merriam-Webster define it for you.

Towards a Healthier, Happier You

A Healthy Mind

Online Psych (KEYWORD: **Online Psych**) has links to all sorts of psychological and mental health resources online, including tests that address IQ, the question "Are You Burned Out?", and a self-scoring alcoholism test. Want to get some family issues off your chest? (I wonder if anyone else's Mom sends Instant Messages as much as mine does?) Have a seat in the Family Room chat area, where you won't have to wait for a receptionist to call you in. The answers to the Frequently Asked Questions in *Online Psych* are worth a look, especially if you need to know quickly—and confidentially—about anything from medications for treating clinical depression to recognizing domestic abuse.

Is there anyone who is completely satisfied with his or her health? Let's face it, even the most fit people in the world have their bad days or can get bummed out. Health isn't just about working off a few extra pounds gained over the last vacation—it's about the ever-fragile state of the mind, about addictions we struggle to conquer, about diseases that strike without warning, and about the inevitable process of aging.

No matter what health or fitness issue I or my family or friends have come up with, I've found great resources, knowledgeable professionals, and supportive communities through AOL. I just drag the favorite places heart for the document into an email message, add a line about how I think this will be a helpful resource, and voilà! It's an especially nice boost for someone trying to stick to something, such as quitting smoking or maintaining a fitness program.

12 Steps and One Click

Our AOL members frequently rave about finding buddies who help them through trying times, like caring for an elder at home, losing weight, or going through cancer treatments. The *Health & Fitness* chats are a strong link to an understanding community—they've been there too.

If you're working your way through the 12 steps, it's only one small click to the *Addiction & Recovery* (KEYWORD: **A & R**) area. How do you identify a gambling, alcohol, or drug addiction in yourself or a friend? Where do you go for help if your child has an eating disorder? In addition to pointing to community resources and articles, AOL hosts 12-step "cybriety" (computers and sobriety) meetings you can get to even if you're suddenly stuck at home with a broken leg or are on a business trip. Many folks in recovery find that having their sponsors available by email makes a huge difference.

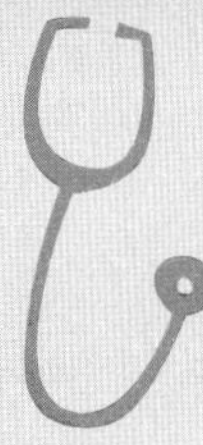

What Should I Say?

The *Online Psych* Grief Forum addresses issues such as being alone during the holidays, what to tell children after a terrorist attack, and down-to-earth guidelines for helping others who have experienced a loss. It's so comforting to know that there are healthy things you can do to help that person (or yourself) get through it.

Getting Better All the Time

The *Better Health & Medical Network* (**KEYWORD: Better Health**) offers a bunch of informational databases, including *Medline* (**KEYWORD: Medline**), which is chock full of articles that will explain all the medical jargon your doctor can throw at you. There are also seasonal features, like info about allergies. Supportive chat groups meet regularly on dozens of topics, including Repetitive Strain Injuries, Procrastinators' Chat, and Depression Mutual Support.

Taking time for something different... You!

Offline, it can be hard to find practitioners of alternative medicine. *Alternatives: Health & Healing* (**KEYWORD: AHH**) explores everything from yoga to yogurt. The searchable database is a terrific way to learn about a variety of non-traditional solutions to health problems and is a great place to learn about stress-busters. My favorite: taking time for yourself. This channel has plenty of ideas and lots of inspiration that will help you to pamper your whole mind and body in that time.

In a Healthy Body

For the fit and those of us trying hard to get there, *Thrive* (**KEYWORD: Thrive**) has a Personal Workout Planner, an interactive tool that allows you to create a custom fitness regime. Thrive@shape, an all-around supportive area, also has weekly chats for Weight Loss Buddies and lots of low fat food hints, because "it doesn't have to taste like cardboard."

Better Health Bookstore

KEYWORD: Better Health Books has health-related books galore and they're all grouped by topic, like divorce, Attention Deficit Disorder, and disABILITIES issues and concerns. I should probably pick up the "Exercise Motivation" book on tape in their "subliminal" section.

Arm Yourself with AIDS Information

KEYWORD: **AIDSLINE** leads you to a database a lot like *Medline*, which contains over 100,000 articles about AIDS and HIV. It's even simpler to search, since it just uses keywords, but you have to be specific or you'll wind up with too much information to handle.

Apparently members use articles from *AIDSLINE* to start conversations with their doctors, and you could certainly use the same information to start difficult conversations with friends and family. Conversations with other HIV-positive people, however, are easy to find—just click on "AIDS Community" for message boards, chats, and selected articles.

This area also links to the informative volumes at the AIDS Bookshelf. If the articles at *AIDSLINE* are too technical, a book might help.

How to Research Cancer at Home

All the latest medical facts about cancer are at KEYWORD: **Cancer J Sci Am**. The online version of *Scientific American's Cancer Journal* has original articles and commentaries on advances in cancer diagnosis and treatment, selected illustrations, and a searchable archive of past issues. When you're done reading, hobnob with colleagues in oncology message boards.

For Doctors Only!

Physicians, this is your place—the *Medical Pearls* area is restricted to discerning doctors. (But since I'm an Insider, the people in charge let me take a temporary peek...)

Once you register at KEYWORD: **MIMS**, you'll see that membership has its privileges. You'll be able to download and update full patient transcriptions, earn CME credits online, rummage through a Sample Cabinet full

Chatter Box

Even I can't keep up with all the health chats going on every day, so I make sure to check KEYWORD: **Healthlive** to stay on top of the scene.

of pharmaceutical information, scan online journals, and instantly access today's health news from Reuters.

Medical Pearls also has the best way yet to keep track of conventions—sort by date, location, and specialty, then buy plane tickets and make hotel reservations at *AOL Travel*.

FREE STUFF!

Drop by the Reading Room at **KEYWORD: AHH** for free alternative medicine resources. Find an AOL-only HIV/AIDS newsletter, articles about nutrition from the *Natural News Digest*, insightful book reviews, and excerpts from books like *Dr. Rosenfeld's Guide to Alternative Medicine*.

House Calls from Physicians and Healers

AOL User, Heal Thyself

Become an alternative medicine whiz or just find out what "alternative medicine" really means with help from **KEYWORD: AHH**. You won't believe all the free stuff hidden here—three newsletters, book reviews, and plenty to download, including logs of past chats and interviews.

Take a crash course in alternative medicine with chats several times a day on subjects such as acupuncture, herbs, AIDS/HIV, and safer sex. Even if you think the idea of beating germs with herbs is "too weird," this area is worth investigating for practical advice like drug-free ways to a better night's sleep and information about chiropractors.

Ask Doctor D!

When you're really sick or injured, you should go to a real-life doctor's office instead of an AOL area—after all, you can't set a broken arm via modem. But for general questions like "What is meningitis?" and "What are the health benefits of goats' milk?" go right ahead and benefit from the knowledge of Leslie Dornfeld, M.D. at **KEYWORD: Dr. D Talks**. Read Dr. D's weekly column on topics such as taking care of your body, medication, and working with your physician.

Learn from Healthcare Pros

You might be surprised to learn that KEYWORD: **Columbia.net** has nothing to do with health insurance. It actually houses hundreds of interesting health-related articles for teens, baby-boomers, the elderly, parents, men, and women.

Scheduled chats provide medical wisdom from guest speakers like a family therapist, a dermatologist, and an obstetrician/gynecologist.

Columbia has a list of healthy recipes, even for desserts and meatloaf. Submit your own! You can also sign up for a free email newsletter and receive advance information about topics that interest you.

Good Stuff!

You too can be an AOL Insider. The weekly newsletter *To Your Health* digs up Health Channel gems and sends them to your email box for the low, low cost of . . . free! Jump to KEYWORD: **Hot Health** to subscribe.

How to Get Free Professional Advice

So many health insiders use AOL that you can find out everything you ever wanted to know about health. Just don't be afraid to ask.

The thriving question-and-answer exchanges at KEYWORD: **Thrive Experts** offer advice in each of the four sections: Eats, Health, Shape, and Sex. Cooking Tips come from the Cheese Wizard and the Great Zucchini, medical attention from *Thrive*'s family practitioner Dr. Bill, tricks for battling the bulge from fitness queen Charlotte Williams, and frank answers about touchy subjects from Delilah.

The "Ask The Experts" button at KEYWORD: **Online Psych** leads you to words of wisdom for troubled minds. It's a safe, anonymous way to ask difficult questions about eating disorders, relationships, and lesbian/gay/bisexual issues. The *Depression Recovery Forum*, KEYWORD: **Depression Recovery**, hosts a panel of psychiatric experts who write columns and answer questions specifically about depression.

Healthy Body

Diabetes Demystified!

So what's the difference between saccharine, aspartame, and acesulfame potassium? What about glucose, dextrose, sucrose, and fructose? The answers about artificial sweeteners and other practical matters are at **KEYWORD: Diabetes.**

Guides to eating at restaurants, buying medical supplies, and getting enough exercise are all available, along with info about how diabetes relates to sexual health, pregnancy, and parenting. When the going gets tough, self-help and support group meetings are held regularly in the conference rooms.

It's also a good resource if someone you know has diabetes and you're too embarrassed to ask questions—find out what to cook to impress your diabetic mother-in-law!

Attention AOL Shoppers!

What are the benefits of melatonin, garlic, and shark liver oil? **KEYWORD: Vitamin EXP** can explain. Read all about it, then request a free catalog or order from their online store.

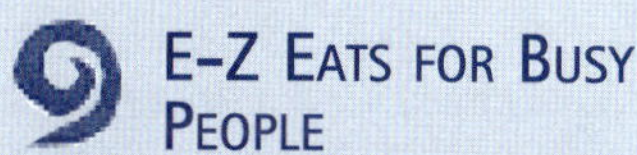

E-Z EATS FOR BUSY PEOPLE

In this age of microwave ovens, it's often faster to whip up a healthy meal than to order pizza. Proof is at **KEYWORD: Thrive@eats,** where Joan's E-Z Eats for Busy People area teaches quick, simple recipes like burritos, stir-fry, and pasta. Even the busiest businessperson can learn how to break the take-out habit and stop skipping breakfast. Because the drive-thru might still occasionally beckon, you'll also find tips for eating out without turning your meal into a grease-fest.

How to Stop the Pain

KEYWORD: Relief tells us that dinosaurs eased their arthritis pain by hanging out in swamps, but the *Pain Relief Center* specializes in more modern information. Today's arthritis patients, for instance, can minimize their suffering by exercising. People coping with other painful conditions can find similar remedies and some empathetic friends at the *Pain Relief Center*.

Specific forums devoted to aches of all sorts help those who already know their problem, but you can also come here to learn more. Maybe you know it's a headache, but what kind? Discover the difference between tension headaches, cluster headaches, and migraines, then figure out what to do about it.

The *Pain Relief Center* also addresses cancer pain, backaches, HIV/AIDS pain, fibromyalgia, temporomandibular disorder (TMD) and other aches and pains such as heartburn and toothaches.

Quit Smoking!

Going cold turkey? Cutting back to a pack a week? Looking into nicotine patches? There are many different ways to quit smoking, so you'll find many different resources at **KEYWORD: Smoking Cessation**, the main screen for kicking the cigarette habit.

Click on the apple for the *Better Health & Medical Network*'s Smoking IQ Quiz, reasons to quit (like the effect of secondhand smoke on your family), and information about why women have special reasons to throw their cigarettes away.

KEYWORD: Thrive@Health has a Quit Smoking Program to keep you educated and motivated. Print out a resolution contract to remind yourself to stay on target, find a quitting buddy to support you in your weaker moments, and read fact sheets on nicotine gum and patches. If a teenager in your life needs to quit, send them to the Great American Smokeout page for age-specific resources.

World Wide Web pages abound, like the sites for Nicotine Anonymous, the American Heart Association, and the American Lung Association. One of the best is the QuitNet. It has a Calendar for Quitting that offers encouragement like "Things should be getting easier by now" and "Remember to keep your guard up!" Interactive quizzes help you learn more about your habit, like why you smoke and how addicted to nicotine you are, and a library of relevant news and guides.

Finally, don't miss the Nicotine Addictions forum at **KEYWORD: A&R**. Get inspired with the stories of members who've quit, and find other hooked-but-quitting soulmates in the message boards.

Attention AOL Shoppers!

For wacky body products like Max the Skeleton, an acupuncture model, and a life-sized, brain-shaped gelatin mold, the only place to go is **KEYWORD: Brainstorms**.

Work Towards a Healthier Heart

Men who eat fish are more likely to survive their heart attacks? Chocolate might actually be good for your heart? It seems like the list of forbidden foods and culinary cure-alls changes every week. *Better Heart Health*, **KEYWORD: BHH**, helps you separate myth from fact.

Get an explanation of the difference between heart attacks and heart failure, and find out how heart diseases can be linked with other disorders like depression and glaucoma. Knowing symptoms of heart disease and methods of screening might help you catch a problem before it becomes severe.

People living with heart disease can look to the Daily Living and Empowerment section for ideas about exercising, sex, dieting, managing stress, cardiovascular organizations, and improving strained relationships with loved ones.

KEYWORD: Heart Disease supplies additional information about cardiovascular disease and strokes. Read a Web newsletter for stroke survivors and their families, assess your risk of heart disease with resources from the American Heart Association, and find out whether your hostile temperament is endangering your health.

Good Stuff!

Be good to your heart and your palate with the American Heart Association's recipes for pizza, shrimp, and BBQ chicken. To find them, look in the Archives of **KEYWORD: Healthfocus** for the "Focus on Low Fat" issue.

How to Work Out in the Urban Jungle

If you think your only exercise option in the city is rollerblading, guess again. **KEYWORD: LocalMotion** has great ideas for sweating in the city and planning the occasional rural excursion. Skiing in Michigan? Camping in Florida? Hiking in Washington, DC? You'll find all these topics and more here.

Spread the Word about Breast Cancer

KEYWORD: Avon Crusade has nothing to do with makeup. It's about breast cancer, and Avon wins Cool Company Points for their commitment to educating women about it—particularly low-income, minority, and older women who often have less access to early-detection services.

Buying a pink ribbon pin, pen, or earrings for yourself or someone you care about will help this important effort. Women can help themselves by taking the Pledge for Better Breast Health.

More information about Avon's *Breast Cancer Awareness Crusade* is on their Web site at *Avon.com*, so fire up your browser to learn more.

Healthy Mind

Meet. . .
the Stress Doc,
a self-titled "psychohumorist" who shares his wit, wisdom, and weirdness at **KEYWORD: Online Psych**. The best part is that he speaks English, not psychobabble or medical jargon!

Get to Know Your Brain

Be careful of the personality tests at *Online Psych*: they really make time fly! Test your self-esteem, IQ, anxiety level, and (Freud would have a field day) your relationship with your mother. These Mind Games are just the beginning of the brain food at **KEYWORD: Online Psych**.

It's not all fun and games, though. *Online Psych* hosts forums for depression, anxiety, domestic abuse, parenting, and suicide prevention, to name a few. You can also search *Online Psych* for articles on any psychological topic.

A group of esteemed experts have virtual therapists' couches at *Online Psych*: Dr. ADD for Attention Deficit Disorder, the Stress Doc, Dr. Love, and others. Other experts are around to help with questions about eating disorders, extramarital affairs, and women's issues. For face-to-face attention, use the Treatment Locator to find a therapist in your area.

Recognize Depression, Then Cope with It

The *Depression Recovery Forum*, **KEYWORD: Depression Recovery**, helps everyone get a clearer picture of the important, misunderstood topic of clinical depression. Depression often goes undiagnosed, so take the Assessment Quiz and learn about symptoms to see if you might be affected. Many people don't know that change in sleep schedule and unintentional weight loss are symptoms of depression—find out more. You'll also find out how to recognize depression in others, from children to coworkers, and how to spot suicide warning signs. Lots more information appears throughout the forum and related Web sites.

Once you've recognized the problem, you can get help. The *Depression Recovery Forum* provides answers about choosing a doctor, insurance coverage, self-help, and the difference between medication and non-medication therapies. Message boards and chats let you know you're not alone, and talking about it often helps the recovery process. Good luck.

୭ ୭ ୭ ୭ ୭

I'm feeling healthier already, even though all I did was sit around and learn a lot. But knowing is half the battle, right? Did you know that additional health facts are hidden in the Reference Channel at **KEYWORD: RefHealth**? A lot of the links there point back to the Health & Fitness Channel, but you might find some new Web pages to explore. At the Fast Food Facts page, find out what you're putting in your body when you eat a Big Mac or a Whopper. Another site, AMA Physician Select, provides information about virtually every licensed physician in the U.S. so you can check your doctor's credentials, choose a specialist in your area, or find a doctor who treats HIV/AIDS-related illnesses. Before you shut down your browser, you can search the Hospital Locator database for information about many hospitals, including services, number of beds, and a map of the hospital's surrounding area.

Good Stuff!

Jog to **KEYWORD: HMFitness** for stretches and exercise routines to get you moving. Don't miss articles about choosing sneakers, swimming, and even America's obsession with abdominals.

Even though I know more about health than I used to, I can't possibly know everything about AOL's health resources. That's because they change with the needs of the members who use them. Every time I type in **KEYWORD: Healthlive**, there is something different going on in the chat rooms. In 24 hours, support chats can include diverse subjects like Multiple Sclerosis, diabetes, infertility, stroke, Lyme disease, depression, endometriosis, thyroid cancer, hypnosis, bipolar disorder, liver disease, acupuncture, family violence, anxiety, scleroderma, monogamy, medications, and body image. And that's just Mondays.

The Health Channel also changes with the seasons. Over the summer, the focus may be on bug bites, bee stings, sunburn, exercising during summer vacation, and preventing heat stroke. Winter woes are different, so expect tips about avoiding frostbite and healing the common cold. Any time of the year, you can count on *What's Hot in Health*, **KEYWORD: Hot Health**, to spotlight interesting health areas.

Speaking of change, writing this chapter got me thinking about my lifestyle. After all, being out of shape isn't a prerequisite for working in an office. *Thrive* gets businesspeople moving with the At Your Desk Workout, **KEYWORD: @shape**. Even if you can't go out for a jog during your lunch break, you can pump iron with a heavy book or do push-ups on your desk.

Maybe after I get used to taking the stairs instead of the elevator, I'll sprint to the *American Running and Fitness Association*, **KEYWORD: ARFA**, to find advice on running, cycling, swimming, exercise shoes, injury prevention, and endurance. Use AOL to become a happier, healthier person—gradually. ;)

It's All in the Family on AOL

What's the most basic community of them all? How about the family? We all started out with the family we were born into, but from there, watch out—anything can happen. Nuclear families with 2.3 kids might be the stereotype, but families in the real world and on AOL are anything but predictable.

Just go to **KEYWORD: Families**, and you'll see what I mean. There are resources for stay-at-home moms and single dads, adoptive parents, and parents of newborns. There are educational resources for involved parents' forums, and child development groups for families with special needs. And there are the Kids areas: be sure to read the next chapter on the Kids Only Channel if you have a child in the under-13 crowd.

The sheer number of diverse families on AOL means that you won't have to search high and low to find information that suits your family's needs.

Remember, AOL interprets the word "family" very broadly—so you should explore the area to see where it intersects with your life. For example, you might not think to look in AOL's *Families* area for finances and money, but if you do, you may find just the right spin on your economic situation. The same is true with pets, religion, travel, and many other topics. The mission of *Families* is "helping you with life at home." So no matter what subject you're pursuing, you may be surprised to

Learn About Online Safety

To ensure that all of your children have a fun and enriching online experience, make it a point to visit *Parental Controls*. This area, located at **KEYWORD: Parental Controls**, allows the holder of the master screen name (the first screen name you selected when you registered your America Online membership) to determine how much Internet access other screen names are allowed. For example, parents can allow children to view only sites geared toward kids (or teens), or can prevent children from viewing any Web sites. Similar controls are available for Mail, News, Chat, and Downloading.

Refine Your Search

If you're searching for members with similar interests, you can refine your search by typing "and" between two words. For instance, if you want to contact parents whose kids have learning disabilities to talk about education issues in your state, you can type:
learning disabilities and
your state name
and get just the parents whose entries include both.

Insider's Tip

Click on The Kid of the Day, on the *Moms Online* opening screen, to learn how to nominate your own special kid.

find out how often the *Families* perspective will be just the one you're seeking.

Family First: Resources for Nuclear, Blended, and Nontraditional Families

Connect with Other Parents

One of the best and fastest ways to tap into family resources on AOL is to fill out a "family profile."

KEYWORD: **Parent Soup** and KEYWORD: **Moms Online** both have them: simply enter your location, the ages of your children, your marital status, and occupation. Then take a few minutes to describe your family.

Now your interests and issues are entered in a database, allowing other parents to find you by filling out a simple Search. I searched for "gifted child" in the *Parent Soup* database, and received 41 matching entries, including educational professionals with experience teaching gifted children.

Remember, these databases work both ways: members can find you, and you can use them to search for other families with similar issues. Don't wait for people to find you. There's no reason why you can't start the ball rolling.

For example, a mother going through a divorce can search for "divorce" or "divorced" and find others in the same boat. In one evening, she can start an instant support group by emailing people who share her situation. A family looking for good hiking trails in Massachusetts can get some great recommendations by searching for "hiking and Massachusetts."

It's important to remember that you can share a great deal of information without endangering your privacy. You can discuss many wide-ranging issues without ever revealing more of yourself than you want to. In fact, some discussions benefit from the relative anonymity of the participants.

Be sure to think about how people will be searching. For instance, if you want to connect with single moms of teens or Jewish moms, be sure to put these search words somewhere in your profile.

Good Stuff!

When in doubt, look it up in the Parents Desk Reference in *Moms Online* (**KEYWORD: Moms Online**), a comprehensive encyclopedia and resource book for parents.

Start an Email Loop

If you find yourself yearning for a focused conversation with a small group of AOL members, consider starting an email loop.

What is an email loop? It's a circle of members who use email to correspond on a daily, weekly, monthly, or hourly basis. And an email loop is not difficult to start: you can begin with just a few people from a favorite discussion group. Run a search on common interests and invite folks, by email, to get to know you.

But before you start, heed these few words of wisdom about email loops from *Moms Online*:

1. When mailing the entire group, it's helpful to keep your comments brief and to have a predetermined form for daily conversations. You might want to have a general header for the day at the top of the page, then add comments below.
2. It's helpful to have one person "manage" the address list. That way you can keep track of which names are currently on it and which have been asked to be removed.
3. Be careful about distributing your address, phone numbers, kids' names, etc., until you feel very comfortable with your loop-ees. You just never know. :(
4. Remember that email is a much freer forum than the public message boards. You can be more candid in your opinions: it's one of the reasons a loop is so much fun!

Software for the Family

The Parent Soup Software Library contains a valuable collection of downloadable software for families.

Some of the popular programs you'll find at **KEYWORD: PS Software** include a math flashcard system, software for creating a baby book, a family tree organizer, and a family scheduler.

Try to think of all the ways people could have phrased an entry relevant to your interest. For instance, people who have an interest in Attention Deficit Disorder could have entered ADD, attention deficit, learning disabilities, special education, Ritalin, and so on.

Meet. . . Pediatrician Dr. Lori Semel

She is also known as LoriDoc, Dr. Lori, AMOM Ped, Dr. Semel, Mrs. Bouraad, Mommy, Honey, and sometimes Hey Doc! You can find her in the Ask the Experts section of *Moms Online*.

Explore Parent Resources

Parents 500 in the *Parent Soup Resource Library*, **KEYWORD: Resource Library**, will take you directly to important information. Simply click on your topic of interest—from Pregnancy to Mothers—and Parents 500 will deliver an up-to-the-minute listing of organizations that focus on the problem. With over 500 groups, you can start building a support system to help you become a better parent. You can even get advice on starting your own group.

Try browsing through the parenting tips section for some helpful ideas. In most cases, these groups can be accessed immediately by phone, mail and, in a growing number of cases, by email.

Vital Resources in *Moms Online* is another valuable resource: a collection of special community areas for families. It features all the content generated at **KEYWORD: Moms Online**—from hosted chats to message board folders, hot tips, essays, and cool Web sites—organized by topic to save you searching time. Looking for information about adoption? Resources on child development? You can find interested communities here.

SAVE TIME: SHOP FROM HOME

If you want to simplify your life (and who doesn't?) why not try to reduce your shopping trips? If you use the Family Channel's Shop at Home recommendations, you can start by eliminating trips to the pet store (try **KEYWORD: Aardvark**), and reduce your back-to-school shopping (**KEYWORD: Lands End**).

Find Support and Advice

When you're looking for advice on family matters, it's nice to be able to alternate between expert opinions and the experiences and support of just plain folks. Fortunately, you can find both in abundance on AOL.

At **KEYWORD: Moms Online**, for example, there's Ask the Pros, which features experts on home economics, childbirth, pediatric medicine, women's health, and postpartum depression. Many of the same issues appear on the message boards, but the tone is worlds apart—there, it's as if you're talking with a neighbor over a backyard fence.

Parent Soup also has an Ask the Experts area, **KEYWORD: Answers**, that features a resident pediatrician, an education and activities specialist, a family counselor, and a nutritionist. Asking a question is as easy as sending an email message. But you may find, as you take your question into one of these "expert" areas, that it has already been answered, and saved, in an accessible archive. In fact, it's a good idea to check the archive first.

Alternately, you can take your concerns to *Parent Soup*'s message boards, or the *Parent Connect* area, **KEYWORD: PS Parent Connect**, and get a very different kind of response to your questions.

Either way, when you're searching for answers to difficult family problems, exploit AOL's resources and search both sides of the service—experts and members—before you make a decision.

A Newsletter for Parents

Every Monday, Susan Weaver, Programming Director of *Parent Soup*, writes a Parent Soup Newsletter. Subscribe for free, at **KEYWORD: Resource Library**. You'll receive a weekly roundup of what's happening in the *Soup*: cool chats and message boards, news of what's going on in our communities, a parenting tip or two, and sometimes even discounts and contest announcements.

Find the Perfect Name for Baby

You might wonder how much there is to learn, and talk about, when the subject is names—unless you're expecting a child. Then, for weeks at a time, you may find it difficult to think about anything else! *Parent Soup*'s *Baby Name Finder* will make your search more efficient and a lot more fun. Located at **KEYWORD: Babyname**, this area has expanded into a variety of related areas. For example, you can find out the origin of over 14,000 names by searching a database. Or you can participate in this area's *huge* baby name message board for spirited discussion on naming issues. Hot topics include "Naming After a Relative," "Religious Names," and "Naming Multiples." Live name-related chats are also scheduled periodically.

Insider's Tip

Click on "The Kid of the Day," on the *Moms Online* opening screen, to learn how to nominate your own special kid.

And no name search is complete without a visit to the Find-o-matic. This popular feature will generate names based on gender, religion, ethnicity, even number of sylla-

> **If You're Expecting**
>
> You'll find a wealth of relevant information in *Parent Soup*'s *Expecting*. **KEYWORD: PS Expecting** features an Expecting Parent message board, a ranking of the top 10 books for pregnant women, and information about La Leche League.
>
> The Pregnancy and Birth Center in *Moms Online* is also resource-rich, with birth stories, product reviews, an Ask the OB/GYN feature, and the results of a Census on Delivery Options.

bles. A related Popularity Finder will tell you how common (or uncommon) a name is. You can also scroll through an updated ranking of the Top 50 boys and girls names. (The top two, as we went to press: Michael and Emily.)

Browse Family-Related Magazines

Dive Into Family Life

There's a natural connection between family life and the magazine format. Both are unpredictable, chock-full of unrelated nuggets of information, and filled with up-to-the-minute concerns that were virtually unknown a few months earlier.

Family Life aims to cover all the bases for parents. From product reviews to surviving your child's adolescence, this online magazine provides a resource for raising children of all ages.

Start at **KEYWORD: Family Life**, and click on "What's New." It will give you the latest on issues inside and outside the home, like Hawaiian vacations, an investigation of organic foods, and helping your child choose a sport.

In Parenting, members will find a valuable clearinghouse of information on the joys and difficulties of raising kids right. Departments include fashion, food, travel, and simply what to do? Reviews give parents a media rundown, ranking books, videos, and more by age, as well as providing concise opinions on each.

Of course parents love to talk about their kids. The message board lets members air their opinions on everything from kids and money to manners.

Good Stuff!

KEYWORD: Jewish Family is a great online collection of all things Jewish. News, chats, message boards—they're all here.

Fine Tune Your Family's Computing

For interesting coverage of the many important issues at the juncture of technology and family life, check out the family-oriented computer magazines *FamilyPC*, **KEYWORD:**

FamilyPC and *Family Computing*, **KEYWORD: Family Computing.**

Family Activities

Find Family Fun

There's no reason why you should have to hear three of the most dreaded words in the English language: "nothing to do." There are just too many ideas for family activities on AOL.

In *Parent Soup*, for example, Kids's Stuff highlights a wide variety of artistic activities, for parents and kids. And *Moms Online*'s Hot Tips area ("By Moms, For Moms") contains an entire listing of Kids Activities, suggested by moms who've had front-line experiences with bored children.

Family Life's Projects also has a lot of great ideas, organized into three categories: cooking, crafts, and activities.

At **KEYWORD: Moms Online**, log into MO Chat to discuss everything from Breastfeeding to Losing a Loved One.

A Place to Chill

Sometimes parents simply need a place to relax, to take a well-deserved break. Anyone want to dispute that? I didn't think so.

But where to go? There are actually a few online spaces designed specifically for that purpose. One is the appropriately titled Time Out in *Moms Online*, **KEYWORD: Moms Online**. In this space you'll find: the Weekday Oasis, a moment of relaxing inspiration every weekday; a deceptively simple Personality Test that will give you useful insights into your relationships and approach to life; and a Comfort Corner, a portfolio of guided visualizations.

Time Out is also the home of the Tiara Treatment, a sweepstakes designed to help moms nurture themselves

Joan Bergstrom

This *Parent Soup*'s Activities Person is your contact if you are stuck for a birthday party idea. Try **KEYWORD: PS Activities.**

Channel Jumping

Got a houseful of kids with "nothing to do?" Click over to Boredom Busters in *Highlights for Children*, KEYWORD: **Highlights**.

Community Builders

There's nothing like finding other members who share your interests.

Here are a few more places to look for kindred spirits.

Families Member to Member, KEYWORD: **FamM2M**, a variety of forums managed and maintained by members like you.

The Exchange. Quite simply, a place where members "exchange" information on an ever-evolving series of topics. See what everybody's talking about at KEYWORD: **Exchange**.

Don't forget the Member Directory, off AOL's main toolbar. Use the Advanced Search option to find other members who share your interests.

with a well-deserved treat. Win fifty dollars in mad money, plus a gift box of Avon products valued at $75.

Finally, the Glimmer of Mirth gives you some humorous perspectives on your frequently overwhelming everyday routine.

Another diverting destination is *Parent Soup—The Game*, at KEYWORD: **PS Games**. This game features family- and parent-related trivia presented in a way that tests both knowledge and quick response.

Gut Instinct, also hosted by *Parent Soup*, has a different challenge: the aim of the game is to pick the answer that you think the majority of people will choose. The faster you answer, the more points you can win.

For example, the question might be, "What President would make the best baby-sitter?" The "right" answer is the one that most people choose. (Am I the only one who thinks Gerald Ford would be a good babysitter? Apparently.)

I can attest, from personal experience, that these games will provide you with a few minutes of valuable diversion.

Find the Best Movies, Books, and Software for Your Family

How often do you rely on other parents for the real lowdown on movies, books, and software? And how often do they steer you wrong? If your answers are "a lot" and "hardly ever," you'll be happy to learn that AOL allows you to dramatically enlarge that crucial circle of parents.

At KEYWORD: **Parent Soup**, for example, the *Parent Picks* area allows you to read hundreds of casual recommendations for entertainment, travel, and baby supplies. A recent edition even featured a review of a traveling circus show.

The Review area at KEYWORD: **Moms Online** also features evaluations *by* moms *for* moms. Books, software, products, movies—this area gives you a casual but unbiased view of what's worthwhile in the latest crop.

KEYWORD: Family Life also maintains an updated Reviews page that covers books, music, software, and videos.

KEYWORD: Kids Reads in The Book Report has a fantastic book review section.

Launch Your Kids on Their Own Online Adventure

Children have their own space on AOL in the Kids Only Channel. But if your children are very young or new to the online world, you may want to initially let them explore areas with you alongside. Plus, you'll be building some family time around their interests.

Kids Only has many outlets for kids to express their creativity. For example, **KEYWORD: Blackberry** leads to a community of kids who write, draw, paint, invent clubs and tell stories in numerous ways. You'll see there's no end to their imagination. **KEYWORD: Kidzine** has a section where your child can become a news reporter. Guide your kids toward these areas to encourage expression of their individual voices.

Both on AOL and on the Web you'll find games and puzzles of all kinds to engage and entertain your kids. One place to start might be **KEYWORD: NetFind**, which has a Kids Only section. Here are popular interactivities and educational games that teach problem-solving, mathematical skills, or are just for fun. **KEYWORD: KO Games** is a veritable toychest. You can either play games with your kids online or download software for later.

AOL is also useful for kids to use in their studies. Instead of helping them with their homework, teach them to help themselves with effective and easy-to-use research tools. Then you can double-check the work when they're done. Researching reports and writing essays on their own may develop your children's sense of autonomy and confidence. **KEYWORD: KO HH** offers *Homework Help* in a variety of ways. Kids can ask a teacher a specific question, learn to look up the answer themselves, or seek tutoring in live chats and on active message boards.

Bank from Home

How can AOL help with life at home? By making it so that you don't have to leave it so often. Let the Families Channel's financial resources help you figure out your family's finances faster, and spend less time trying to figure out how you're going to get to the bank.

Trace Your Family Roots

If you have the urge to go back, waaaay back, check out the Genealogy Forum. This very large, very active area features a special Beginner's Center, five separate chat rooms, an updated Resource Center, and an extensive list of genealogy links on the Internet. You won't forget its **KEYWORD: Roots.**

To understand and encourage your child's interests, Kids Only is a great place to venture together online. Then let them poke around on their own. For more information on what you'll find in the channel, read Chapter 10 of this book, Kids Only: An AOL Just for Children.

9 9 9 9 9

AOL's family resources are about connections—connecting your own family with the broader communities that share your interests and concerns. Once you learn how to tap into the valuable parent-to-parent perspective you get on AOL, it's difficult to give it up. Soon, you'll find yourself scanning the message boards for member advice on everything from movies to gardening.

With every connection you make, your family's resources will grow stronger. The AOL community benefits too: every active, involved family makes the entire service better, broader—a more valuable place for families of all kinds.

Kids Only: An AOL Just for Children

Remember those times as a kid during rainy days or long winters when you went to your pile of games looking for something to do? Remember how those once-fun boxes lost their luster and appeal because you had already played them so many times before? Well, your kids don't have to suffer through those same boredom blues, because the Kids Only Channel is like having a toy store, a lively classroom, a library, a club house, a curiosity shop, and a comic book shelf all in one.

And as computers are implemented more and more in classroom learning, kids will become accustomed to doing much of their research, reporting, and creating online. Here in the Kids Only Channel you'll find multimedia encyclopedias and tutors available to give homework help in chats and via email.

Kids can explore carefully selected and age-appropriate Kids Only material online, or you can download information and games for them to enjoy offline. There are kid-related links to the World Wide Web, which you can leave active or disable. The options for using the Kids Only Channel are diverse, fun, and full of adventure.

Parents can sit down with their children and explore the channel together. Or you can let your kids romp around on their own. After all, it *is* their channel!

Play by the Rules: Kids Only Saftey Tips

When you sit down with your children to discuss using AOL, visit the Kids Only Safety Tips, under KEYWORD: **KO Central**, for a list of do's and dont's. These safety tips also appear whenever your child enters the chat area. For extra emphasis, you could print the safety tips for reference, or you and your child could copy them onto paper and post them near your computer. That way, your kids have the list handy in case they need it.

Upgrade

With the next version of the AOL software you'll be able to assign a password to your Personal File Cabinet. This will ensure that your children won't be able to read your mail.

Define the Parameters of Your Child's Online Experience

Set Parental Controls

Before embarking on a tour of the Kids Only Channel, you might want to check out the exclusive AOL feature at **KEYWORD: Parental Controls**. Since children of all ages use America Online, easy-to-use features have been created to help parents make sure their children have a fun and enriching experience, while limiting access to some features of AOL and the Internet. These *Parental Controls* can be changed at any time, and customized, allowing you to adjust your children's online access as they mature. It's important to note that no system of controls makes up for good old-fashioned parental supervision. One recommendation for monitoring your child's use of AOL is that you make sure your children understand AOL's Safety Tips so they don't inadvertently disclose any personal information such as an address or account password. Before giving your child or teen access to the Internet, check out the options for customizing accounts.

Kids Only on AOL NetFind

AOL NetFind has set aside a special section of their site just for kids. Wacky Web tales, kid-contributed artwork and stories, as well as puzzles and games can all be found here. The search engine here filters results, providing links appropriate for a younger audience. Top Sites catalogs popular Web links for kids' sports, travel, news, and fun. I Spy, Mad Libs, Hangman: classic games join the digital age here. Kids can also do research for homework assignments and get searching help written just for them.

Give Your Children Their Own Screen Names

If you have not yet created a separate screen name for your child, you will need to in order to take advantage of *Parental Controls*. This will allow you to provide a different level of access to the service for your child than you provide for yourself.

Establish a Separate Child Account

A Child account, recommended for children up to the age of 12, is designed for access only to content and services found within the Kids Only Channel of America

Online and to Web sites on the Internet selected for age-appropriate content by Microsystems Software, Inc.

Additional default restrictions on Child accounts: a Child account cannot send or receive Instant Messages, cannot enter member-created chat rooms, and can only send and receive text-only electronic mail (no file attachments are allowed). Remember, these controls can be tailored to your wishes by using Custom Controls, as explained below.

Upgrade

A "content advisor" option under Web Preferences at My AOL will be added to 4.0. It will enable you to customize an Internet ratings system so that you can circumscribe the areas your child is allowed to visit on the Web.

Teen Accounts Range Further

Teen accounts can go anywhere on America Online, and use any AOL feature, but their access to Internet Web sites through America Online is restricted to those sites selected for age-appropriate (13-16) content by Microsystems Software, Inc. They are also blocked from Internet newsgroups that allow file attachments. A search for "teen" at **KEYWORD: Find** will bring up a list of areas on AOL directed specifically toward a teenage audience.

In late 1997 (just shortly after this book has gone to print), there will be a change made to the Teen setting. AOL will provide two more tailored teen designations instead of one. There will be a "mature teen" and a "young teen" option. The "mature teen" account will have access to all of America Online and most of the Web except for those sites blocked by Microsystems' CyberNOT list. "Young teen" accounts will be able to explore most of AOL's content and only age-appropriate material from the Web (13-15). Custom Controls will be available to help you make the right choices for your child.

Channel Jumping

Looking for help from other parents and teachers? Try jumping over to **KEYWORD: Parent Soup** in the Families area. Here AOL members swap talk about homework, birthday games for toddlers, how to get children to write, and how to help kids who hate school. Here you can also access the Parents' book, software, and movie picks.

Use Custom Controls

After designating a screen name as Child, Teen, or General at one of the above categories at **KEYWORD: Parental Controls**, you can tailor the controls for that screen name to suit your needs by clicking on "Custom

Controls." Continuing through the menus that follow, you will be able to adjust the access that each screen name has to any of the following features: chat, Web, mail, Newsgroups, and file downloads.

Let the Games Begin!

There are lots of games scattered throughout Kids Only. Many are designed to be downloaded and used offline. For online fun kids can try several challenging trivia games and contests.

Trek the Trivia Trails

If you and your kids are trivia hounds, you can find endless amusement and knowledge in the many trivia games

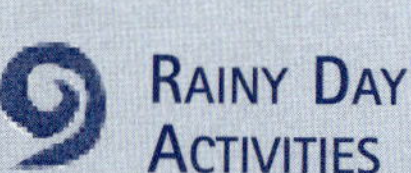

RAINY DAY ACTIVITIES

If you're short on new ideas for stimulating housebound kids, try channel jumping over to Compton's list of fun activities. To access this section, go to KEYWORD: **Education Connection** and then select "Fun activities." Here kids can learn to make an archaeological dig, create fun face-painting designs, build an ant farm, make fossil imprints, and build sand candles. You can look up a description of each activity to help you decide what would interest your child before downloading the files.

Construct a Computerized Game Room

The *Game Grabber* at KEYWORD: **KO Games** turns your desktop into an entire game room. This section is a huge software library where you can download numerous games for free.

Many Shapes Games based on the popular game of Tetris sharpen spatial acuity. A particularly robust section is the Puzzles/Maze/Logic department with challenging games for enhancing memory and object orientation. Secretly, I'm addicted to Broderbund's Mudball Wall.

It's likely that your child will want to download many of these games. A good way to manage all those files would be to first dedicate a folder on your hard drive to serve as a toybox or game room. Then download and store all the relevant files and utilities to that one folder, which your child can have as his or her own personal space.

in Kids Only. *Cartoon Network World's Trivia Toon-up*, in the Game Pad section at **KEYWORD: CNW**, will have you scanning your memory for what's in Mother Hubbard's cupboard and who's the coolest Pound Puppy. Kids who are more into baseball than Batman can take a turn at the plate with *Kids Only Sports Trivia*, **KEYWORD: KO Sports**.

Meanwhile, kids who are more apt to know information about news or kids' television shows might want to check out *News Hound Trivia*, *Nickelodeon Trivia*, and *ABC Kidzine Trivia*. These knowledge games can all be found in their respective main areas, under the Kids Only Central heading.

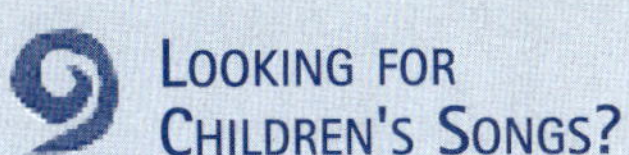

LOOKING FOR CHILDREN'S SONGS?

Ever scour music stores looking for the words to your favorite children's songs? Well, tune in to **KEYWORD: Education Connection.** In the Children's Songs section, you'll find a medley of tunes for youngsters: "Do Your Ears Hang Low?," "Found a Peanut," "Little Skunk's Hole," and "This Old Man," to name a few. Some of these files exist as downloadable text files containing the sheet music; others are Musical Instrument Digital Interface (or MIDI) files. In order to play a MIDI file, your computer must have the proper hardware and software. You can look up the requirements for running MIDI files in Compton's New Media Help File, **KEYWORD: Comptons.**

Kids Quest After Knowledge

KEYWORD: Quest Test provides a popular online guessing game much like the classic Hangman word challenge. The puzzle gives kids a rather difficult clue and they have to guess letters to solve the word puzzle. They can also follow the link to *The Quest* area, which houses message boards where kids can discuss strategies for solving additional puzzles on the CD-ROM.

Make Homework Help a Favorite Place

Ever feel that you need a tutor to help you educate your kids? Are you stuck on a math problem or in need of advice for your child's science project? Then visit *Homework Help*, at **KEYWORD: KO HH**, for helpful hints, ideas, and resources.

Ask a Teacher

If you have a specific question that needs answering and you're not finding the answers in your encyclopedia, who better to ask than a teacher? With *Homework Help*, kids have an insider's approach to studying. Use the Teacher Pager to type in your question, select the general topic it falls under—math, science, English and reading, and social studies—and send it off for an answer. Questions are usually answered within 48 hours. If you are worried about your child sending in an entire batch of homework and then plopping in front of the TV for hours of unproductive time, don't worry. The Teacher Pager volunteers

Channel Jumping

More ideas and resources for your kids can be found in Organizations and Resources in the Education section of Families, KEYWORD: **Education Connection**. Here you'll find descriptions and addresses for organizations like the Children's Art Foundation, Children's Book Council, and Children's Television Workshop.

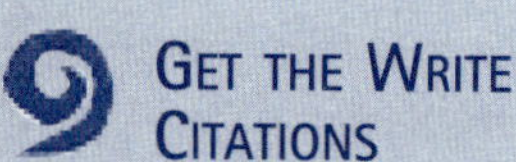

Get the Write Citations

How many times have you or your child worked on a paper and not been sure about how to do footnotes or quotes? The Writing Center at KEYWORD: **Research Zone** offers very helpful tips about finding and gathering materials, taking notes, citing references, avoiding plagiarism, using quotes, and using Internet resources.

Look It Up!

The Look It Up section in *Homework Help*, KEYWORD: **KO HH,** contains several places where you can search for information, including Merriam Webster's kids dictionary and thesaurus and Compton's encyclopedia. If you're not sure how to use online searches, here are some helpful hints:

1. Type the word you're looking for. For instance, if you type "President," you will search for all articles that contain the word "President."
2. You can use the word OR to expand your search. For example, if you type "President OR Vice President" your search expands to articles about either of these things.
3. The word AND can be used to narrow your search. If you type "President AND Vice President," you will now only search articles that are about BOTH Presidents and Vice Presidents.
4. You can also leave out items from your search by using the word NOT. For instance, typing "President NOT Nixon" will search for all the articles about Presidents, but will not include those about Nixon.
5. When you've entered your search words as you want them, simply click on "Search" and wait for the results. Double-clicking on the name of an article will give you the full text of that entry.

promise to help kids with homework, but not to DO it for them: "We are teachers, happy to assist with your learning. You must read your books and do your assignment. The Pager staff will then help you understand confusing things or get you past stumbling points. Do not submit your homework questions or ask us to write your reports. But if you send us your work we will be happy to make suggestions for improvement and fill in the gaps."

Meet...
Dr. Universe

Serious and silly scientists alike will want to visit Dr. U's Cyber Lab, under KEYWORD: **Explore.** Who is Dr. U? He's a scientist named Michael Guillen who makes learning scientific facts fun. This entertaining, enlightening area proves one of Dr. U's scientific philosophies, "Curiosity is Cool," by unearthing weird and wacky facts that are irresistible to kids.

Explore Your World

If you and your kids love knowledge just for the sake of learning, then you'll want to browse the *Explore* section of the Kids Only Channel. Read features about curious topics such as the Yellow Man (an ancient drawing in the Anasazi ruin of Canyonlands National Park), or how veterinarians treat dolphins. Search through fascinating science questions and answers, like why birds fly in vee form, what makes rain, why ladybugs have dots, or how rocks are made.

Budding scientists will especially want to check out Dr. Universe's Cyber Lab, where kids can ask science questions and learn weird but true science facts.

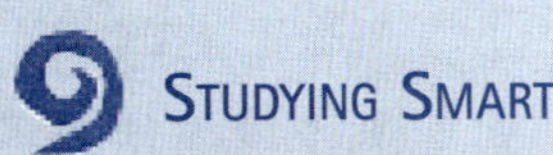

STUDYING SMART

Kids in need of some coaching in study skills can consult the *Study Smart Skills Service* at KEYWORD: **Study Smart.** *Study Smart* helps middle- and high-school students learn faster and study more effectively. The service contains a survey used to help students identify strengths and weaknesses, time saving and effective study strategies, curriculum guidelines, and frequently asked questions about study habits.

Discuss Homework Problems with an Online Tutor

Still looking for help with a homework question? Try searching through *Homework Help's Discuss It* section. Choose a tutoring room about the topic and fire away! Kids can join chat rooms or browse through homework helpers (a virtual library unto itself). You can also post questions on the message boards. One of the most useful online resources is the expansive knowledge AOL members contribute through chat rooms and message boards. For instance, one member offers some tips for memorizing multiplication tables, including the path to a helpful computer program: "KEYWORD: **Filesearch**>>>Click on Education>>>Type 'Multiplication'>>>Press Enter...You must now choose which program you want. I recommend the program that says mult.exe because you do not need anything [else] to run it."

> **FIND RESEARCH TOOLS FOR KIDS**
>
> *Compton*'s has many educational offerings, such as the online Living Encyclopedia. It also offers a spot for parents and teachers to exchange ideas that spark learning and curiosity in kids at the Learning Exchange under KEYWORD: **Comptons.** This series of message boards provides a place to post messages and exchange ideas. Some of the topics included are Educational Technology and Activities for Kids.

Art Galleries for Kids Abound

Big and little kids alike have many opportunities to post their fine works of art on AOL and to browse galleries full of works done by other kids. Throughout the *Create* area, KEYWORD: **Create**, you'll find art mastered by kids of all ages. Encourage your kids to upload their own artwork to the galleries. Easy-to-follow instructions are posted in each gallery.

Post Your Pictures on the Big Fridge

At KEYWORD: **CNW,** The Big Fridge hosts an inspirational array of computer and non-computer art. My favorites are the classic cartoon characters from Scooby Doo, the Jetsons, the Flintstones, Tom and Jerry, and Bugs Bunny. The gallery is the most user-friendly I've visited yet. No need to download the art; you can view it while online and read a brief description about the young artists, with encouraging remarks from *CNW*. Mail art to: Big Fridge on AOL, 1065 Williams Street, Atlanta, Georgia 30309.

Or upload computer drawings using paint programs available in *Create*'s Happening Now section. Don't forget to include the first name and age of the artist!

> **Upgrade**
>
> With the Picture Gallery in AOL 4.0 your kids will be able to show off their artwork in style. When all their drawings are saved in the same file on your hard drive, they can open them all at once through AOL and display them in as if in a real gallery.

A Classic Children's Magazine Invites Readers to Create Their Own Pages

KEYWORD: **Highlights** has a special section for kids to contribute their own pages. Particularly fun to see is the artwork submitted. You'll see imaginative creatures like "A very crazy nerd," "Happy Mean Flower,"

"Mousegiraffe," "Bumbleshark," and "BatBunny." According to one young author, BatBunny "only comes out at night during Easter. They are good creatures and eat bugs and carrots." I'm sure a quick tour through this gallery will spark all kinds of creativity. When babysitting, I visit this site often. My charges and I get a good laugh and we spend hours dreaming up creatures to add to the gallery.

Kids in the Slimelight

Only on Nickelodeon will you find an area of kids in the Slimelight. Hidden under the Nick logo on the main screen of KEYWORD: **Nick**, young AOL members will find a chance to strut their stuff. Here they can share drawings, writing, and even give interviews.

Kids' Creative Community at Blackberry Creek

At KEYWORD: **Blackberry** you'll find a busy creative community for all kinds of interests. Pint-sized Picassos and budding young Hemingways can strut their stuff in this clubhouse. Kids can come to *Blackberry Creek* to talk about what's cool at school, share their creative works, or just hang out.

By creating an electronic scrapbook in this area other kids can find out what you would do if you were an animal, who your best friend is, and how you see yourself in the future. Then they can know more about you and invite you to join clubs they've created right here in the clubhouse.

You can design and send postcards to your friends and family, draw a self-portrait, and choose a frame to show off your work. You can look at drawings by other kids and see what computer creations they've come up with.

Kids can tell tall tales or share stories from their own real lives in the Story Teller section. They can contribute fiction and poems for all the Blackberry Creekies to read or make friendship bracelets with other young members. Kids can get the message out to other kids their age with a newsletter or hang out on the message boards and review movies like real critics.

Good Stuff!

Kids can win big in numerous contests where their creative spirit shines. *Blackberry Creek*, at KEYWORD: **Blackberry**, often has prizes for kids who send in their stories and art, and even well-written book reviews.

How to Amaze Kids with AOL

Kids are impressed with adults who can wiggle their ears, or juggle three tennis balls, or make a coin disappear. Hard stuff.

Have you ever wished you had a cool trick that you could use to astonish kids? I always envied my friends who had one. Because, let's face it, kids are not easily wowed; they have very high standards. Kids are impressed with adults who can wiggle their ears, or juggle three tennis balls, or make a coin disappear. Hard stuff.

Well, here's your chance to raise your status with the younger generation. There are now enough cool AOL areas and features—large and small—that you should be able to sit down in front of any computer that's hooked up to AOL, roll up your sleeves ceremoniously, and proceed to astound, amaze, and dazzle any young'uns in your presence. Here's how I do it:

Opening Acts

First, at the opening screen, I ask conspiratorially, "Have you ever checked behind the AOL logo?" Then I click on it, and, suddenly, Howdy! appears. (**KEYWORD: Howdy** will also take you there.) There's always something funny going on here, whether it's a cartoon or a humorous essay. How funny? I let the kids decide, in Howdy's Rate-O-Rama.

KEYWORD: Random is another astonishing AOL feature: Click on the tiny little roulette wheel, and it will take you to someplace completely unpredictable and totally random. The last time a kid used it in my presence, we wound up at AOL UK (**KEYWORD: UK**). A half-hour later, we were still there, checking out Medieval castles that are open to the public.

Preparation

But wait a minute! I'm getting way ahead of myself. If you really want to be an Amazing Adult, you have to prepare. Here are some areas to check out if you want to dazzle kids.

Moms Online (KEYWORD: **Moms Online**) has some great kid-divertin' ideas for adults in its Hot Tips area. And they are not all computer-centric, not by a long shot. Last time I was there, I picked up a great plan for a Backyard Obstacle Course. The KOFs (Kids of Friends) I was hangin' with that day were amazed at what I was able to do with the lawn furniture!

Family Computing (KEYWORD: **FC**) also features a lively collection of kid-centric stuff—from paint programs to games. The Rec Room (KEYWORD: **Rec Room**) has a cool area, Onscreen Games, that features games you don't have to download. Click on them, and they pop up, ready to play. These are particularly good when you're dealing with young surfers who are impatient with downloads.

Games

AOL Games (KEYWORD: **Games**) has got to be your first destination here. Probably the kids will recognize games you've never heard of, so just turn over the wheel to them. But if you want to compete on your terms, try to steer the action over to the Classic Games area: that's where you can tap your valuable Bingo and Poker experience. The Puzzle Zone (KEYWORD: **Puzzle**) also has some great interactive puzzles.

Snack Time!

Things starting to drag? Two words are magic to kids: "Let's Eat!" The Young Chefs area in the Electronic Gourmet Guide, otherwise known as eGG, (KEYWORD: **Young Chefs**) has a bunch of digestible fun. Cold Drinks, Pita Pockets, Persian rice—take a break and create something wonderful in the kitchen!

Club KidSoft (KEYWORD: **Kidsoft**) also features a bedazzling mix of games, contests, and activities. Download demos, enter contests, chat about cool clothes, and check out Web sites. Club KidSoft also has cool stuff to print out and play away from the computer. Which brings me to my next suggestion. . .

Create

Blackberry Creek (**KEYWORD: Blackberry Creek**) bills itself as "the kid's creativity center," and it lives up to its billing. One of the areas I frequent is "Creativity Software for Kids." In the past I've downloaded paint programs of all levels of sophistication; music programs (Rock Guitar was a big favorite with a teenager I know); and a Crosswords Creation tool.

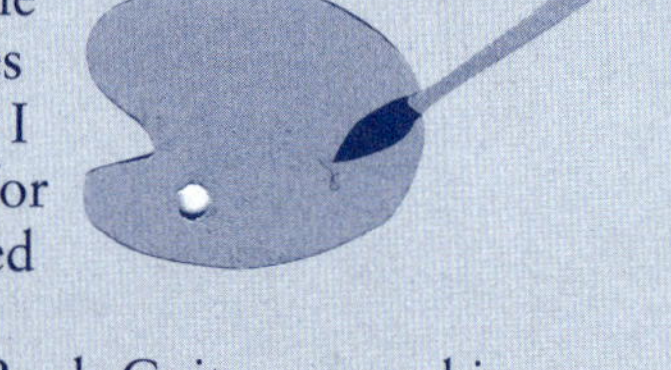

Print It Out

You know that feeling when you've been staring at a computer too long? A friend of mine calls it "Computer Face." Well, if you start feeling that way, or if you see a certain glazed expression come over the faces of your kid companions, it's time to put the printer to work.

My favorite awesome print-out destination is Ted's Lillypad (**KEYWORD: Paperopolis**). Ted claims to be a toad, which may not be true. But there's no denying that Ted has a great collection of free stuff to print out, including Valentines, Crazy Looping Planes, Monster Finger Puppets, and Hairy Gorilla Masks. He also has a bunch of downloadable rude sounds. But I think his paper designs are the best: print 'em out, get out the crayons, scissors, and tape—and you've got an old-fashioned activity break.

Edutainment

Maybe it's just me, but if you're sitting at a computer with kids, it makes sense to at least try to sneak in some educational material, or at least a little brain activity. Maybe they won't notice.

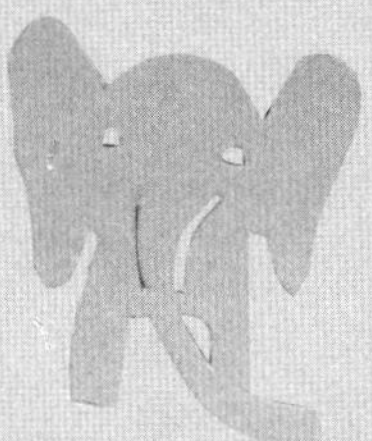

So hop over to Ringling Online (**KEYWORD: Ringling**), the AOL area created by the people behind Ringling Brothers and Barnum & Bailey Circus. They have some fun little brain teasers, like High Low. For example, "King Tusk the elephant weighs 20,000 pounds. High or Low?"

Highlights for Children (**KEYWORD: Highlights**) is another good site for stimulating young brains, especially the Boredom Busters and the Tricks & Teasers area.

On a roll? Then you owe it to yourself to show the kids Homework Help (**KEYWORD: KO HH**). Here you'll find some great reference works, including a Merriam-Webster Dictionary, a Compton's Encyclopedia, and a Merriam-Webster Thesaurus. HH also has Ask a Teacher, where kids can submit a homework question and get a response from a real teacher.

I always make a point of showing my KOFs (Kids of Friends, remember?) Homework Help. I tell them it's a good example of deferred gratification. The first time they see it, they will not be bowled over by radical graphics or light-speed action. But the next time they find themselves hopelessly stuck between a Clueless Parent and a Hard Homework Assignment—Homework Help will suddenly seem. . . awesome!

Surf

Sometimes it's fun just to see all the wacky kinds of stuff that's on AOL, in all its variety. ABC's Kidzine (**KEYWORD: Kidzine**) is great for that. Log in and bounce around for awhile: from News, to News Trivia, to Contests, to Movie Reviews, to Jokez, to Chats...something, and maybe a lot of things, will leap out and flabbergast any kids in the general vicinity.

9 FIND CREATIVE PAINT PROGRAMS

If your kids love to draw and paint, you'll want to look into the shareware paint programs available in **KEYWORD: KO Create.** Under Happening Now, you'll find a section for children's paint programs that offer quite a few different paint programs.

Fill in Coloring Books Online

No need to go all the way to the store to purchase coloring books; just download blank coloring pages from **KEYWORD: DCKids**. Kids can create their own colorful versions of The Flash, Supergirl, Plastic Man, and Captain Marvel. Download the pages and use any draw program to fill them in. If you need a paint program, go to the Children's Paint Programs listing under Happening Now in **KEYWORD: KO Create.**

Write-On!

For the more literary inclined youngster, the Kids Only Channel is full of words and writing challenges.

ABC Kidzine's Write-Stuff in the Brainfood section contains many literary flavors for all sorts of discriminating tastes. Here kids have written about the many things that affect their young lives: animal tales, nature poems, poems about animals, poems about emotions, poems about people, and short stories. If your kids are feeling unsure about their own writing abilities, they can get tips about improving writing skills in the chat rooms at **KEYWORD: Kidzine**.

ABC Kidzine also has an Extremely Tall Tales section where the beginning of a tale is posted and kids send in their own endings to the story.

Insider's Tip

Head to **KEYWORD: Writers** to find a mentor who can help hone your writing skills. A special Teen Writers group lets teens exchange ideas with other literary youth.

Fill in the Blank

Young imaginative writers who love Spider Man and other comic book characters can try their hand at composing an ending to *Marvel Comics* stories. In the Danger Room at **KEYWORD: Marvel** lies the Threaded Web, where *Marvel Comics* posts the beginning of a story and leaves it up to members to finish.

In another section, kids who Wanna Be in Comics can take on the monthly challenge of drawing a Marvel character in the specific frame of a storyline. A template provides only part of the picture, and kids complete the illustration.

Kids' Humor is Taken Seriously

Keep your local pranksters out of trouble for a while by putting them to work composing jokes for The *ABC Kidzine* Joke Book, **KEYWORD: Kidzine**. Here are a few just for laughs:

What would you get if a Vampire crossed a Snow Queen?
FROST BITE.

What is part pig and part tree?
A PORKY PINE!

Good Stuff!

Learn all about *Nickelodeon*'s wacky shows on Nick On-Air at **KEYWORD: Nickelodeon**. Look up your favorite show and find out about its characters, grab some downloadable pictures, and look up information about the different episodes.

Get Your Name in a Super Story

Want to have someone write a story about you or your kids? Type in a name and nine other words and *ABC Kidzine*'s Super Story will send you back some wacky fiction based on your entries. Go to **KEYWORD: Kidzine**, click on "Gamez," and scroll down the listbox to find the Super Story tool. A form prompts you for objects such as a place, famous person, color, and a food you hate. When you send off the form these elements are incorporated into a story that's sent to your email box a little while later.

KEYWORD: Blackberry has two great chats for young writers. On Monday evenings a Book Chat is scheduled and Sunday nights are dedicated to Poetry Mania.

Enter the Clubhouse

What's a kid's world without a clubhouse? In the Kids Only *Club* section (on the main Kids Only screen) you'll encounter a neighborhood full of them. There are clubs about animals, computing, sports, music, and more. In each club you can meet the members, read club organization information, download pictures from the trading post, or enter the club chat. This is an ideal place for children to exchange ideas and opinions about what's going on at their school and in their lives.

Check Out the Music Scene

Kids of all ages will want to check out the Music Club. Discussions range from the most current Pop, Rap, Country music and more to kids making their own music. I was thrilled to see one chat titled "Clarinets are cool," and another on Kid Composers and Song Writers. Kids can talk to other kids about their own music thrills and woes, idols, and dreams.

Channel Jumping

Teens can rant and rave about Kewl Bands in *The Outer Edge*. AOL UK hosts KEYWORD: **TOE**, where British and American teenagers alike can submit their favorite dance, indie, or alternative music.

Pen Pals Connect Here

Lots of kids out there are looking for pen pals, and the members in the Pen Pals Club have all sorts of things to talk about—sports, computers, outdoor activities, art, music, movies, and more. You can find a pen pal either based on age or interest. Just head to the Clubs section of KEYWORD: **Kids Only** to find a friend.

Remind your kids of the Safety Tips found at KEYWORD: **KO Chat**:

1. Don't give your AOL password to anyone, not even your best friend.
2. Never tell someone your home address, telephone number, or school name without asking a parent.
3. Never say you will meet someone in person without asking a parent.
4. Always tell a parent about any threatening or bad language you see online.
5. If someone says something that makes you feel unsafe or funny, don't just sit there—take charge! Call a Guide (KEYWORD: **KO Help**), leave the chat room, or just sign off.

Teens Can Join Service Clubs

Want to help out people in your neighborhood? Or travel around the country building houses in order to build community? You can find a multitude of volunteer opportunities for teenagers at KEYWORD: **Hub Heaven.** Programs such as *Melrose Place* star Andrew Shue's *Do Something* and former president Jimmy Carter's Habitat for Humanity are just two. See which celebrities are using their clout for a good cause. Join in the chats and message boards to see where you can lend a helping hand.

Add to Your Collection

There is no telling what you'll find in the virtual flea market at the Collecting Club. Here kids talk about their collecting highs and lows. . . from their love of Looney Tunes paraphernalia to Beanie Babies to post cards. As in all the other chat sections in the Kids Only Channel, you'll see lots of enthusiasm expressed here. Your kids should feel right at home with the many "I luv"s and rows of exclamation points!!!!!!!!!!!!

Create Your Own Club

Kids are bound to find something that interests them in the *Club* section. Explore beyond the basic categories by looking under More Clubs. You'll see cooking clubs, a science fiction club, photography club, magicians' club, theater and drama club, writers' club, and many others. Kids who don't find what they are looking for can even create their own club. It's a mini city of clubhouses full of kids looking for pals. Don't forget to remind your kids of the safety rules when in chats and club sections.

Insider's Tip

Show your children how to use the Buddy Chat feature on their Buddy List. That way they can set up their own chat room and talk with just their friends.

Sporting Around

All-stars abound in this action-oriented section. At **KEYWORD: KO Sports**, there's talk about every kind of sport, from your typical basketball, baseball, and football to your not-so-typical beach volleyball, bodyboarding, bungie jumping, canoe racing, parachuting, rock climbing, skateboarding, and street luge. You'll find all the areas described below in this section. Keep a restless sports fan happy kicking around in **KEYWORD: KO Sports** during rainy days and off-season.

Meet... Coach Jim

Kids needing solid advice on sports can tune in to *Coach Jim's Corner*, in Play It at **KEYWORD: KO Sports**. Each week Coach Jim, who has coached several different sports, will offer suggestions for improving your game, be it golf, tennis, vollyball, bowling, or running.

Meet the All-Stars

Avid sports fans can access information about some of their favorite athletes. Stargazers can check out the best in the fields under each sport listing, or they can go straight to the stars under Sports Stars. Read interviews about basketball luminaries, biographies about mountain bikers, statistics on ball players, and histories of racecar drivers. Kids can create their own scrapbooks by downloading photos of famous athletes in action. I'm sure thrill-seeking teens will be wowed by bungie jumper Jimbo Morgan's "Off a Bridge," motorcross racer Jeff Emig flying through the air, and world wrestling federation star Andre the Giant striking a fierce pose.

Learn Sports Tips and Tricks

Good Stuff!

Sports tips by kids for kids can be found in **KEYWORD: KO Sports**'s Play It section. Here, kids will enjoy tips from other kids on all kinds of sports, including basketball, baseball, football, soccer, motorcross, tennis, track, and more.

Sports enthusiasts should practice, practice, practice, *and* check out tips scattered throughout the sports section. Some sports categories offer information about succeeding in the sport of choice and about impressing an audience. I just learned how to do a rollerblading backslide (under InLine trick tips), and member TNDSW warns, "When on a half pipe, lean forward when going down. I learned the hard way." Other member messages emphasize the importance of wearing safety gear.

Tackle Sports Jargon

Whether you're a Trad rock climber or a speed ski-sailor, brush up on the sports lingo in current articles and fact sheets. Learn about new things to do on a windsurfer and all the names for those rock climbing gadgets. A school report full of impressive sports lingo and technical terms is only fingers away!

Chatter Box

Monday night is Sports Chat in *Blackberry Creek*. And Basketball fans have their own space carved out on Wednesdays. Check out **KEYWORD: KO Chat** for details.

Chat About Your Favorite Sports

When they aren't out playing the games or cheering on their favorite teams, sports fans can be found online talking about most valuable players, top scorers, fan clubs, and injuries. Here you'll find information on coaching tips, jerseys and logos, trading cards, cheerleading, and more sports than you can probably imagine.

The *ABC Kidzine* also features Coach Jim, who's got a sports tip of the week. To visit Coach Jim's Corner go to **KEYWORD: Kidzine**, click on the "Fanzine" button, then choose "Sportszine" from the listbox. You can post a question to him about nearly any sport and he'll be able to tell you ways to improve your game.

Attention AOL Shoppers!

You don't have to hunt around the mall to find the gaming software your child has been clamoring for. Just go to **KEYWORD: Games Store** to order it and have it delivered right to your door.

Play . . . Games!

What's a Kids Only section without more games? Housebound sports fans can exercise their mental might and learn a thing or two with sports games. To name a few, there's Baseball Power Polls, Basketball Power Polls, sports quizzes, Kids Only Sports Trivia, and the Nickname Game.

What's New in the News?

They may not be up for reading the *Wall Street Journal*, but kids can find out what's hot or what other kids think about current topics at **KEYWORD: KO News**. This site also has an active Speak Out polling section and a You Report It Section, where kids can express their opinions on hot issues.

Good Stuff!

Message boards at **KEYWORD: KO News** give kids the opportunity to report on events happening in their hometowns. If you have a budding journalist in your home, send them to *Kids Only News*.

Kids Report the News

ABC Kidzine's Newz, at **KEYWORD: Kidzine**, contains reports by kids about current topics. My favorite feature is KidViews, where kids put the pen to paper (or rather fingers to keyboards) and eloquently state their views on hot topics like equal opportunity in education, governments worldwide, and women in politics. If you have any budding newshounds in the house, they'll want to check out the information about how to become a KidViews reporter.

Trivia games quiz kids on current events. And their own feature stories are updated weekly, so there's always an opportunity to share what's going on in their surroundings.

Good Stuff!

KEYWORD: **Marvel Kids** has a dynamic Spider Man cybercomic that kids can download and run on their computer. For more fun, popular characters, go to *Shows and Stars* at KEYWORD: **KO SS**.

Subscribe to the Kids Only Newsletter

Kids can subscribe for free to the *Kids Only Newsletter*, where they can find out about new features on the Kids Only Channel, get information about participating in challenges, and read special features. Subscriptions are available through KEYWORD: **KO News**.

Kids Inspiring Kids

I don't know if there is anything more inspirational to kids than seeing the great things other kids do. In the *Kids Hall of Fame*, KEYWORD: **KO Fame**, kids can view a gallery of featured artists, writers, and leaders. Read about young cartoonists and view some of their creations, learn about poets and fiction writers, and get a glimpse of kids who have taken leadership roles. Send in your own nominations and be on the lookout for outstanding kids in your neighborhood.

Whether they are looking for entertainment, homework help, or curiosities, kids of all ages will find something of interest in the Kids Only Channel. Many of the areas also have links to the Web, where kids can expand their potential online. KEYWORD: **KO Web** provides a modified browser that displays age-appropriate content. You can also find excellent links at KEYWORD: **NetFind** with the Kids Only section there.

Since there is so much information in Kids Only, the best use of the channel is to help your child find areas of interest. Add these sites to the Favorite Places folder and you and your kids will have easy access each time you log on.

It's All Fun and Games

Just let me admit it: I love games. Word games. Shoot-'em-up fantasies. Brain-stumping trivia. Sometimes in the middle of my workday, I'll just crave a ten-minute break and, before you know it, I'm playing a quick round of one of AOL's free Game Shows at KEYWORD: **Game Shows**.

When I leave work and I want to relax for a few minutes, a stellar round of bridge gets me going at KEYWORD: **WorldPlay Cards**. Maybe I'll follow that with 30 minutes of *Trivial Pursuit Interactive* at KEYWORD: **TPI**.

What are your favorite games? A good, long game of chess? Roleplaying fantasy? A challenging crossword puzzle? How about an action-filled, head-to-head arcade-style game? AOL has you covered no matter what type of game you love.

Games on AOL are so popular that several have been chosen as Members' Choice selections. And not only are the games themselves fun, but you also get to interact live with people from around the world. You're in control, not just a mere spectator.

Control Your Kids' Access to Premium Areas

AOL's Parental Controls can help you closely watch your kids' time online by controlling access to premium areas. If you would like to allow your child to play premium games, go to KEYWORD: **Parental Controls** and use the Parental Control's Custom Controls feature. To allow your kids to play premium games, you'll have to unlock their accounts by following the online instructions.

Please note as well that no system of online controls substitutes for parental supervision. It is always important to monitor your kids' use of AOL.

Some Games Are Free; Some Carry Added Fees

AOL's recent changes to the Games Channel means that many games are free—that is, they're included in your

9 Allow Permission to Play Premium Games

By default, all screen names other than the primary account are barred from playing premium games until the primary account holder grants them permission. To grant permission, log on with the primary account and go to KEYWORD: **Parental Controls.** Click on the "Premium Services" button. Click to remove the check-mark by any screen names that you want to allow to play premium games. And finally, click "OK".

◆ ◆ ◆ ◆ ◆ ◆ ◆ ◆ ◆ ◆ ◆ ◆

Attention AOL Shoppers!

KEYWORD: **Games Store** has popular games like *Civilization II, Warcraft II*, and *Maurice Ashley Teaches Chess.*

standard access fees—while many others carry additional charges to play. Find all of the free games I mention in this chapter at KEYWORD: **Game Shows**.

For the pay-to-play games go to KEYWORD: **WorldPlay**. The surcharged games, which AOL calls "Premium Games," each carry an additional hourly charge over your basic monthly charge. At press time, the charges were $1.99 per hour of gameplay. KEYWORD: **Premium** has the latest details on surcharged areas.

Throughout this chapter, I will try to point out which games carry an added charge. But to be certain about which type of game you're about to play, watch the online announcements. You'll always be alerted when you're about to enter a premium area. You will be given the option not to play the game before charging begins.

What's in the Gaming Chapter?

It all begins at KEYWORD: **Games**, the main stop for every game on AOL. From the main screen you can discover what's currently offered in the main gaming categories. I might be hedging my bets here, but I think that because AOL covers just about every sort of game you can imagine, you'll probably find that at least one of the following categories suits your interests. This chapter is organized around six main game categories, each of which you'll find represented on AOL:

- Strategy and Action: Smart and Fast-Paced
- Roleplaying and Persona Games: Be Someone (Or Something) Else
- Videogames: Get Reviews, Buyers Guides, and Strategies
- Trivia: Test Your Knowledge
- Puzzles, Cards, and Board Games: Challenge Yourself
- Sports: Create Your Own Teams

KEYWORD: Billing will give you up-to-the-minute billing information on premium game usage.

Good Stuff!

*Quake*ing in your shoes? Download a shareware version of the ultra-popular gore-fest at **KEYWORD: Quake**, or go directly to the message boards to share tips and boasts.

Strategy and Action: Smart and Fast-Paced

Experience Dogfighting Action

Experience what it feels like to be at the controls of a P-51D Mustang looking out of the cockpit at an enemy plane. **KEYWORD: Air Warrior** claims to be the most advanced multiplayer aerial combat simulation available: the detailed graphics and fast gameplay certainly make for some genuinely exciting flying. Beginners will especially like the walk-through that guides them through the setup and initial training flights.

Planes are modeled after one of 35 different WWI, WWII, and Korean War fighters and bombers. GameStorm Online Games runs the show, and holds weekly training sessions for novices and experienced pilots. Attesting to its popularity, *Air Warrior* has been designated a Members' Choice area. If you like it, watch for **KEYWORD: AirWarrior II** coming soon.

TAKE AIM IN SPLATTERBALL

Cover your online opponents in gobs of paint at **KEYWORD: Splatterball.** Choose your weapons: the SplatPistol, SplatRifle, BallonLauncher, or BurstGun, then get ready to be virtually covered in mud and paint. You take on up to twenty other players in this online game of fast and furious paintball. Hide from the enemy as you try to seize their base. You won't come home actually covered in paint, but you just might get covered in sweat. *Splatterball* is a premium game.

Join Warriors in MultiPlayer BattleTech

MultiPlayer BattleTech: Solaris brings you total fantasy immersion in a universe where the ancient code of the warrior merges with futuristic military technology. It's a huge networked game where you'll be walking the streets and hitting the 3-D battlefields with literally hundreds of other players simultaneously. Get the game interface at **KEYWORD: BattleTech**. The download takes about an hour at 28.8, but is well worth the wait.

New players should be sure to take the online tutorial, which helps you learn to navigate the streets and interact live with other players. Join up with a member of a house

Insider's Tip

Although the games forums typically aren't games, they're invaluable: you can get to know other players and learn how to play a game better.

to learn the ropes; many players befriend novices and put them through the paces. You can get involved in clan wars or you might prefer one-on-one combat.

An AOL member and avid player took me step-by-step through training, then we took to team battle. In a 3-D, visually detailed tundra, you can take aim at your enemies and protect your teammates.

Multiplayer Battle Tech: Solaris is a premium game. Before you play, you'll receive on-screen announcements to remind you that it is a surcharged area.

Hang Out in a Virtual Pool Hall

KEYWORD: **Virtual Pool** is one high-tech premium game. Designed with the help of physicists and mathematicians, *Virtual Pool Online* claims to be the most realistic pool simulation ever. The level of realism is high; you've got friction, speed, collision, and roll, as well as true computational ball tracking to give you the feel of real pool. Play 8-ball, 9-ball, straight pool, and rotation. Hang out in one of several pool halls to find an opponent who suits your skills, and then cue up!

Play Chess and Chat with Players Worldwide

From KEYWORD: **Chess,** you can get to the Internet Chess Club (ICC), a very active Web site that allows real-time chess and chatting with players worldwide. To access the ICC, you'll need a special browser called *Blitzin,* which you can download from the chess club library.

Improve Your Chess Game

Chess enthusiasts can play, share experiences, and talk game strategy at KEYWORD: **Chess**. It has convenient regular news reports from the world of professional chess housed alongside game scores and commentary, while resident master Gabriel Sanchez answers members' questions. Other useful parts of the forum: the software libraries and the Instructional Coaches folders where you can get hints and strategies.

KEYWORD: **NYT Chess** links you to the *New York Times* chess area, where you'll find quality chess-related stories and Web links.

Simulate Modern Naval Warfare

KEYWORD: Harpoon brings you combat at sea in a detailed simulation of naval warfare, based on the classic game by Larry Bond. Your job: command NATO or Soviet ships in the North Atlantic. This is not a shoot-'em-up game, but a strategy game that involves skill, intelligence, and experience. It's just like the single-player version of *Harpoon* with the addition of special conference rooms where you can plot strategy with other players and set up online games.

Harpoon is a premium game that carries an additional charge.

Insider's Tip

When playing any roleplaying game, always remember that other characters are real people with real feelings. They should be respected. Obscene or abusive language makes for a negative game experience.

ROLEPLAYERS HELP FELLOW ROLEPLAYERS

When you're new to a roleplaying world, more experienced players will often befriend and assist you so that you can get the most from a game. One member wrote the following about *Legends of Kesmai*: "Arriving in the strange new world of Kesmai I felt alone. Another player took me under his wing and helped me gain some much-needed experience in the dungeons! We traveled around searching for a troll to kill. In our travels I was beaten senseless by an orc, attacked mercilessly by kobolds, and shredded by wyverns. I fought, bleeding and battered." Imagine what would've happened to him without his guide!

Roleplaying and Persona Games: Be Someone (or Something) Else

Where Is the Adventurer's Hub?

KEYWORD: WorldPlay Adventure is the hub of roleplaying games on AOL. It has been said that there are more online roleplaying games than any other game genre. What's good is that it doesn't take a lot of fancy equipment or software to play. Players tell me that it's easy to get immersed in character, living in other worlds, in other times.

Be a Vampire

Antagonist's *Black Bayou* is one very frightening world that you can inhabit each night from 6 p.m. to 3 a.m. eastern time. **KEYWORD: Bayou** brings you roleplaying on the Isle Voletta, Louisiana, replete with vampires, madness, pain, and love.

You get complete control over the development of your character. To make your roleplaying as exciting as possible, remember not to skimp when developing the background of your character: the more detailed you can be about your character's past, the better you'll be at determining how he or she would react to situations that come up during the game.

> **SIMS LET YOU GET REALLY CREATIVE**
>
> *The Simming Forum* at **KEYWORD: Sim** is a free-form gaming area where you might fight it out in space wars, search for the truth in the FBI Paranormal files, or solve a mystery à la Sherlock Holmes in the Victorian era.
>
> What's compelling about Sims is that there are fewer rules than typical roleplaying games, and they have no set ending once a plotline begins. Each Sim is based in a virtual world in which players create a character and act as the character would in the given situations. You play with others in the *Sim Forum*'s own chat rooms—no special interface necessary.

Enter a World of Never-Ending Quests for Glory and Loot

At **KEYWORD: Legends**, you can find a well-designed, intuitive, graphical roleplaying game. Hundreds of players and thousands of computer-driven creatures occupy *Legends of Kesmai*, or *LOK* as it is called by players. Best of all, even if you're just getting started in roleplaying, you'll be immediately immersed, since *LOK* has the best-designed orientation materials I've encountered in an online game.

Read the Fast Start guide in Help: the time you spend there will enrich your gameplaying experience, and you'll learn secrets that could take a while to discover if you simply jump in.

After getting some game background, spend time in the Town of Kesmai so that you can familiarize yourself with moving around and interacting. Later, you can move on to the dungeons where you'll be able to cast spells, meet fellow players and monsters, and—if you're so inclined—search corpses for loot.

Legends of Kesmai is a premium game.

Rolemaster: Magestorm

At **KEYWORD: Magestorm**, engage in magical combat with your team of Mages and vie for control of pools of Earthblood, a special source of magical power. As a new player, you'll create a character, choose a magical realm, and join one of three teams: Order, Balance, or Chaos. Battles consist of Mages casting offensive spells in order to kill opposing players and drain their power. Set in a highly graphical world, this game is played in the first person. A special note: be sure you have the latest version of Direct X installed on your machine; get it at **KEYWORD: GCDirectX**.

MTV Online's Krank

MTV fans can enjoy **KEYWORD: KRANK**, MTV's trivia game that tests music fans with questions like "Who hit big by combining Gregorian Chant with hip dance tracks?" Just to brush up on your musical knowledge, you might want to head over to **KEYWORD: MTV** to study.

Free-Form Gaming Has Fewer Rules

Rules? What rules? Okay, there are rules in the *Free-Form Gaming Forum*, but you'll find no game-masters and no pre-set scenarios. **KEYWORD: FFGF** is dedicated to providing an environment open to anyone interested in roleplaying games, interactive play, and creative development. Learn the basics of roleplaying and creating a persona, or brush up on your skills if you're a seasoned gamer.

Visit the very popular Red Dragon Inn or the Star's End Bar, two roleplaying chat rooms, or the Red Dragon's Great Hall, a conference room. These rooms are usually filled in the afternoon and evening as players weave their elaborate tales. If you're serious about free-form gaming, subscribe to the FFGF-Announcements mailing list by clicking on "News & Information" from the main screen.

Find Your Gaming Niche in the Gaming Forums

The links to nearly all of AOL's gaming forums, with the exception of video games, are conveniently located in one place at **KEYWORD: Gaming**.

Games include live-action, play by mail and email, roleplaying, war and strategy, free-form, dueling, and chess. What's good about the *Online Gaming Forum* is that it caters to the serious gamer—it is not about graphics and machinery, but creative game playing.

Insider's Tip

GamePro's File Vault holds previews of computer and video games not yet on the market, as well as move lists and game walk-throughs that can help when you're stuck and need some clues.

Another good thing in the *Gaming Forum* is the opportunity to talk to designers in the industry for tips on how to turn your original idea for a new game into something others can play. The Game Designers Forum and the Game Publishers Association are just a couple of the weekly live workshop discussions.

Chatter Box

The *Video Games Lounge* at KEYWORD: **Video Games** is full of players 24 hours a day. Listen in as they tout their favorite platforms and titles.

Video Games: Get Reviews, Buyers' Guides, and Strategies

Review Before You Buy; Get Gaming Tips

GamePro Online is the electronic counterpart to the leading videogame magazine, and is a popular AOL Members' Choice area. The best things about KEYWORD: **GamePro** are the monthly collections of codes you can use to become more expert at titles like *Mech Warrior 2* and *Command & Conquer*. You can also find articles and features such as Buyers Beware, in which GamePro's own Watch Dog helps you with your problems: if you're having trouble with your PlayStation or your *Mindscape* game, for example, you can let the Watch Dog know.

Video game players love the reviews of N64, Saturn, PC, and PlayStation titles. Read the reviews so you'll know when the next *Tekken* or *Warcraft II* title will hit the store shelves, and whether they're worth the money.

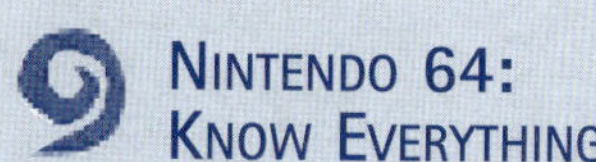
NINTENDO 64: KNOW EVERYTHING

KEYWORD: **N64** is where the latest from Nintendo is praised, reviewed, and conquered by gamers and N64 fans. Get codes for games like *Blast Corps, Turok: Dinosaur Hunter*, and *Doom64*. Before you spend a lot of money on a new title, check the game reviews from members and pros. They can help you make an informed decision before you buy.

Purchase and Download Games

KEYWORD: **Games Store** houses eight categories of games featuring everything from simulation and action to sports and roleplaying. All purchases are backed by AOL's shopping guarantee of a safe and sure transaction. There's no going out to your local store, since you can immediately purchase and download popular titles like *Doom II* and *Duke Nukem* and be playing in almost no time at all. If something a little less intense—or perhaps more traditional—is your style, check out the computer versions of such favorite classics as *Monopoly* and *Trivial Pursuit*.

And if you'd rather have the games on disk, you can purchase them online and have them delivered through the mail as well.

You can even buy a new and improved joystick in the area for accessories.

Download Free Add-Ons and Demos

The *PC Games Forum*'s looks may deceive you, since it's not the snazziest games area on AOL, but the content at **KEYWORD: PCGames** more than compensates for its bare-bones design. In this AOL Members' Choice area, you'll

Join AOL's Most Popular Gaming Community

As the most popular gaming area on AOL, *Antagonist, Inc.* lives up to its reputation with a lot to offer. Probably the finest elements of **KEYWORD: ANT** are the hundreds of games available to download, both free demos and full versions of titles you can buy and play immediately. You can find *Shadow Warrior* from the makers of *Duke Nukem*, or download a copy of *Extreme Assault* or *Esoteria* in the Daily Dose.

The Eye to Eye section holds reviews of the latest releases with opinions from the Antagonist staff. You can quickly find out which games are worth the money, or warn fellow gamers about not-so-great titles.

The advice and opinions run hot at *Antagonist, Inc.* Here's what one member has to say on Nintendo 64 versus Sony PSX: "I think we can all agree that the N64 is far more technologically advanced than the PSX or Saturn, but does that make it the better system to buy? Right now, probably not. PSX and Saturn have a much larger library of games to choose from and they have a higher quantity of good games, although that really isn't saying much about either of the systems."

Discuss the finer points of Nintendo, Sega, and Sony with the multitudes of aficionados, or join the PC Games debate over whether *Quake*'s back-end engine is fully utilized by the game, or could still be driven harder, for even better game play.

Attention AOL Shoppers!

Subscribe to *GamePro*—the world's largest multiplatform gaming magazine—at significant savings off the newsstand price. Click "Sign me up" from the main screen at **KEYWORD: GamePro**.

DOWNLOAD THE TOP 25 DEMOS, FREE

KEYWORD: Top 25 has free demo versions of great games like *Tomb Raider, X-Wing vs. TIE Fighter, Dynamite Joe*, and *Jurassic Primitive War*. The titles change often as newer games come out, so check frequently to preview the latest. The reviews of the games are especially helpful if you're not sure you really want to spend an hour or two downloading. And once you've decided, click "How to Download" for step-by-step instructions if you're new to downloading and installing games.

find help, hints, add-ons, and discussion—but best of all, you can find software, the majority of it free.

In the Software Library, categories for the most popular games make it easier to find what you want, such as add-ons for *SimCity*, or new *Doom* levels. Or you can also search words and phrases. I typed "Warcraft" into the search box and got a list with over 300 separate files to choose from, including new scenarios and guidebooks. To download, simply click on the file you want and choose download now or later.

In addition, the popular message boards overflow with advice on *Diablo*, discussion of 3-D graphic cards, MMX, and *Quake*. You can be playing better in no time at all.

Good Stuff!

If you're really, really smart, **KEYWORD: BrainBuster** has the toughest NTN questions to challenge you.

Trivia: Test Your Knowledge

Trivial Pursuit Interactive: Head-to-Head Competition

"Which of the senses does the olfactory nerve serve?" That's an easy one. But *Trivial Pursuit*, the well-known King of trivia, is ready to stump you in its well-designed and fast-paced online game. Thousands of questions

Meet... **NTN Trivia staffer** Thomas Hall, who says that NTN has over 80,000 questions in its database, and that you'll almost never find an inaccurate question—but when NTN's wrong, they apologize.

Which Trivia Game Suits Your Interests?

Who played Kate Lawrence on the TV show "Family?" For what team did Orlando Cepeda play when he was the 1958 Rookie of the Year? What do you call the slime added to wine or cider to produce vinegar? Do you have a clue? Rock 'n Roll trivia, Comics trivia, Entertainment trivia, and Kids Only trivia are a few of the options you can find in NTN's warehouse of trivial games, **KEYWORD: NTN**. Baby boomers are particularly fond of Retroactive or Nick at Nite trivia, where TV junkies test their knowledge of TV reruns.

play round-the-clock, 24 hours a day. Because no special downloads are required, you can simply go to **KEYWORD: Trivial Pursuit** and start playing immediately.

Each new round of the 30-minute games starts on the hour and the half-hour. In real-time, head-to-head competition with members from around the world, you can demonstrate who knows more by answering questions like "What movie title was also the title of Barbara Streisand's number-one song?" and "Who was the last major league baseball player to bat .400?" Daily winners vie for T-shirts and gift certificates. Even if you don't win, you can still have a lot of fun.

Trivia with an Attitude

The questions, answers, and attitude at *Antagonist Trivia* are a bit in-your-face, but if you don't care about subtlety, this could be the game for you. The under-30 crowd gets a chance to answer questions like "What was Dr. Harry Weston's dog's name on TV's *Empty Nest*?" **KEYWORD: AT** is the place to find this sly variation of NTN Trivia. Depending on how well you do, you can earn tokens to win prizes, everything from a George Winston CD to color digital camera. **KEYWORD: Prizes** has award details.

FOLLOW YOUR INSTINCTS

Play a game in which the majority rules. In *Gut Instinct* it's not the "right" answer that counts: it's being able to predict what the majority will answer that earns you points. Go along with the crowd, and you could be winning in no time. Go to **KEYWORD: About Work,** then select Gut Instinct in the listbox.

Parent Soup: The Game

Test your parenting skills with the *Parent Soup* trivia game. From **KEYWORD: Parent Soup**, select "Play the Parent Soup Game" on the Main Screen. Each game goes for fifteen questions. "What is the fontanel on a new baby?" "Which critically acclaimed TV show is about kids who have no parents?" As you can see, not every question is about parenting, but you can test your parenting knowledge to see how it compares to other players'.

When you enter the game you'll be faced with a question and five possible answers. Try to click on the correct answer as soon as possible. The sooner you answer, the more points you'll get.

Puzzles, Cards, and Board Games: Challenge Yourself

Insider's Tip

Share clues in the NYT crossword chat room. If you can't go it alone, it's easy to get together with people who share your passion for crosswords.

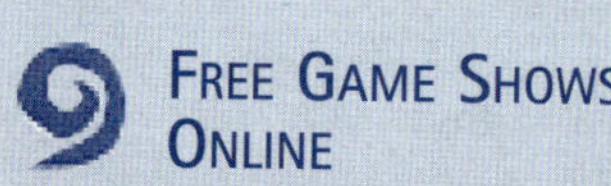

FREE GAME SHOWS ONLINE

KEYWORD: Game Shows takes you and your family to one of the focal points for free games on AOL, which I've described in more detail in the puzzles section of this chapter. Find BoxerJam Gameshows like *Out of Order* and *Strike-A-Match*. There are also other fun family games like NTN studio trivia, *Slingo*, and *Puzzle Zone*.

Solve The New York Times Crossword

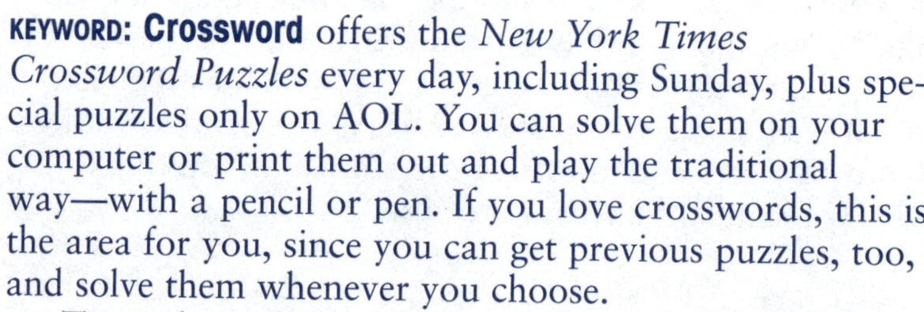

KEYWORD: Crossword offers the *New York Times Crossword Puzzles* every day, including Sunday, plus special puzzles only on AOL. You can solve them on your computer or print them out and play the traditional way—with a pencil or pen. If you love crosswords, this is the area for you, since you can get previous puzzles, too, and solve them whenever you choose.

To work on the puzzles, simply download and install a free program, Across Lite, from the area itself. The online instructions will walk you through the installation process. Once you have Across Lite you'll be able to get a new puzzle every day; the answers appear the following day. If you like to battle the clock, there's a timer and scoring features to keep you up to speed.

Unscramble Words, Head-to-Head

Out of Order is fun and fast-paced. The creator of *Jeopardy* has brought AOL a game show that you don't just watch, you play. At **KEYWORD: Out of Order** you play head-to-head with two other players. The object: unscramble the words based on the clues, and then type your answer. It's social, too, since you chat with your fellow contestants as you play. The special interactive interface downloads automatically in just a few minutes and starts itself the first time you play.

Poker with Sights and Sounds of a Real Casino

At **KEYWORD: Casino Poker**, GameStorm brings you friendly rounds of poker with partners (and opponents) from around the world.

What's nice is that you can play one of the five most popular forms of poker: Seven Card Stud, Five Card Stud, Omaha Hold 'em, Five Card Draw, and Texas Hold 'em. The graphics are topnotch, and the rounds go quickly, so you aren't likely to get bored waiting for other players to play their hands. Go up against other AOL members, or test your skills against artificial intelli-

Interactive Word Puzzles with a Twist

The interactive puzzles at KEYWORD: Puzzle are amazing and fun. They're amazing because they use a special interface that runs on top of AOL and allows you to play against the clock. You get clues as you need them, only when you need them. They're fun because they're clever and probably unlike any game you've ever played before.

Anyone who loves word challenges can find a whole week's worth of colorful games at *Puzzle Zone*, with four new ones every day. Before you play the first time, you need to download the interface, which takes about 3 minutes at 28.8. The software installs itself. From then on, you'll need only a few seconds to download the games each time you return to play. Here's what you'll find:

- *Flexicon* is a 5-minute crossword puzzle that "flexes" to give you more ways to solve the main clue, which is a twisty play on words.
- Find a word in *Strip Search*, a high-tech word-search that gives humorous clues to help you out.
- *Elvis=Lives* is an anagram puzzle that uses scrambled celebrity names. For example: WONDER TRASH is the scrambled clue for HOWARD STERN.
- Link words that have hidden relationships in *Clink*, a stream-of-consciousness game in which you make sense of what seems like nonsense.

gence that was created with help from world-class poker players.

Casino Poker is a premium game which carries additional charges.

SPORTS TRIVIA

KEYWORD: **Sports Trivia** brings you questions that test even the most knowledgeable sports fan. Take your pick from among Hockey, Pro and College Hoops, Baseball, Olympics, and Pro and College Football.

Assess Your Mind; Test Your Brain

Want to take the very popular Love Test? Or maybe you're more interested in knowing how smart you are with an online IQ test? Introverted? Extroverted? Type A personality? Go to KEYWORD: **Online Psych**, then click on "Mind Games" for interesting games, quizzes, and interactive tests to assess just about every aspect of your mind.

Blot Shots is another great game at Online Psych. View a series of inkblots and write the first association that comes to mind. Compare your answers with other members' and see how your imagination contrasts with theirs.

Word-Matching, Quiz-Show Style

Here's where quick and fast-paced games get addictive. From the creators of "Jeopardy" comes *Boxer Jam's Strike-A-Match*, a 15-minute word game that pits you against other AOL members. Try to figure out what the words have in common and be quick about it. KEYWORD: **Strike A Match** plays just like a TV game show: find matching words and click on them as quickly as you can. For instance, if the six words on the board are WALLY, GIRAFFE, MAGNOLIA, THERMOS, BEAVER, and JODHPUR . . .

. . . the two matching words are WALLY and BEAVER, brothers from the '50s show *Leave It to Beaver*. What's exciting about the game is its fast pace and the feature that allows you to chat with others while you play. *Strike-A-Match* has a special interface that downloads in a few minutes and automatically installs itself the first time you play.

Mix Bingo and Slots to Get Slingo

What do you get when you combine ten players, chat, bingo, and slots into one game? **KEYWORD: Slingo**. Get points by filling your card along vertical, horizontal, and diagonal lines. You get extra points when gold coins appear. And sometimes the Joker appears, to be used anywhere in a column to help you make a match. It's a fast-paced game, but you can chat while you play, if your fingers are that quick. It takes just a few minutes to download the colorful, interactive interface, which installs itself automatically.

Enjoy Classic Card Games

KEYWORD: WorldPlay Cards is the place for all of AOL's premium card games. You'll find Bridge, Gin, Hearts, Spades, Backgammon, and Cribbage—with more games always on the way. *WorldPlay*'s technologically advanced card games—like several of the other graphically rich games available on AOL—are fast-paced, social games in which you can chat with other players as you play your hands.

The best thing about *WorldPlay*: each game allows a wide range of play options to suit even the most experienced player. In Bridge, for instance, you can provide your own convention cards, alert or ask questions, and play according to standard bridge rules.

PREMIUM PRICING

What Makes WorldPlay Games Good?

The games are great for two reasons: the people and the technology. The fact that so many people play these games means that you can almost always find a group of players at your skill level, play any time of day or night, and get to know them personally. In effect, the games are highly social opportunities.

Technologically, each game features fast-playing hands, detailed graphics, and the ability to see and "hear" other players as they play using 3-D avatars. You even get to choose and customize your own 3-D representation. **KEYWORD: WordPlay** has a lincup of all the jazzy offerings.

♦ ♦ ♦ ♦ ♦ ♦ ♦ ♦ ♦ ♦ ♦ ♦

Sports: Games and Contests

Play Simulated Sports Matches in Fantasy and Simulation Leagues

In the sport of your choice, you use the stats of actual players to determine the outcome of your team in fantasy or simulation league play. **KEYWORD: Grandstand** is where you can find fantasy games based in real-life baseball, football,

Play Sports, Hard

Choose your sport in the Fantasy and Simulation leagues:

- 50 Yard Line (Football)
- Blue Line (Hockey)
- Dugout (Baseball)
- Net Game (Tennis)
- Off the Glass (Basketball)
- On the Green (Golf)
- On the Beam (Gymnastics)
- Post Time (Horse Sports)
- Roller/Inline Skating
- Sports Cards (Collecting)
- Squared Circle (Boxing/Wrestling)
- The Chalet (Winter Sports)
- The Dojo (Martial Arts)
- The Kop (Soccer)
- Track Talking (Motor Sports)
- Whole 9 Yards (Other Sports)

♦ ♦ ♦ ♦ ♦ ♦ ♦ ♦ ♦ ♦ ♦ ♦

hockey, basketball, tennis, golf, and wrestling. There is a fee for each season (usually between $10 and $20).

You can be a part of live online drafts, participate in weekly owners' meetings, and top it off with playoffs and championships.

KEYWORD: **CyberSports** is the most convenient home base for simulations. Compete in football, basketball, baseball, and even bowling, golf, auto racing, and wrestling using special software.

To participate in the simulation leagues, you contact the appropriate commissioner and then sign up for a team of your own.

How Well Do You Know Your Sports?

Which QB has racked up the most seasons with a 100-plus QB rating in NFL history? Who was named European Soccer Player of the year two years in a row? KEYWORD: **NTN Sports** has answers. Compete against other AOL members in a variety of sports arenas, including hockey, pro and college basketball, baseball, pro and college football, the Olympics, and free-for-all general sports trivia.

New games start every 15 minutes. Hang out with fellow sports fans in live chat areas where you can get to know other like-minded sports fans.

Tee Off with Golf

Enter the green at KEYWORD: **iGOLF** and go 18 holes in the *iGOLF Challenge*. This is an addictive, interactive fantasy golf game. If you seek like-minded golfers, you can find yourself a golf partner for a real-world game in the chat room.

Meet Other Basketball Fans

KEYWORD: **NTN Hoops** is where basketball lovers meet up to compete for fun and prizes against other AOL basketball lovers. Fantasy basketball and pro and college basketball trivia are among the area's most popular activities, especially during basketball season.

Predict the Quarterback's Next Move

Test your football knowledge and strategy skills at **KEYWORD: NTN Playbook**. One of the most amazing features at the *Playbook* is the live interactive game *QB1*: as you watch a live NFL or NCAA football game on TV, you try to predict the quarterback's next call. You go head-to-head with thousands of other players around the country via NTN's Entertainment Network.

Manage (or Invent) Your Own Teams

Ever yearn to create your own dream team, and trade players with others sports fans? If you don't have the cash to buy your own team, the fantasy leagues are your best bet. From **KEYWORD: Usenet**, you can follow the fantasy leagues in several categories. To subscribe to one of the leagues below, click "Expert Add" and type in the names as they appear here:

- *rec.sport.baseball.fantasy*
- *ec.sport.football.fantasy*
- *alt.sports.hockey.fantasy*
- *alt.sport.basketball.pro.fantasy*
- *rec.sport.pro-wrestling.fantasy*
- *comp.sys.ibm.pc.games.sport*
- *alt.games.sports-leagues*

These games aren't part of the *Grandstand Fantasy Leagues* described above. But dedicated fans and fantasy enthusiasts can find games like Email Leagues that are usually free to join.

Sports Trivia Focused on African American Athletes

A.C. Butler, star of the Negro Baseball League from way back, gives his name to one very challenging game of sports trivia. Compete with other members by answering questions about African American athletes and contests from the 1600s to the present day. To play, go to **KEYWORD: NetNoir**, then click "Polls & Games," then "AC Butler."

Even during the off-season there's Football Trivia. Think you know everything about the NFL's legends? What about Heisman Trophy winners? From questions about players and stats to questions about recent games, nothing about football is left untouched.

9 9 9 9 9

Obviously, there's a lot of gaming going on at AOL. The free games are a lot of fun, especially the Game Shows Online. The premium games really dazzle technologically.

Of course, if you play premium games, you can go at any time to **KEYWORD: Billing** to get up-to-the-minute reports on your usage. If you click "Display Billing Detail" you can find out exactly when you've played and how much time and money you've spent on each premium game. If you have additional screen names attached to your account (often called sub-accounts) for your kids or other members of your family, you can see their online activity, too, including time spent playing premium games.

Now that I've gotten all the technicalities out of the way, let's get back to the point of the Games Channel: fun. Take a break from work, expand your mind with trivia, or battle stress as you battle demons from other worlds.

Just remember to check back to **KEYWORD: Games** every so often. As the main gaming hub, it's where you can find out about all the new games AOL plans to offer.

The Sports Channel: Fans, Fantasy, and Fitness

I hate to say it, but when it comes to sports, I don't know the fourth quarter from the fourth inning. I guess you could say I hit the wall (is that a sports phrase?).

Fortunately, my pal Buck, the semi-famous author of the weekly Sports Channel newsletter, has agreed to step in and take a hand off. (Hey, maybe I'm getting the hang of this lingo!) So don't adjust your sets. For the rest of this chapter, Bucky's in charge. Since he's a real sports nut, I fully trust he'll show you the best athletic areas on AOL. I'll meet you back at Chapter 13 (that's Entertainment). Take it away, Buck . . .

Thanks, Meg. I admit it, the Buck doesn't do much besides comb through AOL's Sports Channel, and watch sports on TV. These activities aren't getting me any closer to a Presidential Medal of Honor, but they do give me a keen appreciation of the Sports Channel—maybe even an Insider's view, if you get my drift.

So here's what I've done: I've gone through the Sports Channel and picked out the best, most useful, and most interesting places for athletically inclined AOLers.

Now here's all you have to do: order yourself up a pizza, take thy mouse in thine hand, and follow the Buck on a ride through the Sports Channel.

So without further self-indulgence . . .

Get the AOL Sports Newsletter

Okay AOL Sports fans, I'm takin' names. *Your* names, so that I can send you my free newsletter, *From the Cheap Seats.* It's a weekly guide to sports on AOL, and it's delivered to your mailbox for the cost of a breath of fresh air: *nothing*. Go to **KEYWORD: Newsletters** to sign up.

News, Scores, and Commentary

Get Up-to-the-Minute Sports Information

So you want to know what's happening in the sports world right this minute? Can't wait around for ESPN's Sportscenter or the late news? A great thing about the Sports Channel is that you don't have to wait for sports news, or go looking for it. It comes right out and grabs you by the lapels, right off the top screen of **KEYWORD: Sports**. Whether it's a current scoreboard or the featured story of the hour, it's all one click away. The guys and gals at the Sports Channel have that sportswriter's sense of the big story, and they get it to you quickly.

Good Stuff!

Your season tickets may be lousy seats, but you can get up close and personal with the Sports Pictures of the Week. Find them at **KEYWORD: Sports News**.

The live scoreboards at **KEYWORD: Sports** are as current and accurate as you can get. No matter what the season or the sport, the scoreboards can handle your every scoreboard desire. The real functionality of the scoreboards comes when there are multiple contests occurring at one time. No one can watch every baseball game at once, but that doesn't mean you can't keep track of every game and every at-bat. With the scoreboard, you can watch the changes as the game happens. If you're a fantasy freak and want to know how your players are doing on a certain night, you can check out how Frank Thomas is faring, even in the bottom of the fifth.

Meet... Baseball Critic Brad Ausmus

ABC Sports columnist Brad Ausmus shares his views of Major Leaguers, reports from the clubhouse, and airs his philosophies and predictions. You can catch up with him and send him email at **KEYWORD: ABC Sports**.

Football is another live scoreboard specialty at **KEYWORD: Sports**, allowing NFL fans to keep an eye on each of the games going on simultaneously on Sundays. NBA fans will also have a ball as they watch point totals, assists, and rebounds build along in synch with every game. If you want to stay informed, the Sports Channel scoreboard is the real deal.

Travel the Wide World of Sports on ABC

It's the thrill of victory and the agony of defeat, all right on the Buck's computer screen at **KEYWORD: ABC Sports.** ABC started covering sports on television before the first home computer was even produced, but *Wide World of Sports*, the cornerstone of the ABC sports machine, successfully makes the transition to the Internet at *ABC Sports Online*.

Sure, *ABC Sports* focuses its coverage on ABC-broadcast sports and events. But it covers those events very well. *ABC Sports* does impressive work with World Cup Soccer coverage, explores horse racing thoroughly and completely, and gets to the bottom of both traditional and bizarre competitions from around the globe. Major League pitcher Brad Ausmus writes an enjoyable and highly insightful journal on the trips and travails of a big leaguer.

VIEW CLASSIC SPORTS MOMENTS

KEYWORD: **Slideshows** captures some sports events in words, pictures, and sounds and delivers them to you in AOL's new multimedia technology. View classic plays with the TeamNFL slideshow. Replay Cary Blanchard's victorious field goal kick with the 1997 Pro Bowl slideshow. See how the Extreme Fans area can deliver The Last Shot straight to your email box. Or catch up with NASCAR drivers in a whole new way. AOL *Slideshows* deliver your favorite sports with all new sights and sounds.

Read CBS SportsLine Commentary

Let's look at the new heavyweight on the block, *CBS SportsLine*. KEYWORD: **CBS SportsLine** has put together a fantastic area, covering the major sports with a fervor.

So what do you get? Well, everything. In short, this place is a treasure trove of sports info and fun, so I'll spare you the deserved superlatives to point out some of the brightest spots at *CBS SportsLine*. News is updated as it happens and as soon as *CBS SportsLine* can get it in print and online. A surprisingly extensive and astute group of columnists provide consistently bright and intriguing commentary on the hottest issues in sports.

The site is indexed! For those of you who still don't find the site easy enough to use, there is a handy search function. The Live Radio section lets you hear (you guessed it) live CBS radio, and also provides an archive of *SportsLine*'s best interviews. The City Pages give you access to sports pages from newspapers in every major sports city.

And the capper? If you like to play video sports games, *CBS SportsLine* has an unprecedented lineup of downloadable arcade-style games. Play half-court basketball, try video golf, or test your football passing accuracy against Joe Namath in the Cool Stuff section—a name appropriate to just about everything this area has to offer.

Log into The Sporting News

What the Big Boys Are Made Of

Did you know the Minnesota Twins' Bob Tewksbury draws caricatures of his teammates for charity and has illustrated a children's book? Or that the Oakland Raiders' Napolean Kaufman likens running down the field with a football to the RoadRunner being chased by Wile E. Coyote? Famous athletes share their personal stories, beliefs, and even quirks in *The Sporting News'* Daily Diaries. Every day you can get to know your favorite sports heroes a little better. Mo Vaughn is well-known as a bedrock of inspiration for his fellow Boston Red Sox and stalwart community leader. But what do you know about Green Bay's Reggie White or Denver's John Elway? Meet them here.

All right, let's be blunt. *The Sporting News* is a key resource of the Sports Channel, completely covering every avenue of major sports news.

Where to begin? **KEYWORD: Sporting News** has everything. The Fly updates frequent additions to the site, including articles from some of the most respected commentators on the Web, up-to-date coverage of breaking sports news, as well as scores and stats.

For the educated sports fan—those who want some depth to their coverage—*The Sporting News* columnists are great. T.J. Simers covers pro football with his Interactive NFL Report, and Dave D'Allesandro's NBA Report provides some of the best hoops talk around, while Peter Schmuck and Jerry Crasnick cover all the bases for the grand old game. All of the major sports coverage is constantly—and I mean *constantly*—updated with new articles daily by some of the best sportswriters in any journalistic medium.

Get Complete Previews

Another of the big dogs barking here on AOL is *SportsFan Radio*, one of my favorite areas to preview each and every major sports contest.

For those of you with a flair for predicting the outcome of any sporting contest, **KEYWORD: SFRN** is a valuable source of pre-game info, with every matchup fully detailed with a quality mix of statistics and informed commentary. *SportsFan* covers the four major sports, but is also expert on NCAA football and basketball, concisely delivering the info every fan needs to sit down and make accurate, informed predictions.

SportsFan's message boards are also a pleasantly surprising area for the smarter-than-average poster. Fans compare and trade notes and theories on specific matchups. *SportsFan* also offers a link to live sports odds with Roxy Roxborough and the MGM Grand. *SportsFan Radio* really kicks into gear during playoff time, when the matchups are even more carefully scrutinized and dissected.

Channel Jumping

The Travel Channel can send you off to see your favorite baseball team play in their home ballpark. **KEYWORD: RPMC** delivers vacation packages centered around sports events, including a Baseball Weekend that covers car rental, accommodations, dinner, and tickets to the game.

Tap into Great Local Coverage

Are you living in New York, even though your heart is trapped in San Francisco with the Giants and 49ers? Tired of getting cursory blurbs about the Oilers in Green Bay? Maybe you need to know Nebraska football while stuck in the Alaskan tundra?

Fear not: AOL can bring you great local coverage from almost anywhere in the U.S. at **KEYWORD: Digital City**. Find the city that hosts your favorite team and get ready for some serious hometown pride.

Digital City also keeps you on top of your local scene when you're traveling. Log in as a guest from a friend or family member's account, or use a laptop if you have one. For the truly sports-addicted like the Buck, *Digital City* is crucial to our on-the-road survival.

Some of the Digital Cities with standout sports sections are Philadelphia (**KEYWORD: Philly**), Boston (**KEYWORD: Boston**), Phoenix (**KEYWORD: Arizona Central**), and San Francisco (**KEYWORD: San Francisco**), but they're all good.

Attention AOL Shoppers!

Subscribe to *Sports Illustrated* at **KEYWORD: Magazine Outlet** and save 78% off the cover price. *NBA Inside*, *Baseball Weekly*, and *Football Digest* are just a few of the other magazines you can get on the cheap.

Talk Sports, Whenever You Feel Like It

Express Yourself in the Grandstand

Okay, tired of talking to yourself? Feel strongly about something sporting, but you just can't find anyone to talk to? Then **KEYWORD: Sports Boards** is for you.

AOL's number one chat and message board area, *The Grandstand*, is the place where the sporting community comes to trade opinions, ideas, and the latest news about virtually any sport. Live chats are always filled with sportsmongers, while the message board areas give any AOL member a forum in which to air their diverse views on any number of sports topics. And talk is not limited to the four major sports. *The Grandstand* has a series of areas dedicated to underrated activities such as bowling and gymnastics, and also to newer sports like inline skating and paintballing. That way, members with out-of-the-mainstream interests can find one another more easily.

Insider's Tip

KEYWORD: **Sports Libraries** is the place to go for *The Grandstand*'s first-round picks and cool sports games to download.

One of the greatest qualities of *The Grandstand* is its topicality. Fans at *The Grandstand* jump on the hottest news with fervor, zeal, and a dozen different outlooks. And for those of you with dreams of becoming sports columnists, *The Grandstand* message boards give anyone a venue to be witty.

Talk to the Pros in Athlete Direct

For a change of pace and a radically different point of view, the Buck likes to go right to the source—the athletes themselves—at KEYWORD: **Athlete Direct**.

Good Stuff!

Discover Drew Bledsoe's favorite stadium when on the road. See what's on Corey Nakatani's CD shelf. KEYWORD: **AD Lifestyles** shows top athletes' takes on current movies, restaurants, music, travel, and more.

Athlete Direct has lined up an impressive list of professional athletes on the Internet, each of them writing a journal just for the site. Get to know each of the athletes through that particular person's own words and journal entries. Complete bios will help you put the journals in context as you get first-hand accounts from the athletes on the field. Experience NFL training camp with Drew Bledsoe or Ki-Jana Carter, hit Wimbledon with tennis star Todd Martin, or get up close with Jim Edmonds as he and the Angels make a run for the playoffs.

I really like *Athlete Direct*'s Live chats. Wouldn't you rather be in an auditorium with Dale Jarrett or Michael Chang, posing your own questions, instead of listening to the ramblings of a pizza-stuffed sportswriter like me? Or maybe you think you know all about the top players.

Test your *Athlete Direct* IQ with a Sports Quiz. New questions are posted every other week.

Sports Chat, Live

An easy way to keep track of all upcoming celebrity sports chats is KEYWORD: **Sports Live**. It sure beats yelling at the TV—this way, when you talk to a sports person, he might actually answer. No yelling, though. That means take off the CAPS LOCK, friends.

To find out which athletes are venturing into chat rooms this week, check the Upcoming Auditorium Events listed at *Sports Live*. You have to plan ahead to make sure you don't miss the good stuff. But you'll be glad you did.

All-Night Sports Chat

There are a whole slew of chat rooms that are open for business 24/7:

- Test your baseball trivia skills or mull over highlights at Ebbets Field, KEYWORD: **Sports Rooms**.
- Campfire Chat, at KEYWORD: **Backpacker**, is for outdoorsy types to talk about wilderness travel.
- KEYWORD: **HBN** takes you to the Hunting chat room. You'll find the Fly-Fishing and Freshwater chat rooms there, too.
- Take a pit stop in the Winner's Circle chat room to talk about fast cars. That's right, race to KEYWORD: **Sports Rooms** and click "Motor Sports Chat."
- The place to talk about your golf swing is the First Tee chat room at KEYWORD: **IGOLF**.

If none of these specialized rooms float your boat, there's always good old *Sports Chat* for general discussion. It's at KEYWORD: **Sports Rooms**.

Chat with Fellow Fans

Here's what to do to meet members who share your impeccable taste: go to the Member Directory. Search profiles for the name of your favorite team (like "Yankees"). Click the little box that says "Return only members online." Click "Search." You'll find a whole list of like-minded fans who are readily available to share your enthusiasm. Chat while the game is on and debate the opposing team's strategy play by play.

When there aren't any pros in the neighborhood, talk to AOL sports fans in the chat rooms at **KEYWORD: Sports Rooms**. Some of the most popular rooms: Sports Chat, Baseball, College Football, Hockey, Horses, Pro Football, Pro Hoops, Soccer, Sports Cards, and Tennis.

Where Buck Goes

Find Complete Coverage of the Big Events

Insider's Tip

Find your favorite team quickly and easily. Most have their own keyword to give you player stats, current roster, team news, and trades. Just type in "Oakland A's" or "Packers" or even "Mighty Ducks." Hey, there's no accounting for taste.

Wimbledon? The Indy 500? The Stanley Cup, World Series, Super Bowl, or Final Four—there's a *Fan Central* for all of the biggest sports events, lining up all the material the Sports Channel has to offer for that special game, series, or tournament, all in one convenient area.

Super Bowl freak? **KEYWORD: Fan Central** compiles everything you need to know in one handy site. When your time is valuable (like mine), being able to jump quickly from *The Sporting News* to *SportsFan Radio* to *Athlete Direct* to *ABC Sports* is a blessing.

Also incorporated into the *Fan Central* areas are various chats dedicated solely to major sporting events. For souvenir hunters, *Fan Central* also locates online shopping for those searching for sports fans stuffings. Spare your mouse the endless clicking and head straight to *Fan Central*.

Follow the Recruiting Wars

Attention AOL Shoppers!

KEYWORD: Online Auction is where you can score autographed prints, plaques, jerseys, footballs, and more. You can get great collector's items for a steal.

College hoop junkies go to The Area Formerly Known as Extreme Fans *College Hoops* to keep up with the scene, even during the "off-season." But **KEYWORD: College Hoops** is at its best during recruiting season.

In most sports, recruiting is a part of the game that is taken for granted. In college basketball, recruiting is warfare. High school hoop talent is the lifeblood of every college program, so coaches and alums wage bloodthirsty tugs-of-war over schoolboy blue chippers. Plenty of sites can give you the scores, and every Web site out there covers March Madness, but only *College Hoops* completely covers the recruiting rush. The area also recaps the summer all-star games, as well as the Adidas and Nike summer camps for high school juniors coming into the key recruiting period.

Link Up to the World of Golf

The beauty of **KEYWORD: GOLFonline** is its complete and total coverage of every phase of the game.

If the PGA or LPGA is your passion, *Golf Magazine Online* has some of the best golf coverage and columns on the Web. Coverage runs from each weekly Tour stop to each of the majors, complete with interviews with pros. These guys even cover the Nike and European Tours!

If you need help with your own stroke, check the Instruction section for pointers. Need a place to play? *Golf Online* has one of the most comprehensive course guides around, complete with reviews for your perusal. Or is a resort in your vacation plans? It even offers a weather report so you won't get caught in the middle of a round.

Equipment problems? *Golf Online* reviews all the newest equipment and tells you where to spend your golfing dollars.

Another great area for golfers is *iGolf*. Are you a hacker? A hooker? A slicer? Do you push, pull, short arm, stiff arm, or throw up on your putts? Or do you just like the game of golf, even if you make the turn at a cool 61? Then *iGolf* is a place to experience the game you love, even if you're not trodding the fairways.

The golfers at **KEYWORD: iGolf** are first-rate. It starts right from the First Tee, where *iGolf*'s editors pick out articulate postings on the *iGolf* message boards each week, posting these messages prominently on the Best of the Boards. Take instruction lessons from teaching

Take a Swing at Golf Trivia

So you know everything there is about golf, except how to hit like a pro? Want to put that knowledge to the challenge? Try Golf Trivia at **KEYWORD: NTN**. And don't worry that it's all Tour-based trivia. NTN had the good sense to include questions dealing with golf legend and lore, rules and etiquette, slang names and golf nicknames, so even if you don't know Byron Nelson from Judd Nelson, you'll still be able to answer scores of questions.

pro Butch Harmon, turn to the specialized Instruction section for every level of player, or drop by for Quick Tip Wednesday. There is a board for scores and notes on all the major tours, as well as coverage of the major amateur tourneys.

The *iGolf* Pro Shop has bargains abounding for brand name golf equipment, while you can also get golf course or resort reviews if you're planning a vacation or an outing.

Good Stuff!

KEYWORD: iRace has audio and video clips that put you right in the pit. Hear what Michael Andretti had to say during his final pit stop in the Miami Grand Prix. Or view an Al Unser, Jr. interview.

Get Up-to-Speed with Stock Car Racing

Auto racing is hot, even though you may not know a crankshaft from a camshaft. At least you can try to keep yourself informed with **KEYWORD: Auto Racing**.

Get in on the action at **KEYWORD: iRace**, or at least burn some rubber with racing simulation software and online fantasy racing leagues. The columns of Sparky Plug cover the real world of auto racing while photos, audio samples, and video clips bring the headlines to life. Hear Michael Andretti comment on the Miami Grand Prix, watch a movie of Christian Fittipaldi in action, or flip through the Daytona 500 photo album. Each series, league, and tour has its own folder at *iRace*, so you won't run out of articles to read any time soon.

Meet...
Sparky Plug

iRace has an unusual reporter bringing you the latest from auto racing: a talking spark plug. Sounds silly, but this is one smart auto part. Read all about it at **KEYWORD: iRace**.

Athlete Direct will get you up close and personal with NASCAR stars. At **KEYWORD: AD Auto Racing**, fans can look into the personal journals of Rusty Wallace, Ernie Irvan, Dale Jarrett, Sterling Martin, Richard Petty, and Michael Waltrip to get the lowdown on the season's biggest races. Check out In the Pits with Charlie Harville to get the grizzled veteran's view of the most current NASCAR news.

It may not look like much at first glance, but *NASCAR News* is one of my favorite things at **KEYWORD: Auto Racing**. Dozens of articles are constantly updated and added to the site every week, keeping hardcore car fans up-to-date on the NASCAR Truck Series, the Busch Grand National Series, and the NHRA standings.

Courtside Insights From a B-Ball Expert

Dave D'Allesandro's "NBA Report" in *The Sporting News* (**KEYWORD: Sporting News**) pulls no punches. It's my favorite NBA column, covering the basketball beat insightfully and consistently, even in the off-season.

It's rare to find a reporter who can accurately and intelligently break down a player's game, not simply repeat what a coach or GM tells him. D'Allesandro's independent judgment rates highly.

An added bonus: Dave enjoys receiving mail from his readers. Dave will address particularly good questions in his column. Whatever the response, you can be sure Dave knows what he's talking about.

Chatter Box

Don't agree with what *The Sporting News* columnists have to say? Well, talk back! You can join scheduled chats with these guys and tell them the real deal about your favorite teams and players, all at **KEYWORD: Sporting News.**

Preview Hockey Combat

Puck time! When you want the puck scoop on AOL, *SportsFan Radio* wins on the strength of its game-day previews at **KEYWORD: SFRN**.

Just like NHL players, *SportsFan Radio* can't and doesn't take a night off. Though it doesn't delve into the world of column writing and opinion, I love *SportsFan Radio*'s area because they focus very narrowly on each night's specific match-ups, detailing strengths and weaknesses of players and teams before the puck gets dropped at center ice.

SportsFan Radio kicks into overdrive come Stanley Cup time, going beyond its already comprehensive regular season coverage when it comes down to crunch time. You'll find everything you need to know before you sit down to watch intense playoff hockey action.

Meet...
Matt Williams

Get an inside look at what life in the Show is like for the Cleveland Indians' third baseman at **KEYWORD: Matt Williams**. The veteran ballplayer talks about the pressures and accomplishments of life in the majors.

Check Your Baseball Stats

Ask yourself this question: just how informed do you need to be about major league baseball?

No matter how knowledgeable you are, *STATS Diamond Notes* is stuffed with more info than you could ever need. Mike Mittleman is the madman who composes this abundantly rich column every week, filling it with tasty tidbits of insider info on the players and deals every baseball fan loves.

The beauty of *Diamond Notes* is the depth of Mittleman's knowledge of the game. There isn't a major or minor leaguer Mittleman can't associate with a deal, and, of course, Mike is on the trail of every rumor and trade possibility. Not to overlook the field: *Diamond Notes* astutely captures the keys to both player and team performance, observing the way single players affect the game for better or worse.

You can find *Diamond Notes* at **KEYWORD: STATS BB**, along with a wealth of other baseball material. Mittleman is the star here, but there are plenty of other STATS baseballers you'll want to check out.

Download Icons, Wavs, and Logos

The most popular Windows sports files in the Grandstand Sports Libraries are:

1. ESPN Sportscenter "Da-Da-Da" Wav
2. Sports Icons
3. Football for Windows
4. ESPN Theme Wav
5. ESPN Sportscenter Wav
6. AL Baseball Icons
7. Baseball Icon Collection
8. NBA Icons: 27 teams, NBA Logo
9. BMP: Death to Dallas Wallpaper
10. More Sports Icons

Read No-Frills Tennis Coverage

Comprehensive, current, surprisingly credible, and full of sharp columnists, **KEYWORD: CBS SportsLine** blows you away with information and insight. Covering the ATP, WTA, and the Nuveen Seniors tour, this site outscores other tennis resources. *CBS SportsLine* keeps rankings of the top 100 players up to date and recaps every Tour stop. The Newswire section gives you an unusually deep look into the current state of the Tour and its players, focusing on slumps, hot streaks, and the little differences in every player's game that make tennis interesting.

A special nod of appreciation goes to *CBS SportsLine* for its Pete Sampras area. I was more than impressed with the area devoted to every phase of Pete's life. Sampras keeps his profile so low it's almost underground; fortunately for us, *CBS SportsLine* digs deep.

Find Your Favorite NFL Team

So you're a die-hard, lifelong, to the end, bleeding orange Buccaneers fan. Where do you go on AOL? **KEYWORD:**

Team NFL, logically enough, where you'll find more than you need to know about any NFL team. Of course, we know that the Buccaneers moved away from the bright orange that I loved so much, but if you're a Buccaneers fan, you've learned to live with disappointment.

Here's what you'll find at *Team NFL*: a continuously updated rundown of every minuscule piece of trivial knowledge that fans thrive on. Check the 49ers roster or the Broncos Injured Reserve List. Find a short but informative bio of every player likely to be on your favorite team's roster. Check stats, investigate the coaching staff, download a team schedule, or recap every game.

I particularly like the sense of perspective *Team NFL* has. Each team has an area for all-team single season and career records, as well as fun facts about the stadium each team calls home. You can also research the origins of the organization and the current ownership. *Team NFL* also provides a team directory with phone numbers and addresses for every NFL organization.

I don't think it's possible to get too much info about pro football, but it's fun trying at *Team NFL*.

Insider's Tip

Can't find your sport? Try **KEYWORD: My Sport** for bowling, badminton, cricket, equitation, figure skating, fly-fishing, gymnastics, lacrosse, luge, volleyball, wrestling, and many, many more.

Kickin' It with AOL Soccer

Okay, soccer is the most widely played sport in the world, with leagues and news and players and tournaments enough to give you a headache if you try to follow it all separately. But thank goodness for the *AOL Soccer* area, where all the dribbling, headers, and goals are brought together in one comprehensive area, at **KEYWORD: Soccer**.

First, the World Cup is the biggest sporting deal in the world, so it's perfect for that sporting giant, *ABC Sports* at **KEYWORD: ABC Sports**. But if you're in the mood for something a little more personal—say, reading the journals of some of the greatest soccer players in the world—**KEYWORD: Athlete Direct** might also be a good choice. See what American World Cup and MLS stars like Alexi Lalas and Eric Wynalda have to say about their sport, their careers, and their teams. For you soccer

Good Stuff!

Women have their own playing field at **KEYWORD: WSF**. The *Women's Sports Foundation* comes online to cover the history of women in sports, coed sports, sports careers, and homophobia in the athletic arena.

savants who think you know soccer history, **KEYWORD: NTN Sports** has a specialized trivia game to challenge your formidable soccer intellect.

And of course, Soccer talk at **KEYWORD: Grandstand** is always going on in one of the soccer chat rooms. You can also post your soccer thoughts or treatises in the *Grandstand* message boards area. There's something there for soccer fans in any league.

Download Your Sports

If multimedia is your bag, *ABC's College Football* area has some great stuff for you. For starters, **KEYWORD: ABC Sports** has collected every major college football logo for easy downloading. Then the network stocks its area full of sound clips, video replays, and still shots. What impressed me most was the careful selection of clips from ABC's own broadcasts, giving you access to the most exciting moments of ABC's college football lineup. With both video and sound libraries, you fans out there can take little pieces of ABC for your own.

And for those of you who aren't sure you're capable of making full use of *ABC Sports*' multimedia sports options, there is a handy toolbox that contains answers to common questions, sound players, picture viewers, and other utilities.

Download Stellar GIFs

The most popular GIF files in the *Grandstand Sports Libraries* are:

1. NHL Logos
2. Michael Jordan
3. Basketball Logos
4. Chicago Bulls Logo
5. World Cup Logo
6. New Detroit Tigers Logo
7. Soccer Ball
8. New 95-96 NBA Logos
9. Michael Jordan Dunk!
10. 49ers Logo

Shop for Sports Collectibles

So you want to go shopping, but the thought of trotting up and down the aisles at the mall makes you queasy? Maybe you need a gift for another sports fan, but that couch or computer chair are just feeling so darn comfortable that you don't want to move? I don't want to go anywhere, so I do all my shopping at the *Sports Superstore* at **KEYWORD: Sports Superstore**.

For sports goodies, the Fan Shop is a good place to go. The shop carries a full line of major sports apparel, as well as an extensive group of collectibles and souvenirs for every fan. How happy would a baseball fan be to get a baseball autographed by Ken Griffey, Jr.? What about an autographed Penny Hardaway jersey? The Fan Shop has something for fans of any sport, including NASCAR, so don't despair for those last-minute gifts.

Ordering is easy: simply use the shopping cart feature with secure credit card ordering. And as a special Fan Shop bonus, you can even send the sports collectibles as gifts, with a special personalized message that you can type in yourself over the computer.

The Grandstand Sports Libraries, KEYWORD: **Sports Libraries**, are great places to troll for cool sports-related downloads. Pictures, transcripts, sounds, multimedia files, and games are neatly categorized by sport.

For a general overview of the best sports downloads, check out The Grandstand 1st Round Picks Library, which ranks the current top downloads from all the various sports libraries.

Here are the most popular PC sports files as we went to press:

1. Microputt: Miniature Golf
2. Hockey Game
3. 3D Pool v3.1
4. Season Football v6.3
5. Fantasy Basketball v3.0
6. Air Hockey Game
7. Empire Soccer
8. B-Ball Pro Basketball Game
9. Soccer Game
10. NBA Live 95-96 v2.3 Jordan Update

Games and Contests

Indulge Your Sports Fantasies

Sometimes just watching isn't enough. If you always wanted to be a manager, *The Grandstand* is your place. Fantasy is the name of the game here and you won't find a better-run fantasy zone than KEYWORD: **Grandstand**. Seasonal fantasy leagues include baseball, pro football, hockey, and pro basketball.

The beauty of *The Grandstand* fantasy area is how easy it is to use. The rules are clear—*The Grandstand* Commissioner's office runs like major league baseball's should. There are meeting halls for drafts and discussions about player personnel, and message boards where players can trade notes and theories on fantasy performance.

There are fees for each of *The Grandstand*'s leagues, but *The Grandstand* has such great information services that the cost is worth it. You'll find all the statistics, notes, and transactions you need to run a tight club right at your fingertips.

Show Off Your Sports Knowledge

Okay, you think you know your stuff, but are you ready to put that braggadocio on the line at KEYWORD: **NTN**? *The*

Meet...
Pro Boxers

Fight your way to **KEYWORD: AD Boxing** to read journal entries from Lennox Lewis, Evander Holyfield, and the legendary Sugar Ray.

NTN Games Studio, an offshoot of the NTV trivia made popular in sports bars around the country, specializes in trivia for all the major sports.

Now, I like to think I know what I'm talking about when it comes to sports, but even I was humbled by the challenge *NTN* presents in its seasonal trivia contests. Games run around the clock, and you can click into one at any time to pit your knowledge of athletics against fellow fans from around the world. But beware: some of these people are inhuman, or maybe they scored an answer sheet somewhere—there's no other way they could be that good. *NTN* continually updates scores and leaders of its live, multiple-choice trivia games so you can see where you stand in relation to the rest of the field. In high school, you prayed for multiple choice, and that certainly helps with playing games at *NTN*, where the questions are so inventive and challenging that you'll need all the hints you can get.

Quick: Who threw a perfect game for the Phillies in 1964?

Get Fit

Find Out the Basics

It's good to get the old ticker turning. And as a physical fitness ignoramus, I needed physical direction, and I found it at **KEYWORD: Fitness**.

Channel Jumping

To learn more about fitness, explore all the good-for-you resources of the Health Channel, **KEYWORD: Health**.

Indeed, AOL's *Fitness and Exercise* area is the perfect place for the chronically laggard, but it will also be satisfying and helpful to the most ardent physical fitness buff. It contains information on all the traditional forms of exercise, running, walking, aerobics, weight training, and bicycling.

Fitness and Exercise also offers more obscure, but interesting, areas devoted to physical health. Did you know that yoga is a fitness activity? It just goes to show that you don't have to pump iron to improve your health. Consider taking up tennis, or its faster-paced counterpart, squash. *Thrive* even has an area that tells you how to walk for fitness.

The real wealth of advice from *Fitness and Exercise* deals with nutrition. Turn to any of the areas in *Fitness and Exercise* for solid dietary advice.

How to Bulk Up

So you're feeling a little underweight? Put on weight where it will do you some good at **KEYWORD: Weightlifting**.

Gaining weight is not just about eating 'til you burst, but about adding weight and muscle in a sensible and healthy way. Basically, there are two different variations here, though they are both inextricably intertwined: weightlifting and bodybuilding. If you're a beginner, there are several different areas that will introduce you to either discipline. **KEYWORD: Thrive** will take you step by step through everything you need to do to safely and effectively take to pumping iron. Again, nutrition is just as

Channel Jumping

KEYWORD: Virtues has a lot of worthy fitness tips. Check out the exercise of the week (hacky sack?), and learn how to beat stress by playing pool and going to the movies. Sounds good to me . . .

Get Information and Support

The Personal Fitness Message Boards are filled with helpful discussion on such topics as:

- Vegetarianism
- Weightlifting
- Marathon training
- Nutrition
- Fitness products
- Professional fitness trainers
- Aerobics

The techniques that worked for others may not work for you, but it can't hurt to get some feedback before you start your new fitness regimen.

Meet. . . The Yogi

Megan Lurie McCarver is a certified Yoga instructor in both the Hatha and Kundalini styles of Yoga. She teaches keyboard yoga for stressed-out office workers at **KEYWORD: Virtues**.

important as the weightlifting, and all of the areas here will suggest different dietary changes or supplements.

There are a dozen different sites out on the Web to look into, but the best advice often comes from fellow weightlifters. The folks at the *Grandstand* provide message boards for users to trade techniques and compare regimens.

Explore the Great Outdoors

Channel Jumping

As you can see, there are a lot of sporty getaways out there. But for every possible type of vacation, you've got to explore **KEYWORD: Travel** and Meg's "Great Escape" in Chapter 15.

Find Places to Go

For active vacations, try **KEYWORD: Outdoor Adventure**. Pick an activity, such as ballooning, hiking, or mountaineering, and see your options. Or choose a destination from almost anywhere in the world and see what's available there. You can order a free brochure for several vacation packages, but don't take their word for it—get trip reviews, advice, and "best of" lists from the people at *Outdoor Adventure Online*. Top rock climbing schools, charter sailing in Greece, cattle drive Western vacations (remember the movie *City Slickers*?) . . . there's some pretty interesting stuff here. You can also take online tours, such as CyberSafari.

Attention AOL Shoppers!

Before heading out to scale a mountain or rappel down one, you'll need the proper footwear. Find a variety of inexpensive hiking boots in the Footwear section of **KEYWORD: Sports Superstore**.

Make the Most of Your Time Outdoors

If you're looking for help planning a camping trip, start with *Backpacker Magazine's Basecamp*, at **KEYWORD: Backpacker**.

The Campfire contains message boards on outdoor topics, a Destination Guide, the latest links to outdoors-related sites on the Web, and an extensive primer on the Leave No Trace program, which promotes land stewardship, minimum-impact skills, and wilderness ethics.

The Gear Connection section features extensive Gear Guides, Editor's Choice recommendations, and special areas devoted to must-have items like boots, canoes, and sleeping bags. *Basecamp* also hosts some great resources from the American Hiking Society, the only national nonprofit organization dedicated to establishing, protecting, and maintaining foot trails in America.

Last but not least, there are the resources of *Backpacker Magazine*, including extensive excerpts from the current issue, archives, and gear reviews.

Thrive@outdoors, **KEYWORD: @outdoors**, can also help you plan your getaway. They'll help you test your gear before you take it on the trail, make sure you buy hiking boots that really fit, explain the ins and outs of water purifiers and filters, and give you a backpacking checklist of items you absolutely shouldn't leave home without. Get ideas for weekend hikes, swap adventures at the Saturday Night Campfire chat, and find members' favorite running and walking routes. It even tells you how to fix a flat bike tire—useful information for anyone with a bike, even if you just ride it to and from work.

These resources and many more can be found at the *Great Outdoors* area. **KEYWORD: Great Outdoors** is a good jumping-off point for fun in the open air.

Insider's Tip

Use your Log Manager to keep records of instructive chats. You could end up with a text file of important health and safety tips to avoid injury in a variety of active sports.

Get in the Hunt and Go Fish

The people at the *Hunting Broadcast Network* know what hunters want: hunters want to communicate with other hunters. Isn't that the best way to get information that's reliable and up-to-the-minute? If you want to learn from other hunters, *HBN* is your spot.

Guess what? *HBN*'s sibling site, *Fishing Broadcast Network,* is just as good. Hunters and anglers have a lot in common, and so do these information-packed areas.

Here's what you'll find at **KEYWORD: HBN** and **KEYWORD: FBN**: active chat rooms and message boards, trivia games, and a goofy "Caption It" game. You can also share photos from your latest hunting or fishing trip in the *HBN* photos area. The Gourmet Guides feature everything hunt-able or fish-able, all cooked up.

Virtual hunting is also a possibility, in *HBN*'s software library. My favorite is Prairie Dog Hunt: Judgment

Chatter Box

After a long day of hunting or fishing, trade stories with others in the *Grandstand*'s outdoor sports message areas at **KEYWORD: Sports Boards**.

Day. It's an online version of my favorite arcade game, Whack-a-Mole. Not to be outdone, *FBN* has games like FBN Concentration: it's like the memory game you played as a kid, except with fly patterns.

HBN and *FBN* have plenty of serious resources as well, including Black's Shotgunners Source, and a really cool clickable map that displays the hunting and fishing resources, In Your Neck o' the Woods.

Prepare for Ski Trips

9 HEAD DOWN THE SLOPES

How do you find the best ski resorts, most challenging slopes, coziest winter lodges, and safest equipment? Research the multitude of ski resources on AOL:

- **KEYWORD: Skiing** is the hub for all downhill areas on AOL.
- **KEYWORD: SkiNet** gives you individual mountain coverage and great skiing tips.
- **KEYWORD: Ski Zone** can help you plan an entire vacation package.
- **KEYWORD: Ski Reports** gives you the scoop on weather and snowfall all across America.

Before your next ski vacation, you need to visit **KEYWORD: iSki**. If you're new to skiing, or if your skills are a little rusty, Ski School helps you brush up on terminology and preseason conditioning. The Interactive Lessons section is worth looking at just to see a cool use of computer technology—even if you don't need any pointers.

Ready to make concrete plans? The Mountain Club can save you big bucks on lift tickets and lodging, and the Banditos give you the inside dirt about resorts from Argentina to Colorado. You can also pick up new gear or track the weather at the resort of your choice.

If you can't get to the slopes yourself, follow the adventures of the SnoMads as they travel from resort to resort, chronicling their travels and uploading digital ski photography. Or download some skiing photos—it's not as exciting as racing down the slopes yourself, but at least you can't break your leg that way.

Get Extreme

Find Athletic Adventures

Like taking chances? Like getting involved—way involved? Then check out the *Extreme Sports* area, where sports meets daredevil meets pure rock 'n' roll messiness.

If you love that adrenaline rush, you can get it at **KEYWORD: Extremists**. Follow the X-games, learn about scuba diving (**KEYWORD: Scuba**), and find extreme Web links. Message boards for you adventurous sorts discuss hang gliding, jetskiing, kayaking, fencing, and dirt jumping, to name a few.

Wage War with Paint

Paintball isn't as dangerous as other extreme sports, but it sure is messy. **KEYWORD: Paintball** features Tales from the Front, where paintballers tell stories of successful attacks and humiliating counterattacks. If you've never been involved in paintball combat, find out what to expect from your first battle, what to wear, and what it costs.

In the message board area members share advice on equipment, fields and courses, strategies, alternative weapons, and camouflage. The Meet Your Fellow Paintballers section lets you do just that. Read bios of other members, and submit your own. To find paintball warriors outside AOL, subscribe to newsgroups like *rec.sport.paintball* or visit paintball Web pages.

Meet...
the Surf Doc

Dr. Robert Budman, M.D., answers questions about vertigo, rashes from surfboard wax, stingrays, and other surfing-related hazards at **KEYWORD: Surflink**.

Get on Your Bike and Ride!

Mountain bikers, this is the area that will get your shifters twisting. At **KEYWORD: iBike**, you'll get your hands dirty with mud, dust, and all that's singletrack. For example, if you want to know how to adjust that pesky loose headset, this area's got the lowdown, complete with illustrations. If you don't know what exactly a headset is, don't worry about it. The folks at *iBike* can help with that, too.

Of course there's more than just adjustments here—clicking on the Ride button gives you access to trail and vacation info from around the country, and the Weather button offers news of the mountain biking racing climate, and lets you get local forecasts delivered to your mailbox daily. Not too shabby.

Channel Jumping

Kids have their own coaches, fan message boards, and sports chats in the Kids Only Channel at **KEYWORD: KO Sports**.

Upgrade

AOL 4.0 will let you include pictures in email so you can show off snapshots of ski trips and snowboarding adventures.

Two aspects of this area really make it stand apart from other mountain biking sources. The first is the Punks section, which features thought-provoking hypothetical questions and wipe-out stories. The second stand-out aspect is the Bike Horoscope, which gives predictions like "A spaceship lands in your front yard with huge stenciled letters on the side that say 'Mars Mtn. Bike Team, Ship 2'." You've been warned.

Good Stuff!

KEYWORD: ibike shows you the right way to Accessorize Your Kids to ensure their biking safety. Make sure they use lights, reflectors, and helmets, and teach them how to make their own minor repairs.

If you've gotten this far, you know that AOL Sports is deeper than the mid-winter snow in Aspen. Fortunately, there's one sure protection against a sports information avalanche: **KEYWORD: Sports**. You can't go wrong if you start at the opening screen. The sports nuts who work on AOL Sports know how much they've got, and they spend a lot of their time making sure that the opening screen gives members instant access to the latest, the best, and the most relevant sports content *right now*.

So if you're suffering from information overload, you just have to remember that one **KEYWORD: Sports**. AOL Sports will take it from there.

Maximize Your Entertainment Options

You know how you get to that point in the day when you've earned a few minutes of diversion? For me it comes around 10:30 a.m., after I've taken a sustained crack at everything I *have* to do. That's when I get my daily dose of entertainment. I start with last night's David Letterman's Top Ten list (**KEYWORD: Late Show**), move on to a Dilbert cartoon (**KEYWORD: Dilbert**), then check my horoscope if I have time (**KEYWORD: Astronet**). And the *Celebrity Fix* area gives me all the dish from Hollywood insiders like gossip columnist Matt Drudge.

Sometimes that's all the entertainment I can squeeze in during that morning break, but then I'm often back in the Entertainment Channel—for a few minutes at a time—during lunch, or just after work: I'm in there reading a movie review, or checking to see what new CDs are on the shelves, or looking for a TV listing. It's great for that. If you're a workaholic like me, you won't let yourself take a few hours off to catch a movie, but you can at least use AOL's entertainment resources to maximize the time that you will have later in the day or week. That's how I justify my trips into the Entertainment zone—"Hey, I'm making my entertainment more efficient!"

Also, if half the fun is the anticipation, AOL lets you anticipate and plan for those hours or days (like on the weekend) when you can cut loose with a vengeance.

YOUR TICKET TO THE STARS

The Entertainment Channel's free weekly newsletter, *Star.log*, guides you to the best entertainment features on AOL, spotlights the hottest stars, and lets you know about upcoming online celebrity appearances. Go to **KEYWORD: StarLog** to sign up.

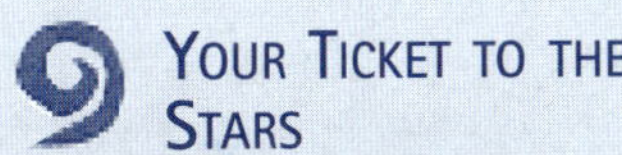

9 Meeting Places for Die-Hard TV Fans

If you missed one crucial episode of *Melrose Place* or you want to know who's going to be on your favorite talk show this week, AOL and its community of members can help.

Get TV celebrity gossip, interviews, and archives at KEYWORD: **TV People.**

KEYWORD: **TV Viewers** has live chats during shows, trivia, and chat transcripts. To see if your favorite show has an AOL forum, check the listing at KEYWORD: **TV Shows.**

Meet the Stars

Chat with the Queen of Nice

Rosie O'Donnell's online area, KEYWORD: **Rosie**, confirms what her fans have always believed: she really is *that* nice. She shows up in the chat room as often as her busy schedule allows, and her sidekick John McD has his own message board where he talks to fans frequently. The RO Safety Reminder tells members how to identify Rosie impersonators, avoid password scams, and play it safe in chat rooms. The staff here really is looking out for the fans.

Fans of the *Rosie O'Donnell Show* will find a lot of exciting things here. Take a peek at Rosie's Scrapbook for a photo of Rosie kissing her idol Tom Cruise or a shot of her with comedy legend Bette Midler. Video and audio clips from the show are archived, in case you missed it when Rosie chatted with Madonna, Hillary Rodham Clinton, or Barry Manilow. Subscribe to a free weekly email newsletter that keeps you up-to-date on both the show and the online area, or join Rosie's official fan club.

There are boards devoted to all aspects of the show—even one for kids—and the chat room is always packed. "I signed up for America Online 11 months ago because of *Rosie Online* and it has been the best time, thanks to Rosie, the great hosts (go Deb!), and all the great Rosie fans," writes one member. "Here's to many more years to come!"

Meet... Oprah

You can email Oprah Winfrey, join her book club and mailing list, and participate in the daily poll at KEYWORD: **Oprah**.

Advice From Oprah

Oprah Online, like the *Oprah Winfrey Show*, tries to help you out. Look for lessons in parenting, romance tips, and advice from Oprah's personal trainer, Bob Greene. You might become happier by participating in the Gratitude area—keep a journal, read inspirational "thoughts for the day," or join in message board topics like "Random Acts of Kindness" and "Items We Treasure."

KEYWORD: Oprah also connects you to Oprah's Book Club, where you can discuss great novels like Toni Morrison's *Song of Solomon* and Wally Lamb's *She's Come Undone*. You'll also find book recommendations that may make your kids fall in love with reading.

Read celebrity interviews, take polls on subjects like stay-at-home parents, or send email to Oprah herself. Of course, you'll find a lot of information about Oprah's show, including schedules, Frequently Asked Questions, pictures, sound bytes, and video clips. If you have a question, one of the dedicated fans in the chat room or message boards can probably answer it for you.

Meet... the ER cast

Get to know the actors and creative team of everyone's favorite blood-and-guts soap opera, *ER*. **KEYWORD: ER** includes an episode guide, staff biographies, and trivia.

Stay Up Late with David Letterman

From the home office in Wahoo, Nebraska, it's **KEYWORD: Late Show**. Even if you're a morning person, you can still be part of the prime-time fun with *Late Show Online*. Catch Dave's opening remarks from the past week, chuckle over last night's Top Ten list, and find out if the guests on tonight's show are worth the potential sleep deprivation.

Only on AOL

KEYWORD: TV People keeps archives of chat sessions with stars of television, movies, and music. If your favorite stars haven't visited AOL lately, they probably have message boards devoted to them anyway.

You'll find everything you love about the *Late Show*—hams and all—but there is plenty of interactive fun here that you can't get by watching TV. Submit to the weekly member-written Top Ten list, or nominate a culinary treat to be Rupert's Sandwich of the Week (past winners include Tuna & Salami and the Boutros Boutros Delight). View Leonard Tepper's suit of AOL disks, salute the Worldwide Pants employee of the week, and get daily updates on Dave's age, weight, and mood. FAQs are available to tell you how to get tickets to the show, and even how to get your Stupid Pet Trick on the air.

Meet... the Late Show Crew

David Letterman, Paul, Biff, and the rest of the gang make **KEYWORD: Late Show** the crazy place it is. Laugh at last night's Top Ten list and dig through the other funny stuff on Dave's Desk.

Finally, no self-respecting Dave fan should miss the Top Ten archives from both Dave and fellow members. Check out the Top Ten Signs You've Been Spending Too

Much Time on AOL—let's just say if your Buddy List has less than 350,000 people on it, you're doing okay.

What's on TV?

Insider's Tip

What's on TV. . . for the next two weeks? Take advantage of your 57 channels with **KEYWORD: TV Source.** Find out when any program airs in your area, from esoteric PBS specials to blockbuster movies on cable.

Tune into ABC

The Test Tube section is the real surprise at **KEYWORD: ABC** is a major network really hosting something this weird? Tune in for out of the ordinary features like the too-dumb-to-be-true stories of Stupid Central and Web links to movie clichés, Shakespearean insults, and the Hollywood Stock Exchange.

You'll also be happy to find all the conventional features you'd expect from something called *ABC Online*. ABC News is obviously brimming with

Working for the Mouse

Spending 40 hours a week at Disney World sounds more like a vacation than a job. **KEYWORD: Disney Jobs** outlines current employment opportunities at the Magic Kingdom. They often need lifeguards, parade performers, and even non-costumed folks like Human Resources people.

How to Find Sci-Fi Hotspots

AOL has a lot of areas devoted to science fiction. Here are just a few.

At **KEYWORD: X Files** you'll get news and multimedia downloads to complement the extreme weirdness and spooky plot twists and that follow Agents Mulder and Scully. The forum can't actually explain unknown phenomena, but it does provide a place for fans to trade theories.

For the latest on the other warped TV show by Chris Carter (the creator of the *X-Files*), turn to the *Millennium Forum*, **KEYWORD: Millennium**.

The *SciFi Channel*, **KEYWORD: SciFi Channel**, is not just for Trekkies. It's also for sci-fi writers, astronomers, and the generally curious. **KEYWORD: Trek** is just for Trekkies, however, and it's a good thing it is—a fanbase this huge deserves its own space.

information, but so is ABC Sports—find game scores, recaps, schedules, and players' stats. ABC Daytime specializes in soap fan interaction with busy chat rooms, opinion polls, and games. There's even a creative, fun, G-rated area for your kids.

Channel Jumping

KEYWORD: Digital City has lots of metropolitan entertainment, including guides to local movies, music, and nightclubs.

Take a Trip Down Memory Lane

This is a great escape hatch when everything on TV looks stale. Take it back a few years, to Nick at Nite's TV Land (**KEYWORD: Nick**).

In a complete role-reversal, the commercials are some of the best things here. "Retromercials" remind you of catchy phrases from Mr. Clean (gets rid of dirt and grime and grease in just a minute), Bounty (the quicker picker-upper), and Ovaltine (it's a winner). If this kind of nostalgia is up your alley, you can download pictures and sound clips from Retromercials and your favorite classic TV shows.

If all this backtracking makes you feel old (or if you're too young to recognize any of the Retromercial quotes) go play at *Nickelodeon Online*. Don't miss the downloadable Digital Toys, a Trivia Challenge, and a chat room called the Nick Blabbatorium.

Music TV from North of the Border

MuchMusic is a little bit of MTV, a little bit of VH1, and a lot of Canada. **KEYWORD: MuchMusic** is understandably loyal to Canadian favorites like Sarah McLachlan, but gives airtime to artists from all over. You can discover many interesting bands with galleries, audio clips, and video samples. If you get hooked, don't worry—more and more U.S. cable affiliates carry *MuchMusic* these days.

Sample Both Flavors of Music TV

Music television tends to flash images across your TV screen at a dizzying pace, but no one can tell you how fast to click your mouse. That means music video fans can take their time at **KEYWORD: MTV**. Click on the "Weekly Schedule" so you won't miss your favorite part of MTV, be it *Singled Out*, *Beavis and Butt-head*, or actual videos. Everything an MTV fan could want is here somewhere—use the refreshingly text-only MAP O' MTV to make sure you find it.

MTV's more grown-up sibling, VH1, is also online at **KEYWORD: VH1**. The forum focuses on the artists who make the music, including biographies, regularly scheduled

SMART TV THAT ISN'T A SNOOZE

The History Channel might have kept you glued to the tube watching the miniseries *Roots* or the movie *Zulu.* Now **KEYWORD: History** keeps history buffs glued to their computer—especially military history devotees. *History Channel Online* also includes prime-time listings so you don't miss an episode of *Year by Year.*

chats, and transcripts of chat sessions past. Speaking of the past, the '70s and '80s return in the Retro Rack, and you can download big chunks of the '90s from the Digital Gallery's hundreds of video clips and sound bytes. Those well-versed in several decades' worth of music should try their hand at the interactive VH1 trivia game. I got clobbered by music know-it-alls, but it was still fun.

Catch Up with the Soaps

Soap operas have a way of getting ahead of you. Take your eyes off them for a few days, or weeks, and half the cast has divorced and re-married. *Soap Opera Digest Online*, **KEYWORD: SOD**, is a great way to keep up with the latest news from both daytime and prime-time dramas. Sneak previews for each show, synopses of the past week, and all the latest comings and goings of characters are posted here. Go into the chat rooms to talk with other fans, and the writers and editors of the *Digest*.

At the *Soap Opera Digest Online* site, you'll get filled in on any shows you might have missed: who did what to whom. Plus, there are listings for events where you can meet and greet the real-life stars of your favorite soaps in your city. And the truly hooked should visit Diva's Hall of Records and read her psychoanalysis of soap characters.

Meet...
Premiere's Movie Critic

Libby Gelman-Waxner's one-of-a-kind take on the movies can be found at **KEYWORD: Premiere**. With column titles like "The People vs. Movie Hype" and "Warhol-ier Than Thou," how can you lose?

At the Movies

Thumbs Up or Thumbs Down?

Before you get to the ticket window, make sure the movie is worth seeing. Start with **KEYWORD: New Releases**. Open any movie's folder to find several opinions about it. **KEYWORD: Movie Reviews** brings in even more expert advice, from top-notch critics like Joel Siegel and Gene Siskel.

A great AOL movie resource is **KEYWORD: Critics**. The staff of *Critic's Inc.* write on-target reviews of movies, music, books, TV, and computer games. A useful feature for parents, is the Kids-in-Mind section, rates movies from "harmless" to "watch out!" in the categories of Sex/Nudity, Violence/Gore, and Profanity. To keep track of new reviews and save time, subscribe to their free newsletter.

Make the Most of Your VCR

So, based on all these great online movie critics, you decide to skip Hollywood's latest offering and rent a video instead. **KEYWORD: Home Video** will let you know what movies arrived on the shelves this week and how good they are. Renting a video is cheaper than going to a movie theater, but you still want to make sure you don't waste two hours or show your kids something inappropriate.

Looking for something more obscure than the New Releases aisle at the video store? **KEYWORD: Movie Review DB** might be able to help. What the *Movie Review Database* lacks in detail, it makes up for by being amazingly comprehensive and extremely big. Kill some time by browsing the archives for short reviews of what seems like every movie made since 1920. Moviegoers in a hurry can search the database for a certain title, star, director, or year of release.

The Ultimate Movie Guide

No film buff should go another day without visiting the Internet Movie Database, *http://www.imdb.com.* Find every possible bit of information about any movie (reviews, trivia, quotes, ratings, plot summaries, cast and crew list, and more). Find out where filmmakers goofed. Download clips. Read the filmography of every crew member who worked on any movie. Brush up on Oscar history. This is the definitive way for movie fans to settle any and all trivia debates!

How to Plan Your Evening

You've called the babysitter. You've made dinner reservations. You have everything you need for dinner and a movie with your spouse except. . . the movie. Figure out what to see at **KEYWORD: MovieLink**. You can search for whatever factor is most important: find out what's playing tonight at a certain time, which movie theater has a certain movie, or the list of movies showing at your local tenplex.

To avoid the mobs at opening night, buy advance tickets online and save yourself the hassle. Other *MovieLink* bells and whistles include downloadable movie trailers, previews, chat, and a Parents' Guide that explains, among other things, the difference between PG and PG-13.

Entertainment Mags and Gossip Rags

Chatter Box

KEYWORD: Live is your source for celebrity chat information. Past guests include actresses, musicians, and Elvis impersonators. The MTV game show *Singled Out* holds an online game every week, too.

Leading actors, principal roles, movie openings: **KEYWORD: Premiere** covers the firsts in films. There are paparazzi photos to download, lengthy reviews of newly released features, and a selection of trivia games like Dead or Alive (Myrna Loy: dead, unfortunately). Libby, columnist for the print version, provides your daily dose of on-target, funny, sarcastic movie commentary. Go Behind the Scenes with the Party Guy, or straight into the Screening Room for the latest news on the most recent releases.

Hollywood News, **KEYWORD: Hollywoodnews**, is updated seven days a week, several times a day. It covers not just film, but also music, books, and all sorts of things that the word "Hollywood" doesn't usually suggest. The Feature Presentations section contains video and sound clips, still photos, full-text movie notes, and Interactive Media Kits—self-contained programs that are interactive samples of upcoming films. Actually, they're sort of online versions of those great trailers that precede the main features in theaters. And, like the trailers, they are often the best thing about the whole production.

Channel Jumping

KEYWORD: NTN has live, interactive trivia games for knowledgeable fans of movies, music, and even *Star Trek*. The Games chapter of this book discusses the wide variety of online trivia games.

Newsboys yelling "Extra! Extra! Read all about it!" used to mean late-breaking news. In these more technologically advanced times, *Extra Online* means the same thing. **KEYWORD: Extra** is updated daily, so it's easy to keep tabs on politics (those crazy Kennedys. . .), the Royal Family, and the latest real-life courtroom drama that you can't help but follow. Because *Extra* is so on top of things, you can also get movie reviews before the movie even comes out. And while news and reviews are all well and good, there's no shame in sitting through a just-okay movie if you're a big fan of the leading man or lady. Actors and actresses are in the spotlight of the STARZ section.

Chatter Box

The *Playbill Online* message boards (**KEYWORD: Playbill Online**) have boards for kids and teens who love the stage, working actors and techies, and amateur theater critics.

How to Break into the Biz

For some, learning about the entertainment industry isn't enough. Maybe you want to be part of the industry yourself. Get ahead of the competition by stopping at **KEYWORD: Acting** on your way to the studio.

Casting calls are posted here for models, actors, actresses, dancers, and singers to be featured in such projects as independent films, theatrical motion pictures, stage productions, and fashion catalogs. You can upload your headshot along with a resume, or two separate modeling shots. While you can leave a resume only, talent tends to get noticed more if you include a photo with the description of your previous work.

Broadway hopefuls can find stage-specific casting calls in the Features section of **KEYWORD: Playbill Online.** If performance isn't your specialty but you still love the theater, look for musical, academic, and administrative jobs.

Channel Jumping

Actors can also talk about the challenges of their jobs in the *About Work* message boards, **KEYWORD: About Work**.

Music to our Ears

Who Shares Your Taste in Music?

KEYWORD: Music is the starting point for online harmony, with member reviews, fan forums, concert information, and other areas I've described below. But what you really can't miss is the MusicSpace Message Center. You'll find other aficionados of whatever discs you listen to, whether you see concerts at stadiums, local clubs, or Symphony Hall. I know what you're thinking: "I bet they don't have a message board for [insert obscure artist here]." Well, every bizarre band I tried had a board, so

Insider's Tip

If you've never heard of the bands at **KEYWORD: Artist Underground**, you're not alone—hardly anyone has, and that's the point. Find out about the best unsigned and independent rockers around.

Good Stuff!

Music 'zines (independent magazines), obscure record labels, and modern rock radio stations can all be found at **KEYWORD: Alternative**.

your tastes are probably represented, too. If not, you can create a board without too much trouble.

There's also a board devoted to musicians working in the industry, or trying to break in. Check here for forums ranging from disabled musicians to marching bands to *a cappella* groups.

Find Everything Acoustic

Fans of folk music might not think to look in the *Country* area (**KEYWORD: Country**), but that's where to find the Folk/Acoustic message board. The Bluegrass & Old Time Music board is there, too.

Country music lovers won't be disappointed, either. Browse tour dates, country music history, and Web pages for many popular country artists.

♦ ♦ ♦ ♦ ♦ ♦ ♦ ♦ ♦ ♦ ♦ ♦

Jam with Other Musicians

Musicians have great resources to play with on AOL.

MusicSpace's *The Studio*, **KEYWORD: Studio**, has links to record companies, online magazines, equipment swapping, and places to kvetch.

The *Creative Musician's Coalition*, **KEYWORD: CMC**, is a worldwide coalition dedicated to the advancement of new music and the success of independent musicians. Swap stories about marketing strategy, resources and education, radio and media, and festivals and fun. Discuss dozens of music genres and read artist profiles in the libraries, which also contain multimedia and sound files.

DRUM Magazine, **KEYWORD: Drum**, can't be beat with its profiles of Industry Insiders such as Craigie Zildjian, and downloadable notations and advice from the Lessons column.

For guitarists from classical to punk, there's GTR, the *Guitar Special Interest Group*, at **KEYWORD: Guitar**, with great hot lists, links, and spots to post requests or ads for lessons, jam sessions, upcoming gigs, and equipment.

Digital musicians hang at the *Composers' Coffeehouse*, at **KEYWORD: Composer**. Here there are links to businesses, music industry data, and MIDI files to download, especially for Macintosh musicians (who will also like the *Macintosh Music & Sound Forum* at **KEYWORD: MMS**).

Craig Anderton's *Sound, Studio, & Stage* has industry news and more at **KEYWORD: SSS**.

Don't Buy the Whole CD From a One-Hit Wonder

Music lovers are constantly bombarded by new albums that may or may not be worth their short supply of time and dollars. Any given artist might be the next big thing, a one-hit wonder, or a total flop. The best way to shop for new music is to get informed—with MusicSpace's *New Releases* area, at **KEYWORD: New Music**. Information about new releases is nicely organized and easily accessible.

Click on the title of the newly released album you're considering for all kinds of information about it. Download sound clips and read reviews by professionals and fellow AOLers. There are also tracklists, photos, band biographies, tour dates, and Web sites. To see what's on the musical horizon, choose "New Releases Full Listing," which includes release dates several weeks in the future.

Classical music aficionados should check out the weekly CD reviews at **KEYWORD: CultureFinder**. If you don't know much about classical music, but would like to learn more, the Recommended Recordings can get you started.

Music Sensations

Paul McCartney, Tori Amos, Whitney Houston, Boyz II Men, Gloria Estefan, Harry Connick Jr., Joan Osborne, R.E.M., Peter Gabriel, Pete Townshend, Madonna, Sting, Seal, Jewel, and others are all profiled at the *VH1 Artist Showcase*, **KEYWORD: VH1**.

Fun in the Aisles of Online Record Stores

What can you do at the areas for Tower Records and Blockbuster Music? Buy music, obviously—but you didn't need me to tell you that. The good news is that each area has unexpected treats hidden amid the rows of CDs.

KEYWORD: Blockbuster sends you to their WWW site, where you can shop for books, videos, and games as well as tunes. But even if you're not in the market for media, you can enter trivia contests and sweepstakes without spending a dime. Sound clips of new music are also free for the taking, to help with the "to buy or not to buy" decision. If there's something you want that they don't have, Blockbuster will special order it for you. So go ahead and track down all those bands you haven't heard since college.

Good Stuff!

Can't remember who sings that song that's been in your head all day? The Tune Finder at **KEYWORD: Tower** lets you search for a CD by artist, album title, or song.

How to Make a Boring Day Fun

You know when you're sick, but not that sick? When your 101 degree temperature or raspy throat means your hypochondriac cubiclemates say, "Stay home! Don't infect us!"

When I was a kid, a day at home wearing my PJs could get mightly boring. And before I got online, I'd go through piles of unread magazines whenever I got the flu. I feel like a potatohead just watching hour after hour of TV—I miss that all-important interactivity I've gotten so used to online.

A Little Bit Dilbert...

I start my day off on AOL with a visit to **KEYWORD: Dilbert**. This time the slogan, "The Dilbert Zone: it's BETTER than WORKING" has a special meaning for me. I'm logged in, appearing on my boss's Buddy List, but blissfully sloppy in my plaid PJs and slippers.

...and a Little Bit Rock 'n Roll

Today my plan is to hang out in all the really fun, slightly slothful parts of AOL that I can't justify visiting on a regular day—including the latest *Rolling Stone* (**KEYWORD: Rolling Stone**). Yep, they really enhance the print version here. Now, it really, literally rocks!

Here, I can rate the cover (cool, sux, or who cares?), download audio from the cover interview and reviewed albums, and find out what the writers really thought about their assignments. Also, there's a whole section where you can submit your photo to be on the online "cover." Ordinary cubicle dweller sick at home? Sure, but at least I can pretend to be Meg, Rock Star Extraordinaire.

Staying home

means a day of "research" on my timesheet instead of a blemish on my perfect health record. See, all of these old media outlets have really cool things happening on AOL, and it's important to experience them the same way as all our members at home do.

The AOL Quiz Show Experience

The play areas are often the first to use the latest and greatest AOL technologies—they jazz up the areas with sound and video files and games galore. Boredom has no place in the Entertainment Channel. For instance, I may never get on a TV quiz show, but I can go up against other AOL members in the live Nick at Night Trivia Challenge. "Who provides the voice for Bart Simpson?" Wait, I used to know that... . In addition to finding out the real answer (Nancy Cartwright), I learn that everyone in the Simpson family was named after someone in Matt Groening's family. Now there's an interesting nugget to use at the water cooler when I'm back in the office.

The same real-time quiz technology is in use at *Premiere*'s area (KEYWORD: **Premiere**), where I score pathetically. I also fail at the "Dead or Alive" game. Raymond Burr died of liver cancer at age 76, on Sept. 12, 1993. Yikes! I'd better read a few of *Premiere*'s in-depth articles and get my Movie IQ up a tad.

All this movie mania is infectious, so my next stop is the *Movie Review Database* (KEYWORD: **Movie Review DB**), where I look up reviews for all the movies showing on cable this afternoon, and figure out how many won Academy Awards (or were nominated), in order to help make my selection.

A Chance to Chat with Rosie O'Donnell

Of course, it'll have to wait until after the *Rosie O'Donnell* show (KEYWORD: **Rosie**). I pop over to see who's the guest today and what I've missed lately. Then I download a couple of photos of Tom Cruise, Rosie's crush (okay, I admit it—mine too), and get the address to write for tickets. Maybe today she'll make one of her regular visits to the chat room and I'll get to toss her a virtual kooshball.

Modem Lady sends me an IM to ask how I'm doing. "Working hard and infecting no one," I reply. "Chicken soup on the stove and research well underway." Yep, all in all, I have to say that staying home sick is a lot more entertaining—and less lonely—than it used to be.

Movies Galore

Whenever I'm not sure where to go, I just try a random keyword to see what'll happen. KEYWORD: **Movies** brings up *@ the Movies*, which links to everything from *New York Times* cinema stories to original AOL member reviews of good flicks for kids in Parent Soup.

Hmmmm...

Soup is a good idea. I head to KEYWORD: **Jewish Foods**, find a recipe from The Israel Foreign Ministry for authentic chicken soup, and take a chopping, stirring, and mixing break. I'll let lunch simmer while I wander around some more online.

Insider's Tip

SPIN Online's section *alt.media* (**KEYWORD: Heavy**) reviews comics, games, Web pages, television shows, books, and movies.

The first thing that caught my eye at **KEYWORD: Tower** was the alluring phrase "CDs Under $10." It wasn't stuff like *The Greatest Hits of Polka*, either—among the selections were Dylan, Nine Inch Nails, Miles Davis, and Bach. The Top 1000 sellers are also available pretty cheap. And if you don't know what the Squirrel Nut Zippers sound like or you've never heard Pat Boone singing heavy metal, the Listening Station is worth a few minutes of your time.

Find a Concert, Then Chat About It

KEYWORD: Spin has a lot of worthwhile material, but the weird-looking icons and vague section titles make stuff hard to find. It's time for *SPIN* 101. Ready?

Sound Bytes has concert tour information in a handy searchable database. While you're writing activities on your calendar, check out the listing of upcoming online chats.

Heavy Rotation includes features, interviews, music reviews, and concert reviews.

In the Downlode section, electronic publishers can upload 'zines, newsletters, and online comics to the Homegrown Digi-Zine library. Likewise, any band or musician can submit sound and video clips to the Cyber Garage. Sound clips, pictures, chat transcripts, and software tools are all available here as well.

Thankfully, the little icon that says "SPIN Mag" is just what you'd think: this month's issue of *SPIN*, uploaded two days before the print version hits the newsstands. Past issues of *SPIN* can also be found in the SPINonline Archives. You can't throw the online area on your coffee table, but otherwise it stacks up to the print version pretty well.

Music From Around the Globe

When you travel to **KEYWORD: World Music** you can visit places like:

- The Bob Marley Supersite, the Jammin' Reggae Archives, and the Reggae and Ska message boards
- *NetNoir* Music, a center for Afrocentric music of all kinds
- *Hispanic Online*'s Latin music area
- The Web page of the world music magazine *Roots World*

Rolling Stone Offers Something Old, Something New

It's good ol' *Rolling Stone*, with a high-tech twist. *Rolling Stone Online* (**KEYWORD: Rolling Stone**) has many of the features we've grown attached to in the paper-bound version, like Random Notes, interviews, and reviews. But the online version has features you can't find in a print magazine, like the interactive Question of the Week (Marilyn Manson: "First Amendment poster boy or an irresponsible hate anathema?") which links to message boards. This month's cover story is here, but it's interactive—you click to turn the page, and you can take quizzes, read notes from the writer of the story, jump to related facts, and download video and sound clips as you go.

Insider's Tip

Fans of Jimmy Buffet or the Iguanas should join the tropical party at the *Parrot Key* area, **KEYWORD: Parrot Key**.

Music Fans Unite

What do Metallica and the Grateful Dead have in common? The fans of both bands are cyber-sophisticated enough to have their own AOL areas.

The *Metallica Forum*, **KEYWORD: Metallica**, is the place to go for all the latest information on tour dates, album releases, album samples, photos, and a discography. The 100 Top Frequently Asked Questions even covers their favorite foods.

Hop on the *Dead Forum* bus and go truckin' down the infobahn at **KEYWORD: Dead**. This psychedelic area features lively message board topics, a store of Dead tunes and paraphernalia, and files on other favorites like Phish. Interviews, retrospectives, and the Rose Garden Chatroom connect Dead past with idealistic future. It's a well-organized, community-oriented way for Deadheads and Fellow Travelers keep in touch in the post-Jerry era.

If neither "Kill 'Em All" nor "Infrared Roses" are your style, **KEYWORD: MusicFan** lists other fan forums and Web pages. For more band fandom than you can handle, try the practically all-inclusive Ultimate Band List at *http://ubl.com*.

Chatter Box

The Grateful Dead chat rooms, **KEYWORD: Dead**, have "busdrivers" who make sure nothing ugly happens—their duties range from telling newbies the rules to kicking out abusive people, but they hope you see them "as friends, not cops."

From Matisse to the Monkees

KEYWORD: Image lets you view and download art from the masters, but I was surprised to also find album covers, city skylines, and posters of celebrities. Subjects with their own "galleries" include Elvis, French advertising, jazz legends, sports, patents and trademarks, Norman Rockwell, animation, Mardi Gras, folk art, food, mousepads, and the Cirque du Soleil.

Rolling Stone Online is a whole lot of flashy fun, but beware: they warn that "this area will explode if your modem speed falls below 14.4," and it's probably true.

Explore the Art World

Getting from Main Street USA to Broadway

You just got tickets for *Cats*, but are they good seats? Find out at **KEYWORD: Playbill**, where theatergoers have access to seating charts for the Winter Garden Theatre and many other venues. *Playbill Online* also helps you plan your next excursion with theater listings, national tour dates, and, for the Broadway-bound, lists of restaurants and hotels in the Big Apple. Watch for industry news, star biographies, and actors' scheduled appearances in the chat room.

KEYWORD: Culturefinder hosts Broadway 101, a guide which will give experienced theater fans the inside track without baffling newcomers. Current Broadway and off-Broadway productions are listed, complete with capsule descriptions, schedules, and ticket information. Broadway 101 reports on venues such as Lincoln Center, offering a CultureFinder Tip for each one. For instance, "Although Carnegie Hall is well-known for its fabulous acoustics, the seats in the balcony offer the clearest sound of all, so as long as you are not afraid of heights, you can actually benefit by saving some bucks." Another money-saving option that Broadway 101 explains is TKTS, which offers discounted theater tickets.

The most discerning theatergoers will appreciate the news and reviews of the *New York Times Theater* section, **KEYWORD: NYT Theater**. It lists the same critics as the print version, and all the reviews of current and past productions are archived and searchable. The directory of major Broadway and Off-Broadway theaters with addresses and phone numbers is a great resource for out-of-towners.

Channel Jumping

Don't know much about the arts? **KEYWORD: CultureFinder** helps with features like Broadway 101, a who's-who list of cultural All Stars, and "cocktail party facts" to drop so you look like you know more than you do.

Take a Crash Course in Culture

Lots of people want to learn more about classical music, opera, dance, and theater, but who knows where to start? If there's one way to get cultured quickly, it's with KEYWORD: **CultureFinder**, the online address for the arts. Not only does this area explain the ins and outs of Broadway and recommend classical CDs, it has a whole New to the Arts? section just for curious beginners.

Dictionaries define terms such as "chamber music" and the CultureBriefs section tells you just enough about important works to get you through a conversation about them. You get the plot of Swan Lake, but also the Cocktail Party Fact that "Tchaikovsky lived to see only the first production of Swan Lake, which was generally considered to be a bomb." The Who's Who in the Arts section compares itself to a collection of baseball cards, with the important statistics about important players on the culture team. More questions? Ask *CultureFinder*'s online arts aficionados.

Chatter Box

The Classical chat room, KEYWORD: **Classical**, is very active and well-organized. It has its own Web site, newsletter, archives, and a schedule of upcoming live events.

Visit Museums from Home

In the past, you'd miss out on many amazing museums unless you visited Washington, D.C. Now you can download images from some of the nation's best museums and view them from anywhere.

The *National Portrait Gallery*, KEYWORD: **NPG**, houses portraits of every U.S. president, not to mention Pocahontas, Ben Franklin, Thomas Edison, Mark Twain, Eleanor Roosevelt, George Washington Carver, Joe Louis, Amelia Earhart, Thurgood Marshall. . . you get the idea. The *Gallery*'s tribute to noteworthy Americans is a sight that no art lover should miss.

The Photo Gallery at KEYWORD: **Smithsonian** features photographs of aviation, space, science, nature, history, technology, art, people, and places. Visit the nation's capital, take a flight with Skylab, or look at early telephone equipment and see how far technology has advanced.

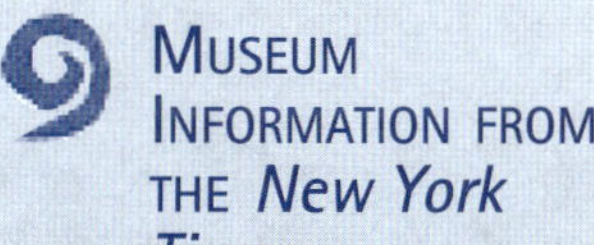

MUSEUM INFORMATION FROM THE *New York Times*

Anyone who lives in or near New York City can easily find the right museum or art gallery in which to spend a rainy Saturday afternoon. KEYWORD: **NYT Museums** has directories and a list of current exhibits, as well as exhibit reviews and art- and architecture-related message boards.

The subject matter is as large as the Smithsonian museums themselves.

Another Smithsonian museum, **KEYWORD: NMAA**, focuses on American art. Special collections highlight African-American art, Hispanic art, women artists, folk art, photography, Native American art, and American landscapes. The *National Museum of American Art* also provides instructions for viewing the images.

Good Stuff!

Visit **KEYWORD: Afterwards** for serious discussion of the arts. Visual artists can upload their creations to the Afterwards Café Gallery, and message board participants include teenage poets, opera enthusiasts, and dancers.

All Things Considered, You Prefer NPR

Like a cool breeze in the media desert, the National Public Radio service has broadcast intelligent news and cultural reporting for the past 20 years. They have more than 13 million listeners coast-to-coast, and can be visited by over 8 million AOL members at **KEYWORD: NPR**.

NPR listeners can catch up with Bob Mondello's film reviews, read the story of *Car Talk* (Tom and Ray went to MIT!), and find out more about the people behind the eloquent voices, including Terry Gross, Linda Wertheimer, and Ray Suarez. You can also find out how to order tapes or transcripts of programs you missed or really loved.

Participate in a discussion of *Talk of the Nation*, NPR's daily call-in program, by entering The Control Room. Numerous debates rage in the Talk about Radio message board area, from the current state of public radio funding to the Bailey White fan club.

JOKE OF THE DAY

Where can you start your day with a laugh? Many areas have a Joke of the Day, including **KEYWORD: Boston**, **KEYWORD: Comedy**, and of course, **KEYWORD: Joke.**

To groan instead of laugh (or just annoy your co-workers. . . heh heh), there are some truly bad jokes for the taking, too. **KEYWORD: WWN** features the Dumb Joke of the Day, and **KEYWORD: HO** boasts the Lame Joke of the Day. Don't say I didn't warn you.

The Laugh Track

Interactive Comedy at the "Online Mardi Gras"

Hecklers Online is not for the squeamish or easily offended, but it's certainly funny if you leave your sense of etiquette at the door. **KEYWORD: HO** has over 80 interactive daily games, contests, interviews, and events to keep you amused, like the daily take-no-prisoners Interactive

Top Ten (with some topics that might make even Dave Letterman squirm), and the Name That Color game.

Start your journey in the Hecklarian faith by viewing defaced pictures in Digital Graffiti or downloading pranks from Hecklers Game Room. Then head straight over to the Hecklers Online Main Screen—certain to offend your other senses, if not your sense of humor. I like the Giggle Box myself with its archive of "Yo Mama" jokes, like: "Yo Mama is so nice, she'll give you the hair off her back." No one needs to be mature *all* the time.

Chatter Box

If you think you can handle it, prepare for more heckling in the Heckler's Hangout chat room at **KEYWORD: HO**. Or, for "your last act of social desperation," try the HO Love Chat.

Knock Knock, Joke's There

"How come the melon had a big wedding? Because it can't elope. Get it? Cantaloupe." ::groan:: There's more where that came from at **KEYWORD: Jokes** (they're not all that clean, either).

Cackle over the Joke of the Day, download funny sound clips, and read interviews with comedians. There is a plethora of message boards on which you can post your best cranks—pick-up lines, misheard lyrics, light bulb jokes, lawyer jokes, truck driver jokes, so-and-so walked into a bar, and whatever else your funny bone desires.

Comics Draw a Big Crowd

Become the Superhero in a Marvel Adventure

At *Marvel Online*, **KEYWORD: Marvel**, you're in control—it's fully interactive! In the Threaded Web, wanna-be writers can develop an ongoing plotline based entirely on your favorite characters. Continue a pro's storyline the way you think it should be written. If you think you know all there is about the Marvel Characters, you can try your luck at Trivia—just don't make a fool of yourself in front of all your rivals.

Chat with comic writers and artists, and post messages about your favorite Marvel characters: Spider Man, the X-Men, Daredevil, the Incredible Hulk, Captain America, and others. Several times a month, AOL members get the exclusive *Spider-Man Cybercomic*. The *Cybercomic* is interactive, too, so you can jump around, find clues, play games, and hear cool sounds as you move along in the story.

Chatter Box

Anime fans are a small (but growing) enthusiastic group. Talk about your favorite movies and episodes in the fast-scrolling Anime Café chat room, **KEYWORD: Japanimation**.

Meet the Whole Warner Bros. Family

Warner Bros. seems to have a very big family, and they all live on AOL.

The WB Network (**KEYWORD: WBNet**) highlights current shows, those in production, and network news.

The Warner Bros. Virtual Lot takes you backstage at **KEYWORD: WB Lot**. Start at the front of the studio gate, and follow the path of a real-life tour, with a Guest Info Booth and everything. In the sky, Superman flies above the lot and gives you access to The World of Superman, including a preview of the New Animated Superman Series, a background of the Original DC Comics Superman, and a link to the newest Lois & Clark: The New Adventures of Superman special area.

Kids WB! Online is at **KEYWORD: KidsWB**, with chats about all the favorite Warner Bros. characters and special fun for kids.

A portrait of Scooby Doo and a Daffy Duck cookie jar can both be bought at the *Warner Bros. Studio Store*, **KEYWORD: Studio Store**.

KEYWORD: Warner brings up the music from Warner/Reprise records and artists like R.E.M. and Tom Petty.

Play Santa Online

It's a little easier to shop for the kids and teenagers in your life with help from **KEYWORD: Entertainment Store.** Choose from the Disney Store, the Games Store, and the Warner Bros. Store, among others—you're sure to find something fun. And you can prove how hip you are by sending the card through email at **KEYWORD: Cardomatic.**

Get a Grand Tour of the DC Universe

All the usual suspects are at **KEYWORD: DC Comics**—Superman, Batman, Wonder Woman, Aquaman, Flash, Green Lantern, Green Arrow, Hawkman, and Catwoman—but you probably didn't expect *MAD Magazine*. *DC Comics Online* represents many facets of animation these days.

For instance, click on the blue arrow near the shady sunglasses-wearing character to see Paradox Press, publishers of graphic novels, the comic magazine *Weird*, and neo-reference books like *The Big Book of the Unexplained*. Back on the DC Comics main screen, a mysterious woman in black leads you to Vertigo Comics' selection of twisted tales like *Hellblazer*, the *Sandman*, and *Swamp Thing*.

Superman swoops over the more traditional DC offerings. Get details on current and upcoming releases, with sneak previews, cover graphics, The Weeks Ahead, and more. Download graphics of your favorite DC hero or heroine from the Who's Who photo-gallery sampler to put on your computer desktop. Look for sections on trading cards, movies and TV, and video games. Graphics from *Lois & Clark*, *Batman Forever*, and *Tank Girl* are available, too.

Good Stuff!

KEYWORD: CNW has a Big Fridge where young artists can hang their work—just like the fridge at home, but with a bigger audience! Send drawings through the mail, or upload computer artwork.

Meet...

DC Comics Bigwigs

Some regularly scheduled chat guests at **KEYWORD: DC Comics** are the editor of the *Superman* books, the Executive Director of Production, and various writers, artists, colorists, and inkers.

If It's Animated, It's Here

Admit it. The first page you turn to when you pick your daily newspaper up off the porch is the funnies page. You use your kids as an excuse to watch cartoons on TV. It's O.K. Just look at Toon Talk in *The Cartoon Forum*, **KEYWORD: Cartoons**, and see how much everybody else loves animation. The selections are a fun mixed bag: classic favorites, new strips on the Web, lighthearted fare on the Cartoon Network, and scathing political cartoons.

The most varied part is the Toon Talk message boards, where "if it's animated, it's here" really rings true. Fans discuss books, strips, shows, movies, and every possible pen and ink genre. When the Biker Mice

TUNE IN TO TOONS

Cartoon Network World, **KEYWORD: Cartoon**, is a great area for kids. Adults who retain their fondness for Space Ghost and Scooby Doo will have fun, too. Walk down memory lane with the Flintstone's Episode Guide, or look up your favorites in the searchable Encyclopedia of Toons database.

From Mars have an enthusiastic online following, you know the boards are comprehensive.

Insider's Tip

Download today's *New York Times* crossword puzzle from **KEYWORD: @times**. Sure, you won't be able to finish it, but who can?

What's Happening Now?

Live Events, Right This Minute!

Try out **KEYWORD: Live** for a one-stop expedition to an assortment of live events happening right now or in an hour or two on AOL.

America Online's largest gathering place, capable of hosting thousands of guests, *AOL Live!* tackles what is important to its online community—political exposés, insightful interviews, groundbreaking social issues, humor, music, radio, TV, film, even night-owl game shows. Chat with any number of celebrities and VIPs about their fields.

Not only is there a variety of live events, but *AOL Live!* provides a potpourri of information and fun things to do: what's going on today, tomorrow, event transcripts, games, contests, interesting, funny and sometimes controversial columns, and special event coverage.

While there are chats for various interest groups (games, Internet, sports), you can also start your own Chat C@fe and invite all your AOL buddies for some virtual coffee.

The majority of live events occur between the hours of 8:00 p.m. and 1:00 a.m. ET, but there are always folks ready for a chat. Recent events range from The Spice Girls' cyberspace debut to Mia Farrow to MTV's Love Doc giving advice on love, sex, and relationship problems.

THROW A PARTY IN A CHAT ROOM

Next time a bunch of your friends are online, why not organize a Buddy Chat? If you have a buddy list, open it (**KEYWORD: BuddyView**), then highlight a screen name (or the word "Buddies") and click the Buddy Chat button. You can use the Buddy Chat button to invite as many members as you want to a private chat room. It's a great way to introduce your friends to each other.

Plan Ahead for Great Live Events

KEYWORD: Live Guide will help organize your online calendar. Too bad AOL doesn't have one of these for my real-life calendar. . . .

Coming Attractions, part of the *Live Guide*, is where to go to find out what's happening when. Discover a full listing of live chats, concerts, question-and-answer sessions with your favorite advice giver, and contests. Every online live event on AOL is covered in this one area, often months in advance, so you have no excuse for missing anything.

Good Stuff!

KEYWORD: **Online Originals** reminds us just how strange the Internet can be. The Klingon Language Institute, the Supreme Silly Putty Collection, and the Shrine to Spam are all here.

Where to Find Online Originals

Try This Trivia Game, If You Dare

Enter KEYWORD: **AT** for a trivia battle where the only goal is to come out standing on top of the carnage.

The eccentrics at Hecklers Online and ANTAGONIST, Inc. have joined forces to bring trivia gladiators armed with attitude a multiple-choice trivia free-for-all, complete with sarcastic hints and a ruthless game timer.

Immediate scores and rankings are posted after each game, and cumulative scores are posted daily. Try to earn as many tokens as you can to cash in on a variety of prizes. But guess fast and guess correctly—or be prepared to run the instant-message gauntlet from your unforgiving opponents.

What to Do When You Can't Sleep

Counting sheep gets boring fast. So does late-night television, where insomniacs are often mesmerized by half-hour infomercials. Since you don't really need spray-on hair or a food processor that slices, dices, and juliennes, give up on the TV and enjoy the late-night lack-of-sleep-induced wackiness at KEYWORD: **Insomniacs**.

Your family, your roommates, and probably your entire block are already asleep, but there's someone to talk to at the *Insomniacs Asylum*. Other insomniacs to cavort with include Rocky Gardiner, who will tell your future in Club Dementia, and the Mystery Woman.

Insider's Tip

KEYWORD: **Entertainment News** has today's headlines about TV, movies, music, theater, multimedia, the Internet, culture, and the people who make it all happen.

Good Stuff!

Seen Elvis lately? What about Bigfoot? The *Weekly World News* is at **KEYWORD: WWN** to satisfy your cravings for psychics, vampires, and horoscopes.

Banter with Naomi, and guess what (and where) her tattoo is. Some other regulars are Roscoe, the owner, bartender, and Jungian scholar; Tony, the programmer with a fondness for caffeine highs and lederhosen; and Xenith, the whip-toting Maiden of the Dark. You may still be awake, but at least you're not bored anymore.

Find Something Different to Do

ZENtertainment, **KEYWORD: Zen**, stars one outspoken man and his uncensored opinions. "I am not part of any big corporation trying to shove their clients or merchandise down your throat," says the editor of *ZENtertainment*, "I'm simply an unemployed slacker with a little too much time on his hands." Mainstream movies and music get their fair share of attention, but the specialty here is offbeat entertainment, like anime, underground comics, documentaries, computer games, amusement parks, indie flicks, and toys.

For a 'zine (short for "magazine") run by one guy, it's kept remarkably current. Subscribe to the free email newsletter to make sure you stay up-to-date. You can also download sound clips, movie trailers, still photos, and more.

Insider's Tip

Getting the dirt on politicians and entertainers is fun, but sometimes you just have to gossip about completely fictitious characters. Join the Monday night *Melrose Place* chats at **KEYWORD: Melrose**.

The Inside Track on Hollywood and Washington

What do the key figures in entertainment and politics have in common? They both generate a ton of gossip, and they both have Matt Drudge hot on their trails. Go to **KEYWORD: Drudge** for the latest gossip, which this online bloodhound defines as "news that just hasn't been confirmed yet." *Drudge*'s mission: to get the latest gossip and deliver it to the public before anyone else gets wind of it.

For a humorous take on political news, skip over to **KEYWORD: Buzzsaw.** Bill Shein skewers politicians and "cuts Washington down to size."

Good Stuff!

Ah, urban legends. You know, like the philosophy student who answered the essay question "What is courage?" with "This is." . . . and got an A. Other clever and not-quite-believable tales are at **KEYWORD: Urban Legends**.

Celebrate Your Lack of Willpower

As the bumper sticker says: "Eat right, exercise, die anyway." Nobody's perfect at *Vices & Virtues*, **KEYWORD: Vices**, so see how your transgressions compare to others'. Confessions are made freely, and the featured Obsession of the Week details weird quirks of human nature, like our uncontrollable desire to collect complete junk.

If you care about becoming a better person, there's a Digital Conscience that can keep you in line by sending nagging email. But if you'd rather hang onto your bad habits (after all, they're kind of fun!), gather in the forums devoted to the arts of eating, drinking, smoking, and sex.

Keeping Your Kids Entertained

Letting your kids go online can be scary, but there's plenty of age-appropriate fun available. Just keep an eye on the youngsters and suggest areas like these.

KEYWORD: DCComics for kids has puzzles, online coloring games, downloadable comics covers, and message boards just for younger fans.

Children can read other kids' writing and get their creative juices flowing at **KEYWORD: Kidzine**.

Nickelodeon Online (**KEYWORD: Nick**) features episode guides, Frequently Asked Questions, character profiles, downloadable Digital Toys and other games, a Trivia Challenge, and the Nick Blabbatorium chat room.

The WB also has a kids-only area at **KEYWORD: KidsWB**. Download a Tazmanian Devil Coloring Kit and chat live with beloved cartoon characters like Daffy Duck.

Kids will holler "Yabbadabba do!" for the *Cartoon Network*, **KEYWORD: Cartoon**. They offer over 8,500 animated titles, including Scooby Doo and the Jetsons. Have the kids draw some cartoons and post them here for the world to see.

9 More Ways to Indulge on AOL

Yield to your sweet tooth with *Godiva Chocolatier* (**KEYWORD: Godiva**) and *Eli's Cheesecakes* (**KEYWORD: Cheesecake**).

Southern Californians can find the best brew pubs with some help from the reviews of **KEYWORD: LA on Tap.**

Those who enjoy a good smoke often relax at **KEYWORD: Cigar Café.**

To enjoy decadent food, frosty beverages, *and* a cigar, visit **KEYWORD: FDN.**

Channel Jumping

More G-rated areas can be found at **KEYWORD: Kids Only.** If you're really worried about what the young ones see, you can use **KEYWORD: Parental Controls** to block all areas except the Kids Only Channel.

The Wine Guy and the Schizo Gourmet may be doomed, but they're having fun in the meantime. Message boards also help the vice-ridden get together. I'll admit I spent quality time bonding with other chocolate fiends when writing the Health & Fitness chapter got me down ;)

૭ ૭ ૭ ૭ ૭

Of course there's lots more on AOL that's entertaining than what I've written here: for instance, all those computer games require a separate chapter (Chapter 11).

Try the International Chapter (Chapter 14) for entertainment from around the globe. Life hasn't been the same since I discovered Canadian humor at **KEYWORD: Beavers**, where they celebrate Beavers and Butt-head, "drink" Absolut Nonsense liberally, and discuss the Canadian Conspiracy. **KEYWORD: Japanimation** sums it up by saying they're "serving all your anime and manga needs." If you're not into anime yet, you can download video clips to try it out.

One of my favorite forms of entertainment doesn't get much time in the Entertainment Channel, so I jump to **KEYWORD: Books** to revel in the written word. The Learning Channel's *Books & Writing* area can keep me online for hours discussing authors, reading reviews, and deciding which novel to delve into next.

So whether it's a morning horoscope, an afternoon soap opera update, or a late-night trivia game, I think we've found enough fun to fill up at least a day, if not a week or two, in AOL's Entertainment offerings.

A View of the World: AOL's International Flair

Getting an educated, accurate world view means expanding your horizons: I soak up all the culture I want in the International Channel.

I read news stories reported directly from the countries where the action is happening. American media can only report events through the filtered lens of the U.S. perspective, but **KEYWORD: Intl News** provides direct contact with the people most affected by the issues. And the *World-Wide Weather* area is a powerful tool for travelers leaving the States on international business or touring.

With over 200 countries and territories profiled in this channel, I can steep myself in the cultures of Europe, Asia, South America, and the Middle East. Just picking a keyword like **Bangladesh** or **Cameroon** transports me to a foreign country. I can absorb some of the idioms of the language, download the national anthem, and explore the history and traditions of the people there. Maps and photos of the region also create a lush visual backdrop.

New sites are always being added to explore more fully the cultural nuances of and current social issues in a country. From what I've heard around the office, the upcoming *India* cultural site sounds like it will have a lot to offer. Unfortunately, **KEYWORD: India** isn't launching soon enough for me to tell you about here. But go online and take a look at the world outside your Windows; explore the International Channel.

The Economist Intelligence Unit

Investors with global accounts will surely be amazed at the amount of hard data to be found at **KEYWORD: EIU.** Whether your business concerns lie at a national or regional level, you'll find GDP figures as well as other determining factors from social and political spheres.

The Country Alert section offers market-influencing news and the Global Forum is where in-the-know speakers discuss political analysis and pressing topics like the status of the European Economic Council.

Get a Taste of Foreign Culture

Explore Irish Heritage

KEYWORD: Irish Heritage proves there's more to Irish culture than just leprechauns and limericks. One of the many business etiquette tips you'll find here is that Dubliners find it rude for guests to leave a party early. If an Irish client takes you to a pub for an after-work pint, expect to stay a while.

Beyond the online pub crawl, *Irish Heritage* is rich in folklore, mythology, and literature. Fairy tales come alive in the picturesque landscapes of the Emerald Isle, and you can take an interactive tour of them in this area. Listen to sound files of the traditional drum of the bodhrán or contemporary Irish musicians. You don't have to kiss the Blarney Stone to tell your own tales of Eire, but you might want to try learning some ancient Gaelic phrases in the chat room.

Insider's Tip

KEYWORD: Intl Access gives you those all-important access numbers so you can log on to AOL from over 100 foreign countries.

Learn Japanese Customs and Etiquette

Gray skies overhead
Rain quietly whispering
The earth renews
An AOL member

The well-designed haiku section of **KEYWORD: Japan** allows you to try your hand at the artform as well as read examples from the masters. Buddha's birthday, martial art techniques, the tea ceremony: many treasured Japanese traditions and customs are detailed in *Japan!* This area has a playful side, featuring sumo wrestling facts, members' karaoke performances, and even reviews of Godzilla movies.

But members with a dedicated work ethic similar to that of the Japanese will find invaluable resources here, too. Financial tycoons can keep a watchful eye on the Nikkei and daily news from the Pacific Rim. Practice

Good Stuff!

Remember the dueling national anthem scene in the classic Bogart film *Casablanca*? Recreate it on your desktop with sound files of over 200 national anthems available in the International Channel.

common phrases with sound files from the Japanese phrase library and flip through the mini guide to Japanese etiquette. Think you've got a handle on the cultural intricacies? Take the Decorum Quiz to double check.

JOY TO THE WORLD

Some of the best international areas are temporary ones that crop up at different times of the year. Special holiday seasons like Chinese New Year, Oktoberfest, and various wintertime festivities are celebrated with contests and interactivities. Cinemaniacs will appreciate the live coverage from the Riviera during the annual Cannes film festival. Bastille Day and the 4th of July mark independence for two nations in the same month, and you can cheer here.

Read News from Israel

Israel is the Holy Land to believers of many faiths. Whether you belong to Jewish, Muslim, Christian, or Baha'i sects or are just following the struggles and history of the nation, look at **KEYWORD: Isr@el** to see the true soul of the country.

To hear the voices of Israel, read Jordanian and Palestinian news publications and *The Jerusalem Post Daily*. *Isr@el Interactive* has also posted its own foreign correspondent, Judy Tashbook, a writer originally from Lubbock, Texas, who made Aliyah (the immigration of Jews to Israel) in the summer of 1996. She sends weekly Letters from Israel describing what it's really like to live in such a sacred land.

If you want to make the journey yourself, this area links to many opportunities for learning and employment. Find connections here to study the Torah at a Yeshiva or university, or embody the Zionist idea of working the land on a kibbutz. You can also participate online in the scheduled Peace Talk chats and by writing essays on controversial topics such as the quandary "Is Israel a Jewish State?" Cast your vote here and see whether other members agree.

Take an interactive tour of Jerusalem, learn the significance of the Wall, or read the poetry that is as important to understanding Israel as hearing the news.

Say G'day to Australia

What exactly is a "didgeridoo?" A "dingo?" Check out the dictionary in the *Great Southern Land* (**KEYWORD: GSL**), which you can read either from American to Aussie

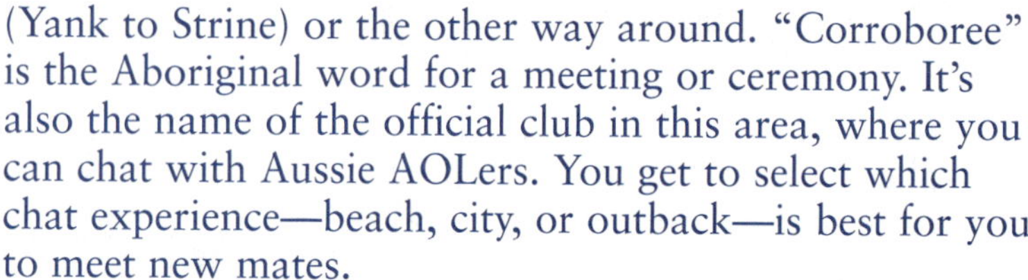

(Yank to Strine) or the other way around. "Corroboree" is the Aboriginal word for a meeting or ceremony. It's also the name of the official club in this area, where you can chat with Aussie AOLers. You get to select which chat experience—beach, city, or outback—is best for you to meet new mates.

The quirkiest feature of this area is the history of Vegemite, the popular concentrated yeast extract used as a sandwich spread. You can visit the Tuck Shop for recipes and cooking tips; whip up some Swaggies Soup and get a list of American substitutes for hard-to-find Australian ingredients.

Insider's Tip

A clear Usenet heirarchy will lead you directly to international Internet discussions. Try *soc.culture* followed by the country you're looking for. There are over 150 to choose from.

When Aborigines "walkabout," they leave home to follow invisible songlines, or ancient paths, etched in the land which constitute their shared history and mythology. While not quite the same spiritual undertaking, the Paget family travels throughout Australia and shares

Visit Every Nation Under the Sun

Honduras, Suriname, Rwanda: the heart of the International Channel is the world itself, and all the countries it encompasses. Each has its thumbprint embossed on the area with its flag and national anthem, which you can download and listen to. Every country profiled has message boards where you can exchange tips on places to visit, discuss customs and politics, or search for family ties and lost friends. Whether a war-torn country or a bastion of peace and prosperity, you'll find online elements that give you a snapshot of the region:

- Top news stories from local papers
- Society and culture newsgroups
- Links to the best Web sites

There are well over 200 countries and territories covered in the entire channel, so your heritage is sure to be included.

Good Stuff!

You can stay abreast of what's happening across the globe with **KEYWORD: Intl News**. Online versions of international newspapers are stored in this area, delivering stories directly from the nations where the events take place.

their stories online in an educational cyberdocumentary in this area.

Tell Us How Your Family Came to America

Tell Us Your Story (**KEYWORD: Tell Us**) offers an opportunity to share the story of your family's migration to and early days in the United States. For some this is a keystone in genealogy, as surnames were often changed at Ellis Island. You can post queries on the message boards to research your lineage or visit the virtual immigration museum at The Statue of Liberty—Ellis Island Foundation, Inc.'s Web site.

The Fact of the Day provides fascinating milestones in immigration history. Members chat in their family's native language and debate assimilation and the concept of America as a "melting pot." But the crux of this area is the members' tales. On the From South America message board, one member relates his journey to America from Brazil at age 13 and how he adapted to a new country: "This is home now. I've been here longer than I was there, so there's no other place for me. I will go back to Brazil someday, to visit, but if home is where the heart is, I'll be going on a round trip."

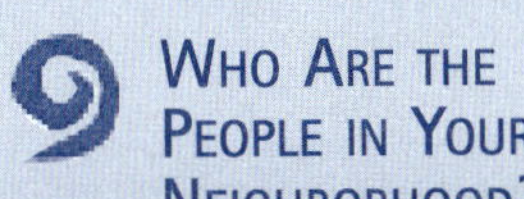

WHO ARE THE PEOPLE IN YOUR NEIGHBORHOOD?

America being the melting pot that it is, the best introduction to international culture might be in your own backyard. Mrs. Nagramada who lives four doors down might make the county's best lumpia, and you might never know. But if you checked in with your Digital City you might find a calendar of local cultural events—maybe even a Filipino food festival. Or organize a block party on the message boards and make your Digital City truly reflect your town's local color.

Dine with the Global Gourmet

True tastes of the world are found at **KEYWORD: GG**, with authentic recipes from around the globe. Learn how to make Spanish tapas, Greek moussaka, Thai chicken satay, or West African kabobs. Take a culinary tour of Belize or discover spicy treasures from Argentina to Tunisia to Vietnam in the Cookbook.

Along with international recipes you can sample the cultures of various nations; just how do women in the Middle East eat while wearing a veil?

One of the most dynamic message boards in this area is the Global Chefs Exchange. Kitchen gurus who cook for a living swap hors d'oeuvres ideas, advice on catering, and the particulars of a career as a sous chef.

Captivating Travelogues Tell You Where to Go

At *Lonely Planet* (KEYWORD: **LP**) British globetrotters contribute great summaries of travel destinations with specifics about the quickest or most scenic travel routes, the best time to go, what to do, and how much money you should expect to spend. Writers On the Road share their outrageous adventures of rickety bus trips on Himalayan roads and close encounters with mammoth icebergs. Download color maps or check out their guide to world festivals and events. They cover everything. Really. From the Moose Dropping Festival in Alaska to the National Yo-Yo Championships to the Tomatina (tomato-throwing) Festival in Spain.

Look Up Foreign Phrases Easily

KEYWORD: **Foreign Dictionary** gives you translations from Australian Aboriginal to Zulu to English and back again. You can double-check your writing to ensure you've transcribed Swahili accurately. Better than a printed pronunciation guide are the multimedia audio lessons streamed directly into Web pages. You can hear Hindi expressions and greetings online as if you were in a listening lab on campus.

Encounter the Parisian Lifestyle

Vive la difference! The distinctions between French and American attitudes is one of the more fascinating aspects of KEYWORD: **Bonjour**. From different takes on flirting to impressions of who's the rudest, you can debate with French members on various cultural customs. *Bonjour Paris* also has real insider guides to visiting landmarks, seeing the sights with the kids, matching wines with boulangeries, finding cybercafés, chic boutiques, and don't-miss events like beret tossing contests.

If you need to brush up on your translation you can take Leland's language lessons right in this area. Look at the portraits of famous Parisians, caricatures, and commentary from the French equivalent of Garrison Keillor.

Another pivotal area to explore French culture is the *Paris Guide* at AOL France. Go to KEYWORD: **International**, click on "World of AOL" and select AOL France. In the Voyage folder in the list box you'll find the *Paris Guide*. It covers famous monuments, museums, restaurants, and great places to stroll all throughout the city. Members should note this area is written entirely in French.

Talking with People Around the World: Make International Friends

Connect with Members Overseas

Exchanging email is an innovative way to learn a foreign language, especially by encountering a particular person's regional dialect and getting a command of the language's practical, everyday usage. **KEYWORD: Special Delivery** has a searchable database where you can find an international pen pal.

If you're looking for a new pal, or just someone with a similar interest or profession to correspond with, use the customized search to select the country, language, and age of the person you want to meet. For example, you might find yourself talking with Salvatore, an Italian student, or Stephanie, a German girl who spends part of her summers hiking in the Alps. Or else just enter an interest like "Flyfishing" and see who's in the database.

Meet. . . Madame X at **KEYWORD: Intl Love.** She'll tell you how couples maintain long-distance relationships, how to accept another culture without compromising your own, or how to communicate with foreign in-laws.

Chat in a Foreign Language

KEYWORD: Bistro is the hub of the international chat community on AOL. Members can have conversations in five different languages: French, German, Italian, Japanese, and Spanish. Just enter the room that suits your taste.

The message boards are active as well. Members looking for friends or family overseas may want to post inquiries here in their respective language. Students learning a new language can get some practice in their writing skills.

There are special language-specific versions of AOL software you can use to access the content of AOL France, Germany, and Japan. While AOL 4.0 will accommodate certain diacritics like accent marks and umlauts in email, AOL Japan can only be used with special software (and a keyboard that types kanji).

Good Stuff!

What's the equivalent of a "come hither" look in a chat room? The sound file of a pickup line in a foreign language. You can download one from **KEYWORD: Intl Love**.

AOL Is Getting the World Wired

Considering I've been working here for about 30 years in Internet time (that's kind of like dog years), I've watched AOL grow and expand not only in its range of services, but also in its reach. America Online is now almost a misnomer; we've got members from all over the world joining our community. Did you know that the French, German, British, Japanese, and Canadians all have their own full-scale services with original content? Their main screens have channels similar to yours when you log on. You can see for yourself. Go to the International Channel and click on "Europe" for access to AOL France, AOL UK, or AOL Germany. They reflect the unique style of each country—AOL France is a little provocative whereas AOL Germany is more proper.

Many of these areas are entirely written in the country's indigenous language. If you're looking for some more entertainment und Sie sprechen Deutsch, check out AOL Germany's KEYWORD: **Media Control**. Parlez-vous francais? Try AOL France's KEYWORD: **Modes**. And of course you'll be able to read all of the great stuff on AOL UK and Canada.

Japan is a whole different story. You have to have the correct software—and a keyboard that can type kanji. But with AOL 4.0 you can type in your accent marks so the difference between "if" and "yes" is clear en espanol. You can include umlauts and tildes, too—all those diacritics that are important when writing in a foreign language are embedded in the 4.0 client. And you'll also have complete access to every foreign language area. With AOL 3.0 you can only sample a few of those services. With AOL 4.0 you'll be able to reach all the keywords in AOL France and Germany. So keep checking KEYWORD: **AOL Insider**—I'll let you know when 4.0 is available.

4.0 Upgrade

With 4.0 you can use accent marks, umlauts, and other foreign language diacritics in your email to the international pen pals you meet at KEYWORD: **Special Delivery**.

Insider's Tip

You can register to be a beta tester of international versions of AOL software. Apply in the World of AOL section at KEYWORD: **International**.

Get a Passport to Love

Love makes the world go 'round—and *Passport to Love* can take you around the world searching for that special someone. With love letters, advice, and explanations of various cultural romantic customs, you can be an international heartthrob without having to book passage on the Love Boat. Just enter **KEYWORD: Intl Love.**

Le Swoon-O-Matic love letter generator is an incredibly fun feature, with fill-in-the blank, pre-written mash notes in English, French, German, and Spanish. For a more tongue-in-cheek approach, head over to **KEYWORD: Cyrano**. These love letters aren't brimming with eloquence from a loquacious bard, but they're fun. Need to make a quick apology? Send the "I'm an Abject Jerk and Beg Your Forgiveness" letter.

If you need more help with the nuances of courting, consult *Passport to Love*'s Madame X. She explains customs around the world and culturally diverse romance rituals. Submit your questions to the cosmopolitan queen of amore who offers advice to the lovelorn.

In Europe, It's not Football

You know that what Europeans call football is known in America as soccer. But did you know that the heaviest professional sumo wrestler weighs in at 606 pounds? Cricket, fencing, and the Tour de France: the International Channel covers the worldwide arena in depth. You can get the latest sports news on rugby teams, auto racing, world figure skating, and those legendary Romanian gymnasts. And, of course, soccer.

Global Fun and Games

Brush Up on Your Latin – and French, German, Spanish...

Learning translations and conjugations can be difficult. But you can tame the beast with some humor by turning language lessons into a game. **KEYWORD: Word Game** throws you some quizzes in Latin, French, Spanish, Italian, and German. Test yourself on individual words or take a crack at entire phrases. Choose a category such as Travel, Office and Business, or Mixed Bag and see how many words you can translate correctly. If it's been ages since your last semester of college French, don't worry: there's a cheat sheet here to help you out.

Around the World in 80 Mouse Clicks

Most of us don't have enough time, money, or frequent flyer miles to experience other countries first hand. But when the only international flavor in your town amounts to multicultural flapjacks at the local IHOP, it's definitely time to go online. Just click your way across the continents to get some culture. I took a whirlwind worldwide trip through AOL to show you how it's done.

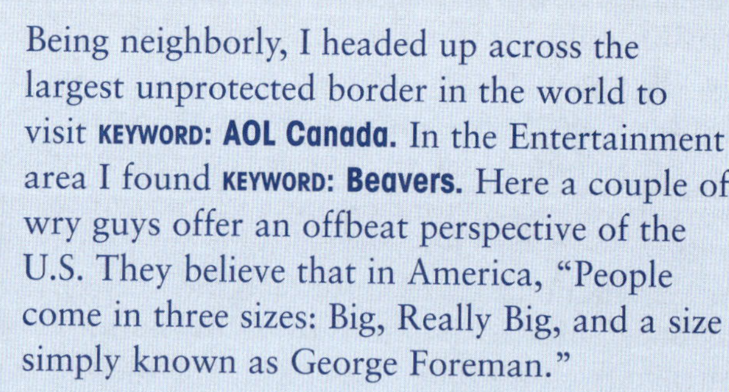

Being neighborly, I headed up across the largest unprotected border in the world to visit KEYWORD: **AOL Canada.** In the Entertainment area I found KEYWORD: **Beavers.** Here a couple of wry guys offer an offbeat perspective of the U.S. They believe that in America, "People come in three sizes: Big, Really Big, and a size simply known as George Foreman."

But the Beavers' sarcastic tips for American visitors sent me running in the opposite direction to Mexico. I was looking for a chimichanga. Instead I found the Chupacabra. KEYWORD: **Parascope** has a multimedia extravaganza devoted to the mythical part-bat, part-kangaroo, part-alien goatsucker reportedly sighted in Mexico and Puerto Rico. Fascinating, sure. But not very savory. So I consulted KEYWORD: **Global Gourmet** to rustle me up some good Mexican food. Not only did I uncover a recipe for charred habañero salsa, but I also found authentic Austrian appel strudel and Ethiopean honey yeast bread. Hmmm. World travel through the tastebuds. Not a bad way to go.

In need of a siesta from all that food, I just wanted to relax. So I turned my desktop into a Jamaican resort by downloading some reggae sound clips from KEYWORD: **World Music.**

Winding my way down into South America, I changed my tune to a Brazilian beat at KEYWORD: **Hispanic Online**, where I could really follow the rhythm of the Hispanic community with Latin world news, politics, the arts, and a local cultural events calendar. More history was to be found in Argentina at

KEYWORD: Evita, where I learned stories about the real woman versus fiction about the icon.

Leaving la Tierra del Fuego and swinging up eastward, I landed in Africa in the International Channel, which covers every country from Algeria to Zimbabwe. But the Black experience on AOL can really be found at **KEYWORD: NetNoir,** "the Soul of Cyberspace." A special section of that area highlights anything and everything on AOL each week related to Black culture, including links to specific articles and chats. Rosa Parks, the Harlem Renaissance, Kwanza holiday traditions: the celebration of African-American heritage and identity continues at **KEYWORD: Black History Reference**.

Another culture in our own backyard comes from the outback. When I sailed across the Indian Ocean to **KEYWORD: Australia**, I found that the member-requested message board "Australians living in America" had filled up (reached 500 posts) in only 45 days. Maybe I should volunteer to run a new message board—"Americans living in Australia". . .

Actually, I could do a stint on another, entirely different island. During a visit to **KEYWORD: Japan!** I picked up some culture by learning chanoyu, the traditional tea ceremony. Even tried my hand at haiku:

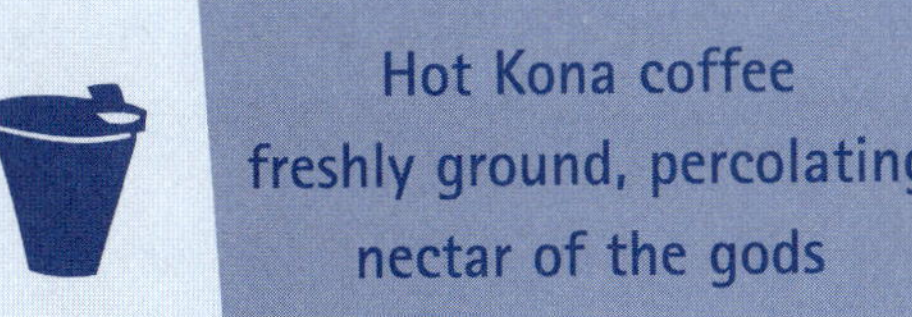

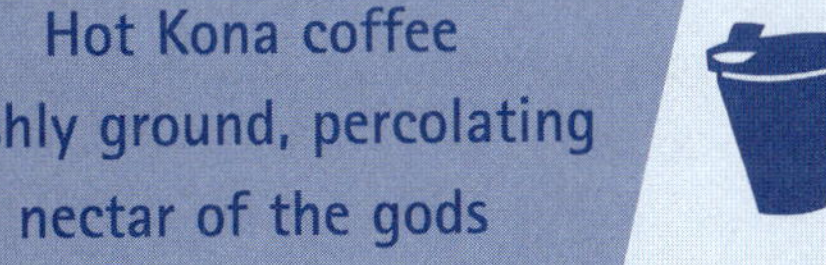

Hot Kona coffee
freshly ground, percolating
nectar of the gods

O.K. So I'm not quite Basho. Maybe I'd be better in the Japanese graphic art of anime. At **KEYWORD: Japanimation** I downloaded some cels and animations to raise the coolness quotient of my email stationary. And before I said, "Sayonara" to Japan, I slipped some Zen koans in my pocket.

The most unexpected leg of my journey was at **KEYWORD: OAO**. Outdoor Adventures Online has unique, offbeat trips that could be the adventure of a lifetime. They can send you kayaking on Lake Hovsgol in Mongolia or horseback riding in little visited eastern Tibet, a highly spiritual locale.

Between outdoor excursions and my new koans, I'd reached a quiet, peaceful state. Thoughtful. Respectful. Open-hearted. I was prepared. The time had come to make my contribution to world peace.

Online.

I went down to **KEYWORD: Isr@el** to join the "Peace Talk" chat room. AOLers don't shy away from controversial discussions, and plenty of chat forums provide room to hear all opinions and perspectives. *Isr@el* isn't the only place to participate in solutions to global problems. Up in Romania, many children need families. And at **KEYWORD: Adoption**, I found an entire message board dedicated to them, as well as the discussion of the international adoption process. Meanwhile, Americans interested in or already belonging to a German exchange student program have their own bilingual magazine on AOL at **KEYWORD: Oskar's.**

Of course, my own heart's desire, gay Paris, was calling me. And **KEYWORD: AOL France** has it all: museums and galleries, restaurants and runways. I spent some time strolling down the beloved Boulevard des Mondes. When I needed more exposure to Parisian style, I meandered over to **KEYWORD: Bonjour Paris**. Their Viva la difference section explains the distinctions between American and French culture. And the fashion gossip flows faster than the Seine.

For a proper look at English life, I visited **KEYWORD: AOL UK**. Here I discovered some great pubs, venues to hear up and coming British pop bands, and the ins and outs of the game of cricket. Digital City London also provided a perfect tour. I then scooted up to Scotland to check out Digital Cities Edinburgh and Glasgow, the latter of which hosts the annual T in the Park music festival.

I went from kilts to Celts by crossing over to the Emerald Isle at **KEYWORD: Irish Heritage**. There I took a scenic tour of the country, learned the origin of leprechauns, and downloaded some fairy-tale landscapes. (By now my download manager looks like the requisite projection of vacation slides.) After the pub crawl, I was pooped and ready to rest my weary head back home in the States.

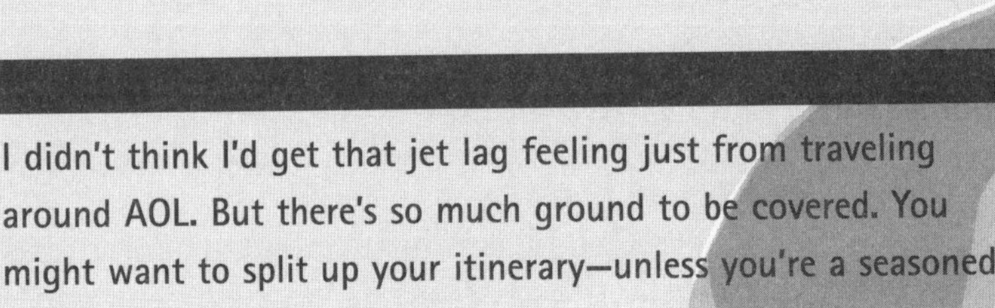

I didn't think I'd get that jet lag feeling just from traveling around AOL. But there's so much ground to be covered. You might want to split up your itinerary—unless you're a seasoned world sojourner. Bon voyage!

Flaunt Your Knowledge of International Trivia

Join other worldly members at **KEYWORD: Intl Trivia** to compete in a fast-paced game and test your knowledge of geography, history, culture, language, and entertainment.

A new game begins every 15 minutes. Answer multiple-choice questions about topics with an international twist as fast as you can. Race against both the clock and other players for the highest score.

Attention AOL Shoppers!

The International Marketplace abounds with foreign language CD-ROMs, international magazines, and even transatlantic flower delivery.

Name That Flag

Pledge allegiance to **KEYWORD: Flag.**

Your mission, should you choose to accept it, is to match the flag posted with the appropriate country. Some of the flags featured will be familiar ones, but others will prove more of a challenge. Don't be discouraged—the elusive countries can all be found, with a bit of sleuthing, in the country areas of the International Channel. There's a new Mystery Flag every day, so international trivia buffs and online detectives are never without a brainteaser.

FIND INTERNATIONAL PEN PALS

I found one of the best places to meet other AOLers at **KEYWORD: Special Delivery.** The atmosphere is very casual and friendly—a great place for finding email pals just looking to chat and make friends and not be hassled for romantic encounters. You must be 18 or older to participate, but if you're looking for pen pals for your kids, try **KEYWORD: KO Clubs.**

Play with Our Neighbors to the North

Not all Canadians play professional hockey and make maple syrup in their cabins in the woods, but they can laugh at the image. Discover Canadian humor with a bite at **KEYWORD: Beavers.**

Beavers is where Canadians and Americans come to have a little fun at the other country's expense. You can even find a few scathing tips for the American traveler in Canada. DON'T wear a baseball cap that says, "Guns, Freedom, or Death"—it makes Canadians nervous. DO visit Winnipeg: no Canadians want to and they could use the business.

In Beaver Tales, share sketches, stories, and songs. Each week you can find a tale to be read around the virtual campfire. The Beaver Damn is bursting with

Meet the International Channel Insiders

Social butterfly that I am, I love having the opportunity to run around AOL headquarters and meet all the people who make this online community experience happen. There are two I'd especially like to introduce: Marta Grutka and Laura Sheahen. These worldly women are the International Channel producers, responsible for bringing some of my favorite areas to the service.

With a Masters degree in International Relations and expert command of the French and German languages, Marta has edited corporate publications involving trilingual interpretation. She also spent time in Brussels, Belgium, analyzing European industries such as aerospace equipment and communication services, before coming to AOL.

Laura has always been fascinated by other cultures, particularly Russia. She combined her studies of Russian literature with as many international expeditions as possible. Her travel high point: watching snow fall on the Kremlin at night. Travel low point: being arrested by the Egyptian police for climbing the pyramids at Giza without a permit (luckily, a $13 bribe paid them off).

What both Marta and Laura appreciate most in their AOL work is the tremendous help they get from their "community leaders." These are the members who volunteer as ambassadors throughout the International Channel. You often see them hosting scheduled foreign language chats at **KEYWORD: Bistro** and answering message board queries. If you'd like to become a community leader, send mail to screen name Intfl Apply. Want to contact Marta or Laura? Go to What's Hot in International, click on "Suggestions," and send off a note in the Contact Us section.

KEYWORD: Bistro is the best place online to practice a foreign language or converse in your native tongue. Tagalog, Swahili, Gaelic: Volunteer to host a chat in your language!

not-too-nice opinions about the news of the day, whether it's life in Canada, things that drive those Canadian Beavers crazy, or what makes 'em laugh.

Insider's Tip

The International Channel has a bi-weekly newsletter, *Around the World with AOL*, that tells you about new areas and teaches foreign phrases in each issue. You can subscribe at KEYWORD: **Newsletters.**

Sneak a Peek at Japanese Animation

Fans of Japanese animation—including both anime and manga—finally have their own area at KEYWORD: **Japanimation**. Admirers of this artform can read the latest issue of *Anime Today*, a newsletter of video releases and titles, not to mention the industry's top news stories.

The key to *Japanimation Station* is the library of free daily downloads of quicktime movies, audio files, and artwork, so fans can enjoy some animation online. Anyone wanting to purchase new CD-ROM games, comics, or other related paraphernalia should pay a visit to Mangamania, the area's animation store.

Discover Royalty Around the World

Channel Jumping

KEYWORD: **Vacation Plan** and KEYWORD: **Destination Focus** in the Travel Channel often highlight key cultural facts about foreign cities such as common idioms and menu items.

At KEYWORD: **Royalty** you can discuss the rise and fall of worldwide monarchies—particularly that of England. On message boards members mourn the loss of Princess Diana and wonder what will become of the British throne. Trace royal genealogy and learn more about the lineages leading to the crowns of Denmark, Sweden, and Monaco. Read royal histories or take the Tower of London Virtual Tour.

Does your own family have a coat of arms? Search for your surname's crest, seal, heraldry, history, and even your family's tartan, if you have one.

Sample the Virtual Baguette

AOL France has a number of intriguing areas. KEYWORD: **Modes** is a popular section on fashion, but it's all in

French. If you hop over to their Vogue section (it's a folder in the listbox) you'll find a bilingual Web-based magazine affectionately titled *The Virtual Baguette*. When you first pull up the site the French version will appear. To access the English version, just scroll to the bottom of the page and click "anglais."

This online magazine (or 'zine, for short) runs several serial pieces, including episodes of an interactive thriller, an innovative, convoluted comic strip narrative, and an ongoing *X-Files* parody. My favorite feature here is the new Virtual Tapisserie. It's a gallery of "tapestries," or illustrations that you can use as wallpaper for your desktop. A new, original image is added to the gallery every two weeks. Just select the one you like, choose the resolution you want, and when the graphic finishes loading, right-click on it. Select "Set as Wallpaper" from the pull-down menu and voila! You've added some French finesse to your system.

To reach AOL France, go to **KEYWORD: International**, then click on "World of AOL." From there you can reach any of the international AOL services.

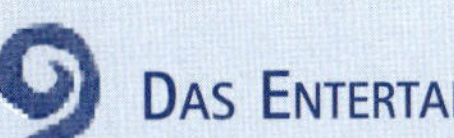

Das Entertainment

AOL Germany, France, UK, and Canada all have full-fledged Entertainment Channels of their own. Particularly popular are Germany's **KEYWORD: Media Control**, France's **KEYWORD: Modes**, the UK's **KEYWORD: Artist Underground**, and Canada's **KEYWORD: Beavers.** These areas keep you current on what's evolving in the worlds of visual media, fashion, and music, and sometimes take a tongue-in-cheek stab at current events around the globe.

Become an Aficionado of German Cinema

KEYWORD: EGO stands for *Entertainment Goes Online*. This film magazine is written entirely in German, but worth looking at if you have even the slightest command of the language. Popular foreign films are covered with news, previews, and interviews, as are American films.

The O-zone is an interactive club where you can chat about the cinematic works of Wim Wenders such as "Wings of Desire," or deconstruct the film "The Tin Drum."

AOL Germany also has **KEYWORD: Media Control**, which covers not only film and video but television, books, CD-ROMs, and music. Also completely in German, *Media Control* lists the top-rated titles in Germany in these mediums, providing an interesting slice of life from the entertainment perspective.

I think one of the most powerful uses of the International Channel is tracing your family's history and origin. The message boards alone are a tremendous resource that can put you in direct contact with distant relatives—quicker than a letter ever could. I also love the holiday areas celebrating Oktoberfest, independence days, and winter festivities worldwide. They're a great way to incorporate some international traditions into your own family gatherings.

I hope you enjoyed the tour. If you're planning an international excursion be sure to check out all the resources in the Travel Channel. Or just keep reading and I'll show them to you. . .

The Great Escape: Travel Resources on AOL

Normally, I race around the third floor, hopping from meeting to meeting with executives, trying to get all my work done. It makes for a full week. But packing up my cubicle and taking it on the road often extends my workday into the wee morning hours. Between picking up the rental car, logging in on the laptop at the hotel, and returning hordes of phone calls, I don't have any time to hunt for a decent place to eat. So before I visit an unfamiliar city, I go to **KEYWORD: Zagat**. Their guides have restaurant reviews written by ordinary people like me, which can be more insightful than the opinion of someone with a gourmet palate. *Zagat* survey participants rate the food, atmosphere, service, and cost of restaurants all over America. You can even get specific and find a restaurant that delivers, that your kids will enjoy, that's open at 1 a.m., that prohibits smoking . . . the list goes on.

For instance, if I've got a trip scheduled for New York, I check out reviews in the downtown neighborhood. According to the guide, Carmine's Restaurant in TriBeCa is reasonably priced and open on Sundays. "Around since 1903 (and looks it), this inexpensive red-sauce Italian fish house at the Seaport resembles the belly of a boat, as patrons sit elbow to elbow enjoying both its sustenance and high spirits."

Business Travel Center

Some work takes you away from the office. But with AOL you can stay connected with headquarters while learning foreign business etiquette. **KEYWORD: Business Travel Center** gives you personalized business news, phone and address directories, maps and directions, financial resources, and international access numbers so you can log on from Hong Kong. Or invite your colleagues back home into a private chat room for an online conference with prospective international clients.

Chatter Box

M-I-C. . . see how to avoid pitfalls on your next Disney adventure. Join the monthly Disney chat at **KEYWORD: Family Travel Network** and be sure to enter their contest.

Of course, I always remember to file the dinner receipt for my expense report. And I try to keep costs down even when I'm not footing the bill. *Dining à la Card*, **KEYWORD: D a la Card**, has a dining program that gives members 20% cash back on their dining charges—including beverages, tax, and tip—when dining at participating restaurants and paying by credit card. You can also earn 20% cash back at participating hotels, resorts, transportation services, food shops, cruises, and even pro sports games. When you enroll in the program your initial rebate checks will be applied toward the annual $49.95 annual fee. Afterward, you'll get rebate checks directly.

Business trips being inherently hectic, it's a good idea to plan ahead with AOL's travel resources.

The World Is Your Oyster: How to Know Where to Go

Find the Key Guide to Florida

Miami Beach hosts nearly two million visitors each year. That's a lot of potential sand kicked in your face if you don't know how to get around the constant crowds of tourists. Maybe that's why *Destination Florida*, **KEYWORD: Florida**, was voted a Members' Choice area. It has tips on the best ways to get around, where to stay, and how to save money while traveling in the Sunshine State.

Sidestep Tourist Traps

Go through the "back door" of a European country: an underrated picturesque town, unhyped natural wonder, or uncommercialized cultural spot. Expert sojourner Rick Steves has spent the past 20 summers exploring Europe, making mistakes, and taking notes. At **KEYWORD: ETBD**, you can learn from his errors instead of making your own.

The amusement parks are obviously a big attraction. If you're planning a family vacation to Florida, the Theme Parks section of this area is invaluable. Magic Kingdom Tips had this gem: "Unlike some of the other Orlando attractions, Disney does not sell its tickets at a discount, either at its own gate or discount-ticket shops. However, you can cut down on costs if you have a Magic Kingdom Club Card, are an AAA member, or if you buy a multi-day pass to one or more theme parks." Find

ATM locations beforehand, learn how to avoid long lines, and target the best places for young kids.

Destination Florida also covers the alternatives to the theme parks. Jetty Park, a public beach, provides one of the clearest spots to see a NASA shuttle launch. And Key Largo provides spectacular diving. To find all there is to see and do throughout the state, check here.

Prepare for European Travel

There's an indispensable tool at **KEYWORD: Destination Europe**—the Travel Kit. It has an online currency converter, distance calculator, packing strategies, and lists voltage and adapter needs for differences in overseas electricity. Money Matters for the Traveler includes tips on getting the best exchange rates, such as using ATM and credit cards to earn rates from 2–7% better than cash or travelers cheques.

The train is probably the best way to traverse all the countries of Europe. Here you'll find maps and timetables in addition to Eurail Pass prices. Those who prefer the road less traveled might enjoy the offbeat offerings of Rick Steves' *Europe Through the Back Door*.

Even while exploring new countries, you can keep the comforts of home. American Express users won't want to leave home without looking into European AmEx offices, while devoted AOLers can find out how to log on from faraway lands.

Traveling around the world doesn't disconnect you from the World Wide Web. With **KEYWORD: Intl Access**, you can log on to AOL from the four corners of the globe. Get the list of access numbers for your country and follow the step-by-step process for connecting right here.

Plan Your Itinerary

KEYWORD: Travel Corner has a network of correspondents in more than 220 countries who provide concise, accurate, and frequently updated profiles of major U.S. and worldwide cities. If you're headed for a new city and are looking for the must-see's and must-do's, this is the place to find them.

For each major city, *Travel Corner* provides the addresses and phone numbers of major attractions. Top

Good Stuff!

Travel Corner's editors bring back more than T-shirts from their travels abroad. Enter a contest to win beautiful, exotic, and sometimes kitschy souvenirs from foreign lands.

Insider's Tip

Travelers on international business should learn the cultural protocols described in various areas of the International Channel.

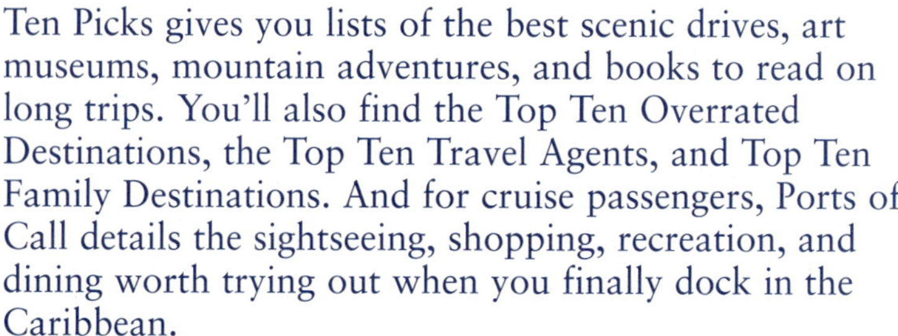

Ten Picks gives you lists of the best scenic drives, art museums, mountain adventures, and books to read on long trips. You'll also find the Top Ten Overrated Destinations, the Top Ten Travel Agents, and Top Ten Family Destinations. And for cruise passengers, Ports of Call details the sightseeing, shopping, recreation, and dining worth trying out when you finally dock in the Caribbean.

Recipes from around the world and snapshots uploaded by members to the Vacation Photo Album can give you a glimpse of foreign lands. But to design a more personal experience, take the interactive Travel Personality Quiz. It can tell you whether you and your traveling companion are actually compatible. If you like to crowd as much activity as possible into every possible moment, then you might not want to book that cruise with the coworker who's a couch potato.

Camp Across America

KEYWORD: **Travel America** also offers profiles of major American cities. But this area's most valuable aspect is its store of state park information that's otherwise hard to find. *Travel America* works directly with state recreation agencies to bring AOL members the details on individual parks that are usually omitted from most travel guides. Divided by state, you'll find directories of national parks, forests, monuments, and historical sites.

Upgrade

The new AOL Image Gallery provides a simple way to store digital versions of your vacation photos. Look at several simultaneously or send them to friends in email.

However, not everyone is comfortable "roughing it" in the great outdoors. Visa cardholders opting for a more urban landscape might profit from TAO's Traveling with Visa section. It highlights preferred dining spots in San Francisco and Monaco, a Visa ATM locator, and exclusive discount opportunities with the world's best hotels, resorts, and cruise lines, as rated by Conde Nast Traveler. In addition to exclusive benefits and extra savings, Visa Rewards often have special giveaways and sweepstakes such as a free weekend for two at Marriott hotels.

Find the Cruise That's Right for You

Thinking of sailing the seven seas? At **KEYWORD: Cruise Critic** members contribute candid reviews of more than 100 ships, and you'll find a Top Ten list in Editor's Picks. Yet the best way to find the right cruise for you may be to use the Cruise Selector—an online interactive ship finder that asks you to match several variables (cruising region, budget range, and lifestyle) to locate a package that suits you to a sea.

Cruise Tips offers a trove of information, including advice about how to select a cabin, when to tip, and what to do when ashore in various ports. Scan the Cruise Board for helpful comments from recent travelers. One AOL member recommends holding a family reunion on a cruise: "You get more for your money (meals, activities, entertainment, etc.). There is something for everyone to do around the clock. . . . Several cruise lines have special programs for the kids, so they have fun while the adults visit and do what they enjoy." You can also stop in at the Cruise Café for discussions with other sea-faring members or the monthly conversation with Editor-in-Chief Anne Campbell. Though there are classified ads in the Ship Shop that may offer good deals, the benefit of this area is truly shared member experiences.

Good Stuff!

Budget or luxury liner. Honeymoon or singles cruise. Nightlife or family adventure. Click on your interests and destination and the Cruise Selector will find the right ship.

Don't Leave Home Without 'Em

Travelers cheques, that is. American Express card-members can purchase this convenient form of travel currency right online at **KEYWORD: ExpressNet.** If you're not a member, you can apply for a card and enroll in the ExpressCash program. Locate AmEx offices abroad in case your cheques are lost or stolen. Or you could safeguard your trip ahead of time by buying insurance online in this area.

Viva Las Vegas

I always try to squeeze in some fun downtime on my business trips. **KEYWORD: Unofficial Vegas** gave me the inside track on cruising the famous strip after a day of schmoozing with conventioneers. I wouldn't dream of leaving Las Vegas without seeing Wayne Newton, so I found him in the Entertainment and Nightlife section first. I also learned to play it smart before setting foot in a casino. Blackjack, craps, roulette—get the house advantage down pat. And playing **KEYWORD: Casino Poker** gave me the upper hand.

The Practical Traveler

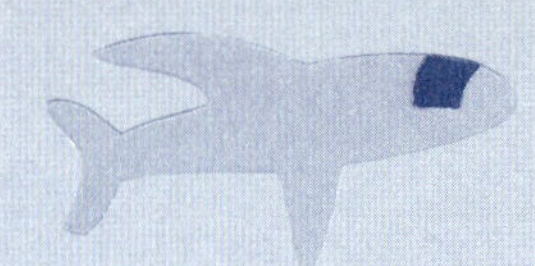

I need a checklist.

I even need an entry on the checklist that says, "Double-check checklist." Neurotic? Maybe. Helpful? You bet. I start online, of course, with a folder of favorite places that comprise the Art of Pragmatic Travel.

Mapping Out the Essentials

Planning is the key to a hassle-free trip. The obvious and most basic step is to check the weather in your destination so you know what to pack. At *Weather News* (KEYWORD: **Weather News**) there are current and long-range forecasts for both American and international cities. Business travelers will find weather updates for the U.S., Europe, and Asia, and if your company sends you off to a convention in Colorado, you can plan to sneak in some Alpine shooshing with the ski reports here.

To some extent, packing the right clothes can prepare you for a foreign climate, but there's more you can do to preserve your health while away from home. At the *Better Health and Medical Network* (KEYWORD: **HRS**) you can find information on how to regulate your sleep pattern while changing time zones, how to shake off jet lag, and even discover the tell-tale signs of malaria. Stocking up on tips from this area can help ward off common travelers' ailments, which can ruin an entire vacation.

And I don't know about you, but I have to have any product that makes my traveling that much easier. I've found some great gadgets online at *Hammacher Schlemmer* (KEYWORD: **Hammacher**). Their Traveller's Edge department carries keyless luggage locks, world time zone alarm watches, air pressure relieving plugs, and a packable trench coat.

Someone once said, "Getting there is half the fun." Clearly this person never got motion sickness, had the directional instincts of a carrier pigeon, and knew how to pack a linen suit with nary a wrinkle.

Beyond Our Borders: Traveling Abroad

If and when I ever get to go to Paris, I'll be completely prepared—especially with *Destination Europe*'s (**KEYWORD: Destination Europe**) practical Travelkit. Use the interactive distance calculator to find out how far it is from one city on your itinerary to the next. The kit also clues you in to voltage and adapter needs overseas, packing tips, and strategies for keeping your money safe. A mark, a yen, a buck, or a pound? Find out how much your American dollars are worth in your destination country with the currency converter. Or make money matters simple with travelers cheques. *ExpressNet* (**KEYWORD: ExpressNet**) lets you order American Express Travelers Cheques right online and shows you where to find their travel service offices all over the globe.

Before you jet off to unknown parts for excitement and adventure, safeguard yourself with updates from the U.S. State Department at the *Travel Advisories* area (**KEYWORD: Travel Advisories**). Locate embassies and medical facilities ahead of time just in case you need them during your journey.

And if you're bringing a laptop (and vowing to actually use it), *International Access* (**KEYWORD: Int'l Access**) keeps you plugged in to AOL with instructions on how to get access while going abroad. You may want to bookmark some key Web sites from the Business Travel Center, including interactive maps and directions and an address locator.

How to Talk to the Locals

Looking to navigate little-known dialects in remote villages without a translator? Take some foreign language lessons and get practice online first. Brush up your translation skills with the *International Word Challenge*, **KEYWORD: Word Game**, a fun game that includes a folder to test you on travel-specific phrases. And you can chat live around the clock in *Bistro*, **KEYWORD: Bistro**, in French, German, Italian, Japanese, and Spanish. Hourly, scheduled chats are listed for additional languages such as Polish, Dutch, Russian, Chinese, Gaelic, and even Esperanto. If you've got time, take a full-fledged foreign language course online. You can find them in the Learning and Culture Channel.

Hmmmm...

I wonder how you say "permanent relocation" en francais.

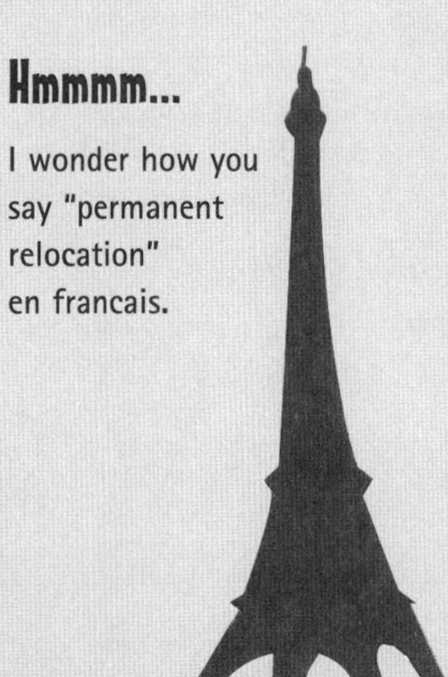

Top Ten Family Destinations

Members and *Travel Corner* staffers weighed in on the best places for family vacations:

- Washington, DC
- Orlando, FL
- Yellowstone Park, WY
- San Diego, CA
- Museum of Science & Industry, Chicago, IL
- Mount Rushmore, ND
- Tuscon, AZ
- Branson, MO
- Mackinac Island, MI
- Steamboat Springs, CO

♦ ♦ ♦ ♦ ♦ ♦ ♦ ♦ ♦ ♦ ♦

Meet. . . the "Cruise Critic"

Anne Campbell once served as a travel consultant to the Brazilian Government Tourism Association. Now the host of *Cruise Critic*, you can get her advice, too.

Taking the Kids, Pets, and Other Stowaways

Families Share Their Travel Experiences and Advice

KEYWORD: **Family Travel Network** has an easy-to-use, searchable database of vacation destinations appropriate for the whole family. You can look for family travel spots either by region or activity. Important information listed for each place includes the phone and fax numbers, dates open, type of accommodations and dining available, rates, activities, and more.

Both parents and kids send in details about their experiences, so you can benefit from stories of hits and misses of their trips. One message board is devoted to taking the kids on business travel. One AOL member says, "New York can be great. I took the LimoTour with their VIP limousine with a see-through roof. The kids loved [it]. They know how to cater to the whole family. Their drivers are professional tour guides and stories of New York even amazed the kids. Found out about them through the New York City Convention and Visitors Bureau. A must."

Travelers even send in pictures to the photo album. And a family reports to you live from their vacation with images and impressions of their expedition in Virtual Vacations.

The *Family Travel Network* shines a spotlight on a particular destination, describing all the specific don't-miss wonders that the city has to offer. There are also contests, where you can win prizes or cash, in addition to weekly featured travel bargains and specials.

KEYWORD: **Parent Soup** also has family travel ideas in the Resource Library. The Educational Vacations section is mostly comprised of popular museums, such as the hands-on Exploratorium in San Francisco, where you can take a sensory tour of science exhibits. And members rave about their favorite vacation destinations in Travel Picks.

Bargain Hunting and Reservation Booking

Learn the Art of Budget Travel

Legendary travel writer Arthur Frommer scours the globe for the best travel deals: airfares, hotel rooms, cruises, restaurants, and more. You can find bargains typically only known to travel agents, such as unadvertised budget airfares, right here at **KEYWORD: Arthur Frommer**.

In Best of the Bucket Shop, learn how to get great deals from consolidators. Find the "Poor Man's Spa" and discover "foam-rubber bus travel" or consider inexpensive "alternative" travel like political excursions and resorts that stretch your mind.

Rather than pay to see exotic lands, why not work your way around the world? Become a part-time travel agent or a one-person tour operator—look into Careers in Travel. Learn the Art of Budget Travel to take advantage of "youthless hostels" and free sightseeing. And of course, Arthur's got some Travel Opinions of his very own.

Meet. . .
Arthur Frommer

For 40 years Arthur Frommer has been candidly reporting on travel destinations with a practical, nuts-and-bolts style. Learn a systematic approach to covering your travel needs in his online area.

Keep Business Travel Costs Down

A minimal expense report will make you look especially good in front of the boss—or increase your profit margin if you are the boss. *Travelers Advantage*, **KEYWORD: TA**, offers discounts, travel agent services, and specials to their members. Sign up online to become a member or find out how to get in touch with *Travelers Advantage* by phone or mail.

In this area you can find full information on their money savings programs like the 5% Cash Bonus, where you receive back 5% of your purchase price on tickets purchased through *Travelers Advantage*. They also offer Hotel Savings of 30–50%, Travelers Advantage Full Money Guarantee, and a 24-Hour Reservations Hotline.

Attention AOL Shoppers!

Join *Travelers Advantage* for a 5% cash bonus on travel and 50% off hotel rates. Members also enjoy special deals on airfare, cruises, and vacation packages.

If you're looking for information on travel, cruise, hotel, or resort packages, *Travelers Advantage* also features Vacation Specials. Or, if you want to find out if your favorite vacation destination has a hotel participating in the *Travelers Advantage* Hotel Savings programs, just search the international listing of participating hotels by criteria.

For information on what to do when you get there, *Travelers Advantage* has weekly events focusing on popular travel destinations. Miss an event? They're archived in the Transcript Library. And the sweepstakes gives

Get a Personalized Map

KEYWORD: Time Savers coordinates several powerful Web resources to get you where you need to go in a hurry. Sites like Mapquest and the AAA Map'n'Go CyberRouter will give you door-to-door street maps and turn-by-turn driving directions that you can print out and take with you. You can get a map of major highways across the country and then zoom in to a street atlas of a particular city.

Be Your Own Travel Agent

Window seat over the wing. Vegetarian meal, or kosher if available. Usually coach, sometimes redeye, always the lowest fare possible. These are my preferences when booking an airline ticket. And *Preview Travel* already knows, since they've got my profile stored at **KEYWORD: RESERVATIONS**.

It keeps track of all my frequent flyer account numbers, too. In fact, I haven't had to call an agency to book a trip for me since I started using AOL and began choosing my own adventures. With *Preview Travel* I can:

- Find the cheapest flight with Farefinder
- Plan an itinerary based on interests and activities with Tripfinder
- Make airline, car rental, and hotel reservations 24 hours a day, 7 days a week
- Purchase tickets online
- Get tickets home-delivered via UPS, at no extra cost
- Contact a *Preview Travel* agent via phone or email if I encounter any problems

Multiple profiles let you keep business and vacation travel separate—though I recommend a mixture of both.

snowbound northerners a chance to win trips to sunny locales such as Orlando or the Bahamas.

Book an Entire Vacation Online

Preview Travel Vacations, **KEYWORD: Vacations**, features great deals on all-inclusive excursions, air fares, and accommodations. Or go vacation window-shopping: there's a great collection of photos, video clips, travel tips, information on special attractions and activities, and maps. It's like having a travel agent and a vacation library all in one place.

It's easy to find what you're looking for. If you know where you want to go, just select a vacation by geography. If you're unsure about a specific destination, you can check out great vacations by type—family, couples, singles, sports, beach, city, or culture.

You can request booking information right online with just a mouse click. Check out prices and availability. Cyber-travel agents get back to you via email with more specific details. You can also call directly to speak to an agent to book your trip and confirm reservations.

Chatter Box

KEYWORD: Traveler has scheduled chats for seniors on the go, RV travel, and a monthly Disney chat to get you started.

Make the Most of Frequent Flyer Miles

Maximize your frequent flyer program with *InsideFlyer Online*, **KEYWORD: InsideFlyer**. The digital version of this popular print magazine gives you the latest news on how to stretch your miles to get free flights, upgrades, and deals on rental cars and hotel rooms.

Extensive reviews of various airline's mileage programs explain and rate their level of customer service, earning ability, and award choices, and are given an overall rating.

You can also learn how to get the most miles and points from each paid flight, manage miles on different airlines, and get advice from FF guru Randy Petersen, the Mileage Advocate. For instance, he offers five pros and cons for companies retaining their employees' business

Insider's Tip

Find the weather forecast of your destination, then store the area's link in your Favorite Places folder. It's a quick way to keep an eye on what to pack, right up to the moment of departure.

Chatter Box

The main Travel screen now has a link to Travel Talk, a comprehensive schedule of all travel-related chats, sorted by room.

travel points. On the one hand, "It provides accountability to all levels of cost control in the company," but it can also "create employee antagonism (when introduced wrong)."

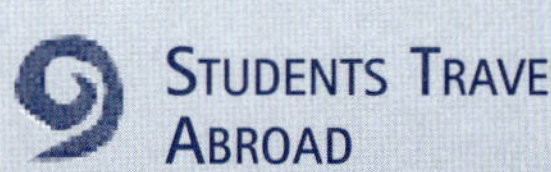

STUDENTS TRAVELING ABROAD

Students should take as many breaks as they can get—including travel discounts. If you can't afford to send your kid abroad for a semester, negotiate a deal for a month or a summer Eurailing. The *Independent Traveler* has a scheduled student travel chat and special bargain packages. And consult the *Traveler's Resource Center* for a guide to youth hostels.

♦ ♦ ♦ ♦ ♦ ♦ ♦ ♦ ♦ ♦ ♦

Traveling Savvy, Safe, and Stylish

Become an Independent Traveler

You could consult dozens of guidebooks and still not find all the useful information to be uncovered at **KEYWORD: Traveler.** Develop the skills to become the quintessential Independent Traveler with tools in this area.

The *Travelers' Resource Center* offers tips to stretch your dollar while on the road, such as cheap airfare strategies and insightful advice on car rentals. In the Bargain Box you can find the latest and greatest airline ticket deals with updates on the airfare wars and promotions. If that's not the ticket, you could check the specifications on being an air courier—just agree to haul someone else's package and you can fly for a fraction of the standard cost.

If you're interested in advice from fellow vagabonds, drop in on the Travel Boards, where you can get recommendations for hotels, restaurants, or sightseeing hot spots from people who live where you're going. Better yet, pull up a chair in the Travel Café to talk with them live. Or find out what expert sojourner Rick Steves has to share about his experiences traversing Europe through the Back Door.

Ask Arnie About Specific Travel Needs

Inquiring AOLers want to know:
"Have you ever been to Belize? Is it safe for two women to travel alone?"

"My fiancée and I have dreamed of getting married in Cancun. However, we don't have a clue how to begin planning this . . ."

"I am traveling to Las Vegas for a convention in February and am planning on having my wife and daughter join me at the end of the week . . . Do you have any suggestions on surrounding attractions . . . that would be appropriate for a family of three?"

Submit a question to the Travel King himself, and if it's creative enough, he might just answer it in his next column. Arnie Weissmann writes weekly about travel concerns, ideas, and obsessions. You won't find his wise-crack approach in many guidebooks, but at **KEYWORD: Ask Arnie** you'll find witty solutions to varied travel situations. And if you disagree with what he's got to say, Talk Back to the man. Send Arnie email with your thumbs up or down on his suggestions.

Attention AOL Shoppers!

Charming hotels, little-known sights, romantic spots for two: find them with a pocket guide in the *Travel Bookstore* written by those in the know.

Map Out Your Journey

The American Automobile Association is more than just emergency breakdown service. Pick a pleasure cruise with confidence, obtain a good map of the national parks, or get simple advice on driving from Boston to Bethlehem (PA, of course). *AAA Online*, **KEYWORD: AAA**, delivers all this and more—with the outstanding level of competence you've come to expect from them on the road.

Travel insurance is just one of the many services offered by AAA. With an AAA membership card, you also get discounts at hotels, restaurants, and even some theme parks. Membership benefits often include senior discounts. You can search the benefits available to you just by typing in your zip code in a quick search.

AAA also occasionally hosts auditoriums on topics ranging from How to Plan A Cruise to Help for First-Time Car Buyers. Check the forum schedule for chat dates and times.

Channel Jumping

Climbing Mt. Kilimanjaro is about as off-the-beaten-track as you can get. *Outdoor Adventures* (**KEYWORD: OAO**) in the Sports Channel can send you off on safari or in a hot-air balloon.

Travel Safe with Advisories from the State Department

U.S. tourists concerned about political climates can find out whether it's a good time for overseas travel with **KEYWORD: Travel Advisories**. If you're planning a trip to a foreign country, but are concerned about the recent guerrilla uprisings and the last malarial outbreaks, then make a quick trip online to *Travel Advisories* before you venture out in person.

In this area, travelers can access the U.S. State Department's Consular database for all types of news about travel to foreign countries—entry requirements, registration and embassy location, areas of instability, medical facilities, crime, highway travel, and more.

In addition, all current Travel Warnings are listed alphabetically by country. Usually a result of civil unrest, natural disasters, or outbreaks of serious diseases, these warnings are issued when the State Department decides, based on all relevant information, to recommend that Americans avoid all travel to a particular country, especially to the problem areas.

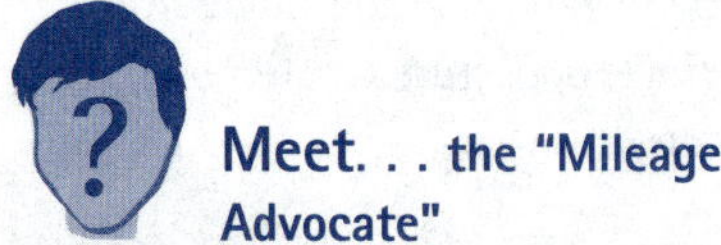

Meet. . . the "Mileage Advocate"

Frequent flyer guru Randy Petersen is available exclusively to AOLers at **KEYWORD: InsideFlyer**. Email him any questions you have about your airline's program.

Find Needed Travel Supplies Online

It's a law of the universe that travelers will always forget to pack something. Visit **KEYWORD: Travel Store** for a checklist of what you need to get where you're going.

For trips to the far reaches of the globe, there are foreign language CD-ROMs. The Pet Travel Center is an excellent resource for finding kennels and self-feeders for furry and feathered companions. And all travelers need maps, travel books, cameras, and luggage for pragmatic packing.

Everything for the trip can be easily ordered here and delivered to your home. Innovations like computerized maps, atlases, language instruction kits, and trip planners—combined with old reliables like Swiss Army knives—will get you prepared.

Channel Jumping

KEYWORD: Digital City is the Insider's guide to the urban landscape. Chat with the locals, get their recommendations on restaurants, or be a tourist in your own town.

Vacations Off the Beaten Path

Gays and Lesbians Venture Over the Rainbow

"Dear Auntie Em: Hate you. Hate Kansas. Taking the dog. –Dorothy"

Don't let a twister deliver you to some random vacation destination where you have to surrender your travel dollars to unappreciative establishments. **KEYWORD: Over the Rainbow** clues you in to gay-friendly areas of American and international cities and gay-owned hotels and stores to help keep you on that yellow brick road.

Most of the writers contributing reviews to this area are residents of the cities they cover, so you'll get the insider perspective not usually available to a travel writer who just breezes in for the weekend. For instance, don't overlook Provincetown in the off-season, but skip the Overblown Tourist Sites in San Fran. Find accommodations where the clerk won't raise an eyebrow when you two book a room with a single bed. Restaurants, sites and attractions, cultural events, and shopping centers that cater to the gay community are profiled, with addresses and phone numbers, and there are tips for HIV+ travelers. While Castro Street is certainly not the only avenue where you'll find gay literature and queer gear, where exactly would you go in Delaware? Find out here.

Insider's Tip

Got film? Mail in your rolls to *Mystic Color Lab* (**KEYWORD: MCL**) for developing and home delivery within 24 hours of receipt.

TRAVEL BARGAIN WEB SITES

The Web is full of deals on airfare, train tickets, and car rentals—if you know where to look. Here's a quick list of some great sites:

- Shoestring Travel *http://stratpub.com/*
- Budget Travel *http://www.budgettravel.com/*
- TravelBids *http://www.Travelbids.com*
- The Savvier Traveler *http://www.savtraveler.com*
- Travel Deals *http://www.travelassist.com/mag/a50.html*

Design an Exotic Getaway

Plan an imaginative vacation based not on location, but on a spectacular event at **KEYWORD: RPMC**.

Hear the famous Three Tenors in London. See NASCAR races in person. Maybe the package Jamaica Shaken, Not Stirred is more enticing to you (it's a James Bond festival at the Renaissance Jamaica Grande Resort). Whether you're up for a safari or not, don't miss the photos of the Costa Rica Ecosafari, one of RPMC Travel's Adventures.

Good Stuff!

Get the most requested recipes from popular bed and breakfasts all over the world at **KEYWORD: B&B**.

Not tempted? Maybe you would enjoy the fabulous wine train that winds its way through the Napa Valley vineyards in California. Enjoy the ambiance of a romantic meal by candlelight and picnic at famous vineyards tasting the world-famous wines.

Each vacation plan comes with an itinerary that makes planning a snap.

Get Cozy with Lanier's Bed and Breakfast Guides

KEYWORD: B&B covers all areas of innkeeping, for both owners and guests. Here Lanier Publishing brings their *Bed & Breakfast Guide* online with locations and phone numbers, amenities, types of meals served, accessibility for the handicapped, accommodations for children and pets, and price ranges of over 14,000 inns worldwide.

Search for accommodations by state or look for inns by specialty. Inn News and Message Center highlights the Inn of the Week—inns that focus on romance, sports, and contests. A favored feature of the area is the catalogue of the best-loved, most requested recipes from every region and for every season, including brunch and tea-time treats.

Innkeepers have a special corner all to themselves, with articles, information, and real estate listings of inns for sale. Find out about innkeeping seminars and conferences that'll show you how to own and operate your own little resort.

Channel Jumping

Research and Learning has the indispensable and objective consumer's guide to Walt Disney World at **KEYWORD: Unofficial WDW**.

Add These Dependable Planning Tools to Your Favorite Places

Subscribe to the Official Travel Channel Newsletter

The free biweekly newsletter from the Travel Channel is a good way to keep up with online resources for trip planning. The newsletter always highlights special deals so you can take optimum advantage of current airfare wars.

The Great Escape previews what's coming up in Destination Focus and the Vacation Plan areas. You can subscribe to the newsletter from **KEYWORD: Travel** and find an archive of past issues.

Insider's Tip

Subscribe to *The Great Escape*, the free biweekly email newsletter that updates you on what's going on in the Travel Channel.

Get a Complete Vacation Plan

KEYWORD: Vacation Plan pulls together a complete package of information, guides, and stories about a particular destination. The standard travel tips, weather forecasts, maps, and stats that you'd expect to find are here. But what this area also gives you is a glimpse of a city or country's culture and couches its essence in a visitor's context.

For instance, Colloquialisms and a Menu Guide can acquaint you with a different dialect, be it a foreign language or the vernacular of New Yorkers. The Dos and Don'ts list critical cultural facts to absorb. And for more extensive guidance, it's a good idea to peruse the related books featured in Barnes and Noble's Travel section.

Good Stuff!

Check out O'Reilly & Associates/Songline Studios' *NetTravel: How Travelers Use the Internet* from the Travel Books section of **KEYWORD: Barnes and Noble**. It provides more extensive tips on how to use online resources for planning your trips.

Vacation in the Magic Kingdom

"Meg! You've just finished writing the Travel chapter! What are you gonna do now?!?!"

. . . well, you know what comes next. But knowing that "The Happiest Place on Earth" can also be one of the most crowded, I'd spend some quality planning time so I don't wind up Grumpy. **KEYWORD: Unofficial WDW** can get you around all the parks in record time, help you select a hotel, and provide you with tips on traveling with seniors, kids, and disabled guests. And Digital City Orlando hosts **KEYWORD: Theme Park Central** with member reviews of the rides and updates on weather and park events.

The only guaranteed drawback of taking a vacation is that I have to return from it. If I didn't bring the laptop, there's that backlog of email to conquer. And the papers in my inbox (yes, we still use paper around here) are stacked so high that they begin to topple precariously. I keep thinking they'll morph into the Leaning Tower of Pisa, but it never happens.

At Your Leisure: Explore Your Interests on AOL

While chatting online and exploring the Web can be considered modern leisure activities, the real benefit of many forums and links on AOL is the support for all those things you do offline. Swap practical ideas with other members. Get expert advice from professionals. Or just proselytize about your favorite hobby. You'll find many diverse interests just at KEYWORD: **Hobby** alone. You never know what kind of people share your enthusiasm for an esoteric subject or who might crawl out of the proverbial woodwork to talk it over with you.

Satisfy Your Appetite for Eating, Drinking, Cooking, and Entertaining

Expand Your Cooking Repertoire

Opening up the Cookbook at KEYWORD: **Cooking Club** gives you access to over 20,000 (and growing) tried and true recipes supplied by AOL members across the nation. Appetizers, entrees, salads, desserts, low-fat and no-fat cooking—there's an abundant array of dishes here. But the invaluable resources of this area are the preparation

All You Can Eat at AOL

One way to access many of AOL's cooking, drinking, and dining options is with KEYWORD: **Food**. Besides housing such interest areas as *The Cooking Club* and the *electronic Gourmet Guide*, it also launches you to other palatable places such as the *New York Times* and *Woman's Day* food sections. Sample blueberry muffins with *Lanier's Bed & Breakfast Recipes*, keep it kosher with *Jewish Community Food*, sharpen your culinary skills with Julia Child at *Good Morning America Recipes*, or eat your way to a healthier lifestyle in *Thrive@eats*.

procedures, such as using room temperature eggs for a fluffier soufflé, or seasoning a cast iron skillet to brown meat without sticking.

If you need to put together a quick, healthy meal after a long day at work look to **KEYWORD: Food** for daily dinner ideas, complete with recipes, shopping lists, and pantry item necessities. Food is centered on a different theme each day, so you can put together a really harmonized meal.

Good Stuff!

Dining out again? Check out Cuisinenet at **KEYWORD: eGG** for synopses of major city restaurants categorized by such unique criteria as al fresco dining, brew pubs, and fusion.

Transform Everyday Dishes into Gourmet Meals

The electronic Gourmet Guide's searchable database at **KEYWORD: eGG** offers an efficient way to locate hundreds of recipes, party ideas, and preparation techniques specifically tailored to your cooking needs. Just typing in "brussel sprouts" brings up 27 recipes, articles, and lessons. You can learn to spruce up this much-maligned vegetable with a pecan glaze or gratin à la Mornay, as well as read what Julia Child has to say about reheating leftover sprouts. And the *eGG*'s Gourmet Glossary is a kindly reminder that this versatile miniature cabbage is really called Brussels sprout.

eGG members and staff also dish out helpful Cooking Tips on converting and figuring measurements, baking holiday sweets, and adding extra flavor and spice to old standards.

Channel Jumping

The *Global Gourmet* in the International Channel, **KEYWORD: GG**, prepares travelers for successful, respectful dining experiences abroad.

Educate and Entertain the Kids with Cooking

Another useful tool provided by the *electronic Gourmet Guide* is **KEYWORD: Young Chefs**. This area provides a creative and instantly gratifying outlet for hungry, energized kids looking for fun after-school activities. With the Peppered Leopard cartoon chef as their guide, kids can whip themselves into Pastamania, or stuff their afternoon blues into Pita Pockets. Chef LePep keeps kitchen safety, food handling, and basic hygiene in mind, as he presents kids with easy-to-follow recipes for special holiday treats and everyday snacks.

Learn More About Vegetarianism

How does a vegetarian obtain sufficient protein and calcium? Can you combine vegetarianism with a diabetic diet? What's the best way to minimize water retention and lower cholesterol levels?

Registered dietitians respond to pertinent queries about vegetarian nutrition concerns at KEYWORD: **Vegan**. *Vegetarians Online* also debunks myths about vegetarianism and provides international, gourmet, and basic recipes that please both children and adults.

This area serves as more than a meatless cookbook, however. Most notably it is a lively conduit and resource for vegetarians active in political, environmental, and ethical issues. You can join discussions about Earth-Friendly Living, Preventative Nutrition, and locating cruelty-free products. *Vegetarians Online* is a comprehensive, supportive starting point for members considering making the move toward a vegetarian lifestyle.

One member coaches another on the message boards by saying, "You probably need to start out gradually, like you're already doing. First cut out red meat. . . . Subscribe to a vegetarian magazine and read whatever you can on the subject. Join a vegetarian society if you have one. You will probably have many setbacks, but don't beat yourself up over it. Just get back on track as soon as you can. You can do it!"

Channel Jumping

The Travel Channel has *Zagat Restaurant Surveys* for those times when you want to get out of the kitchen. The reviews at KEYWORD: **Zagat** are provided by ordinary patrons, not professional reviewers, so you don't need a gourmand's palate to appreciate them.

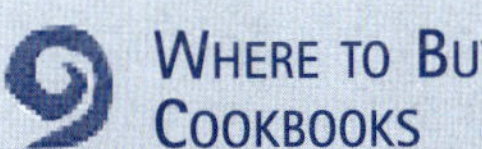

Where to Buy Cookbooks

The Book Shop at KEYWORD: **eGG** summarizes hundreds of publications, taste-tests recipes, and tells you how to order books online. The Bookish Cook at KEYWORD: **Cooking Club** recommends the best in culinary mysteries (when the protagonists are restaurant critics or chefs). And KEYWORD: **Vegan** reviews vegetarian cookbooks, many of which can be bought online in the Vegetarian Store.

Pore Through Beer and Wine Reviews

Though KEYWORD: **FDN** acts as a comprehensive site on both dining and imbibing, the real strength of the *Food and Drink Network* lies more in the drink than the food. Of particular interest are BrewBase and WineBase. These large, searchable databases disclose the tasting results from the Chicago-based Beverage Testing Institute (BTI)— the nation's only full-time product testing service specializing in beverages.

Assisted by technical advisor Dr. Harry Lawless, a Cornell University professor and sensory scientist, the BTI testers rate the "pleasure factor" of each selection. Here's what BTI's BrewBase had to say about Sam Adams Dark Wheat:

Score: 88 (out of 100)
Brewed in Massachusetts
Awards: Silver Medal, Best Buy Awards
Description: Orangish amber color. Roasted malt dominates aroma, with nutty and fruity touches. Crisp and light-bodied, with a delicate maltiness. Finish toasty, with lingering caramel flavors.

A little-known hops resource for Los Angeles residents is **KEYWORD: LA on Tap**. Not quite as structured or scientific as the BTI, reviewers delve into the nitty-gritty of what makes each LA brew pub unique, often launching into their own personal narratives.

How to Find Fine Wine on AOL

Wine connoisseurs hoping to expand their collections and fine-tune their palates can access several areas for assistance.

KEYWORD: FDN has a searchable database with ratings, vintage years, and prices, *Wine Enthusiast* magazine, links to Web sites with winery photo journeys, a winery directory, and a wine dictionary.

KEYWORD: Food takes you to some of the premier wine areas on the Web where you'll be able to find wine racks, cellars, corkscrews, and crystal stemware.

Host a Wine Tasting Party

Wine Made Easy by Paterno can help you throw a wine tasting party with The Tasteful Gathering Dinner Planning Guide at **KEYWORD: Paterno**. Choosing the wine, planning the menu, tasting techniques and vocabulary; find all you need to know. Paterno Imports, a family business with 50 years of experience, along with the esteemed magazine *Wine Spectator*, have imaginatively laid out instructions on how to evaluate the appearance, bouquet, and taste of a wine. Menu and presentation suggestions are partnered with these guidelines, as well as general recommendations for choosing the best wine to accompany a meal. Paterno also directs you through the intricacies of wine labeling, and traces the histories and landscapes of the Lungarotti, Frescobaldi, and Masi Wineries.

Turn Your House into a Home

Get Help with Selling or Buying a Home

The United Homeowners Association Forum offers several convenient ways to ease the costly and overwhelming process of buying or selling a home. **KEYWORD: UHA** houses several functional tools, including the Home Price Line. Described by *Money Magazine* as one of the smartest homebuying ideas around, the Home Price Line will tell you the comparable selling prices of houses in a particular zip code or area. By maintaining 23 million accurate records of the top 50 U.S. metropolitan areas, Home Price Line ensures up-to-date, reliable information.

Fill out and send an online Buyer's or Seller's Profile form, and *UHA*'s Buy/Sell Rebate Program will assign you an American Realty Referral counselor. This real estate professional will then match you with an appropriate realtor in your area. The real bonus? Following sale and settlement, you'll get a rebate check for one-third of the realty referral fee, which is usually .25–.35% of the price of the home.

From the Homeowner Services, you can also sign up for the *UHA*'s Mortgage Rate Shopper Service. This safe, free service presents your mortgage profile to hundreds of potential lenders, giving them a chance to offer you a much better rate. To discover what it takes to qualify, and to prepare yourself for negotiating the best deal possible, wend your way through *UHA*'s Mortgage Maze. Study the loan types that are best for your income level and employment status, or look up definitions in the terminology dictionary. Mortgage Maze also gives you a handy checklist summarizing all the documentation necessary to close a loan with a lender.

Good Stuff!

Take a tour of *Home Magazine Online*'s House of the Year at **KEYWORD: HomeMag**. You'll get a 3-D look at every room from every angle by downloading the software and using the mouse as your guide.

Calculate How Much House You Can Afford

The Real Estate Desk, **KEYWORD: OurBroker**, offers four interactive calculators that help homebuyers and refinancers figure out how much house or mortgage they really can afford. Made available by HSH Associates, the nation's largest publisher of mortgage and consumer loan information, these resourceful tools take you through a variety of "what if" scenarios. Figure monthly or biweekly payments; generate full amortization schedules; determine the income necessary for affording certain monthly payments; or calculate the amount needed to end your loan within a certain time.

HSH Associates reminds you, however, that actual mortgage lenders will still serve you better than a computer program. To find a regional list of lenders, use the *Real Estate Desk*'s Mortgage Information Center. There you'll also uncover rules for lenders, rate listings, and tax tips.

Attention AOL Shoppers!

Home Magazine Online houses an online Flea Market where anyone can post places for rent and houses for sale, or buy and sell antiques, furnishings, and any other household items.

Pick the Perfect School for Your Children

For most families moving to a new home, the quality of neighborhood schools plays a key role in choosing a location. **KEYWORD: SchoolMatch** aids this decision-making with a tool that incisively researches the facts for you. For a nominal fee, which is further discounted when you order online, *SchoolMatch* will profile the top 15 public and/or private schools in your area. With a database comprised of all 15,825 American public school systems, as well as all accredited private schools, you need not worry that a school has been overlooked. Included among the statistics provided are national SAT and ACT averages, expenditures per pupil, district population, educational level of residents, academic rigor, and tuition costs. Even parents who are not relocating, but have a child with disabilities or want options for artistically gifted children, can use *SchoolMatch* for identifying acceptable educational institutions.

To receive straightforward answers to questions such as: What is an at-risk program? or, How does a state's tax base affect education? parents can also turn to the Glossary of Education Terms, Comparisons of State Resources, and General School and Enrollment Statistics areas of *SchoolMatch*.

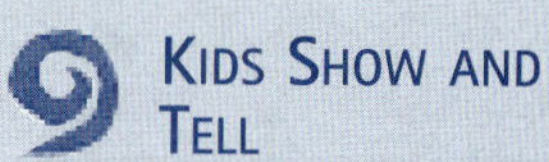

KIDS SHOW AND TELL

In the Kids and Pets area of the *Pet Care Forum*, your children can show and tell about their own dogs, ferrets, and fish with stories and photos in the file libraries, and discussions on the message boards. Better yet, they can take a trip to KidZoo on the Web to play animal identification games, hear the sounds of elephants and velociraptors, and learn the ins and outs of becoming a veterinarian or zoo keeper.

Take Excellent Care of Your Pet

A long-standing Members' Choice area has been the popular Pet Care Forum. The chats and message boards here are extremely active, with people who are passionate about caring for their dogs, cats, birds, fish—you name it. It was the first place I checked for advice on locating a new vet for my dog. I figured enough people here would contribute their experiences with the quality of care their pets have received. You'll find extended animated discussion on related newsgroups such as *rec.pets.dogs.breeds* and *rec.pets.cats.health+behavior.*

KEYWORD: **Pet Care** has its own Veterinary Hospital section. A crucial tool that makes use of the speed and convenience of online research is the handy First Aid Emergency Care for Cats and Dogs. There are illustrated examples of muzzling a dog properly, rescue breathing and basic CPR, and extensive tips on preventative medicine. For instance, beware of toxic household items such as pennies, garden supplies, antifreeze, and poisonous plants.

AOL also hosts a private forum for professionals at KEYWORD: **VIN**. The *Veterinary Information Network* provides information, consulting, database, and continuing education for veterinary doctors and scientists. The network requires a paid yearly subscription—call the 1-800 number listed to find out about fees before submitting the form with your credit card number.

For an idea of pets' effects on human health, check the Animals and Society section. Those grieving the death of a companion animal will find support for their loss here. The Rainbow Bridge is an especially touching passage among a list of readings appropriate for this tough time. A file library stored here allows you to upload words and pictures in memory of your departed pet.

Meet...

Gina Spadafori

She's the Pet Connection columnist for the *Pet Care Forum*, KEYWORD: **Pet Care**. Animal owners can depend on Gina for her well-researched syndicated articles on topics like pet nutrition, the first steps in owning a puppy, and how to live with pets and allergies.

Attention AOL Shoppers!

KEYWORD: **Aardvark** is the place to find a comfy sherpa bed for your favorite feline or plush toys for your new pup. Carriers, water bowls, and high-fashion collars—much of what your pet needs (and maybe desires) can be bought here online and delivered right to your home.

Build Your Dream Home

If you have ever envisioned designing or constructing a house of your own, **KEYWORD: HomeMag** can help make that dream a reality with their Build Your Own Home: Best Selling Home Plans. This collection of articles lets you select from a number of starter, mid-sized, or luxury homes that suit different lot and wallet sizes.

A large kitchen for catering parties? A recreation room for the children? Along with a floor plan and a colorful illustration of the front exterior, *Home Magazine* explains the special features that may make the house appropriate for you and your family. All floor plans can be viewed online or downloaded. If you decide to build a house based on one of the home plans, you can download an order form for the reproducible masters and construction packages.

For more home design ideas, look through the Building it Better folder in the message boards. Here, you'll find suggestions for house design software and for locating materials, contractors, and architects.

Meet... "Pet Shrink" Steve Aiken

If your cat is more Sphinx than Felix, animal behaviorist or "Pet Shrink," Steve Aiken at **KEYWORD: Pet Care** will help you unravel the mystery of that whiskered enigma. For additional counsel, visit the Cat Forum staff and other feline friends in the Cat Forum message boards.

Derive Interior Design Inspiration

Each month, *Metropolitan Home Online*, **KEYWORD: Met Home**, takes you on a photographic tour of an exceptional home that combines livable space with refined furniture and elegant trimmings. For those who can afford it, these "open houses" offer a visual springboard for remodeling or refurnishing their own home. Featuring the work of some of the nation's foremost interior designers, Home of the Month gives you a close look at how the professionals interplay color, form, and style.

Editor's Choices point shoppers to unique, luxury objets d'art, furnishings, and gardening items carefully selected by the trained eyes of *Metropolitan Home*'s staff. Experts answer readers' questions. And on the message boards you'll find renovation innovations, popular trends, and tips from members.

Consider Doing Your Own Home Improvement

At **KEYWORD: HouseNet**, home improvement authorities Gene and Katie Hamilton and other expert decorators, plumbers, architects, and electricians help you determine whether to hire a professional or do the work yourself. With cozy, user-friendly graphics and language, *Housenet*'s Do It Yourself. . . or Not? compares the cost of contracting with the expenses of buying or renting the equipment. It also estimates the number of labor hours, and considers the extent of exertion and expertise needed to do the job well. For example, to remove a tree stump, a pro will take 2 hours and charge you $145. You can get rid of the stump yourself in 3 hours for $90 in equipment, but you better be handy with a chain saw and a grinder. And don't forget to wear protective glasses!

If you decide to do it yourself, the formulas found in Go Figure! will help you carry out necessary metric conversions and measurements, and the interactive calculator will gauge how much paint you need to buy.

Not sure where to buy all the necessary tools and materials to complete the job? Flip through the Sourcebook database for phone numbers, descriptions and addresses of over 1000 manufacturers, associations, and services.

GARDENING ON AOL

Ideas for planting flowerbeds, vegetable gardens, or cultivating a gorgeous lawn can be found in various areas of AOL. The *New York Times on AOL* has gardening Question and Answer articles at **KEYWORD: NYT Gardening.** The popular *HouseNet* area has an extensive Garden Works section. At **KEYWORD: Housenet** you'll find out how to move a tree, protect your garden from pests, learn how to cut back an overgrown garden, and discover what's involved in seeding and sodding a lawn. A special chat room lets you get advice from other members about maintaining your yard.

Learn Backyard Basics

Home Magazine Online's Gardening area at **KEYWORD: HomeMag** provides a fruitful resource for the beginning gardener. Gardening 101 maps out the basic steps for selecting and planting seeds, and warns you against pruning hazards. The illustrated Hand Tool Guide will point new tillers to the shovels and spades that work best for the job at hand. More advanced gardeners will probably want to skip straight to the Plant Guide, which recommends the tastiest vegetables found in mail order catalogs, and the latest exotic flowers available in shops.

Looking for bulbs to plant in the fall? Buy them online at **KEYWORD: Garden Escape**.

Grow an Organic Garden

As world-wide concern for the environment increases daily, many more green thumbs are turning to organic fertilization and pest control for their gardens and lawns. To that end *Garden Spot* has two lively folders dedicated to organic gardening. Here people from all zones exchange research as well as personal discoveries. Requests for techniques and supplies often inspire a bounty of suggestions. One member hoping to reduce dandelion growth received many innovative replies, ranging from improving soil with a seaweed fertilizer to harvesting the "weeds" for dandelion wine.

From **KEYWORD: Garden** you can also link to the *UHA*'s Garden and Landscape Resources, which houses lists of organic suppliers as well as articles on organic yard and project ideas.

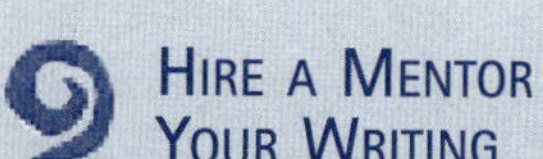

Hire a Mentor for Your Writing

The *Writer's Club* sponsors a mentor program which pairs aspiring writers with more established pensmen and women. At **KEYWORD: Writer** volunteer mentors can teach you how to do the following:

- Make the most of the *Writer's Club* resources
- Find an agent
- Locate a receptive publisher
- Improve characterization, plot, and language

Listen to Your Literary Voice

Get Sneak Previews of Upcoming Novels

Some bibliophiles fear online content will kill the reading of books and existence of libraries. But if any AOL area shows how unfounded that stance is, it's *The Book Report*. **KEYWORD: Book Report** has probing interviews with authors and highlights upcoming books with discerning reviews of novels, children's books, and works of nonfiction.

The Book Report also secures exclusive excerpts to give AOLers sneak previews of potential bestsellers before they hit the bookshelves. And the increasingly popular phenomenon of book clubs has an online manifestation here as well. Joining an online book club may encourage you to plow through that thick novel or biography that's been languishing on your bedside table, or prepare you with questions for the author in a live chat.

Daytime talk show diva Oprah Winfrey helped the resurgence of book clubs. You can find out what she and

Unearth Your Family Roots

The *Genealogy Forum*, at **KEYWORD: Roots**, enables you to dig much deeper into your family's history than an annual glance at grandma's photo album. This easy-to-use forum guides you step-by-step through the vast arena of genealogical research. Listed here are just a few of the exhaustive resources and lessons to be amassed. If you are just getting started, you can take advantage of these options:

- A beginners' center with basic lessons and methods for a successful research project
- Ways to locate, access, and understand vital records using public agencies and archives, such as libraries, county histories, census indexes, and genealogical societies
- Suggestions for genealogy software, and programs to download and demo

As you advance up the branches of your family tree, you'll want to check out these resources:

- Clever ways to organize your search, and those growing stacks of documents
- Important skills for preserving photographs and paper documents
- Methods to investigate family histories by ethnicity, or geographical region
- Actual archives of church, death, and marriage certificates, immigrant ship passenger lists, census indexes, and other records to download
- Opportunities to contact families who share your surname, such as message boards organized by geography and name
- Online family reunions
- Beginner, general, and special interest group chats
- New and old immigration stories

Chatter Box

Join the Online Book Clubs in the chat rooms of **KEYWORD: Book Report**. Sing the praises or lambaste the prose of classic, contemporary, children's, horror, and new age books.

Insider's Tip

You always laughed when Dad insisted Jesse James was your great-great uncle. But what if it were true? Find out if you're related to any politicians, celebrities, or historical figures in the Famous Ancestors message boards at **KEYWORD: Roots**.

her viewers are all reading in her own book club at **KEYWORD: Oprah**.

Buy Books Online

Good Stuff!

Experience the almost lost entertainment of serialization. At **KEYWORD: Book Report** you can read classics like *Huckleberry Finn* in serial form online, or download them for later.

To read up on the effect of the Internet on literacy, you can check out these titles:

- *The Gutenberg Elegies: The Fate of Reading in an Electronic Age* by Sven Birkerts
- *Virtuous Reality* by *HotWired*'s Netizen columnist Jon Katz
- *Being Digital* by MIT Media Lab's Director Nicholas Negroponte

To immediately experience the effect of the online world on reading, check in at **KEYWORD: Barnes and Noble**. With over one million titles available on their virtual shelves, you may find the convenience of ordering novels, essays, and short stories for home delivery increase the amount of reading you do.

Another popular bookstore, whose bookshelves exist only in cyberspace, is the Amazon.com Web site. Often in both these areas you're able to purchase books at a discount and have rare or out-of-print titles hunted down and special-ordered for you.

Specialty books can also be found in areas that have their own stores, like Parents Soup, Pet Care Forum, and the *Travel* Channel.

Chatter Box

Nearly any time of the day (and especially at night), writers pack the chat areas of **KEYWORD: Writer** to decompress after a long session of prose, poetry, or—"gulp"—writer's block.

Improve Your Writing with Critiques and Contests

Inspired by his 13-year career as a "performance writer," Dan Hurley, aka "The Amazing Instant Novelist," has devised a site at **KEYWORD: Novel**, where AOL members can refine and show off their own writing talents. Anyone who has a novel, story, or poem in progress can post their work to The Writer's Block, where staffers and members constructively critique, encourage progress, and pose suggestions for improvement. The environment remains relaxed and open, so that writers feel comfortable putting their words on display.

Weekly contests offer plenty of other opportunities to put your writing skills to the test. Thousands have entered their most original essays on open-ended, thought-provoking, and nostalgic topics such as the Christmas Spirit, Weddings, and Expressions of Fear. In addition to being eligible for a prize, each submission receives gut reactions, accolades, and criticisms from reading members and staff.

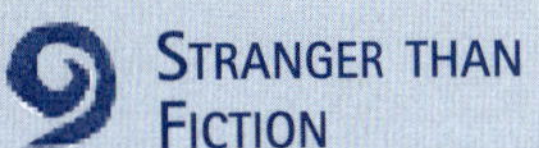

For an unconventional angle on the literary world, check out EXCLUSIVE! at KEYWORD: **Book Report.** Any kind of literature-related news, events, speeches, opinion pieces, or panel discussions that may shock, or at least surprise you, is stationed here and in the archives. Examples of past exclusives are: Anne Rice's *New York Times* political ads; a second look at Tupac Shakur as a poet; and reader responses to *The Rules*.

Turn Your Writing Habit into a Career

The *Writer's Club* at KEYWORD: **Writers** opens its pages to new and experienced authors who intend to earn a living by writing. Wondering how to promote your just-released novel? Avoid copyright complications? Or just plain get published? The Articles and Columns and the Business of Writing areas brim with candid insights from established editors, lawyers, writers, agents, and publishers. In addition to providing detailed essays on marketing, publishing, and legal issues, these areas offer experts poised to answer your individual inquiries.

Novelists, poets, journalists, and screenwriters can also fine-tune their skills with the *Writer's Club*'s frank, instructive essays written by published writers and editors. These articles explain such important fundamentals as how to keep track of characters, hook the reader, create believable dialogue, and explore the poetic voice.

Insider's Tip

An inspirational letter submitted to the editors of *Woman's Day Online*, KEYWORD: **Woman's Day**, will bring you a bit of cash if your words get published.

Indulge Your Zeal for Wheels

Visit the Auto Center

Auto Center is the main garage that stores all AOL's car resources. You'll find the latest Car and Driver Buyer's Guide, where hundreds of vehicles, including economy, mid-price, and luxury cars, plus convertibles, station wagons, vans, minivans, sport utility vehicles, and pick-up trucks, have been test driven and rated. Another essential car-buying tool is in the Buying section of KEYWORD: **Auto Center**. The Auto Loan Calculator will help calculate how much financing you need to get the car you want. And the Classifieds are an excellent resource not only for finding cars but for parts and services as well. A new catalytic converter or foreign import may be easier to find than you think.

Some parts of this area, like tips from master technician Erik Nielsen, will give you expert information on choosing and maintaining the vehicle that's right for you. But other areas are designed just for auto-lovers who enjoy the thrill of the road and compare rides. Chats, Web sites, newsgroups, magazines, and even an online

Insider's Tip

The Buying section of KEYWORD: **Auto Center** is a perfect example of how online resources can help you accomplish tasks in your everyday life. Here you'll find a buying guide, auto loan calculators, and articles on financing and leasing your next car.

Meet... Master Technician Erik Nielsen

KEYWORD: **Auto Center** brings you the indispensable advice of ASE Certified Master Technician Erik Nielsen. With a flair for writing on the layman's level, Erik gives in-depth, honest answers to questions such as: "Where can I get performance parts for my Saturn?", "Do I really need a format injection clearing?", and "How soon do I need to change the timing belt on my Honda?"

Research Before Buying a Car

Before buying a new car, investigate KEYWORD: **Car and Driver**. *Car and Driver* test drives 300 cars, trucks, and vans a year, reporting on up to 200 of them. Their straightforward writing style makes it easy for anyone to follow the details of their comprehensive road tests, buying guides, and first drives. But, getting opinions on the message boards from drivers who already own the car you're eyeing often offers more information than specs from a review. *Car and Driver*'s message boards are filled with people passionate about cars who are revving to reveal their own experiences and knowledge.

For more comparison shopping, cruise *Road & Track* for their richly written Buyers Guide and Road Tests. At KEYWORD: **Road**, handling, braking, and fuel economy are all covered within the context of the test conditions. Reviewers also weigh initial prices against possible maintenance costs. To arm yourself for a trip to the dealers, download their "cheat sheets" of the specs and photos.

car show provide a space for auto enthusiasts to expound upon the qualities of their prized automobile.

Chatter Box

Car and Driver's scheduled and open chats let auto enthusiasts share their love for driving, get an insider perspective from engineers in the industry, and stay on top of growing advancements in technology.

Find the Inside Scoop on the Auto Industry

KEYWORD: **Car and Driver** offers up-to-the-minute, keen reporting on the auto industry that will give you the upper hand in negotiating your next automotive purchase. The Daily Auto Insider at *Car and Driver Online* exposes marketing techniques used by manufacturers to make a sale, announces upcoming technological innovations, and divulges covert political maneuverings in the industry. Find out what's winning awards, who's making money, and where the money's being spent. The Daily Auto Insider also sums up stories from other publications, including information on best-selling sedans and recalled parts.

Good Stuff!

KEYWORD: **Classifieds** has a vehicles section where you can buy or sell a car. In addition to autos, trucks, and recreational vehicles, you can advertise parts and services. At the time of this writing you can run an ad for two weeks for $9.95 or one full month for $15.95.

Buy Your Next Car Online

KEYWORD: **AutoVantage** can give you free dealer invoice pricing, quotes on the specific vehicle you want, and $20 worth of free gasoline. In addition to exclusive discounts, AutoVantage provides its members with individual car buying assistance. Experts will walk you through the whole process. Consult with them on whether you should buy or lease a vehicle, and even call them from the dealership if you're wary of what the salesman is telling you. You can sign up for a three-month trial for $1 to sample the benefits of the club.

One resource in their online area that is available to everyone is the Used Car Lot. It has classified ads where you can buy or sell a used car. A free Car Alert service will notify you when a car that matches what you're looking for becomes available. But to get AutoVantage's used car valuations, trip routing, and roadside assistance, you have to become a member. You can apply online and receive $20 worth of free gas just for signing up for the three-month trial.

Channel Jumping

Find an effective design for a home office that fits your decor but remains functional. Head to the *WorkPlace* channel for ideas on setting up space for a home-based business.

Take Flight with Aviation Areas

Hone Your Knowledge of Specialty Aircraft

The *Aviation Forum*, **KEYWORD: AVForum**, offers a non-stop resource for over 400 annual airshows in North America. Schedules, locations, rosters of performers, and sometimes ticket information of private and military shows are offered several months in advance. Smaller air-craft—like model airplanes—are covered here, too. ATC Mallard, Cessna, and Navy jet fighters: there are message boards and software related to specific airplane models of all types and sizes.

Contruct All Kinds of Model Planes

KEYWORD: Model Planes is the launching pad for exploring Web sites dedicated to radio control, scale model, and paper airplanes. Aviation hobbyists can link to Philip Edelbrock's paper on how to design and fly the ideal Hand Launch Glider, go on a tour of the model airfield at The Icelandic Modeler's club Thytur, or learn to distinguish between different glider styles at Sailplane Modeler.

Read All About Aviation

Flying professionals and hobbyists will want to make an occasional landing at *Flying Magazine Online*, **KEYWORD: Flying Magazine**, to read The Flying Experts' fascinating and informative columns. Each expert's personality seeps through these entertaining collections of essays. Especially notable are Peter Garrison's Aftermath columns. Rather than sensationalize, Garrison's analyses of airplane accidents attempt to objectively present the facts, as well as help pilots avert future flying disasters. Gordon Baxter's soulful, nostalgic Bax Seat column lends a personal voice to *Flying Magazine*. At 73, this former pilot refers to himself as a "teller of tales" dedicated to keeping *Flying Magazine* at the top of the heap. Earnestly sharing some oddball experiences as a commercial airline pilot is Thomas Block's periodic Flying the Line column. And you can catch some humor and commonsense tips from I Learned About Flying From That, or ILAFT (pronounced "I Laughed"). These reader-written articles share flying stories of survival and stupidity. You'll also find frameable wall posters featuring reproductions of *Flying Magazine*'s covers from special times in aviation history.

Attention AOL Shoppers!

Collectors of memorabilia, antiques, and Americana can swap, buy, and sell to their heart's content at **KEYWORDS: Antique, Collectors, Civil War**, and **Model Trains**.

Become a Savvy Techno-Shopper

Choose TV and Video Equipment with Confidence

While researching and budgeting for TV, video, and home entertainment equipment, sift through the well-researched test reports found at KEYWORD: **Video Online**. If the small number of reviews relative to the market size surprises you, keep in mind that *Video Magazine* only reviews the top 100 products each year, filtering out the weakest models. With extreme attention to detail, the reviewers direct you to the hidden features while pointing out which devices function better than anticipated, and which do not fulfill expectations. For faster reference, you can skip over to each test report's short form with just the specs and its "by the numbers" listing of basic parts and price. Reviewers stay on top of the latest technological advances, covering such groundbreaking innovations as hybrid TV/PCs, direct-broadcast satellite, and DVD technology.

Insider's Tip

Fly virtually everywhere. Join one of three flight simulator clubs at KEYWORD: **AVForum.**

Get a Personal Perspective on New and Used Stereo Systems

Though *Stereo Review Online*, at KEYWORD: **Stereo Review**, performs thorough test reports of new audio equipment, you can receive longer-term, more personalized viewpoints from AOL members in the "Sound Off" message boards. Knowledgeable members provide genuine, bias-free advice on your potential purchases. One member advises, "Regardless of whether or not you want DTS eventually, you definitely will want Dolby Digital capability, as it is the standard audio format for a growing number of things (DVD included)."

Another key perk provided by the Sound Off boards is the full-blown treatment given to smaller components and parts usually not covered in magazine reviews. The Soundings folder, for example, has more than 3,000

Computer Magazines Update You on the Latest Technology

With the advent of WebTV, computer and television technologies are melding. One hot technology on the horizon, DVD, is covered in both video magazines such as *Video Online* as well as computing and online magazines such as Communications Week, Interactive Week, and CNET. To keep current on all fronts of technology, visit KEYWORD: **Magazine Rack** in the Computing Channel.

posts on speaker cables alone. Sound Off visitors can also seek out other members for advice on electronic mishaps and installation assistance, or to buy and sell equipment.

Focus on Photography and Art

Channel Jumping

Kids have their own artistic playgrounds in the Kids Only Channel. You'll find a Big Fridge online where they can showcase their drawings like they do at home, coloring pages to print out, and contests galore.

Ask Todd About Marketing Your Art

Starving artists can end the famine with the marketing and publishing wisdom found at **KEYWORD: AskToddArt**. Post a question to art business world maven Todd Bingham, and secure an answer that both advises and illuminates.

Broad questions such as: "How do I photograph artistic paintings for promotion?" receive lengthy answers that look at all possible angles. After laying out the necessary steps to hiring a professional photographer, Todd continues with this advice: "If you have a cash flow issue...the very best way to shoot them from an amateur point of view is to take 'em outside and lean 'em up. Natural sunlight is the most authentic and very best way to light artwork to photograph it."

An answer to your question may already exist in Previous Q & A's, in Frequently Asked Questions, or in The Basics of Marketing, which offers guidelines on negotiating gallery commissions, creating a portfolio, and finding an agent or publisher. Dealers, publishers, and gallery owners on the lookout for undiscovered talent or new markets will also want to check in on *AskToddArt*.

Attention AOL Shoppers!

Popular Photography, **KEYWORD: PopPhoto**, tests and reviews the top 35mm cameras, making your search for a new camera simpler. You can download the test graphics and complete specs for future reference.

Learn to Take Stunning Travel Photos

Traveling to new destinations often offers serious amateur photographers the best chance to make the most of their hobby. The Taking Travel Photos section of *Popular Photography*'s How-To Area, **KEYWORD: PopPhoto**, features instructive photographic essays of several vacation and sightseeing spots. Each essay recommends special landmarks and events that make excellent compositions. They also problem-solve potential obstacles to ideal shots, such as using different filters, films, and lenses to accommodate for hazy skies or poor access. A trip to Las Vegas inspired photographer Elinor Stecker-Orel to give these tips on shooting the Mirage Hotel: "Inside. . . you'll find a tropical paradise with real orchids and splashing waterfalls. It's best to use flash, although fast film will work under the skylight areas. The best photo op at the Mirage? The outdoor man-made 'volcano.' Every 20 minutes after dark it erupts with a roar and a blaze of fire and smoke. Flaming 'lava' even runs into the lake in front of the hotel—another marvel for your SLR or camcorder."

Even if you're not planning to travel, you can brush up on your picture-taking skills in the Tech and How-To Area. This accessible resource offers a package of pointers on Getting Started, and a Complete How-To Guide with lessons on maximizing depth of field, and shooting in very low light (good tip: focusing on the eyes will make your subject look sharper). You can also scan reviews of how-to books on the market.

Meet...
Todd Bingham

Active in the art gallery business for 20 years and current director of Planet West Publishers, Todd Bingham lends his marketing expertise to inquiring artists at KEYWORD: **AskToddArt**.

Exchange Photography Advice and Equipment

While not as visually arresting as *Popular Photography*, the *Kodak Photography Forum* practically short circuits from the constant flow of photographers posting to their Message Center. One of the more popular message boards at KEYWORD: **Kodak** is Photography Buy and Sell, where you can do business with items not under the Kodak brand, such as Canon, Nikon, and Polaroid. There are a ton of digital cameras being exchanged in this area, so if your interest is in moving from the medium of celluloid to pixels, I'd recommend this forum for getting a used digital camera on the cheap.

Look also to KEYWORD: **Classifieds** to see if you can find a slightly used digital camera. Click on "Computing," then "Peripherals," then "Other."

Digitally Enhance Your Photography

If you're wondering how to choose from the growing selection of digital cameras and related products, check out *Popular Photography*, KEYWORD: **PopPhoto**. Their writers review the latest digital cameras, and also keep you updated on all the new gizmos from the trade shows. For additional information, pay Pete Davison a visit at KEYWORD: **Kodak**. Davison, an expert in imaging technology, hosts a "New to Digital" chat on Monday nights.

Enrich and Improve Your Craftsmanship

Get a Handle on Woodworking Tools

A quick foray into the Tool Reviews at **KEYWORD: Wood** can save woodworkers a lot of time, money, and disappointment. *American Woodworker*'s experienced staff spends long hours and concentrated energy performing hands-on tests of newly released tools on the market. The results of these laboratory and workshop tests get funneled into honest, easy-to-read reviews and comparisons that expose false manufacturers' claims, and reveal

Insider's Tip

American Woodworker's Tool Reviews tell you what equipment rates highest with the magazine's editors. But the best parts of posting the magazine online are the ability to search articles easily and the daily quiz. Web links also take you to more woodworking resources, such as the *rec.wood working* newsgroup.

Patch Up Your Quilting Skills

You can increase your productivity and diversify your creations with the many resources at **KEYWORD: Quilting**. Probably the best aspect of *The Quilting Forum* is the fabric exchanges. You can receive a constant influx of patterned, plain, and hard-to-find fabrics by joining one of these monthly swaps. Some of the other noteworthy areas of the forum include:

- Online lessons, which give you project patterns to download, and directions on how to cut, design, and stitch
- Hints on how to enroll in a local guild and locate hidden quilt shops
- Calendars of quilting shows
- Opportunities to meet other forum frequenters offline to shop, or to craft quilts for charitable causes
- A Quilting Exhibit to post photos of, and comments on, your most prized creations

Good Stuff!

KEYWORD: Quilting offers a free, online newsletter called the NinePatch News. In addition to the forum's chat schedule and notes from readers, the newsletter includes a calendar of upcoming quilt shows and retreats. To sign up for NinePatch, go to the *Quilting Forum* and follow the subscription instructions.

the workability and overall performance of the tools and machines.

Members can also access reports on "classic" tools, since *American Woodworker Magazine Online* has archived every back issue since 1988. And if a particular review does not contain the accompanying chart originally in the print version, it's possible to order an article reprint from the Online Store.

Insider's Tip

Sew News is replete with essential tips on topics such as sewing machine maintenance, fabric texturizing, and patterns for reversible kid's clothing. But the best resource at **KEYWORD: Sew News** may be the message boards, where you can get specific questions answered by both the *Sew News* staff and fellow members.

Join an Online Crafting Community

Since craft work often goes hand-in-hand with communal activity, the chat room at **KEYWORD: Crafts Magazine** fittingly fuels innovative crafting ideas during its open and regularly scheduled sessions. These sessions include a series on quilting methods, help in finding mail order product sources, and techniques for rubber stamping. During the hosted chats, handiwork experts answer questions in practical, artistic terms as demonstrated by this quote from *Crafts Magazine* staff member Judy Brossart: "There is a really cute clay pot favor you or your kids can make for Mother's Day. Simply fill the pot with a foam shape, cover it with Spanish moss, then add yo-yo flowers. You can buy the pre-made yo-yo's, add a button center and also add a stem. Then poke the flowers into the pot, add a few eucalyptus stems and you're finished." In the spirit of community, *Crafts Magazine* also houses Moms Helping Moms—an area which lists Internet and street addresses of organizations that donate finished products or extra materials to homeless shelters, hospitals, and other charitable causes.

Find More Crafts and Home Decoration Ideas

KEYWORD: Woman's Day has an elegant Crafts and Home section with sewing suggestions, crafts notions, and articles on sprucing up your house to truly make it a home. You can also put your flair for design to work with **KEYWORD: Ideas for Better Living.** Also hosted by *Woman's Day*, this area has downloadable files to help you create festive ornaments, decoupaged plates, sweaters, scarves, and other gifts with a personal touch.

Download Craft and Sewing Patterns

With *Crafts Magazine Online* and its subsidiary publication, *Sew News: The Fashion How-to Magazine*, at **KEYWORD: Sew News**, you can easily download the graphics and text of hundreds of instructional articles. Each

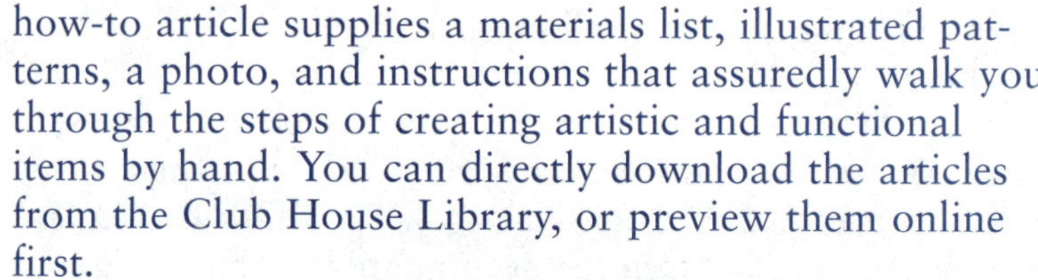

how-to article supplies a materials list, illustrated patterns, a photo, and instructions that assuredly walk you through the steps of creating artistic and functional items by hand. You can directly download the articles from the Club House Library, or preview them online first.

Insider's Tip

Does your interest in fashion compel you to pursue a career in the industry? *Wilhelmina Agencies* offer model and design career advice, as well as opportunities to get exposure and potentially jump-start your career at KEYWORD: **Wilhelmina**.

Crafts Magazine Online proves especially useful for making homemade gifts and decor during holidays and special events. Within the Painting, Needlework, Fabric Art, Florals, and Special Features areas, you'll discover ideas for theme-based pieces, such as a graduation T-shirt, a clay pot Christmas tree, and wedding accessories.

Prepare to Tie the Knot

While roping together all the particulars of the wedding ceremony and reception, the whole family can remain sane with KEYWORD: **Knot**. During the initial planning stages, *The Knot: Weddings for the Real World* puts the billion dollar wedding industry into perspective, directing you through the processes of choosing a band and taste-testing cakes. You may even want to hire a photographer, florist, or clergy person from *The Knot*'s vendor message boards.

To keep emotions under control, there are several areas which give brides expert and "from the trenches" advice on issues in intimacy, family, and solving unexpected emergencies. Meanwhile, mothers and bridesmaids learn to deal with everything from groom grudges to makeup smudges from The Wedding Party area.

And you can decide between a ritzy island retreat or a more rugged destination with the honeymoon research tools at Great Escape.

Good Stuff!

Save money on wedding affairs by making your own guestbook, place-settings, and trinkets for the guests. KEYWORD: **Woman's Day** has many ideas for wedding crafts in their Crafts and Home section.

Meet the Martial Arts Masters

Learn the Dojo

From the Reference area of *Martial Arts Worldwide Network*, **KEYWORD: MAW**, you can connect directly to Action Theatre. This downloadable collection of free video clips features highly skilled instructors and world champions demonstrating ancient and contemporary methods of self-defense, self-improvement, and inner power. Included among the disciplines are ju-jitsu, aikido, and kickboxing. Hollywood film clips with movie stars like Bruce Lee and Chuck Norris also grace Action Theatre! Free software to run the videos can be downloaded if you need it. You can also order full-length instructional videos from the *MAW* Video Library online store.

Channel Jumping

KEYWORD: Japan in the International Channel has more information on the Martial Arts in the Sports section. Karate, judo, shotokai: the forms are quite diverse. Learn the differences among them here.

Let Martial Arts Experts Train You

Students of Martial Arts can also benefit from the online training tips given by kickboxing heavyweight champion Joe Lewis, and three-time national karate tournament champ Keith Vitali, at **KEYWORD: Karate Int**. Both of these skilled athletes have written articles detailing effective approaches, and tips on mind preparation for tournaments. Photographs of the techniques and moves accompany many of the articles.

Karate International Magazine also caters to those less interested in learning martial arts maneuvers, and more fascinated with the machinations of the movie industry. Written by martial artist and Hollywood writer and director Keith W. Strandberg, Facts, Rumors, Lies, and Half-Truths offers a critical insider's look at action flicks. Strandberg digs up the dirt on films in production, makes actor salaries public, and analyzes the shooting, budgeting, and writing from his expert standpoint. Jackie Chan, Jean Claude van Damme, Bruce and Brandon Lee are only a few of the stars Strandberg covers.

Insider's Tip

The *Women Warrior Network* at **KEYWORD: MAW** offers streetwise safety and martial arts self-protection techniques designed for women. It also links you to the Assault Prevention Information Network and Fighting Women News Magazine.

Get a Closer Look at the Ultimate Fighting Championships

Wondering what all the hype is over *The Ultimate Fighting Championships*? A stop by **KEYWORD: UFC** will bring you face-to-face with photos and profiles of champs Vitor Belfort, Oleg Taktarov, Mark Coleman, and other oversized contenders. Use the download library to access exclusive action shots of past championships, photo portraits of favorite champions, and interviews with fighters. But perhaps the most action of this site resides in the message boards, where fans have a fighting chance to grapple over upcoming fights and past legends.

> **WHERE TO GET A PSYCHIC READING**
>
> You have several options for gaining advice from psychics. Some are free, and some have fees—it all depends on whether you'd rather spend time or money. At **KEYWORD: Crystal Ball** you can sign up for a free, public reading in the Tarot room, or treat yourself to a longer, live, one-on-one or private email reading. Prices vary. At **KEYWORD: Astronet** you can get a free mini-reading in the Reading Rooms or hire a professional for a longer session.

Explore Mystical Powers and Other Psychic Phenomena

Uncloak the Mysteries of the Mind and Universe

Has a vivid dream, powerful déjà vu, or extraordinary meeting of the minds ever prompted you to explore the realms of clairvoyance, astrology, and psychic readings? The bustling message board at **KEYWORD: Mystic Gardens** gives curious members an opportunity to question and experiment with such phenomena as astral projection, psychic healing, and Celtic Runes. Exchange stories about soul mates, compare characteristics with those who share your sign, muse over unexplained phenomena, and interpret dreams.

Learn to Use Metaphysical Powers

You can gain insight into several ancient sciences of prediction and healing with the *Crystal Ball Forum*'s

Metaphysics Learning Center, **KEYWORD: Crystal Ball**. The Center familiarizes curious beginners with the terms, techniques, and processes of such oracles as Tarot, Numerology, and I-Ching. These lessons, which have been authored by scholars and professional practitioners, take you beyond bland, textbook definitions and into the heart of each method. Incorporating helpful photographs, charts, and drawings with interesting text, the lessons teach you how to do readings and interpret signs.

Good Stuff!

Use your psychic powers to solve crimes, find adoptive parents, and explain paranormal experiences with The *Crystal Ball* Psychic Investigations Team at **KEYWORD: Crystal Ball**.

Get a Free Psychic Reading

To see where your destiny lies, or to better understand your emotions and motivations, queue up for a free, live reading in the *Astronet* Reading Rooms, at **KEYWORD: Astronet**. Using the wisdom and prophesies of astrology, channeling, tarot cards, and various other oracles, the professional readers on *Astronet* offer daily relationship, financial, and career counsel.

Not quite satisfied with your reading? Get a second opinion—or a third, fourth, or fifth—from a long list of experienced teachers, writers, healers, radio personalities, and others with their own unique perspectives on the heavens. Profiles of the readers can be screened in Meet Our Readers. Check the Reading Rooms schedules to see when your chosen psychic will appear. Be forewarned, however, that the readers can only perform between 6 and 10 readings per two-hour session. Plan on arriving as early in the rooms as possible to secure a spot for yourself.

If the line's too long in the Reading Rooms, you can instead take advantage of *Astronet*'s interactive software programs. Provided by Matrix, Inc., an award-winning pioneer in metaphysics and technological innovations, these programs help you to determine past, present, and future horoscopes, and acquire answers to yes and no questions from the Runes and I-Ching. *Astronet*'s trivia game is a fun way to learn more about astrology.

Meet...

Melissa Townsend

At **KEYWORD: Tarot to Go**, Melissa Townsend combines astrology, tarot cards, and her own psychic abilities to offer personal readings in live chats and on the message boards.

Good Stuff!

With the guidance of the Zodiac, and a look at members' profiles, you may just find your match in the Astromates lounge, where romance sparkles. **KEYWORD: Astronet**.

This chapter is really only a sampling of the kinds of topics covered throughout AOL. All kinds of hobbies and interests have vital forums and active message boards where you can share your enthusiasm and experiences. It's your input that drives these areas, proving once again that often the best resource on AOL is the members themselves. And since common interests often build active communities, that's what I'm going to write about next.

17 Communities: Finding Friendship, Advice, and Support

How many communities do you belong to? On America Online that's not an easy question to answer. For me, it often depends on the day, and the time of day, and my workload, and how adventurous I'm feeling. But without getting into specifics, I'll make a wild estimate and claim citizenship in ten, maybe twelve, overlapping AOL communities.

Sound high? I'm willing to bet most veteran AOLers belong to just as many. How about you? No matter how you define yourself, there are bound to be several communities on AOL that reflect each of the varied parts of you. Let's see: Monday through Friday, you're a professional. Then after work, you return home and you're a spouse. Maybe you're a parent—your role now becomes simply "Mom" or "Dad." Or perhaps you're single and looking. On the weekends, you become a tennis enthusiast, hiker, or would-be writer. Now are you starting to see what I mean?

Among the communities on AOL, you'll find religion and belief areas, places that celebrate racial diversity, supportive gay spaces, women's networks, hangouts for retired people, areas that encourage volunteerism, and resources for military servicemembers. And we won't leave out the extensive number of places to find your match in love and romance. Are your communities starting to add up yet?

Find Chat Friends

You'll see that there are plenty of opportunities on AOL to meet like-minded people and to build community. Chat is just one more great way to talk with people around the world on topics that interest you most. You'll find conversations on careers and family, for seniors, teens, and women. Talk with hobbyists, musicians, and neighbors in cities throughout the country such as Denver, Miami, NYC and many others. To join in, go to KEYWORD: **Chat**, select "List Rooms," then click on the category of your choice. You'll be talking in no time!

What Do You Believe?

Explore the World's Religions and Beliefs

Chatter Box

People of vastly differing opinions debate and learn about hot topics in Christianity, Islam, Judaism, New Age, and Paganism. If you're spiritual, join in by clicking "Chat" at KEYWORD: **Religion**.

While KEYWORD: **Religion** initially appears to be divided into four major areas—Christianity, Judaism, World Beliefs, and Spiritual Mosaic—it's really divided into scores of sub-communities. *Religion & Beliefs* is the common forum where you can learn more about your own faith and those of others. Get in-depth knowledge of your own religion, and explore the beliefs of others.

From Ask a Rabbi to Catechism for Beginners to Wiccan ritual descriptions, there are many resources for the spiritual seeker. You'll also discover plenty of opportunities to meet members of your own faith—or one you've always found interesting. And whether it's Ramadan, Easter, or Passover, there are plenty of useful holy day resources like recipes, art, and prayers.

Islam, Judaism, and Christianity currently have the most extensive offerings, with the Catholic Community area particularly robust. You can use the terrific pointers to the Web and discussion areas for many other faiths, including Sikh, Atheism, Baha'i, Hinduism, Unitarian Universalist, Islamic/Muslim, Pagan/Magick, Native Spirituality, and Interfaith.

Connect with the Christian Community

Good Stuff!

Subscribe to *Christianity Online*'s free newsletter. Every Friday you'll know exactly what's new with the Christian Community. Sign up at KEYWORD: **CO**.

The congregation at *Christianity Online*, KEYWORD: **CO**, extends well beyond any parish borders to bring Christians of all denominations together. You are invited to share your religious experiences and the role of faith in your daily life in this AOL Member's Choice area.

Before you start, you can go on a tour of the expansive AOL area at KEYWORD: **CO Tour**. Children talk to each other about what it's like to grow up being a preacher's kid, having "strict" parents, and celebrating their faith in youth groups and in camps at KEYWORD: **CO Kids**.

Ministers exchange ways of struggling with the tough issues facing their churches at **KEYWORD: CM**. Single, married, and divorced men and women discuss how their beliefs and personal relationships with God help guide their relationships with one another.

The most prominent resource of this area is the active participation and interaction of the community's members. Fellowship Halls One and Two are full 'round the clock with Christians sharing prayer requests, encouraging one another, or discussing theology. For all the Christian chat, go to **KEYWORD: CO Live**.

The Internet tools at **KEYWORD: COWEB** help you get to excellent Christian Web sites.

Discuss Faith with the Catholic Community

At the sound of the bells, you'll know you've reached the Catholic Community area, **KEYWORD: Catholic**. There's a lot of information here: church history and practice, current debates, messages from the Vatican, and all the international news and issues that concern Catholics today. You'll have access to messages from church scholars as well as laymembers from across the country. The Catholic community is growing and changing online!

Discuss your beliefs with fellow church members or those of another denomination. If you've forgotten, or are teaching a younger Catholic, the Web Resources include a link to a site on How to Pray a Rosary. The message boards are huge: one interesting resource is the Q&A with Father Ken Roberts.

Attention AOL Shoppers!

Save up to 48% on religious magazines at **KEYWORD: Magazine Outlet**. *Guideposts*, *Catholic Digest*, and *Hope* are here. Just click the category "Lifestyles & Interests," then click "Religious."

Your Jewish Heritage

Youth groups, synagogues, and other Jewish organizations create strong bonds. The *Jewish Community* area, **KEYWORD: Jewish**, is no exception. From kids (**KEYWORD: Jewish Youth**) to Jerry Seinfeld (**KEYWORD: Jewish Arts**), you've got all the most interesting aspects of Jewish culture.

Insider's Tip

Matchmaker, matchmaker, make me a match at **KEYWORD: Jewish Singles**. Search for Jewish mates who share your interests or live in your state. Their singles chat is one of the most popular on AOL.

Channel Jumping

Visit the Holy Land at *Jewish Community*'s **KEYWORD: Israel** and the International Channel's **KEYWORD: Isr@el**. Take note of the "@" sign or you'll miss the second area entirely.

One of the most popular features is **KEYWORD: Ask a Rabbi**, which attracts 50 to 60 email questions per day and inspired an article in *Wired* magazine. *Ask a Rabbi* allows Jews in rural communities without a local synagogue, curious non-Jews, and many others to get their Judaism-related questions answered. The rabbinical replies arrive within a week or two; in the meantime, read through the Q&A archives to learn more about the Jewish faith.

Jews who keep Kosher and anyone who appreciates good potato pancakes will enjoy **KEYWORD: Jewish Food.** Search a database of Kosher restaurants and find all new fillings for your Hamentashen (Purim cookies). You'll find recipes for every holiday, including a guide to setting up your Seder table. Additional holiday and spirituality resources can be found at **KEYWORD: Jewish Holiday.** Download a Jewish calendar or read commentary on Torah passages.

A section of *Jewish Community* is dedicated to getting more out of your Jewish heritage, even if you hated Hebrew school or don't go to synagogue. As of this writing, the area was at **KEYWORD: Why Be Jewish**, but look for it with a new name soon.

Where's Your Faith on AOL?

Think you can't find your religion at **KEYWORD: Religion**? By going to **KEYWORD: WorldBeliefs** or one of the individual keywords below, you'll find links to forums that include hugely popular message boards, Web resources, and download libraries.

The forum of the world's youngest independent religion, **KEYWORD: Baha'i** takes you to resources of followers who strive for world peace and harmony, and an end to politicized religion. Come discuss the central theme of Bahá'u'lláh's message, that humanity is one single race and that all of humankind is truly one global society. In the message boards, members delve into their beliefs about how traditional barriers of race, class, creed, and nation are giving way to create a universal civilization.

If you want to know more about the teachings and following of Siddhartha Gautama, the Buddha, just go to **KEYWORD: Buddhism**. One Buddhist member writes: "Refrain from speaking what is not true." Other wise aphorisms abound in the message boards: "There are two wings to the Dharma, study and meditation. If overweighted on one side you cannot fly."

If you want to follow the religion that has no single creator and upholds great respect for an ideal way of life, **KEYWORD: Hinduism** is the place to go. Karma yoga, Krishna consciousness, and Hindi teens are popular discussion threads. Here's what one teen had to say about discrimination in school: "I can totally relate . . . so many people at my school get the wrong idea of Hinduism . . . they think it's a cow-worshipping religion. We've had a few skits in some of our classes—so many of them mock Hinduism and Indians!!"

One does not have to journey to Mecca during Hajj to celebrate Islamic faith—**KEYWORD: Islamic** has your resources. On the active message boards members debate topics like whether women wearing hijab is a humble submission to Allah or suppression by men. Does hadith

Atheism-Agnosticism Forum

Skeptics and nonbelievers need not be left out of the online religious community. **KEYWORD: Atheism** or **KEYWORD: Agnostic** takes you to the *Atheism-Agnosticism Forum*, where freedom of religion also means the freedom not to practice religion at all. The message boards here discuss all aspects of being a nonbeliever in a world where most people are part of an organized religion. Atheists and agnostics have separate boards (both are interesting) where they talk about relationships with believers, trade ideas for coping with religious holidays, point out songs with atheistic themes, tackle philosophical issues, and try to define what agnosticism really means.

Good Stuff!

The Atheism-Agnosticism Forum of **KEYWORD: Atheism** has links like the Celebrity Atheist List. It catalogues famous atheists and agnostics such as Jodie Foster, Bill Gates, Kurt Vonnegut, and Billy Joel.

Different Religions Come Together

Divisiveness is often the norm among peoples of differing religious faiths. **KEYWORD: Interfaith** helps members to foster goodwill among and between different religions and beliefs. Jewish/Muslim friendship, religious tolerance, and interfaith marriages are some of the dozens of topics in the message boards.

Channel Jumping

KEYWORD: India leads you to a Hindi Language Resources page that features spiritual terms, audio lessons, and Hindi magazines.

really illuminate the holy Quran, or contradict its teachings? Are followers of Louis Farrakhan representative of Muslims in America? Members of all faiths can learn about these issues and enlighten themselves about the religion. Texts on the Jihad, methodology of the prophets, and pictures of Mecca can all be downloaded from the software library.

Pagans have their own place to discuss such topics as religious intolerance and parenting at **KEYWORD: Pagan**. Witches, Wise Ones, MagicDancers, Faeries, Magickians, Astrologers, and others network with fellow spiritualists. Find everything you ever wanted to know about Ceremonial and High Magick, for instance. Congregate in a live Pagan chat just about every night of the week.

Racial Harmony

Hispanic Schools, Cities, and Success Stories

Enrich Your Latino Business

Grow your business with the resources and networking for Latinos at **KEYWORD: Hispanic Online.** Once you click "Business" you'll find weekly live chat with other professionals and extensive message board discussions of topics such as Latino biz and the Net. The business success stories tell of successful Centros Medicos Latinos, restaurants, and one very savvy 19-year-old marketing genius.

If you've ever been to *Hispanic Online*, you know that the chat room parties never stop. Chats focus on young people, singles, professionals, and Spanish-speakers. The message boards cover everything Hispanic under the sun. But for those times when you don't feel like talking, don't forget that **KEYWORD: Hispanic Online** has a lot more to offer.

Students and parents should check out the Education section, which ranks the top 25 colleges for Hispanics and lists a bunch of scholarships that can ease the financial burden of college. Young people can also find many Latino and Latina role models here, like famous athletes, brilliant scientists, well-loved entertainers, and successful entrepreneurs.

Your career gets a boost from a list of organizations which help Hispanic businesses and articles about job success. Know where to work, or just which companies to patronize, with information on the 100 best U.S. companies for Hispanics. The companies are evaluated based on recruitment and hiring practices, education, minority vendor programs, and support for Hispanic organizations. Other "best of" lists rate restaurants that cook it (almost) like Mom and the best cities to call home.

Black Voices

Imagine a neighborhood coffee shop where locals from all walks of life gather to sip a beverage and talk about life. What you get is Black Voices—a news, information, and discussion area of special interest to African Americans and all AOL members. Most anyone would feel at home in this open community.

It's an all out exchange of ideas and philosophies. Certainly there is lots to talk about, and most anything is fair game. Meet live online with black entrepreneurs, join the Black Voices book club to discuss novels like "Sister, Sister," or get together with other young students in

Chatter Box

Black Entrepreneurs. Over 40. Nation of Islam. Young Ebony Scholars. These are just a few of the more than 20 live discussions that you can participate in. Go to KEYWORD: **Black Voices** then click on "BV Chat Rooms."

Your Heritage Is Represented

If you're not Black or Hispanic, you may not have found an AOL community for people of your ethnic background. Rest assured, it's there.

Go to KEYWORD: **Exchange** and click on "Communities." Message boards bring together Native Americans, Asian-Americans, and people of European descent (from Holocaust survivors to Scottish clans). Native Americans also have a scheduled chat every Wednesday night and a full library of pictures, treaties, and articles.

If you're biracial, multiracial, or involved in an interracial relationship, the Multicultural message board at the Exchange will address your concerns. KEYWORD: **Black Voices** also has a section called Ebony and Ivory that talks about hardships that come with black/white relationships and the raising of biracial children.

Young Scholars chat. Seven nights a week, the discussion and information exchange in Black Voices is hopping. Another place to share your views is the Black Wall, a huge message board on the Web which includes interesting talk on women in business, teens, and interracial relationships.

So that you'll never be lacking for hard news, follow the links to the in-depth online newspapers in Baltimore, Charlotte, and Orlando. At each of these great news resources, you'll find columns and regular features to keep you up with the latest opinions by respected community leaders.

NetNoir: The Soul of Cyberspace

Meet... HeartBeat

KEYWORD: NetNoir's resident relationships expert, HeartBeat, offers down-to-earth advice about sustaining a relationship in the '90s. "We do not play here," *NetNoir* warns, "and the answers you get will be FOR REAL!"

The self-titled "Soul of Cyberspace," **KEYWORD: NetNoir** takes an Afro-centric look at education, business, music, and sports. The forum is huge! Diverse interests for a diverse crowd means articles and areas that cover just about any subject: Minority Golf Association, Martin Luther King, reggae, and Historically Black Colleges (great for the college-bound).

NetNoir's weekly newsletter keeps you in touch with new happenings in the forum, including a list of authors and entertainers live in chat rooms. Sign up by following the link to the *NetNoir* Web site.

The Internet resources are strong in the section called Black Web, or you can go straight to other AOL areas of particular interests to African Americans by clicking the icon Black AOL.

Take a peek at the Celebrity Spotlight for live guests in fields such as politics, business, literature, entertainment, religion, and self-empowerment.

Most of all, *NetNoir* is about the people in the community. Business, romance and erotica, genealogy, books, college, and youth discussion threads—these are just a few of the topics you can discuss in the enormous and popular message boards.

Queer Connections

Find Queer Fellowship at onQ

Talk about communities within communities! Gays, lesbians, bisexuals, and transgendered persons. Parents and Friends of Lesbians and Gays. The Gay and Lesbian Alliance Against Defamation. Straight Friends. It's easy to get lost in the many levels of community at **KEYWORD: onQ**. But, of course, the inclusiveness and diversity are points of pride as *onQ* serves the variety of queer interests.

Get questions answered, meet people, and find support. The Home & Family section contains great marriage resources including an analysis of legal matters, and message boards on popping the question. Here's what a member warns you should be prepared for when you have a wedding ceremony: "(1.) People who are uncomfortable showing up late and sitting in the back, like parents. (2.) Friends to shy away from you after the service—often people see you in a different light (even other gay friends) and you drift apart. (3.) Crying (4.) Screaming just a little too."

Sub-communities are well-represented: women only, leather, trans, and the first ever group for active duty servicemembers, Military onQ. In Military onQ, for instance, discussion is entirely anonymous so that servicemembers can freely discuss issues important to them without fear of investigation. The transgendered forum includes the only daily TG news service. You don't have to worry about where you'll fit in.

Good Stuff!

Who's that warrior princess? Xena, of course. Join in at **KEYWORD: Gay Chat** every Sunday at 11 p.m. ET to laugh at that ubiquitous "whoosh" sound and dish about her relationship with Gabriel.

Instant Support for Gays, Friends, and Parents

Distraught mother of a lesbian daughter? Just coming out? Gay parent? There's a chat for you every night of the week at **KEYWORD: Gay Chat**. *OnQ*'s chat provides anonymity (if you prefer) as you seek support, make friends, or just relax with a group of like-minded comrades. Check the other chat schedules, too, for Bisexual discussion, Gay youth, and casual talk in the Lambda Lounge.

PlanetOut: Fun and Informative

KEYWORD: PlanetOut moves a little more to the lighter side of queer life in comparison with its AOL cousin, *onQ*. But it also has great resources for when you're in a more serious mood. Where *onQ* is more comprehensive, *PlanetOut* is irreverent. The two forums really serve to supplement and balance each other. From parents, politics, and parties to coping and comics, you're sure to find the news, fun, information, and community resources you're looking for.

PlanetOut's popular and well-stocked queer moving image collection helps you select movies that might matter to you. **KEYWORD: PopcornQ** lists the newest releases, highlights gay film festivals, and serves up movie news. Want to see hundreds of films recommended by famous queers? Just select Queer Top Ten. Bust out laughing with well-known funnies *Dykes To Watch Out For*, and *The Mostly Unfabulous Social Life of Ethan Green.*

Take a quick trip to the best queer resources on the Internet with **KEYWORD: NetQueery**. Every day, you can find the daily Top 20 most popular sites, as well as the Top 20 sex sites and the Top 20 "people" sites by gays worldwide.

Support resources come out in droves, too. Check out all of the national organizations making a difference in your world, including: Parents and Friends of Lesbians and Gays (PFLAG), the National Gay and Lesbian Task Force (NGLTF), and the Gay and Lesbian Student Teacher Network (GLSTN).

WOMEN AT WORK

Get to the top of your profession with the copious work resources at **KEYWORD: Women.** Be inspired by featured profiles of women who've gotten the jobs and careers they've wanted, like human resource manager. Learn the 100 top companies for women: among them are Xerox, Lucasfilm, Ltd., and Hewlett-Packard.

Women's Network

Network with All Kinds of Women

The message boards and scheduled chats in *Women's Network* show how truly diverse the women of AOL are. Talk to mothers, stepmothers, women trying to have children, and women who are childless by choice. Trade recipes with dieters, or share stories with the members of Loving Ourselves Fat Today. Straight, bisexual, and lesbian women. Young, middle-aged, and elderly women. Married, single, divorced, and widowed women. White women and women of color. They're all at **KEYWORD: Women**, talking about the issues that matter to them.

Women's Network is a prime example of women sharing their experiences. A typical quandary: to stay in an unsatisfying job or move on. "I too am trying to get up the courage to leave my job of 18 years and go back to school," a member writes. "I'm having a hard time overcoming the fear. I have been so complacent the past few years in my job and I really want to go to school full-time and can probably afford it for the first time in my life but I can't make the break. But I do have an interview for another job tomorrow and that's at least a step in the direction of leaving my security net and taking a risk."

In addition to providing space for women to get together, *Women's Network* scours AOL and the Web for relevant information. For example, they link to *Business Week's* features on women and business that investigate sexual harassment, maternity leave, and the glass ceiling. They make sure you didn't miss the article in the Travel Channel about women vacationing alone. The Women in Action section addresses political and social topics like domestic violence, single mothers, martial arts, and women in leadership positions.

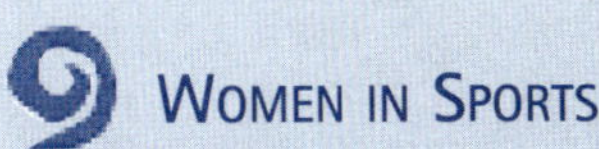

WOMEN IN SPORTS

Women's achievements in sports plaster ABC's special area at KEYWORD: **ABC Women.** In-depth profiles of women in sports range from swimming, gymnastics, and track and field to basketball. You can make your opinions heard by taking the Wide World of Sports Poll, like "What sport do you predict will see the biggest rise in popularity?" Ninety-five percent of respondents said basketball. What do you think?

Magazines for Women Who Do Too Much

If you're looking for fashion, beauty, or diet information, I don't have to tell you where to find it. You're a smart lady, and that stuff is everywhere. But there's more to women's magazines than that, including features that every woman can use—even if your idea of high fashion is wearing the *new* bluejeans.

KEYWORD: **Woman's Day** has an Easy Living section that might make your life, well, easier. Get car advice and help dispel that myth about women being lousy drivers. Learn strategies for making money at home, and find suggestions (suitable for either gender) about choosing a pet and avoiding financial pitfalls. You'll also find recipes inspired by Mom's home cooking, ideas on boosting your self-confidence, and tips for family women who are trying to make their days less hectic.

Coping with Your Divorce

The *Club for First Wives* is a community of divorced women getting used to being single again. Participants in message boards talk about custody issues and look at many divorce situations: "I left him," "I left him for her," and "It was his mid-life crisis" are only a few. It's also okay just to rant about your ex's worst qualities and to plot revenge . . . as long as you don't actually do it. ;)

KEYWORD: **First Wife**'s weekly poll lets you compare your experience to that of other online divorcees. See the results of surveys like "Who left?" and "Who cheated?" You may feel like the only one who's ever been tempted to re-marry your ex, but 3.4% of the members who took that week's poll already have.

Generations

Where the Teens Are

Cyber-savvy teenagers probably already know about *Seventeen Online* at KEYWORD: **Seventeen**, *MTV Online* at KEYWORD: **MTV**, and *Spin Online*, KEYWORD: **Spin**. Those three popular areas provide you with plenty to read and listen to, but there's even more to discover at KEYWORD: **Teens**.

KEYWORD: **Plug In** is multifaceted enough that you can vent one day and party the next. Write about this week's hot topic in Rave & Rant, speak your mind in an audio poll, and de-stress in the message boards—lots of other people are going through hard times, too. On the lighter side, read about computer games, find cool Web pages, and let loose in nightly chats.

Chatter Box

Visit KEYWORD: **Teen Hangout** for the quickest shortcut to the Teen Chat room, plus message boards, pictures of other members, and a schedule of who's hosting which chats.

Learn more about computers, surf the Web, and make new friends at KEYWORD: **Youth Tech**. *Youth Tech* was created by kids and teens, so you're bound to find members here who are on your wavelength. Do you have to be a young computer guru to hang out there? "Nope," says the *Youth Tech* staff. "You can just be here for the fun of it all!"

A fairly new area, the *Book Bag*, recommends diverse page-turners from *Paradise Lost* to *The Mystery Science Theater 3000 Episode Guide*. In the message boards at KEYWORD: **BookBag**, see what students at other schools are reading in English class and talk about your favorite authors.

Poets, student journalists, and other creative souls have their say at KEYWORD: **Teen Writer**. Enter a writing contest, research teen-friendly publishers, and find a mentor. The goal of *Teen Writers* is to be a safe haven—if you're getting tormented at school for your bookish nature, it won't happen here.

Another online safe haven is *!OutProud!*, an area for queer youth. Learn what to expect when you come out to your parents and what your rights are at school. The chat room has a lively under-21 crowd that will befriend you within minutes, and the message boards span a wide variety of topics: the prom, falling in love, school from junior high to college, political activism, Boy Scouts, and entertainment. You can find *!OutProud!* through KEYWORD: **TEENS** or KEYWORD: **OutProud**.

KEYWORD: **Teens** will also lead you to areas for homework help, snowboarding, computer games, activism, and the arts—all intended for a young audience.

Channel Jumping

Cher's Clueless Site, KEYWORD: **Clueless**, is a must for fans of the movie or TV show. The Cher-speak glossary is particularly wicked, way awesome, and fully chronic.

Good Stuff!

Readers of *Seventeen Magazine* have a lot in common! Find out just how much in the message boards at KEYWORD: **Seventeen**.

Teens Exist on the Outer Edge

The Outer Edge, KEYWORD: **TOE**, is AOL UK's teen hangout, featuring offbeat topics like independent music, skateboarding, and the paranormal. The chat room is a great place to meet teens from all over, but remember the time difference between your hometown and England–if that makes it hard to find a conversation, try the message boards. *The Outer Edge*'s Vault has lots of fun downloads: Alvin and the Chipmunks singing the *Macarena*, electronic sheep that wander your computer screen, and *.bmp* files to replace your current desktop wallpaper.

What Teens Do Online

I spent some time hunting out the best of the best. I looked at the statistics on what's really popular for teens, and asked a few of the teen guides what they thought was cool—or "phat," as they put it.

They recommended a combo of useful, fun, and hip. So there's teenager life offline and there's teen life on America Online, and here's the difference...

Recently, I volunteered to give a demo at a local high school about AOL and what's available for teens. But I realized that I've gotten old—in fact, ancient—by teenagers' time. I mean, when I was in high school, girls were in love with the guys in Duran Duran and *The Breakfast Club* was the movie that summed up our lives. So, basically, I was out of touch. What would they like: artsy stuff? fashion? games?

OFFLINE vs.	AMERICA ONLINE
"There's nothing to do."	Join teens who are making a difference at **KEYWORD: Do Something**
Gangs threaten to beat up computer whizzes	Gangs of computer whizzes at **KEYWORD: Youth Tech**
Worrying about the prom	Getting prom advice from real teens who've been there at **KEYWORD: Plug In**
Teens hang out at the mall, listening to the radio	Teens debate the best radio stations in the country at **KEYWORD: Teen Hangout**
Stay after school for a special SAT prep class from the world's most boring math teacher	Take a free online test prep class, visit college home pages, and speed ahead at **KEYWORD: Road to College**
Watch airplanes fly over your house	Join a squadron and shoot down a few enemy planes live at **KEYWORD: Air Warrior**

OFFLINE vs.	AMERICA ONLINE
Sit in your bedroom reading an old copy of *SPIN* magazine and wishing you were old enough to buy tickets for the next Bosstones show	Have a chat and get daily tour updates from Nate of the Bosstones at **Keyword: SPIN**
Watch *Star Trek* reruns on TV	Become a cadet and move up the ranks on a Federation Starship at **Keyword: Space Fleet**
Pore through stacks of used comics for months looking for that special Braniac trading card or DC Comic	Write to the comics' creators, swap cards with other fans, and find out about upcoming conventions at **Keyword: DC Comics**
Doodle in your notebook at school	Chat with the editor of *Anime Today* and swap stories about your favorite manga at **Keyword: Japanimation**
Throw in the towel and flunk that Physics test	Ask a teacher to explain what the heck Einstein was talking about at **Keyword: Homework Help**
Send away for dozens of college applications and start typing	Fill out an online registration form and send it to multiple colleges with the click of a button at **Keyword: Back to School**. In your extra time, look over Business School options

So how did my presentation go? Great! The high school kids went nuts—there was something for everyone from the class wonk to the class artist. And the teacher was pretty pleased, too. Luckily for me, she didn't teach math!

Remember When with Baby Boomers

If you think baby boomers are part of the "silent generation," then you've never visited *Baby Boomers*. This garrulous group at **KEYWORD: Baby Boomers** will remind you—loudly and often—that they belong to the communication era. You can revisit the era of the '60s, transformed into the AOL message boards of the '90s.

If you'd like to share some memories, talk about the music from the '50s and '60s, rehash some classic TV or seek advice on real, contemporary issues from people who grew up when you did, join the club.

Chat on the Message Boards and join the 49ers with others born in 1949. Some 49ers never miss a high school reunion: "It looks as though I may be the senior member of this 49er Club. I was born 1-1-49!!" a member writes. "I've been to many combined high school class reunions . . . . We had a great bunch of people and even though many of us are spread throughout the world, we manage to keep abreast of almost all of our classmates." This member's post just about sums up the point of *Baby Boomers*—keeping in touch with people in your generation.

Go on a Friend Search, or find your Birthday Twin. Got The Beatles on your mind? This might be the place for you. Do you ever ask yourself, Where Did We Go? Hook up with boomers from Queens to Los Angeles and find out. Or answer the eternal question in How Did You Meet Your Mate?

Twenty- and Thirtysomething Space

Post–baby boomers have their own forums in the Communities section at **KEYWORD: Exchange.** One Gen Xer wrote: "We don't like the hype of the boomer era. We grew up with advertising and frankly don't trust it." How's that for starting some intergenerational mudslinging? Members in their thirties wonder, "Is there life after 30?" One member's answer: "I don't (often) feel the need to prove myself to anyone anymore."

Seniors Congregate Around Their Computers

If you're an older adult looking for a little mind-expansion, try **KEYWORD: SeniorNet** and discover new ways to use your computer. And while you learn, you can relax and interact with your peers. Spend a minute in the highly popular chat room and you'll discover that there's probably more talk about grandchildren than microprocessors. People meet and greet old friends and make some new ones. The casual, friendly atmosphere makes you feel right at home, no matter what your level of familiarity with AOL or online chat is.

New and more advanced computer users will appreciate the articles and message boards in the Computer Learning Center. A participant here gives some processor advice that could save you some money: "Now is the time to pick up a Pentium 90 for what a 486DX2 cost six months ago. It should be fast enough for us 'geezers' who don't have to be on the leading edge of technology (unless we can afford it, that is!)." No matter whether you come for the technical information or just the company, the Community Center is a friendly meeting place to chat and reminisce.

Seniors really are talking up a storm in AOL's TownSquare. Any time of day you'll find people "brightening up one another's day"—as a chatter said when I looked in on the conversation. To get there use **KEYWORD: Chat**, then click "List Rooms" then "Life" then look for the senior rooms in the list in the right-hand box. And remember, never give your password or account information to anyone online.

Prepare for Retirement with AARP

Retirement can comprise the best years of your life. However, ensuring happiness in retirement requires preparation and research. It is a good thing, then, that the *American Association of Retired Persons* online area provides guidance about retirement issues, from handling your finances to maximizing your leisure time.

KEYWORD: AARP gives you access to government resources, insurance issues, tips on managing your money, health know-how, and consumer advice. All the information is tailored for the specific needs and concerns of older Americans.

Experienced, sagacious members are ready to help in the member bulletin boards and chat rooms. They form a community of older people who are able to answer many retirement questions like how to cope with managed care and which retirement communities are great to live in. One member wrote: "I live in a retirement community near Beaufort, South Carolina. It is Dataw Island and was developed by Alcoa Aluminum. I think it is a wonderful community. If you like golf, fishing or boating, it's hard to find a better place."

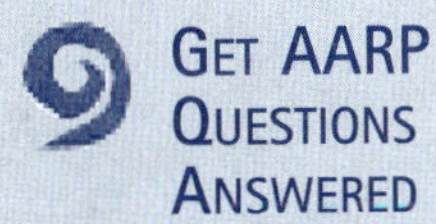

Got a question about AARP or need help finding information online? Every Tuesday through Friday in the Events Chat room at 2 p.m. ET, an AARP Online staff member will be available to answer your questions about membership, benefits, or other issues. **KEYWORD: AARP.**

Married to the Military

"Civilians don't get it," says one article in the Married to the Military section of KEYWORD: **NMFA**. If you've ever felt that way, read these stories of wives, husbands, and fiancées of servicepeople. Topics include Hollywood depiction of the military and dealing with frequent relocation.

AOL Salutes the Military

Services for Servicepeople

You might already know that *Military City Online*, KEYWORD: **MCO**, provides news, Web links, and R&R for active military personnel, veterans, and their families. But did you know that it can save you money?

The Medical Center explains military health care eligibility, veterans' insurance, benefits for your family, and dental plans. To help you manage your money, the Pay & Benefits section offers a military tax guide, pay chart, variable housing allowance rates, and software that will help you calculate it all. Even *Military City Online*'s advertisements are useful, offering insurance and benefits just for military people.

To find what you need in this big City, click on "Index" on the bottom of the screen for an alphabetical listing.

Find an Old Army Buddy

Trying to track down the friends you served with? Try the *Locator and Reunions Center*, KEYWORD: **Brats**. You can search national phone books, link to Web sites specifically for finding military personnel, scan the Looking for People boards, or post a "locator notice." Considering AOL's millions of members, even a locator notice as simple as "I am looking for James Harris. He was stationed at Fort Carson in 1957–1958" might yield results. Reunions are also listed so you don't miss the boat if your Navy buddies decide to get together.

Insider's Tip

USO-GRAMS are email messages that can be sent to overseas Navy personnel. Find out more about keeping in touch at KEYWORD: **MCO**'s Chat section.

Remembering Veterans

If you can't make it to the nation's capital, you can still visit the *Vietnam Veterans Memorial* at KEYWORD: **The Wall**. Anyone who has seen the Wall in person knows that sitting in front of a computer screen won't be exactly the same, but this well-done area captures the emotional experience of visiting the memorial. There are also some tributes online that aren't at the memorial site, like kids' letters to veterans and pictures of offerings left at the Wall in the past. You can search through all the names of those who died to find a loved one.

The popular, moving message boards serve as a space to salute a veteran or contact lost friends or family. One folder even includes a space for comments for the "Online Wall."

As a service to the friends and families of those who died in the Vietnam War, the Vietnam Veterans Memorial Fund provides free rubbings of any name on the Wall. You can request one through email.

Community Service

Help Build Better Communities

AOL Community Matters invites you to join their mission: helping people help themselves and others by building better communities both online and off, just a little closer to home. **KEYWORD: Community** is the hub of volunteering and making a difference on a personal level. With the many resources listed both on AOL and on the Internet, you can go directly to the main informational pages of organizations like Big Brother/Big Sister, AIDS Ride, Differently Abled Associates, Special Olympics International, and the Girl Scouts. About 70 other groups are also represented; clearly, you will never be lacking a good cause.

The prominently featured link to Action Without Borders (at *www.idealist.org*) takes you to an enormous database of organizations needing your help: Want to fight for civil liberties? Just enter "civil liberties," and you'll get a detailed list of several organizations to contact. You can do the same with animal rights, voting, gay rights, and consumer protection.

A Volunteer's Paradise

10,000 non-profit jobs and volunteer opportunities. Books and videos on education, human rights, and the environment. A chance to make a difference in the community of your choice. Go to *www.idealist.org*, or follow the link at **KEYWORD: Community**.

Think Globally, Act Locally

Do some good right in your own backyard. Many of the Digital Cities have special sections that list local volunteer opportunities. **KEYWORD: Washington DC** has a slew of ways you can help out, like DC Tech Corps, an organization that helps bring the latest technology to schools. Try any of the following keywords for well-organized listings: **Chicago, Boston**, or **Twin Cities.**

♦ ♦ ♦ ♦ ♦ ♦ ♦ ♦ ♦ ♦ ♦ ♦

Channel Jumping

What's your sign? The Astromates section of **KEYWORD: Astronet** will help you find "astro-compatible partners."

Youth Get Involved

KEYWORD: Heaven is an umbrella site for a number of activist organizations, mainly directed at getting youth involved in their communities. Find out what the issues are and how to get involved. Learn from celebrities and regular Joes and Joannas who make a difference daily. Discover where you can go in your city or town to become a part this growing community of activism and volunteerism!

Heavenly Bodies highlights celebrities who actively participate in the volunteer community, and tells you how and why they got involved. Maybe you'll follow in their footsteps. The section called Good Company highlights people and large companies that do good.

The message board is like an ever-growing community center full of volunteer suggestions like this one:

Do Something. . . Volunteer

Do Something knows there's more to young people than watching MTV. It's a national non-profit organization that provides training, guidance, and financial resources to young leaders working for local change. **KEYWORD: Do Something** organizes parents, teachers, and young people to make their communities better places to be, with projects like Homework In the Hood, a study group for Santa Ana, California, students.

The *Do Something* online area excels as a forum to exchange ideas with other community activists and learn more about leadership. One of the *Do Something* resources is *Build Magazine*, a publication by and for people under 25, who believe that all young people are visionaries. Local *Do Something* describes the programs in Boston, Newark, Selma, and Washington, D.C.; *Get Involved* provides applications for grants and programs.

"Don't forget your local animal shelter or humane society always needs help. If you can't help with time, they can always use food, blankets, towels, leashes, toys, money. How about having a garage sale and giving the profits to the shelter. Put a jar on your desk at work for pennies for puppies."

Good Stuff!

Are you on a steady diet of Harlequin novels? Maybe you'd like to become a romance writer yourself. The Romance Writing area of KEYWORD: **Romance** educates writers and entertains readers.

Find a Match That Fits

Fall in Love@AOL

Love@AOL, KEYWORD: **Love at AOL**, is a hub of online dating activity. Take a look at the Photo Personals to meet your potential mate, or post your own photo+. Pay a visit to the Love Shop, where you can find romantic gifts for your lover, read your love-related horoscope, practice flirting skills in the game Score, or take a weekly poll.

Chat in The Hot Bed or the For Play Café where you'll find some of the steamiest discussions in all of AOL. The Love@AOL message boards are full of dating anecdotes like "My Best Pick-Up Line Is . . . " and "You Know You're In Love When . . . "

Are you losing hope? Get advice from Jaid Barrymore, Dr. Kate, or G. Gaynor McTigue ("the king of what NOT to do in a relationship"). On the other hand, if your relationship is blossoming, you can hold a Cybervows ceremony and marry your sweetheart on AOL.

The Romance Hub on AOL

Are you on a steady diet of Harlequin novels? Maybe you'd like to become a romance writer yourself. *The Romance Writing* area of KEYWORD: **Romance** educates writers and entertains readers. For a list of like-minded meeting places for live discussion, click on Chat.

See Who You're Chatting With

It's a common problem: you're bad at names (or screennames), but you never forget a face. If you're curious about what your new-found online friends look like, flip through the photo album at KEYWORD: **Gallery** to find out.

You don't need to know how to scan a photo or upload a file to have your own portrait added. Just mail it in to the address provided in the area, have it scanned for free, and let members see the real you. Support is available for any *Portrait Gallery* technical problems that might arise.

Understand Your Relationship

When you're in love, your heart pounds—but your head has something to do with it, too. Gain a better understanding of your relationship and yourself with the *Relationship Forum* at **KEYWORD: Online Psych.**

Meet Your Neighbors

The Internet has sparked many a long-distance relationship, but you can also use AOL to meet people who live near you. Select a city at **KEYWORD: DC Personals**, then read personals ads or place your own. Specify age, ethnic category, and religion (the last two are optional) to narrow your search.

Ads are free and run for 21 days. The only rules? You must be over 18 years old, and you cannot violate AOL's Terms of Service.

Find Love Overseas

What if Mr. or Ms. Right lives several thousand miles away? Find out by searching for your beloved at **KEYWORD: Intl Love**. You can locate a mate based on looks, profession, or religious beliefs. If you're tired of making the first move, enter your own profile so your potential soul mate can find you.

The intricacies of courting may seem overwhelming—especially when they vary greatly from country to country. Courting customs around the world and culturally diverse romance rituals are explained here. Find out how couples in long distance relationships keep it all together, how to accept another culture without compromising your own, or how to communicate with in-laws who speak a different language.

Chatter Box

Every Tuesday, contestants on *Singled Out Online* (**KEYWORD: MTV**) go through the audience in MTV's Arena and pick four people to vie for their affection. The winners get a free date online and MTV prizes.

Dating Resources for the Gay Community

Looking for a same-sex date can be frustrating—sometimes the "Men Seeking Men" ads can get lost in a sea of "Men Seeking Women." But *Relationships onQ*, **KEYWORD:**

H2HonQ, specializes in personal ads from gays, lesbians, and bisexuals looking for love.

The personal ads here are posted in message boards. There are boards just for gay men, lesbians, bisexuals (men and women post in the same board), the transgendered community, HIV+, teens, the leather community, and members just looking for platonic friends. Stick to the boards that fit your description—for instance, adults posting in the Teens board will not be tolerated.

Feel free to make suggestions and ask questions. *OnQ*'s message board managers look forward to member input and will usually answer all questions in the message boards.

Meet Christian Singles

"Christian DJ seeks outgoing woman for relationship." "Pentecostal CF seeks Pentecostal CM." "Single white Baptist man seeks godly wife." These are just some of the headlines in KEYWORD: **CO Singles**. If you're looking for a relationship with someone who shares your Christian values, this is a good place to start looking.

Member ads include age, location, marital status, what you're looking for in a date, education, job, interests, a self description, favorite Bible verse, and a personal religious testimony. If you join the *Singles Connection*, you can post your own profile and receive a singles newsletter. Message boards and chats round out the area, providing a place for Christian singles to discuss life and love.

Connect at the Jewish Matchmaker

Single Jewish men and women who prefer to date other Jews can meet plenty of new people at KEYWORD: **Jewish Singles**. Member profiles in the Matchmaker dating service include age, religious observance, education, occupation, smoking and drinking habits, home town, and hobbies; some ads include photos, too. Search for any of

Searchable Personals in AOL's New Classifieds

Place your own highly visible personal ad in AOL's new classifieds section, KEYWORD: **Classifieds**. When you place an ad on the many personals message boards mentioned in this chapter, members have to click through the ads to find you. But when you place a spotlighted ad in *Classifieds*, your ad becomes part of a huge searchable database. Members who are searching for mates can find you more easily—their search words can get them directly to the ads that match what they're looking for. Your personal will be spotlighted for two weeks for $6.95 or for one month for $10.95.

these attributes, or browse listings of men and women in your state.

Other ways to connect with Jewish singles include chat rooms and message boards. Boards bring together singles from various parts of the U.S. and Canada, college students, widows and widowers, gays and lesbians, and single parents.

Channel Jumping

Anyone planning a walk down the aisle will benefit from the wedding advice at KEYWORD: **Knot**.

Keep Your Online Relationship Alive

If these tactics for meeting people online succeed, you'll have a whole new set of issues to deal with. But never fear: online relationships are the specialty at KEYWORD: **NetGirl**. Ask NetGirl a love-related question, and she may share her wisdom with you.

The message boards here are packed full of members' musings and theories about cyber-relationships. Anyone—men and women—with any questions at all about relationships will find something worthwhile here.

Several times a week, you can chat with NetGirl and other AOL members to discuss a wide variety of themes, including meeting people online, coming out online, dealing with online embarrassment, gender-switching online, and online resources for people dealing with divorce.

Meet... Dr. Kate

Dr. Kate Wachs, a clinical psychologist who specializes in relationship issues, dispenses advice at KEYWORD: **Love at AOL**.

So what do you think? Did you find a category or two in this chapter that you fit into? Yes? I hope so. But remember, what's here is just a start—you can find communities spread throughout AOL. Meet people who share your interests in pets, jogging, food, cars, gardening, health, and fashion. To find more information on the activities and pastimes you enjoy, just jump in this book to the chapters on families, interests, games, and sports.

That's a Wrap

♦ ♦

There's More to AOL than Meets the Eye

When I first sat down to start this project, I thought I knew almost all there was to know about AOL. After all, I work here. But with each chapter I kept learning more. I discovered content I'd never seen. I found new ways to use the tools. Writing the Kids Only chapter made me look at AOL from an entirely different perspective. And I got more psyched up about Sports than I ever thought I could with Buck's enthusiastic tour of the channel. I've even started subscribing to his newsletter, "From the Cheap Seats."

Being engaged so deeply in the service while digging up the best tips gave me the opportunity to get to know all the benefits of AOL membership. I can't imagine learning all this great stuff in just a few sessions. It really takes an explorer's mentality to research the entirety of AOL. Fortunately, now that I've done all the footwork, you don't have to. You hold the map in your hand.

Many people become accustomed to learning software and using it in a particular way and returning to what is familiar. We know that. That's why we invented Favorite Places. But I hope this guide has introduced you to many more ways to integrate AOL's resources into your life. Perhaps you didn't know about **KEYWORD: News Profiles**. Or you thought Personal Finance was the sovereignty of Wall Street investors. Maybe now, after reading this book, you're getting instant news dispatches about issues that really concern you, and you're

doing all your banking online. That would make me feel a lot better about my frequently overwhelming job!

What's Next?

As I'm typing these last few lines I can see a lot happening on the AOL horizon.

For example, AOL is planning to debut a feature that may eventually replace your phone altogether: AOL Talk. If you have a sound card and a microphone, you'll be able to talk to other members live through Instant Messages.

Invitation-only chats in the new Society Channel may serve as the online salons of the future. Here the culturally savvy and literati can philosophize, discuss the current works of premiere artists, or exchange opinions about haute couture. You could become part of the Inner Circle and interact with notable people in the business world and the arts—the newsmakers featured on the front pages impacting our society and culture.

And AOL Today is coming. Captivating personalities will host different areas of the service, informing and entertaining you like never before. So you see, it's not just AOL's software interface that's changing; the entire AOL world is constantly evolving.

Look for More Tips Online

If you want to keep up with the very latest on AOL, go to KEYWORD: **AOL Secrets**, where you'll find other AOL employees sharing their Favorite Places and hot tips.

And of course, stop in for the latest tips and suggestions at KEYWORD: **AOL Insider**.

AOL is not going to stop for anybody, you or me. So log on and let's all head into the future together. See you on AOL!

AOL Members' Choice Areas and Web Sites

Members' Choice AOL Areas

When you see the Members' Choice seal on an area, you're visiting a site that other members value and visit often. To find all the Members' Choice areas listed in one spot, go to **KEYWORD: Members Choice**. The links here will take you to the fifty most popular areas on AOL. If you want to go where the most members congregate, this is an excellent launching point. Here's the list of the top fifty AOL areas as this book is going to press:

Area Name	Keyword
ABC Kidzine	Kidzine
ABC Online	ABC
Antagonist, Inc.	ANT
ASTRONET	ASTRONET
Aviation & Aeronautics	Aviation
Better Health & Medical Network	Better Health
Cartoon Network World	CNW
Christianity Online	CO
Dow Jones Business Center	DJBC
Extreme Fans Sports	FANS
Fictional Realm	Fictional Realm
First Call Earnings	FirstCall
GamePro Online	GamePro
The Genealogy Forum	Roots
Grandstand	Grandstand
Hecklers Online	HO
Historical Quotes	Historical Quotes
Hoover's Business Resources	Hoovers
Independent Traveler	Traveler
Jewish Community	Jewish
Love@AOL	Love at AOL
Market News Center	MNC
Marvel Comics Online	Marvel
Military City Online	MCO
Moms Online	Moms Online
Morningstar Mutual Funds	Morningstar
The Motley Fool	Fool
MTV Online	MTV
Music Message Center	MMC
The New York Times	Times
NICK at NITE	Nick
Nickelodeon Online	Nick
NTN Studio	NTN
Online Psych	Online Psych
onQ	onQ
Oprah Online	Oprah

PC Games Forum	PC Games
PC Graphics Forum	PGR
PC Music & Sound Forum	PC Music
Pet Care Forum	Pet Care
PlanetOut	PlanetOut
Preview Travel	Preview Travel
Quotes & Portfolios	Quotes
Rosie O'Donnell Online	Rosie
Seventeen	Seventeen
Soap Opera Digest	SOD
The Sporting News	The Sporting News
STATS, Inc.	STATS
Thrive	Thrive
WWF	Superstars

Members' Choice Web Sites

AOL members also gravitate toward certain Web sites. Find the most popular ones at **KEYWORD: Web Keywords**. This area provides direct links to AOL Members' Choice Top Web Sites, such as:

Keyword

Switchboard
ZDNET
Deja News
Magellan Internet Guide
MTV Online
Riddler
Sportsline USA
The Weather Channel
Warner Bros Online
Mapquest
HBO
Jumbo
Gamespot
Liszt
NetGuide
iGuide
Tripod: Tools for Life
HomeArts
Windows Internet Magazine
NetGuide Live
Extra
Salon
City.Net
DC Comics
Macromedia
Zippo's Usenet News Service
The Electronic Newsstand
Total NY
Firefly
Home PC
Urban Desires
Motley Fool

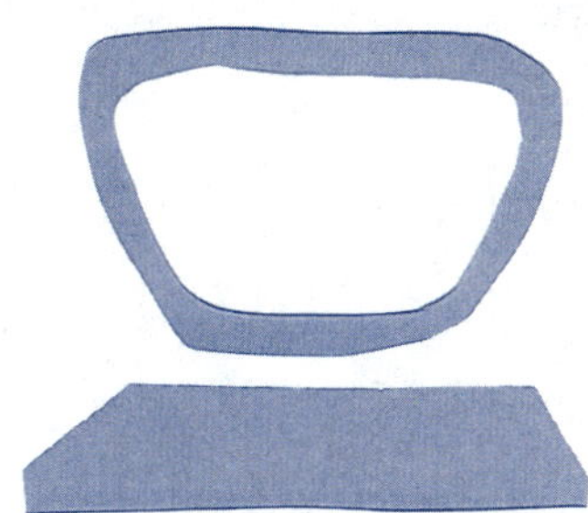

Keyword Your Way to the Web

In addition to the Members' Choice Web sites, there are many more popular and resourceful sites worth visiting. AOL has made it easy to get to them without having to know the exact URL. We've given them keywords. Below is the directory of Web sites you can access by keyword. Look for sites being added at **KEYWORD: Web Keywords**.

Keyword

Adobe.com
American Photo
Angelfire
Apple.com
Atlantic Financial
Big Yellow
BigBook
Bingo Zone
Boston Globe
Careerpath
CBS
CDnow
Census
City.net
CNN.com
Compass.com
DejaNews
Digits
Discovery.com
E-mail Address
Edmunds
Electronic News
Elle.com
Epicurious
ESPN
Family Tree
Firefly
FOODTV
Four11
GA Tech
Gameplayers
Gamespot
Garden.com
Gateway2000.com
Go Florida
HBO
Home PC.com
HomeArts
Homes
HotWired
HP.com
IBM.com
IDSoftware
iGuide
Indiana University
Intel.com
Intellicast
Internet Movie Database
Ivanhoe
Jumbo
LA Times.com
Link Exchange
Liszt
Look Up
Macromedia.com
Mapquest
McDonnell Douglas

Microsoft.com
Monster
MSU
MTV.com
Nando.net
Nasa.gov
Nascar.com
Navy.mil
NBA
NBC.com
NetGuide Live
NetGuide.com
Netscape
Nintendo.com
Novell.com
NY Times.com
ON.com
Pathfinder
Purdue
Quantum Group
RealAudio
Riddler
RIT
Rockwell Automation
Salon
Sci Fi.com
Search.com
Sierra.com
Slate
Sony
Sportsline
Stanford University
Switchboard
TechWeb
The Weather Channel
Total NY.com
Travelocity
Treasury
Tribune.com
Tripod
U Iowa
U Mich
U Penn
U Texas
UIUC
UMD
United Media
Universal
Urban Desires
USAToday.com
Vacations.com
Warner Bros.com
Washington Post
Washington University
Webtivities
White House.gov
WinMag.com
Wisc
WSJ
ZD Net
Zippo

◆◆◆◆◆◆◆◆◆◆◆◆◆◆◆◆◆◆◆◆◆◆◆◆◆◆◆◆◆◆◆◆◆◆◆

AOL Shoppers' Guide

AOL Ensures Customer Satisfaction

Shopping on AOL is Safe and Secure

AOL is committed to ensuring that your transactions in the Shopping Channel are safe and secure. The Certified Merchants that comprise this online mall have been selected carefully to provide you with the best shopping experience possible. They meet and often exceed AOL's set standard of customer service. For instance, these stores will process your order within one day of receipt and monitor their inventory closely to make sure that the merchandise advertised is available.

You may have read the headlines about the dangers of shopping on the Internet. Fortunately, those stories don't apply to AOL. That's because the Certified Merchants have been subjected to rigorous screening and ongoing monitoring by AOL. And AOL guarantees your protection against any liability reported promptly to your credit card provider. For all the details, go to **KEYWORD: Shopping**, click on the 100% Total Satisfaction Guarantee button in the top right corner, then click on "More About Security" at the bottom.

Complete Satisfaction, Guaranteed

All AOL Certified Merchants offer generous return and refund policies that are backed by AOL's unconditional money-back guarantee of satisfaction. Online customer service departments are immediately available in each store. If you need additional assistance, you can send email to the Shopping Channel's general customer service department. You'll get a response to your questions within one business day.

Discover the Most Convenient Way to Shop

Shop Around the Clock

AOL's stores are open 24 hours a day, 7 days a week. This means you can do all your shopping without having to drive endlessly looking for a parking spot or push through crowds of shoppers at the mall. You can shop in your pajamas if you want to. You can even have gifts shipped directly to friends and family instead of having to find the right size box and get it to the post office in time. This is ideal during the bustling winter holiday season.

You can take a guided tour of the stores at KEYWORD: **Shopping** to window shop. An automated gallery shows you a new store every ten seconds, and you can Take a Closer Look to go straight to the store. Or just consult this directory to keyword your way to the merchandise you're seeking.

Get the Real Deal

You can also sign up for several free services for added convenience. A free newsletter, *The Weekly Goods*, keeps you up-to-date on bargains, creative gifts and specialty items, and products you'll only find online. Another free newsletter, *Real Deals*, delivers the best bargains right to your email box every week. You can sign up for both *The Weekly Goods* and Real Deals at KEYWORD: **Newsletters**. Select AOL Official Channel Newsletters from the listbox and you'll see them listed at the top. You can also subscribe to *The Weekly Goods* from KEYWORD: **Shopping**.

Sign Up for the Free Gift Reminder Service

You never have to forget another birthday. At KEYWORD: **Reminder** you can create a calendar of your friends' and relatives' special occasions, and the *Reminder Service* will send you email before the event. The *Reminder Service* sends a note directly to your email box two weeks before the event and, if you wish, four days before the big day—giving you plenty of time to send a present. Plus, if you're stumped on gift ideas, the service will send you suggestions.

An easy-to-use form makes registering your reminder requests simple. Just enter the dates you need to remember and select when you want to be reminded. You can edit your reminder calendar at any time, and set dates to automatically repeat annually. The *Reminder Service* is completely free of charge, making it one of the best deals in the Shopping Channel.

Buy and Sell Used Goods

AOL Classifieds is a high profile place to put an ad for a car, a computer, or even real estate you're trying to sell. Buy an airplane ticket on the cheap. Find used sporting equipment, garden tools, electronics, and more. This is also an excellent spot for members on the lookout for antiques and collectibles.

A prime feature of **KEYWORD: Classifieds** is the Help Wanted section. If you're looking for a job you know how much time is wasted searching through employment ads in the newspaper. *AOL Classifieds* streamlines the process, since it's much easier to filter through the listings online to find the position you want. You can either read the postings from Employers Offering Jobs, or post your own ad so employers will see you. Click on "Place an Ad" to see the different prices for various placements.

Browse the Stores

1-800-98-PERFUME

KEYWORD: 1-800-98-PERFUME

Get discounts on authentic, classic, name-brand scents for men and women. Search for your favorite cologne or perfume or see what's on special for the day. Holiday and gift sets are available. Join the free membership and reminder FragranceNet Club to get your gifts out to friends and family on time.

1-800-FLOWERS

KEYWORD: 1800FLOWERS

Catch the bouquet every time with this online florist. Find flower arrangements, fruit baskets, and sweets and treats for all occasions. Learn fun facts about which flowers are in bloom this month. Discover floral design tips to spruce up your home.

Aardvark Pet Supplies

KEYWORD: Aardvark

Find gifts for the pet who has everything: catnip and squeak toys, sophisticated collars and leashes, sherpa beds for lots of comfort. There are also essential items for caring owners, including grooming kits, airline approved carriers, and paw print picture frames to keep your pet close by.

alle' Fine Jewelry

KEYWORD: alleJewelry

Superior quality jewelry at up to 50 percent off manufacturer's suggested retail price. Gold, diamonds, gemstones, watches, sterling silver, pearls, and much more at discount prices. Look for end-of-season clearance sales, too.

American Greetings

KEYWORD: American Greetings

Your one-stop shop for the best personalized greeting cards, chocolates, and gifts. Send an electronic card that moves, talks, and sings! Animated Greetings are a fun way to wish someone a happy birthday or just let them know they're loved.

AOL Computing Superstore

KEYWORD: CSS

Make the most of your computer in the Superstore. Shop for PCs, printers, modems, virus protection software, and the latest, most cutting-edge peripherals and gadgets. You'll find a range of digital imaging equipment and cool tools like Internet phones.

AOL Magazine Outlet

KEYWORD: Magazine Outlet

Spectacular savings and special deals on hundreds of magazines. Save 78% off the cover price of *Sports Illustrated*. Order computing, fashion, health, fitness, entertainment, travel, news, music, and many more magazines. Women can find their favorite monthly magazines, such as *McCall's* and *Ladies Home Journal*, for far less than newsstand prices.

AOL Online Auction

KEYWORD: Online Auction

An exciting way to shop. Bid, browse and beat your friends to hot deals on computer equipment, cameras, rare books, collectibles, jewelry, and much more. And you won't be purchasing antiques by mistake if you scratch your nose.

AOL Shoppers Advantage

KEYWORD: Shoppers Advantage

Over 250,000 brand name products at 10 to 50 percent off manufacturers' suggested retail prices. Member Benefits include a low price guarantee, warranty protection, and advanced searching capabilities. Best Buys are featured each week and there are contests to win prizes such as a Caribbean Cruise. To quote the lowest price available, the service asks for the zip code to which merchandise will be shipped. If you're not a Shoppers Advantage member you can enroll in a three-month trial for just $1.

AOL Store

KEYWORD: AOL Store

Software, hardware, books, modems, and special AOL merchandise. Check out the Editors' Reviews and Best Sellers. Look like an official Insider with AOL logo jackets, sweatshirts, and baseball caps. Apply for the America Online Visa card in the AOL Services section and earn free months of online time.

atOnce Software

KEYWORD: atOnce

Download hot software products such as a 3-D editor for Quake. Picks of the week, real deals, and free stuff, too. Join the club to get freebies and additional discounts. You can search the store by category or look for a specific software title. Get software immediately. Upon paying by credit card, you can download software such as games to play right away.

AutoVantage

KEYWORD: AutoVantage

They're driven to save you money. Request a quote, get car buying and roadside assistance, trip routing services, and discounts on car rental. Get free dealer invoicing and personal assistance when buying a new car. You can even call your agent from the dealership to make sure you're making the right choice and getting the best deal. Non-members can browse the classifieds section for a used car. But to be notified when the wheels you're looking for appear on the lot, you have to join. Try a three-month membership for $1 and get $20 worth of free gasoline.

Avon

KEYWORD: AVON

Cosmetics, skincare and beauty products for women and men. You'll find their popular product lines Anew and Skin-So-Soft, as well as makeup, fragrances, and items for your bath or home spa. You could get an additional bonus, such as a free gift when you make a purchase online. If you're accustomed to personal service from an Avon representative, you can request to have one call on you with a simple form here.

BarnesandNoble@AOL

KEYWORD: BARNES AND NOBLE

The world's largest bookseller online. Over one million titles at discount prices. Check out the Bestsellers to see what America's reading. If you're active in a book group on AOL you'll find the reading selections readily available here.

The Body Shop

KEYWORD: Body Shop

Fragrances, moisturizers, bath and beauty products from a name you trust. The Body Shop doesn't test their products on animals and its products have minimal impact on the environment. Socially concerned and responsible shoppers will enjoy the fragrant soaps, lotions, moisturizers, and other bath products here.

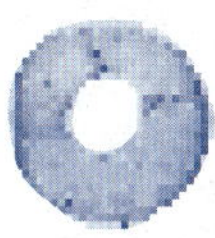

Chef's Catalog

KEYWORD: Chefs Catalog

Professional restaurant equipment and high-quality cookware for the home chef. Get all-important cutlery. Save on stainless steel pots and pans. High-end electric equipment such as sturdy blenders and powerful food processors make great gifts for serious cooks. This store also has a Gift Concierge to help you select the ideal housewarming or wedding present.

Cyberian Outpost

KEYWORD: Cyberian Outpost

PCs, laptops, memory, modems, printers, monitors, and software available for next day delivery. Find games, academic assistance software, and extra memory for your computer. An Order Tracking service helps you keep an eye on your package.

CyberShop

KEYWORD: CyberShop

Brand name appliances, home furnishings, and gourmet food. Shop four specialty boutiques for romantic wedding gifts, unique birthday surprises, ideal presents for true gentlemen, or trinkets that have a personal touch. A search function allows you to easily shop the entire store for a specific item. Browse the online aisles by department or by name brand.

Disney Interactive

KEYWORD: Disney Interactive

No one knows family fun and entertainment better than the Walt Disney Company. Find engaging and fun multimedia, educational, entertainment, and creativity software galore. Helpful utilities, hints, and program patches can be downloaded from this area. Troubleshooting information is available, as are message boards where fans of Winnie-the-Pooh share their experiences with the animated storybook.

Disney Store Online

KEYWORD: Disney Store

Mickey, Minnie, Goofy, and your favorite videos, apparel, and gifts. Send a Pooh Gram and let that honey-loving bear deliver birthday wishes, thanks, or congratulations to a good friend. Find toys, watches, and CD-ROMs featuring beloved characters.

Eddie Bauer

KEYWORD: Eddie Bauer

Quality clothing, gear, and furnishings for people who love the outdoors. This is the place to come for field gear such as functional and sporty backpacks and travel accessories. You'll find footwear for both men and women and items for the home as well as outdoors. Furniture, bedding, linens, floor coverings, and more bring classic looks to your interior decorating.

FAO Schwarz

KEYWORD: FAOSchwarz

Welcome to a world of toys where dreams come true for children of all ages. Classic collectibles abound in these aisles, such as the perennial favorite Madame Alexander dolls. The Best of FAO section features popular games, stuffed animals, preschool toys, action figures, and arts and crafts paint sets and pint-sized studios. Barbie has her own department and sports a wide-ranging repertoire of looks. You also have the option to shop the store by price, as well as category.

Fossil

KEYWORD: Fossil

Hundreds of watches, sunglasses, belts, bags, and wallets, plus gift ideas. In addition to solid, dependable timepieces the Prize-o-rama offers chances to win free items such as CDs and videos. Visit Fossil Town USA to learn fun facts, trivia, and read the history of the famous Fossil tin.

The Fragrance Counter

KEYWORD: Fragrance Counter

Designer perfumes, cosmetics, and an interactive Fragrance Advisor to help you choose your ideal scent. Looking for a romantic evening style? Or a more classic, casual scent for every day in the office? The Fragrance Advisor will guide you toward appropriate perfumes, colognes, skin care items, and even gift suggestions.

FreeShop

KEYWORD: FreeShop

Great offers and trials—free. Try before you buy. Get information on satellite systems and audio book clubs. Find mail order catalogs offering everything from shoes to electronics. Find products for personal finance, business and career, entertainment and hobbies, home and lifestyle, and more.

Garden Escape

KEYWORD: Garden Escape

Design, research and buy your dream garden. Discover the proper bulbs to plant right now. Order the appropriate tools to plant them. Perennials, roses, peonies, heaths and heathers, and orchids are among some of the plants you can order online, in addition to seeds and bulbs. You'll also find essential green house supplies and irrigation equipment. Bird feeders and houses can enliven your garden by attracting wildlife. Or start composting and learn the art of planting an organic garden with the help of beneficial insects.

Gift Sender

KEYWORD: Gift Sender

Gourmet food, beverages, flowers, baskets, and stuffed bears for your special someone. Send your favorite student a campus care package. Instead of flowers, have a bonsai tree delivered on Mother's Day. Gourmet foods are a great gift to send someone who may not indulge themselves otherwise. And teddy bears always deliver the message that you care.

Godiva Chocolatier

KEYWORD: Godiva

Satisfy your soul with Godiva chocolates, coffees, and desserts. When it comes to chocolate, one can never be too decadent. Sample the seasonal and holiday collections. Or peruse the Chocolate Guide to find scrumptious morsels like the Amaretto DiSaronno Truffle and Vanilla Caramel.

Hallmark Connections

KEYWORD: Hallmark

High-quality, custom-designed greeting cards and gifts. Featured in this store are unique designs for computer paper so you can quickly design party invitations, create special announcements, or jazz up your snail mail correspondence. Animated, electronic greetings are a fun way to say "Hi." You can preview them right in your browser window or download them.

Hammacher Schlemmer

KEYWORD: Hammacher

Unique and innovative gifts for travel, home, office, and relaxation. The High Tech Showcase features innovate electronic and computer equipment. The Tested as the Best section highlights products that have been rated in comparison tests by the Hammacher Schlemmer Institute and proven to be the best in their class, so you know you're getting the highest quality possible.

Health & Vitamin Express

KEYWORD: Vitamin EXP

Stay healthy, wealthy, and wise with an array of vitamins. Boost your energy level, prevent seasonal sicknesses, and augment your daily nutritional intake. You can request a free catalog online and get the latest health news on topics such as melatonin, antioxidants, beta carotene, ginkgo, and homeopathy.

Hickory Farms

KEYWORD: Hickory

Delectable cheeses, meats, desserts, and coffees that are easy to give—and receive. Explore the store for unique foods for entertaining, such as apricot dips, sweet potato souffle, and green bean almondine. You can even purchase a turkey with all the trimmings for Thanksgiving dinner. The Gourmet Marketplace serves up equally innovative cuisine with treats from around the world. And you can shop Mission Orchards for fresh fruits and a variety of nut assortments.

JCPenney

KEYWORD: JCPenney

Clothes, appliances, and furniture direct from the famous department store. You can order online any item that appears either in the area or in their print catalog. From casual sportswear to elegant jewelry, you'll find what you need for yourself and your family. You'll also find answers to specific fashion needs such as uniforms and scrubs and maternity clothing.

JCPenney Plus & Talls

KEYWORD: Plus & Talls

JCPenney combines style and value with what you want most. Find the fashions that fit your life. Lingerie, separates, jeans and more. Order classic lines such as Hunt Club pants and skirts online or from the JCPenney print catalog.

Lands' End

KEYWORD: Lands' End

Classic activewear, outerwear, luggage, and overstocks at great prices. In addition to getting their catalog, you can get information about professional opportunities within the company as well as internship programs.

Lillian Vernon

KEYWORD: Lillian Vernon

Unique gifts, garden ornaments, and children's products. Find neat ideas for decorating your home or office—or your home office! Send a personalized gift. Get holiday curios to celebrate special seasons. Festive kitchen gadgets brighten every day meals. Convenient travel and car accessories make life easier for those who are always on the go.

Nystyle

KEYWORD: NY Style

New York's vibrant chic, as captured by the city's premier manufacturers and retailers. Find ladies dresses and suits for daytime and evening. Mothers-to-be can secure a stylish nine-month wardrobe. Discover a unique line of therapeutic skincare products. Get everything you need to be the toast of the town in Manhattan.

OfficeMax OnLine

KEYWORD: Officemax

Office supplies, furniture, computers, printers, and accessories—from your keyboard to your door. Find all the equipment to get your business buzzing. One key feature of this area is that you can search for the exact product you need, be it just toner for the copy machine or an entire suite of office furniture.

Omaha Steaks

KEYWORD: Omaha

World famous premium steaks, meats, and fine gourmet foods. Aside from ordering foods, you'll also find instructive tools such as a steak-cooking chart, food safety and handling tips, and recipes for cooking beef, poultry, fish, veal, pork, and lamb.

One Hanes Place

KEYWORD: Hanes

Save up to 50 percent on intimate apparel from L'eggs, Bali, Hanes Her Way, and Champion. Slightly imperfect lingerie can be had for a steal. You'll also find important accessories such as open-weave mesh bags to protect fine delicates and hosiery in the washing machine.

Online Postcards

KEYWORD: Cardomatic

A great new way to send electronic greetings to your friends and family. Birthday, anniversary, get well, and thank you cards aren't all you'll find here. You can also select from this area's featured collections of Dilbert, astrological, Hecklers, and gay and lesbian postcards.

ONSALE Auction SuperSite

KEYWORD: Onsale

Bid for great deals on computers and electronics in the world's largest live online auction. It's easy. When you see an item you want to bid on, click the Place Bid button on the item's catalog page. Enter the amount you wish to bid, quantity you wish to buy, your billing and shipping addresses, and your credit card information. If your bid is currently winning, it will appear on the item's catalog page within a few seconds of placing your bid. This is how you can watch to see if someone is outbidding you, and you can up the ante. When the auction closes, you'll be notified by email if you are a winning bidder.

Parsons Software

KEYWORD: Parsons

Your one-stop software shop. Guaranteed! Genealogy, tax preparation, financial, legal, creative, business, and bible study software. Free newsletter spotlights great deals. This area also keeps you posted about industry news that may affect you as a consumer and notifies you about products that are being discontinued.

The Sharper Image

KEYWORD: Sharper Image

Special gadgets, collectibles, and fitness products. Find necessary equipment for the outdoor enthusiast. Get the most cutting edge technology for the wired executive. The Auto Club section features miniature model cars and accessories for your life-size vehicle. Classic gifts are offered in addition to the innovations you've come to expect from this store.

Sports Superstore

KEYWORD: Sports Superstore

Fitness apparel, footwear, and sports equipment from a leading sporting goods retailer. There are departments for extreme athletes who pit themselves against nature in the great outdoors and for those who prefer to find fitness in the gym. A special section is devoted to golfers, where you'll find bags, carts, drivers, fairway woods, and more.

Starbucks Coffee

KEYWORD: Starbucks

Exquisite beans, coffee accessories, and exotic gifts. Send some aromatic coffee to a deserving friend. Get a coffee grinder to make the most of the bean and brew it properly. Find espresso accessory kits and cappuccino cups for the perfect cup o' joe. Consider adding something special like Fontana syrups or try a coffee sampler to try new flavors. You can even learn a little about "coffee culture."

Tower Records

KEYWORD: Tower

Browse the Top 1000. Search with Tune Finder. Sample at the listening station. Buying music has never been so much fun. You can do a quick search by artist to find the albums you're looking for. Can't remember the name of the band? Try the Tune Finder, which lets you search by artist name, album title, or song title. You'll also find a discount section with CDs for under $10.

Travelers' Advantage

KEYWORD: TA

Join this club for a 5 percent cash back bonus on travel, exclusive weekly specials, 50 percent off hotel rates, and many more benefits. Save on cruises, airline tickets, and even entire vacation packages. Enter contests to win prizes like a trip to Jamaica. You can enjoy immediate benefits by enrolling in the membership for three months for just $1. For instance, get two American Airlines® Saving Certificates worth up to $200 and a Free Hotel Night Certificate that entitles you to stay at any participating hotel or motel of your choice.

Virtual Vineyards

KEYWORD: Virtual Vineyards

Wonderful wine, fabulous food, and gourmet gifts from a leading wine expert. The resident experts here, Peter Granoff and Tim Gaiser (affectionately known as the Cork Dorks) can point you toward the best Cabernets of 1994 and participate in online "tastings" of outstanding Sauvignon Blancs. You can view wines by category, winery, or variety. Find samplers, a monthly wine program, and wines under $15. Learn how to pair wines with appropriate dishes and get wine news by email. Gift certificates are also available.

Warner Bros.

KEYWORD: Warner Store

Clothing, accessories and toys branded with Bugs Bunny, Sylvester, and your favorite WB characters. You'll find Looney Tune classics and items from your favorite movies and TV shows. Follow the yellow brick road by viewing Wizard of Oz ornaments in the gallery. The Kids section has Scooby-Doo figurines while adults can join the Collectors Guild and acquire classic animation stills.

Z Auction

KEYWORD: ZAuction

The computer store where you set the price. You could continually follow computer news magazines to track the prices of hardware, laptops, and peripherals and wait for the best deal. Or you could just come directly to this area and put down the amount you're willing to pay. Hard drives, motherboards, scanners, digital cameras, and printers are only a few of the many items available on the auction block. Visit this area often to see if what you need is up for bid.

Index

A

AAA Online, 291
ABC Television Network, 52, 63, 143, 187, 193, 214–215, 226, 238–239, 333
About Work, 74
acting, 243, 250
ActiveX technology, 47
activities and hobbies, 316–318
    AOL Live!, 256
    concerts, 248, 256–257
    cooking (see food)
    family-oriented, 171–174
    fitness (see exercise and fitness; sports)
    games (see games)
    Insomniacs Asylum, 257–258
    local movie schedule, 241–242
    online adventures for kids, 173
    outdoors, 230–232, 272
    photography, 314–315
Adams, Cecil, 144–145
addictions, 152–154
address book, images in, 41–42
Advice and Planning, 101
aerial combat simulation, 197
African-Americans, 329–330
    cultural history, 132, 271
    financing education, 140
    news, 56
    sports and, 211
AIDS information, 156
airlines, 289–290, 312
allergies, 147–148
alternative medicine, 155, 157
American Association of Retired Persons, 339
American Automobile Association, 291
American Express, 80, 282
American Woodworker, 316
animation, 117, 254–256
    Japanese anime, 254, 271, 276
Antagonist, 203
AOL
    AOL Community Matters, 341
    AOL Insider Tips, 5
    AOL Live!, 256
    Child accounts, 176–177
    daily tips, 144
    help on, 105
    installing at multiple locations, 26–27
    international access, 262
    logo, clicking on, 184

AOL (*continued*)
- parental controls, 176–178, 196
- Teen accounts, 177
- top 25 questions on, 44–45
- version 4.0, 37–50

Arizona, 58
Army servicepeople, finding, 340
art, 250–252
- fashion, 318
- galleries, 182–183, 188–189
- interior design, 304
- marketing, 314
- (see also entertainment)

Arthur Frommer, 287
ASCII text, 7
AskToddArt, 314–315
Astronet, 320–321
astronomy, 131
Atheism-Agnosticism Forum, 327
Athlete Direct, 218–219
attaching files to email, 42
audio (see sounds)
Australia, 263–265, 271
Auto Center, 309–311
auto racing, 222
Automatic AOL (Flash Sessions), 30, 45
Aviation Forum, 312

B

Baby Boomers, 338
baby names, choosing, 169–170
background images, 41
backpacking, 230–231
banking, 99–100, 173
Barnes & Noble, 308
baseball, 223–224
basketball, 210, 220–221, 223
BattleTech, 197–198
BCC (blind carbon copies), 7–8
Beaty & Company, 88
Beavers, 270, 274–276
Bed & Breakfast Guide, 294
beer reviews, 299–300
Better Health and Medical Network, 148, 155, 283
Better Heart Health, 161
biking, 233–234
bill paying online, 99
Bistro, 267, 275, 285
Black Bayou, 199–200
Blackberry Creek, 183, 186
Blacks (see African-Americans)
blind carbon copies, 7–8
Blockbuster, 245
blocking IMs, 17
bonds, 86
Bonjour Paris, 266, 272
books, 260, 306–309
- coloring books, 188
- cookbooks, 299
- on health, 148
- libraries (see libraries)
- Oprah Winfrey's book club, 237, 306
- previews of, 306
- references (see references online)
- for teens, 335

books (*continued*)
- travel, 295
- (see also writing)

Boxer Jam's Strike-A-Match, 208
breast cancer (see cancer)
Broadway (see theatre)
Brokerage Center, 80–82
browser (see Web browser)
browsing (see finding)
Buddhism, 327
Buddy Chats, 13–14, 256
Buddy Lists, 13, 18–19
Buffet, Jimmy, 249
business
- AOL at work, 26–31
- *Business Week* magazine, 72
- community service programs, 190, 341–343
- companies in the news, 85
- finance (see finance)
- finding employment, 238
- home-based business, 30, 67, 72–73
- job searches, 73–75
- news, newsletters about, 65, 72–73
- professional networking, 66
- researching companies, 83
- retiring from, 99, 134, 339
- searching for businesses, 34–35
- small businesses, 66, 69
- travel, 279, 287–289
- Web-based business, 68
- women and, 76

buying online (see shopping)

C

C-Span Interactive, 60
Canada, 270, 274–276
- investment resources, 88
- maps, 135

cancer, information and forums, 152, 156, 161
card games, 206–209
cards (see greeting cards)
career (see business)
cars, 309–311
- American Automobile Association, 291
- auto racing, 222

cartoons, 64, 179, 255
- Japanese anime, 254, 271, 276

Casino Poker, 206–208
Catholicism, 325
CBS SportsLine, 215–216, 224
CD drives, playing sounds off, 16
CD-ROMs, reviews of, 122
chat, 323
- Buddy Chats, 13–14, 256
- common phrase abbreviations, 12
- in foreign languages, 267, 275, 285
- hosting chat rooms, 16–17
- preferences for, 25
- private rooms, 13
- recording with Log Manager, 14
- rich text in, 42
- sounds in, 15–16
- support groups, 150–154, 162–163

chess, 198
Chicago, Illinois, 56–58

children (see kids; teens)
Christianity, 324–325, 345
cigarettes, 160
cities
  exercise in, 161
  rated, 133–134
  (see also Digital Cities)
Civil War history, 132
classes (see education/schooling)
classical music, 245, 251
classifieds, 57, 76–77, 311, 345
clip art (see images)
Club for First Wives, 334
clubs for kids, 189–191
College Hoops, 220–221
colleges (see education/schooling)
coloring books, 188
Columbia Concise Encyclopedia, 125
comics, 253–256
  Dilbert comic strip, 64, 246
  Marvel Comics, 188, 253–254
community service programs, 190, 341–343
companies (see business)
Company Connection, 121
Composer's Coffeehouse, 115, 244
compressed files (see zipped files)
Compton's Living Encyclopedia, 125, 182
computers
  computer camp for kids, 122
  Computing Superstore, 120
  family and, 167, 170, 172
  help on, 104–108
  learning tool, 140
  news on, 118–120
  online classes about, 116–117
  references for, 129–130
  seniors and, 338–339
  shopping for, 103, 120–122
  (see also hardware; software)
concerts, 248, 256–257
Congress (U.S.), 60
connection speed (see performance)
Consumer Reports, 58
cookies, browser, 48–49
cooking (see food)
copying email messages to others, 7–8
country music, 244
crafts, 316–318
credit cards, 99
  American Express, 80, 282
Crossman, Craig, 120
crossword puzzles, 206
cruises, 282
Crystal Ball Forum, 320–321
culture
  African-American, 132, 271
  Culture Finder, 250–251
  ethnic background, 329
  international, 262–266
  U.S. immigration stories, 265
customizing
  email, 25
  Go To Menu, 23–24
  inclusion in Buddy Lists, 18–19
  news profile, 58
  newsgroups, 12
  parental controls, 176–178, 196
  personalized stationery, 40–41
  sounds, 24–25

D

database programming, 108
dating online, 343–346
David Letterman, 237–238
DC Comics Online, 255
Dead Forum, 249
Deaf and Hard of Hearing, 151–152
debates (see online discussions)
decompressing files (see unzipping files)
delays (see performance)
Democratic party, 61
depression, information on, 158, 162–163
desktop, Favorite Places on, 23
desktop publishing, 115
Destination Florida, 280
diabetes, information on, 159
Diamond Notes, 223–224
dictionaries, 128–130
  Australian, 263–264
  Dictionary of Cultural Literacy, 127
  language translations, 266, 269
  medical, 153
Digital Cities, 134, 342
  cultural events, 265
  news, 51, 57
  sports coverage, 217
  weather, 55
Dilbert comic strip, 64, 246
Dining à la Card, 280
disABILITIES Forum, 150
discussion groups (see online discussions)
Disney World, 238, 280, 295
Do Something, 342
doctors, references for, 156–157
downloading
  dangers of, 9, 109
  Download Manager, 30
  files, locating after, 111
  games, 202–204, 215–216
  help for, 130
  scheduling for another time, 30
  shareware, 103
  software, 110–111
  sounds, 15–16
  sports files, 224, 226–227
  stuff for kids, 185
Drudge, 258
DRUM Magazine, 244

eating (see food)
economics, 89
Edit Go To Menu option, 23
education/schooling
  choosing a school, 302
  colleges, information on, 137–140
  computer camp for kids, 122
  financing, 138–140
  help with homework, 136, 139
  home schooling, 140–141
  online classes, 116–117, 135–136
  in science, 131
  standardized tests, 137–138
  student travel, 290
  study skills, 139, 181
  teaching resources, 140–143
  writing mentor program, 306

Electric Library, 126
electronic mail (see email)
email
- attaching files to, 42
- blind carbon copies, 7–8
- Buddy Chat for, 14
- common phrase abbreviations, 12
- customizing, 25
- email loops, 167
- formatting messages, 7
- hyperlinks in, 8
- junk messages, 6
- mailing lists, 109–110
- to overseas Navy personnel, 340
- personalized stationery, 40–41
- pictures in messages, 39
- signatures in, 10
- speaking, not typing, 26
- spell checking, grammar checking, 39–40
- version 4.0 improvements in, 39–42
- viruses and, 9

emoticons, 12
employment (see business)
encryption, 43, 48
encyclopedias, 125
England, 273, 276, 335
entertainment, 235–260
- art, 182–183, 188–189, 250–252
- concerts, 248, 256–257
- *Entertainment Goes Online*, 277
- gossip, 258
- international, 260, 269, 274–277
- for kids, 259
- magazines, 242–243
- movies, 240–243
- music (see music)
- *The New York Times* listings, 53
- newsletter, 235
- sports (see sports)
- television (see television)

ER (television program), 237
ERIC database, 140
European travel, 280–281
exercise and fitness, 161, 164, 228–230 (see also health)
expiring newsgroup postings, 12
ExpressNet, 80, 282
Extreme Sports, 232

F

facts, resources for, 125–127, 143, 163
family, 165–174
- computers and, 167, 170, 172
- games for, 172
- *Genealogy Forum*, 173, 307
- home schooling, 140–141
- how to amaze kids, 184–187
- magazines for, 170–171
- parental controls for kids, 176–178, 196
- profile of, 166–167
- rating Web site content, 49
- reunions in chat rooms, 13
- travel with, 286
- working parents, 75
- (see also kids; parents)

Fan Central, 220

FAQs (Frequently Asked Questions lists), 11
- art, 314
- computer-related, 107–108
- multimedia, 112
- on mutual funds, 88
- on newsgroups, 11, 33
- (see also references online)

fashion, 318

Favorite Places, 8
- moving to desktop, 23
- version 4.0 improvements, 46

files
- attaching to email messages, 42
- downloading, 9
- helper files, 21
- locating downloaded, 111
- zipped/unzipping, 16, 111

film, 240–243, 247, 277

finance
- advice on, 86–89, 94–96
- banking, 99–100, 173
- bonds, 86
- buying a home, 301–302
- college education and, 138–140
- information about, 128–129
- international, 89, 96
- investing, 80–86, 89, 94, 144
- market quotes, 85
- money management resources, 97–101
- mutual funds, 82–83
- news on, 54, 86, 94, 96
- Personal Finance Channel, 80
- searching for information on, 80
- stocks, 81, 83–85
- taxes, 100
- travel budgets, 287–290

finding
- businesses, 34–35
- downloaded files, 111
- employment, 238
- Find a Business (Switchboard), 34–35
- Find in Top Window, 21
- Find utility, 20
- kid-enabled, 176
- NetFind search engine, 32–35
- news, 53
- newsgroups, 11
- particular religions, 326–327
- people, 134
  - AOL members, 20, 56, 172
  - computer industry professionals, 120
  - government officials, 61
  - international pen pals, 267–269, 274
  - investors, 95
  - medical professionals, 157–158
  - musicians and music fans, 243–244, 249
  - news correspondents, 52
  - online dating, 343–346
  - other kids, 190
  - other parents, 166–169
  - parenting experts, 169
  - professional networking, 267–269, 274
  - in science industry, 131
  - seniors, 338–339

finding, people (*continued*)
sports fans, 219
teachers, 141, 179–182
women, 332–333
in your neighborhood, 56, 344
queer communities, 293, 331
software, 110
sports and sports teams, 220, 225
work, 73–75
fishing, 232–232
fitness (see exercise and fitness)
flags, 274
Flash Sessions (see Automatic AOL)
Florida, 280
Disney World, 238, 280, 295
Orlando Sentinel, 56
Flying Magazine Online, 312
fonts, 115
food
Dining à la Card, 280
international, 265–266
Jewish, 326
for kids, 185
recipes/cooking, 149, 297–300
football, 211, 224–225
(see also soccer)
formatting
chat text, 42
fonts for, 115
text, tools for, 7
France, 272, 276–277
Paris, 266, 272
Free-Form Gaming Forum, 201
Frommer travel guides, 287
funds, 82–83

G

games, 185, 193, 195–197
card games, 206–209
cost of playing premium, 195–197, 212
downloading, 202–204, 215–216
family-oriented, 172
GamePro magazine, 203
international, 269, 274–277
for kids, 178–179
paintball, 233
puzzles, 206–209
role-playing games, 199–201
simulation, 197, 200, 209–210
sports-related, 209–212, 215–216, 227–228
(see also sports)
strategy games, 197–199
trivia (see trivia)
video games, 202–204
gardening, 305–306
gay (see queer communities)
Genealogy Forum, 173, 307
geographical location
cities, rated, 133–134
gay-friendly, 293
jobs by, 77
maps, 135, 288, 291
(see also Digital Cities; travel)
George magazine, 59, 62
Germany, 277
GIFs (see images)
Glenna's Garden, 152
Go To menu, 23–24

golf, 210, 221–222
"Goodbye" sound, changing, 25
government, 59–64
grammar, checking email for, 40
The Grandstand, 218, 226–227
graphic arts, 113, 116
graphics (see images)
Grateful Dead, 249
greeting cards, 34, 41
Grolier Multimedia Encyclopedia, 125
guitars, 244

H

Hammacher Schlemmer, 283
hardware
  ratings of, 118–119
  shopping for, 120–122
Harpoon, 199
headers, newsgroup postings, 12
headlines (see news)
health, 147–161
  alternative medicine, 155, 157
  depression, information on, 158, 162–163
  fitness (see exercise and fitness)
  Health Magazine, 149–150
  medical reference, 125, 153, 156–157
  support groups, 150–154, 162–163
heart-related health issues, 161
Heavenly Bodies, 342
Hecklers Online, 252–253
help, 22–23
  AOL, 105
  computers and software, 104–108
    downloading, 130
  FAQs for (see FAQs)
  helper files, 21
  with homework, 136, 139, 179–182
  Windows operating system, 106
hiding from Buddy Lists, 18–19
Highlights for Children, 172, 182–183, 186
Hinduism, 327
Hispanic Online, 270, 328–329
history, 132–133, 144
  African-American, 132, 271
  History Channel (television), 240
  stock quotations, 84
  news (see news)
hobbies (see activities and hobbies)
hockey, 223
holidays, 263, 326
Holocaust, 133
home/house, 301–302, 304–306
  home-based business, 30, 67, 72–73
  home decoration, 317
  Home PC, 104
  home schooling, 140–141
homework, help on, 136, 139, 179–182
hosting chats, 16–17
humor, 252–253
  comics, 64
  for kids, 189
  political satire, 63–64
hunting, 232–232
hyperlinks in email, 8

I

iBike, 233–234
icons, adding to toolbar, 43–44
ignoring particular IMs, 17
iGolf, 210, 221–222
images
    in address book, 41–42
    animation, 117, 254–256, 271, 176
    AOL photo galleries, 38, 343–344
    background email images, 41
    clip art, 116
    comics/cartoons, 64, 179, 188, 253–256
    creating, 113–114, 116
    in email messages, 39
    financial news graphs, 54
    galleries, 53, 182–183, 188–189, 251–252
    graphic arts, 113, 116
    news, 52–53
    photography, 314–315
    scanning, 113
    from specific geographic areas, 57
    sports, 214, 226
    tools for, 114
    weather forecasts, 55
IMs (Instant Messages), 13, 17, 19
Inc. Online, 73
InsideFlyer Online, 289–290
Insomniacs Asylum, 257–258
installing
    AOL at multiple locations, 26–27
    .wav files (sounds), 16
    Web browser plug-ins, 25–26
Instant Messages (IMs), 13, 17, 19
insurance, 89, 291
interactive games (see games)
interior design, 304
international, 261–278
    AOL access, 262
    dating, 344
    financial news, 89, 96
    foods, 265–266
    games and entertainment, 260, 269, 274–277
    music, 270
    networking, 267–269, 274
    news, 89, 96, 264
    sports, 269
    travel (see travel)
    trivia, 274
    weather, 56
Internet, 108–110
    references for, 129–130
    publishing on (see publishing on Web)
investment (see finance)
iRace, 222
Irish Heritage, 262, 273
iSki, 232
Isr@el Interactive, 263, 272

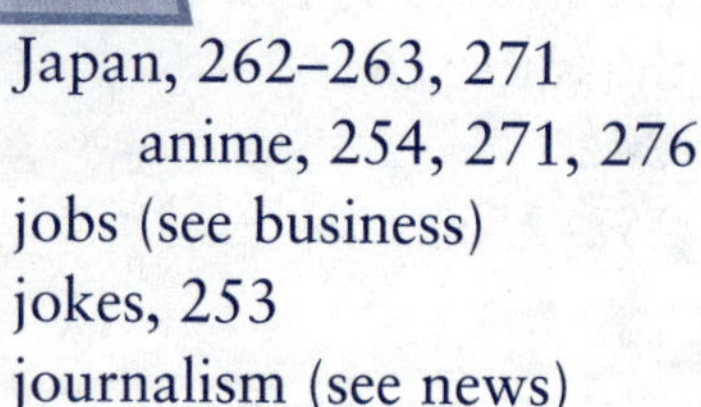

J

Japan, 262–263, 271
    anime, 254, 271, 276
jobs (see business)
jokes, 253
journalism (see news)

journals (see magazines/journals)
Judaism, 325–326
- dating, 345–346
- *Holocaust*, 133
- *Isr@el Interactive*, 263, 272
- recipes, 247, 326

junk email messages, 6

karate, 319
kids, 175–192
- Child accounts, 176–177
- choosing schools for, 302
- clubs for, 189–191
- computer camp, 122
- cooking and, 298–299
- entertainment for, 259
- games for, 178–179
- how to amaze, 184–187
- image galleries for, 182–183, 188–189
- *Kids Hall of Fame*, 194
- meeting online, 190
- *NetFind Kids Only*, 35
- news and newsletters for, 193–194
- online adventures, 173
- parental controls, 176–178, 196
- rating Web sites for, 49
- schooling (see education/schooling)
- Science Fair, 136
- screen names, 176
- service programs for, 342
- sports for, 191–193
- (see also family)

The Knot, 318
Kodak Photography Forum, 315
Komando, Kim, 107

language translation, 266, 269, 285
Lanier's *Bed & Breakfast Guide*, 294
Las Vegas, Nevada, 282
Late Show Online, 237–238
legal advice, 124
Legends of Kesmai, 200
Letterman, David, 237–238
Libertarian party, 61–62
libraries
- *Electric Library*, 126
- movie database, 241, 247
- New York Public Library, 126
- sports, 227

links in email, 8
LiveGuide, 256–257
loans, 99
local, 51
- cities, rated, 133–134
- community service programs, 190, 341–343
- cultural events, 265
- exercise ideas, 161
- images, 57
- meeting people in neighborhood, 56, 344
- movie schedules, 241–242
- news, 51, 56–59
- professional networking, 67

local (*continued*)
- sports coverage, 217
- television programming schedule, 238
- weather, 55
- (see also Digital Cities; geographical location)

Locate button, 13
Log Manager, 14, 21
logging chat contents, 14
Lonely Planet, 266
Love@AOL, 343

M

magazines/journals, 54, 64
- *Backpacker Magazine*, 230–231
- *Business Week*, 72
- *Car and Driver*, 310–311
- *Consumer Reports*, 58
- crafts, 316–318
- database of, 126
- *The Economist*, 89
- electronic equipment, 313
- entertainment, 242–243, 277
- family-related, 170–171
- *Flying Magazine Online*, 312
- *GamePro*, 203
- *George*, 59, 62
- *Golf Magazine*, 221
- *Health Magazine*, 149–150
- *Highlights for Children*, 172, 182–183, 186
- *Home Magazine*, 301, 304–305
- *Inc. Online*, 73
- *InsideFlyer Online*, 289–290
- music-related, 244, 246, 248
- *Newsweek*, 54
- *Popular Photography*, 314–315
- *Scientific American's Cancer Journal*, 156
- *Soap Opera Digest*, 240
- *SPIN*, 248
- sports-related, 217
- *Woman's Day*, 317, 333

Magestorm, 200
mail (see email)
mailing lists, 109–110
manager, chat rooms, 16–17
maps, 135, 288, 291
Market News Center, 54, 86
martial arts, 319–320
Marvel Comics, 188, 253–254
Maven, 121
Media Control, 277
medical information (see health)
Medical Pearls, 156–157
Medline database, 153
Member Orientation, 6
Member Services, 22
members
- local, 56
- photo gallery for, 343–344
- searching for, 20, 172
- names for (see screen names)
- (see also finding people)

Members Helping Members, 22
Merriam-Webster, 128–129
Metallica Forum, 249
MetaTools, 114

Metropolitan Home Online, 304
Military History Forum, 132
military, 340–341
Model Planes, 312
modems, 108
Moms Online, 166–169, 171–172, 185
money
  banking, 99–100, 173
  cost of playing premium games, 195–197, 212
  credit cards, 80, 99, 282
  management resources, 97–101
  paying bills online, 99
  shopping online (see shopping)
  travel budgets, 287–290
  (see also finance)
mortgages, 99
Motley Fool, 79, 86–87
movies, 240–243, 247, 277, 332
MTV, 201, 239
multimedia, 112
  animation, 117, 254–256, 271, 176
  encyclopedia on, 125
  Multimedia Showcase, 25–26
  version 4.0 improvements, 46–48
multiplayer games (see games)
multiple screen names, 27
music, 243–245, 248–250
  composing, 115, 244
  concerts, 248
  international, 270
  for kids, 190
  MTV, 201, 239
  VH1, 239–240, 245
  (see also sounds)
mutual funds, 82–83
My AOL, 25
mystical phenomena, 320–321

N

names
  baby, choosing, 169–170
  having written into stories, 189
  of members (see screen names)
national (see United States)
National Museum of American Art, 252
National Public Radio, 252
naval warfare games, 199
Navy personnel, writing to, 340
neighborhood (see local)
NetFind search engine, 32–35, 176
NetGirl, 346
NetNoir, 271, 330
networking (see finding people; professional networking)
New York Public Library Desk Reference, 126
The New York Times, 53, 131, 206, 250–251, 305
news, 51–60
  ABC News, 52, 63
  Afro-centric, 56
  book-related, 309
  business-related, 72–73
  companies in, 85
  computer-related, 118–120
  customizing profile for, 58
  entertainment gossip, 258

news (*continued*)
- financial, 54, 86, 94, 96
- hourly summaries of, 144
- international, 89, 96, 264
- for kids, 193–194
- local, 56–59
- national, 52
- National Public Radio, 252
- online discussions on, 63
- politics, 59–64
- scientific, 131
- searching for, 53
- sports, 214–217
- today's headlines, 51
- weather (see weather)
- (see also newsletters)

newsgroups, 109–110
- FAQs for, 11, 33
- NetFind resources on, 33
- searching, 11
- setting preferences for, 12
- sports-related, 211
- (see also online discussions)

newsletters, 64
- business-related, 65
- entertainment-related, 235
- finance-related, 102
- for kids, 194
- parenting, 169
- sports-related, 213
- travel-related, 294–295

newspapers
- Arizona, 58
- *Chicago Tribune*, 56–58
- database of, 126
- *The New York Times*, 53, 131, 206, 250–251, 305
- *Orlando Sentinel*, 56

Newsweek, 54
Nickelodeon, 183, 239
Nintendo, 202
NPR (National Public Radio), 252
NTN Trivia, 204, 221, 227–228

O'Donnell, Rosie, 236, 247
Online Campus, 136
online classes (see education/schooling)
online discussions (see chats; IMs; mailing lists; newsgroups)
Online Gaming Forum, 201
Online Investor, 89
Online Psych, 154–155, 162, 208
onQ, 331, 344
Oprah Online, 236–237, 306
organic gardening, 306
Orlando Sentinel, 56
Out of Order, 206
outdoor activities, 230–232, 272
The Outer Edge, 335
!OutProud!, 335
Over the Rainbow, 293

Pagan religions, 328
paging, 30

Pain Relief Center, 159
paintball, 233
parentheses, email addresses in, 7–8
parents
    contacting other, 166–169
    home schooling, 140–141
    how to amaze kids, 184–187
    Parent Soup, 166–167, 169, 172, 205
    parental controls, 176–178, 196
    parenting trivia, 205
    resources for, 168
    (see also family; kids)
Paris, 266, 272
passwords
    for Personal File Cabinet, 49
    reporting solicitations for, 18
PC Graphics Arts Forum, 113
PCs (see computers)
people (see members)
    finding (see finding people)
    talking to (see chats)
performance
    browser, improving, 106
    connection speed, 19–20, 27, 108
    optimizing for PC, 105
periodicals (see magazines/journals; newsletters; newspapers)
Personal File Cabinet, 25, 49
personal fitness, 229
Personal Publisher, 48, 115–116
pets, 303
phishers, reporting, 18
photo galleries, AOL, 38, 343–344
photography, 314–315
    (see also art; images)
Photoshop, 114
pictures (see images)
PlanetOut, 331–332
Playbill Online, 243, 250
Playbook, 211
playing .wav files, 16
plug-ins, 25–26, 47
poker, 206–208
politics, 59–64, 258
Popular Photography, 314–315
portfolio, investment, 81
preferences (see customizing)
PreferredMail, 6
President (U.S.), 59–60
Preview Travel Vacations, 289
PrimeHost, 30, 68
private rooms, 13
Professional Forums, 66
professional networking, 267–269, 274
profile, news, 58
programming, 107–108
psychic phenomena, 320–321
public service programs, 190, 341–343
publishing on Web, 68, 112, 115–117
punctuation, checking email for, 40
purchasing (see shopping)
push technology, 13–14
puzzles, 206–208

Que's Computer and Internet Dictionary, 129–130

queer communities, 331–332
  dating, 344–345
  teen, 335
  travel, 293
quilting, 316
quotations, 128, 144
quoting newsgroup postings, 12

R

Random, 184
rating Web site content, 49
The Real Estate Desk, 301–302
recipes (see food)
recording chat contents, 14
references online, 123–146
  encyclopedias, 125
  fact resources, 125–127, 143, 163
  for kids, 180
  medical, 153, 156–157
  parenting, 168
region (see geographical location)
religion, 63, 324–328
replying to newsgroup postings, 12
Republican party, 61
research (see references online)
reservations online (travel), 288
restaurants (see food)
retirement, 99, 134, 339
Revolutionary War Forum, 132
rich text format (see RTF)
role-playing games, 199–201
Rolling Stone, 246, 248
romance writing, 343
Rosie O'Donnell Show, 236, 247
Royalty, 276
RTF (rich text format), 7, 42

S

Sage School, 81–82, 87–88
satire (see humor), 63–64
saving chat contents, 14
scanning images, 113
Scholastic, 141
SchoolMatch, 302
schools (see education/schooling)
science, 131, 136, 181
science fiction television, 239
screen names
  for kids, 176
  length of, 45
  multiple, 27
  switching without disconnecting, 45
searching (see finding)
SEC reports, 83
security
  downloading, dangers of, 9, 109
  encryption, 43, 48
  online banking and, 99
  parental controls, 176–178, 196
  reporting password solicitations, 18
  safe travel, 292
  self-defense, 319
  sounds on CD drives, 16
  version 4.0 improvements, 48–49
  viruses, 9, 104–105
Self Help, 151

selling a home, 301
selling online (see classifieds; shopping)
sending greeting cards, 34
seniors, 338–339
    retirement, 99, 134, 339
service programs, 190, 341–343
sewing, 317–318
shareware, 103
shopping, 168
    books, 308
    buying a home, 301
    for cars, 310–311
    classifieds, 57, 76–77, 311
    computer supplies, 103, 120–122
    Consumer Reports for, 58
    electronic equipment, 313–314
    gardening supplies, 305
    Hammacher Schlemmer, 283
    music, 245
    pet supplies, 303
    sports collectibles, 220, 226–227
    travel supplies, arrangements,
        287–290, 292–293
    video games, 202
signatures (sigs), 10
The Simming Forum, 200
simulation games, 197, 200, 209–210
sites (see Web sites)
skiing, 232
Slingo, 209
Small Business Administration, 69
small businesses (see business)
smileys, 12
Smithsonian museums, 251–252
smoking, 160
soap operas, 240
soccer, 225–226
software, 110–111, 119
    family-oriented, 167, 172
    games (see games)
    imaging, 114
    searching for, 110
    shareware, 103
    shopping for, 120–122
solicitations for passwords, 18
sounds, 114–115
    in chats, 15–16
    customizing, 24–25
    downloading, 15–16
    installing .wav files, 16
    speaking email messages, 26
    (see also music)
space (astronomy), 131
spam, 6
speaking email messages, 26
Special Delivery, 267–269, 274
speed (see performance)
spell checking email messages, 39
SPIN Magazine, 248
sports, 213–234
    athletes, stories of, 216
    event coverage, 217, 220
    extreme, 232–234
    finding a sport or team, 220, 225
    games about, 209–212, 215–216,
        227–228
    images, 214, 226
    international, 269
    for kids, 191–193
    magazines and newsletters, 213, 217

sports (*continued*)
- martial arts, 319–320
- news, 214–217
- newsgroups on, 211
- online discussions about, 192–193, 217–220
- outdoor activities, 230–232, 272
- previewing events, 216
- shopping for collectibles, 220, 226–227
- talking to athletes, 218–219
- trivia, 208, 210, 221, 227–228
- *Virtual Pool Online*, 198

SportsFan Radio, 223
SSL encryption, 48
standardized tests, 137–138
stationery for email messages, 40–41
STATS Diamond Notes, 223–224
Stereo Review Online, 313–314
stock car racing, 222
stocks (see finance)
strategy games, 197–199
streaming technology, 46
Strike-A-Match, 208
student travel, 290
study skills, 139, 181
support groups, 150–154, 162–163
surfing, 233
Switchboard, 34, 134

T

taxes, 100
TCP/IP, and connection speed, 27
teachers
- resources for, 140–143
- talking to, 179–182

Team NFL, 224–225
technical support (see help)
teens, 122, 177, 334–337 (see also kids)
television
- ABC Network, 52, 63, 143, 187, 193, 214–215, 226, 238–239, 333
- *C-Span Interactive*, 60
- *Cartoon Network*, 179, 255
- *CBS SportsLine*, 215–216, 224
- MTV, 201, 239
- *Nickelodeon*, 183, 239
- programming schedule, 238
- shopping for, 313
- soap operas, 240
- talk shows, 236–238
- VH1, 239–240, 245

Tell Us Your Story, 265
tennis, 224
text
- capturing online, 21
- fonts, 115
- rich text format (see RTF)

theatre, 243, 250
Thrive, 149, 155, 160, 229, 231
Time Savers, NetFind, 33–34
toolbar, AOL 4.0 improvements, 43–44
TOS Files screen name, 9
TOSspam screen name, 7
Tower Records, 248
traffic (online), avoiding heavy, 19–20

travel, 266, 279–296
accessibility for disabled travelers, 150
budgeting, 287–290
for business, 279, 287–289
family and, 286
newsletter, 294–295
reservations online, 288
safety and, 292
skiing packages, 232
Travel Advisories, 284, 292
weather and (see weather)
trivia, 204–205, 247
international, 274
for kids, 178–179
NTN Trivia, 204, 221, 227–228
sports, 208, 210, 221, 227–228
trojan horses, 9

U

The Ultimate Fighting Championships, 320
The United Homeowners Association Forum, 301
United States
government, 59–61
immigration stories, 265
maps, 135
National Museum of American Art, 252
news, 52
political parties, 61–62
references on, 135
travel in, 282
Vietnam Veterans Memorial, 340–341
universities (see education/schooling)
University of California, 135–136
unzipping files, 16, 111
URLs in Go To menu, 23
Usenet (see newsgroups)
users (see members)
USO-GRAMS, 340

vacations (see travel)
vegetarianism, 299
version 4.0 of AOL, 37–50
veterans, 340–341
Veterinary Information Network, 303
VH1, 239–240, 245
Vices & Virtues, 259–260
video games, 202–204 (see also games)
Video Magazine, 313
videos (movies), 241
Vietnam Veterans Memorial, 340–341
Virtual Pool Online, 198
virtual reality, 114
viruses, 9, 104–105
vitamins, 159
voice-recognition software, 26
VRML (Virtual Reality Markup Language), 114

W

- waiting (see connection speed)
- Wall Street (see finance)
- .wav files (see sounds)
- weather, 51, 55–56, 283
  - international, 56
  - ski reports, 232
- Web-based business, 68
- Web browser
  - improving performance, 106
  - plug-ins for, 25–26, 47
- Web preferences, setting, 25
- Web publishing, 68, 112, 115–117
- Web sites
  - content ratings, 49
  - designing, 30, 47–48, 116
  - reviews of, 32
- weddings, 318
- weightlifting, 229
- White House, 59–60
- *Wilhelmina Agencies*, 318
- Windows operating system, 106
- wine reviews, 299–300
- Winfrey, Oprah, 236–237, 306
- WinTune program, 105
- *Woman's Day*, 317, 333
- women, 332–334
  - business and, 76
  - self-defense, 319
  - sports, 225
- woodworking, 316–317
- words
  - dictionaries (see dictionaries)
  - language translations, 266, 269, 285
  - puzzles, 206–208
  - resources for, 127–129, 143–144
  - (see also writing)
- work (see business)
- writing, 180, 308–309
  - kids and, 188–189
  - mail (see email)
  - mentor program, 306
  - references for, 127–129
  - romance writing, 343
  - teens and, 335

- yoga, 229
- "You've got mail", changing, 24
- *Your Business*, 66
- *Youth Tech*, 334

- Zagat guides, 279–280, 299
- *ZENtertainment*, 258
- Ziff-Davis, 119
- zipped files, 16, 111